Life Reimagined: A Practical Guide to Recovery and Growth

Emma Gardner

Forward Thinking Publishing

First published 2025

Published by Forward Thinking Publishing

Text © Emma Gardner

The moral rights of the author have been asserted.

All rights reserved. No part of this book may be reproduced by any mechanical, photographic or electronic process, or in the form of a phonographic recording; nor may it be stored in a retrieval system, transmitted or otherwise be copied for public or private use, other than for 'fair use' as brief quotations embodied in articles and reviews, without prior written permission of the publisher and author.

The information given in this book should not be treated as a substitute for professional medical advice; always consult a medical practitioner. Any use of information in this book is at the reader's discretion and risk. Neither the author nor the publisher can be held responsible for any loss, claim or damage arising out of the use, or misuse, of the suggestions made, the failure to take medical advice or for any material on third party websites.

A catalogue record for this book is available from the British Library.

ISBN: 978-1-916764-09-5

Published by Forward Thinking Publishing

Contents

Introduction 1
   Understanding Cravings and Recovery 1
   The Science of Cravings 1
   Understanding Cravings as a Need to Replace a Habit 3
   Strategies for Managing Cravings 3

The Psychology of Addition and Cravings 4
   The Brain's Reward System 4
   Tolerance and Withdrawal 4
   Healthy Alternatives to Boost Dopamine 5

How this Book Helps 6
   Primary Coping Mechanisms 6
   How to Use This Book Effectively: A Practical Guide 7
   Making the Most of This Book 9

Why 6 Months of Activities are Powerful for Addition Recovery 11
   Summary Table: Benefits of a 6-Month Activity Program in Recovery 13

My Contingency Plan 14
   Example of a Trigger Based Contingency Plan 16

Activities 17
   Activity 1. Make A Smoothie 18
   Activity 2. Write a 6-word story 21

Activity 3. Perform a plank challenge 23

Activity 4. Practice facial exercises 25

Activity 5. Do a quick face mask 27

Activity 6. Give yourself a hand massage 30

Activity 7. Paint rocks with inspiring words 32

Activity 8. Try a new herbal tea 34

Activity 9. Do a 6-minute HIIT workout 36

Activity 10. Make energy balls 39

Activity 11. Try dry brushing 40

Activity 12. Do a quick aromatherapy session 42

Activity 13. Practice speed reading techniques 45

Activity 14. Delete & unsubscribe from unwanted emails (and trust me, if you are like me it will take much longer than 6 mins!) 47

Activity 15. Press Flowers 49

Activity 16. Do a wall sit for as long as possible 51

Activity 17. Create a small mosaic 53

Activity 18. Prepare overnight oats 55

Activity 19. Organise a junk drawer 57

Activity 20. Identify different bird species in your yard 59

Activity 21. Leave positive reviews for local businesses 61

Activity 22. Engage in a quick social media interaction 63

Activity 23. Practise & Hold Power Poses 65

Activity 24. Upcycle an old t-shirt into a reusable bag 67

Activity 25. Make a DIY Natural Air Freshener 70

Activity 26. Make flavoured water 72

Activity 27. Set up a digital calendar..75

Activity 28. Practice portrait photography..77

Activity 29. Try a walking meditation 79

Activity 30. Make a mini volcano (or use your head!) 81

Activity 31. Observe plant growth 83

Activity 32. Do a set of burpees..84

Activity 33. Learn a traditional dance move..86

Activity 34. Set SMART goals 87

Activity 35. Practice positive affirmations..89

Activity 36. Do a stress-relief colouring page..91

Activity 37. Try acupressure points for stress 93

Activity 38. Do a quick journaling session..96

Activity 39. Try EFT tapping..98

Activity 40. Create a dialogue exchange..101

Activity 41. Sketch a quick self-portrait..104

Activity 42. Prepare a healthy snack..106

Activity 43. Practice desk stretching 107

Activity 44. Do a quick facial massage..109

Activity 45. Read a chapter of a book 111

Activity 46. Update your device's software..113

Activity 47. Clean up your social media friends list..114

Activity 48. Make a bird feeder..116

Activity 49. Identify constellations..118

Activity 50. Create a nature scavenger hunt list 120

Activity 51. Create a bookmark – Personalise for you or your favourite book 121

Activity 52. Grow crystals 122

Activity 53. Perform squats and lunges 124

Activity 54. Take photos for a colour challenge 127

Activity 55. Practice a body scan meditation 129

Activity 56. Create a dream catcher 131

Activity 57. Try calligraphy 133

Activity 58. Make a DIY cleaning product 135

Activity 59. Create eco-friendly gift wrap 138

Activity 60. Try Cold Water Therapy (CWT) 140

Activity 61. Create a Memory Jar 143

Activity 62. Do a proprioception activity 146

Activity 63. Do a jigsaw puzzle 149

Activity 64. Water your plants 150

Activity 65. Create a playlist 151

Activity 66. Do a quick-self-acupressure session 153

Activity 67. Clean out your wallet or purse 155

Activity 68. Do a quick health check 157

Activity 69. Play with bubbles 159

Activity 70. Solve a Sudoku puzzle 161

Activity 71. Do some vocal warm-ups 163

Activity 72. Sculpt a tiny clay figure 166

Activity 73. Speed clean a room 168

Activity 74. Try body percussion exercises 170

Activity 75. Learn a magic trick 172

Activity 76. Try a quick Pilates routine 174

Activity 77. Write a letter to your future self 176

Activity 78. Practice good posture exercises 177

Activity 79. Do a quick manicure 179

Activity 80. Experiment with food plating 180

Activity 81. Start a mini book review 182

Activity 82. Create a photo story in 6 images 183

Activity 83. Decorate a picture frame 185

Activity 84. Try a loving-kindness meditation 187

Activity 85. Learn basic coding concepts 189

Activity 86. Try pronouncing words in a new language 192

Activity 87. Practice time management techniques 194

Activity 88. Tighten loose screws 196

Activity 89. Set a Short-Term Savings Goal 198

Activity 90. Have a 6-minute dance party 200

Activity 91. Learn basic First Aid 202

Activity 92. Play a quick game of darts 205

Activity 93. Make a keyring/chain 207

Activity 94. Identify Your Personal Values 209

Activity 95. Create a vision board 211

Activity 96. Take a brisk walk around the block 213

Activity 97. Write down any fears you want to overcome and how to tackle them 215

Activity 98. Create a miniature origami animal 218

Activity 99. Do a water displacement experiment 219

Activity 100. Research traditional costumes 221

Activity 101. Try the Method of Loci Technique 223

Activity 102. Practice juggling 226

Activity 103. Upcycle an old item 228

Activity 104. Make beeswax wraps 230

Activity 105. Create a comic strip 232

Activity 106. Wipe down kitchen counters 235

Activity 107. Groom a pet 237

Activity 108. Sort through old papers 239

Activity 109. Practice Laughter Yoga 241

Activity 110. Write & Reflect on your Personal Values 243

Activity 111. Create shadow art using household objects 245

Activity 112. Do a quick foot rolling exercise for plantar fasciitis prevention 248

Activity 113. Make a Lava Lamp 250

Activity 114. Observe and record wildlife 252

Activity 115. Do jumping jacks for 6 minutes 254

Activity 116. Clear your browser cache 256

Activity 117. Make a list of everything that makes you happy! 258

Activity 118. Create a quick salad 260

Activity 119. Plan a random act of kindness 262

Activity 120. Start a compost bin – even without a garden 264

Activity 121. Try Pointillism art...267

Activity 122. Make a solar oven..269

Activity 123. Research local attractions..271

Activity 124. Create a travel emergency kit or one for your home, you never know when you might need it! 274

Activity 125. Practice cloud watching and imagination 276

Activity 126. Solve a riddle 278

Activity 127. Take macro photos of nature 280

Activity 128. Update your CV..282

Activity 129. Improve your work area ergonomics 284

Activity 130. Practice Visualisation techniques................................287

Activity 131. Do a quick yoga flow 290

Activity 132. Try fruit and vegetable carving.....................................292

Activity 133. Practice nonverbal communication skills 294

Activity 134. Give yourself a foot rub 296

Activity 135. Read inspirational quotes..299

Activity 136. Organise your desktop icons..301

Activity 137. Make a terrarium..303

Activity 138. Learn how to deal with Chronic pain 305

Activity 139. Create a mini scrapbook page 308

Activity 140. Practice progressive muscle relaxation 310

Activity 141. Write a list of goals...312

Activity 142. Update your online profiles 315

Activity 143. Plant microgreens 317

Activity 144. Do a Mindful Eating Exercise 319

Activity 145. Practice Balance Exercises 321

Activity 146. Observe and Record Weather Patterns 324

Activity 147. Research Traditional Foods 326

Activity 148. Do a Quick Personality Assessment 328

Activity 149. Clean Window Tracks 330

Activity 150. Organise a Spice Rack Plus Other Ideas 332

Activity 151. Create Care Packages 335

Activity 152. Research Money-Saving Tips 337

Activity 153. Do Some Gardening or Weeding 340

Activity 154. Plan a Day Trip 342

Activity 155. Start a Fundraiser 345

Activity 156. Practice remembering phone numbers 347

Activity 157. Create nature rubbings with paper and crayons 349

Activity 158. Write Thank-You Notes 351

Activity 159. Practice Mindful Listening 354

Activity 160. Practice Decision-Making Skills 356

Activity 161. Research a Dream Destination 358

Activity 162. Create a sound map 360

Activity 163. Try colour therapy 362

Activity 164. Start coin collecting 364

Activity 165. Sign Up for a Volunteer Opportunity 366

Activity 166. Create a DIY pet toy 368

Activity 167. Create a found object sculpture 370

Activity 168. Practice interview questions 372

Activity 169. Create a paper quilling design 375

Activity 170. Practice mime techniques 377

Activity 171. Learn to tie different knots 379

Activity 172. Do a Sensory Awareness Exercise 381

Activity 173. Update Your Budget 383

Activity 174. Try ink blowing art 385

Activity 175. Do A Strengths and Weaknesses Analysis 387

Activity 176. Learn basic sign language 389

Activity 177. Try Beatboxing 392

Activity 178. Design a mandala 394

Activity 179. Make homemade pet treats 396

Activity 180. Read poetry 399

About the Author 403

Dedication

To my husband, David, who reminded me about Little Emma's need to play.
To Mum and Nanna Bob, who are looking down and saying, "What on earth are you doing now, Emma?!"

Out of death is new life. To Benji: remember to grow up trying new things, playing, and laughing every day.

And to everyone in recovery: remember, people may not understand the amazing skills and abilities you possess. Use them wisely and teach the world.

CHAPTER 1

Introduction

Understanding Cravings and Recovery

Addiction recovery is a journey that often involves managing intense cravings and although these decrease over time, you never know when they might strike or you may be triggered by something, even years after giving up a substance or behaviour. Getting into a healthy coping routine early on gives more chance of knowing where to turn when a sniff of a crisis is on the horizon. This book is designed to help you navigate these challenging moments by providing daily activities and challenges to engage in when cravings strike and to keep the mind as healthy as possible.

The Science of Cravings

Most addictive cravings are relatively short-lived, lasting between 3 to 10 minutes, with an average duration of 6 minutes. Understanding this can provide hope and motivation during difficult moments. When a craving hits, your brain isn't actually craving the substance itself, but rather the dopamine release associated with it, so we reach for the behaviour we are most used to, to satisfy this need.

Please remember that addiction is any repeated behaviour that affects our quality of life but we still cannot stop it. The obvious one's being drugs and alcohol, but there are so many more:

• Alcohol addiction • Nicotine addiction • Opioid addiction (e.g., heroin, prescription painkillers) • Cocaine addiction • Marijuana addiction • Amphetamine addiction • Benzodiazepine addiction • Hallucinogen addiction • Inhalant addiction	• Gambling addiction • Internet addiction • Video game addiction • Sex addiction • Shopping addiction • Food addiction • Exercise addiction • Social media addiction • Internet addiction
• Caffeine addiction • Tanning addiction • Plastic surgery addiction • Spiritual obsession • Cutting or self-harm • Hoarding addiction • Sugar addiction	• Work addiction (workaholism) • Love addiction • Adrenaline addiction (thrill-seeking) • Smartphone addiction • Selfie addiction • Cosmetic surgery addiction

Can you recognise any of these in yourself? Or see how they can become an addiction or behaviour to cope with life?

I am in recovery from alcohol, although just from this list I can recognise another six in my lifestyle, behaviour and coping strategies!

When individuals use addictive substances, they are often trying to escape from a variety of emotional, psychological, and environmental challenges. Here are some common things people may be trying to escape:

1. **Emotional Pain and Trauma**: Unresolved trauma, emotional distress, or feelings of shame and vulnerability. This can stem from childhood experiences or adult life challenges. Individuals who have experienced physical or emotional abuse may turn to substances to numb the pain and avoid memories of these events. Grief from losing someone close can lead people to use substances as a coping mechanism for their emotional pain.

2. **Stress and Overwhelming Life Situations**: Temporary relief from stress, financial problems, relationship issues, or other life obstacles that feel insurmountable, such as unemployment, job stress, unstable housing or homelessness, parental divorce, conflict and social isolation.

3. **Negative Emotions and Mental Health Issues**: Substances may be used to self-medicate and temporarily alleviate symptoms of depression, anxiety, PTSD (to get rid of flashbacks or nightmares) or other mental health conditions, such as ADHD. Individuals use substances to alleviate them although it makes their conditions worsen over time.

4. **Reality and Daily Responsibilities**: Some individuals use substances to escape the mundane aspects of life or to avoid dealing with problems directly, preferring a state of intoxication over facing reality. Pressure from social networks to fit in or to manage social stress.

5. **Physical Pain and Withdrawal** : When stopping an addiction, people may feel pain or withdrawal symptoms like headaches, shaking, anxiety, or the return of old health problems. It is tempting to reach for painkillers, but this is just replacing one substance with another, there are healthier alternatives.

Cravings can be linked to the need to replace a habit. When stopping an addiction, cravings can be intense and difficult to manage, stemming from both physical withdrawal symptoms and psychological factors, such as the emotional need for a coping mechanism or a sense of fulfilment.

Understanding Cravings as a Need to Replace a Habit

1. **Addiction Replacement**: Cravings can lead to what is known as "addiction replacement," where individuals substitute one addictive behaviour for another. This can include moving from substance use to behaviours like overeating, excessive shopping, or compulsive exercise. This highlights how cravings can drive the need to replace one habit with another.

2. **Emotional Needs**: People often use substances to fulfil emotional needs, such as managing stress, anxiety, or trauma. When they stop using substances, they may seek other ways to meet these emotional needs, which can manifest as cravings for alternative behaviours or substances, especially in times of stress.

3. **Habit Formation**: Habits, including addictive ones, are deeply ingrained in the brain. When one habit is removed, there can be a void that the individual may try to fill with another habit. This is why replacing unhealthy habits with healthier ones is a common strategy in recovery.

Strategies for Managing Cravings

- **Healthy Alternatives**: Engaging in healthy activities like exercise, hobbies, or creative pursuits can help manage cravings by providing alternative sources of fulfilment and distraction.
- **Therapy and Support**: Cognitive Behavioural Therapy (CBT) and support groups can help individuals identify, reducing the need to replace one habit with another.
- **Mindfulness Techniques**: Practices like urge surfing can help individuals acknowledge and ride out cravings without acting on them.

Understanding this dynamic and employing strategies to manage cravings can help individuals avoid replacing one addiction with another. Remember addictive behaviours are only a temporary relief, and ultimately lead to financial difficult, broken relationships, trouble with the law, further illness and ultimately in many cases of alcohol and substances, death.

CHAPTER 2

The Psychology of Addition and Cravings

The Brain's Reward System

Addiction fundamentally alters the brain's reward system, which is primarily driven by dopamine. When cravings strike, the brain isn't actually craving the substance or activity itself, but rather the dopamine release associated with it.

Dopamine and Pleasure

Dopamine is one of the body's "feel good" hormones. In the context of addiction:

- It reinforces behaviours perceived as pleasurable or rewarding.
- It creates a sense of satisfaction, encouraging the repetition of these activities.
- Addictive substances or behaviours cause an excessive release of dopamine, producing intense feelings of euphoria.

Formation of Habits and Compulsions

- Large surges of dopamine "teach" the brain to prioritise addictive activities over others.
- This process results in the formation of habits and compulsive behaviours.
- The brain learns to associate these activities with significant rewards, leading to dependency.

Tolerance and Withdrawal

Two key psychological impacts of addiction are:

1. **Tolerance:** The brain adapts by reducing its sensitivity to dopamine, leading to needing larger amounts of the substance to achieve the same level of pleasure.

2. **Withdrawal:** When the substance is not present, withdrawal symptoms may occur, driving individuals to continue using to avoid discomfort rather than to achieve pleasure.

Healthy Alternatives to Boost Dopamine

To satisfy dopamine cravings without substances, consider incorporating these activities:

Physical Activities

- Regular exercise can significantly increase dopamine production.
- Outdoor activities expose you to natural sunlight, which helps regulate dopamine production and supports mood.
- Remember to exercise in moderation, as it can also become addictive if overdone.

Dietary Approaches

- Consume foods rich in tyrosine, such as almonds, avocados, bananas, eggs, lean meats, and green leafy vegetables.
- Include probiotics in your diet to support gut health, which is linked to dopamine production.
- Ensure adequate protein, vitamins, and minerals to support overall dopamine production.

Mental and Social Activities

- Set achievable goals to improve focus and potentially increase dopamine levels.
- Listen to music and engage in social activities.
- Practice mindfulness and meditation to reduce stress and potentially boost dopamine.

Lifestyle Adjustments

- Prioritise quality sleep, aiming for 7-9 hours per night to help regulate dopamine levels.
- Try cold showers, which can increase dopamine levels and benefit skin health.
- Engage in creative activities like photography, drawing, or knitting to achieve a meditative state and potentially boost dopamine.

CHAPTER 3

How this Book Helps

This book offers a variety of activities across different categories, including art, exercise, mindfulness, and personal development. These activities are designed to:

1. Distract you during the crucial craving window

2. Stimulate dopamine release naturally

3. Provide alternative coping mechanisms

4. Promote overall well-being and personal growth

Primary Coping Mechanisms

When faced with a craving, you can employ three main strategies:

1. **Urge surfing**: Ride out the craving, focusing on the fact that it will pass within minutes. Easier said than done! Although with understanding and time, you can acknowledge that the feeling is with you, thank it for reminding you it is still there ready to pounce and then continue with whatever you were doing, without reminders of guilt or shame over your using days, just the empowerment of who you are and what you do.

2. **Distraction activities**: Engage in safe and healthy activities that stimulate dopamine and serotonin release. In this book there are 180 activities to do over a period of 6 months. Please make notes of some more that you think of and would like to try. This book is for you to find new interests, find what works best for you and note how they help. You might sleep better after moving more, you may eat better when you start going outside more etc.

3. **Coping techniques**: Utilise specific tools to respond to cravings and triggers. This will give you a great head start!

How to Use This Book Effectively: A Practical Guide

- **Daily Engagement**: Commit to trying a new activity each day to create a positive routine.

- **Flexibility**: Adapt activities to suit your interests or comfort level.

- **Reflection**: Use the Journaling Page Recovering Activities (template at the book of the book which can be printed or copied into your own journal and/or downloaded from my website) to record your thoughts and experiences.

- **Track Progress**: Monitor your growth over time as you progress in your recovery.

- **Holistic Approach**: Engage in activities that support various different aspects of your well-being.

Remember, consistency is key in recovery. By engaging with this book daily, you're creating new habits and coping mechanisms to support your journey towards a healthier, addiction-free life.

This book is designed as a versatile tool to support your recovery, personal growth, and emotional well-being. You can approach it in several ways, depending on your preferences, needs, and current state of mind. Here's a comprehensive guide to making the most of it:

1. Open and Dive In

- Feel free to open the book at any page and start with an activity that appeals to you. Whether it's a quick mindfulness exercise, a creative task, or a physical challenge, engaging spontaneously can boost motivation and curiosity.

- You don't have to follow a strict sequence. Trust your instincts—if a particular activity resonates today, do it.

2. Page-by-Page Approach

- Alternatively, you can commit to working through the book systematically, page by page. This structured approach helps build a routine and ensures you don't miss out on activities designed to address different aspects of your well-being.

- Set aside a specific time each day or week for this, turning it into a habit that supports your recovery journey.

3. Skip Activities if Needed—But Reflect

- If you choose not to do a particular activity, ask yourself *why*. Is it due to lack of interest, physical limitations, or emotional resistance? Journaling these reasons can uncover underlying barriers and help you address them.

- Remember, it's okay to skip activities temporarily. Use your journal to explore your feelings about skipping—are you avoiding discomfort, or is the activity genuinely not suitable right now?

4. Use Household Items and Be Creative

- Many activities are designed to be accessible and budget friendly. Before purchasing new supplies, look around your house for items you can repurpose—such as using a mug for a facial massage, old magazines for collages, or jars for homemade remedies.
- Creativity is encouraged! Adapting activities with household items can make them more personal and meaningful.

5. Journal Before, During, and After

- For each activity, record your feelings and thoughts:
  - Before: How are you feeling? Anxious, hopeful, indifferent?
  - During: Did the activity bring up any emotions? Joy, frustration, nostalgia?
  - After: How do you feel now? Relaxed, energized, overwhelmed? Did it help you, or would you like to modify it?
- Journalling helps track your emotional responses and progress over time, making it easier to identify what works best for you.

6. Adjust the Difficulty

- Feel free to modify activities to suit your current ability or mood:
  - Make the exercises easier by reducing duration or intensity.
  - Increase challenge by adding repetitions, weights, or complexity.
- This flexibility ensures activities remain engaging and prevent feelings of frustration or boredom.

7. Reflect on Enjoyment and Habit Formation

- After each activity, ask yourself:
  - *Did I enjoy this?* If yes, consider making it a regular part of your routine.
  - *Could this become a healthy habit?* How might it support your recovery long-term?
- Building enjoyable routines increases the likelihood of maintaining them, turning activities into positive habits.

8. Attempt Every Exercise—Surprise Yourself

- Even if an activity doesn't appeal at first glance, commit to trying it at least once. You may be surprised by how it makes you feel or the insights it offers.
- Approach each exercise with an open mind and remember that every attempt is a step forward in your journey.

9. Track Your Progress

- Recreate the Journalling Page, as this supports reflection, habit tracking, and self-compassion—core elements of this book's philosophy and effective recovery practice.
- Use a journal, sticky notes, or a simple checklist to monitor completed activities.
- Celebrate small wins—completing a week of daily activities, trying something new, or noticing emotional shifts.
- Recognising progress boosts motivation and reinforces positive habits.

10. Be Kind to Yourself

- Recovery and self-improvement are ongoing processes. Some days will be easier than others.
- Use this book as a gentle companion, not a taskmaster. Celebrate your efforts and forgive yourself if you miss a day or don't feel like doing an activity.

This book is a flexible, empowering resource. Feel free to open it whenever you need inspiration, follow it systematically, adapt activities to your circumstances, and always journal your feelings and progress. Remember, the goal is to support your well-being, foster self-awareness, and build resilience—so approach each activity with curiosity and compassion. You might just discover new passions, strengths, and habits that will serve you well on your recovery journey.

Making the Most of This Book

Embrace Nostalgia and Playfulness

- Allow yourself to enjoy childhood activities without judgment.
- Recognise that simple pastimes can offer unexpected benefits, serving as meditative exercises or evoking cherished memories.
- Embrace moments of joy and laughter in our fast-paced world.

Keep an Open Mind

- Don't dismiss activities too quickly; read through the entire day's entry.
- Look for variations or simpler alternatives that might suit you better.
- Stay open to stepping out of your comfort zone and trying new things.

Reflection and Adaptation

If you didn't try the day's activity:

- Journal your thoughts about why you skipped it.
- Explore your emotions and consider if your feelings might change in the future.
- Try adapting the activity to better suit your interests or comfort level.
- Try the Contingency Plan below to help you plan and be more adaptive.

Accessibility and Resources

- Most activities can be completed at home with common household items.
- While some may involve minimal costs, the book is designed to be budget friendly.
- If you discover a new passion, you might choose to invest in equipment or supplies to further develop your skills.

Tracking Progress

- Use sticky notes or bookmarks for activities you'd like to practice often.
- Reflect on past experiences with similar activities to assess your progress.
- Identify areas for improvement and use these insights to enhance your current experience.

Remember, the primary objective of these activities is to stimulate your mind, ignite your creativity, and support your recovery journey. Don't hesitate to adapt them to match your comfort zone and personal interests!

CHAPTER 4

Why 6 Months of Activities are Powerful for Addition Recovery

A six-month program of daily activities is a strategic and evidence-based approach to supporting individuals in addiction recovery. Here's why this duration is particularly effective for forming new habits, developing healthy routines, and fostering long-term change:

1. Aligns With Standard Rehab Recommendations

- Six months is commonly recommended as a minimum period for structured addiction treatment or aftercare because it allows enough time for the brain and body to begin healing from substance use and for new, healthier neural pathways to form.

- By providing six months' worth of activities, your book mirrors the structure and duration of many professional recovery programs, offering a familiar and supportive framework.

2. Supports Habit Formation and Routine Building

- Habit formation science suggests it takes consistent repetition over weeks or months to establish new behaviours. While the oft-cited "21 days to form a habit" is an oversimplification, research indicates that forming complex, lasting habits often takes 2–6 months of daily practice. Notice the word 'practice', it's about doing it and not thinking about doing it, like I did for years.

- A six-month program provides enough time for individuals to:

    o Replace old, unhealthy habits with new, positive ones

- Experiment with different activities to discover what works best for them
- Reinforce routines through daily repetition, increasing the likelihood of long-term adherence

3. Addresses the Critical Early Recovery Window

- The first six months after quitting a substance are often the most challenging, with heightened risk of relapse due to intense cravings, emotional volatility, and lifestyle adjustments.
- Having a structured set of activities for this period gives individuals practical tools to manage cravings, distract themselves during vulnerable moments, and fill the void left by addictive behaviours.

4. Encourages Consistency and Accountability

- Daily engagement with the book's activities helps establish a sense of purpose and routine, which are crucial for recovery.
- Tracking progress over six months allows individuals to see tangible improvements in mood, coping skills, and overall well-being, reinforcing their commitment to recovery.

5. Facilitates Personal Growth and Self-Discovery

- Six months is enough time for individuals to try a wide variety of activities—creative, physical, social, and reflective—helping them rediscover interests, passions, and strengths that may have been neglected during addiction.
- This diversity supports holistic growth, not just abstinence, and helps build a fulfilling, substance-free life.

6. Promotes Long-Term Change and Resilience

- Consistent engagement with healthy routines over six months helps "rewire" the brain's reward system, making it less dependent on substances for dopamine and pleasure.

By the end of six months, many individuals will have developed a toolkit of coping strategies, self-care practices, and new habits that support ongoing resilience and reduce relapse risk.

Summary Table: Benefits of a 6-Month Activity Program in Recovery

Benefit	Why It Matters in Recovery
Mirrors clinical recommendations	Builds trust and structure
Supports habit formation	Rewires brain, replaces old behaviours
Covers high-risk period	Reduces relapse risk during vulnerable months
Builds routine and accountability	Encourages daily progress and self-reflection
Fosters self-discovery	Helps find joy and meaning in sobriety
Enables long-term change	Sustains recovery beyond initial detox

A six-month activity-based recovery book is not just a distraction tool; it's a scientifically grounded, practical resource that empowers individuals to build new habits, routines, and identities. By guiding users through the crucial early stages of recovery, your book offers a bridge from old patterns to a healthier, more resilient life

CHAPTER 5

My Contingency Plan

In times of ultimate stress and craving when you feel you need help immediately always to come to your contingency plan because:

1. **Immediate Support**: A contingency plan provides immediate support and strategies to manage cravings and stress. This can include calling a sponsor, reaching out to a support group, or engaging in a pre-planned activity to distract from the craving.
2. **Prevents Escalation**: Acting quickly can prevent the situation from escalating. The longer you wait, the more intense cravings can become, making it harder to resist the urge to use substances.
3. **Reduces Impulsive Decisions**: Stress and intense cravings can lead to impulsive decisions, such as relapsing or spending your savings on a big un-needed purchase. A contingency plan helps individuals make more thoughtful choices by providing a structured response to these situations.
4. **Maintains Progress**: Relapsing can undermine progress made in recovery. I personally do not see a relapse as a negative thing, although at the time it can feel like you have let the world down and can lead to a dangerous downward cycle. By using a contingency plan, individuals can protect their hard-won gains and continue moving forward in their recovery journey.
5. **Builds Resilience**: Relying on a contingency plan during stressful moments helps build resilience and confidence in your ability to manage challenging situations without resorting to substance use.

A well-crafted contingency plan typically includes:

- **Emergency Contacts**: A list of people to call for immediate support, such as a sponsor or trusted friends.

- **Distraction Techniques**: Activities like exercise, meditation, or hobbies to shift focus away from cravings.

- **Safe Environments**: Places to go where one feels safe and supported, such as a support group meeting or a trusted friend's home.

- **Self-Care Practices**: Strategies for managing stress and emotions, such as deep breathing or journaling.

By having a contingency plan in place and using it during times of stress and craving, individuals can effectively manage these challenges and maintain their path towards recovery.

You can download a blank Continency Plan and Journalling Page for Recovery Activities for you to print and use at www.evolve-recovery.co.uk.

My Contingency Plan Example

1. Identification of Triggers

- **Internal Triggers**: Emotions like stress, anxiety, or depression.
- **External Triggers**: Places, people, or situations associated with substance use.

2. Coping Strategies

- **Relaxation Techniques**: Deep breathing, meditation, or yoga.
- **Physical Activity**: Exercise, walking, or sports.
- **Creative Outlets**: Painting, writing, or music.
- **Social Support**: Supportive friends, family, or a sponsor.

3. Emergency Plan

- **Contact Information**:
  - Emergency contacts/Sponsor
  - Therapist
  - Supportive Family Members/Friends
  - People from Rehab/Aftercare
  - Support lines, AA/NA/CoDa/Samaritans

- **Safe Places**: Locations to go during a crisis, such as a support group meeting or a trusted friend's home.

- **Immediate Actions**: Steps to take when feeling overwhelmed, such as calling a support hotline or engaging in a pre-planned activity.

4. Relapse Warning Signs

- **Emotional Changes**: Increased irritability, mood swings, or feelings of isolation.
- **Behavioural Changes**: Withdrawal from social activities or neglecting responsibilities.

5. Regular Self-Assessment

- **Weekly Reflections**: Regularly evaluate progress, identify areas for improvement, and adjust the plan as needed.

6. Healthy Lifestyle Practices

- **Nutrition and Sleep**: Focus on maintaining a balanced diet and adequate sleep.
- **Leisure Activities**: Engage in hobbies or activities that promote relaxation and enjoyment.

7. Professional Support Therapy Sessions: Regular attendance at therapy sessions to address underlying issues.

- **Support Groups**: Participation in support groups like AA or NA.

Example of a Trigger Based Contingency Plan

Trigger	Coping Strategy	Emergency Action
Stress	Deep breathing, exercise	Call sponsor, attend support group
Social Pressure	Assertiveness training, avoid triggers	Reach out to therapist, engage in a hobby
Negative Emotions	Mindfulness, journaling	Contact emergency contacts, practice self-care

Positive Reinforcement: While this is not a direct component of a contingency plan, incorporating elements of positive reinforcement (e.g., rewarding yourself for milestones achieved) can enhance motivation and engagement in recovery. Therefore, list some milestones and/or some rewards that you will give yourself for your hard work and achievements.

Activities

Activity 1. Make A Smoothie

Smoothies can be beneficial for everyone and for individual in recovering there are many reasons to start drinking them.

1. **Nutrient Replenishment**: Substance abuse often leads to nutrient deficiencies due to poor dietary habits and impaired nutrient absorption. Smoothies, rich in fruits, vegetables, and other nutrient-dense ingredients, can help replenish essential vitamins, minerals, and antioxidants that support overall health and recovery.

2. **Detoxification Support**: The antioxidants and enzymes in smoothies can aid the body's natural detoxification processes, which is crucial during the recovery phase.

3. **Mental Clarity and Energy**: Nutrient-rich smoothies can improve mental clarity and provide a natural energy boost, helping individuals stay focused and engaged in their recovery activities.

4. **Customisation and Palatability**: Smoothies can be tailored to individual tastes and dietary needs, making them a palatable and enjoyable part of the recovery process. I cannot stand the taste of milk and also, if I drink too much in my coffee, I begin to feel sluggish with stomach pains, so I usually have my shakes with fruit juice, coconut water or coconut milk. Do not feel you have to follow the recipes directly if you do not like something, but I would say try it first, or reduce and quantity of the product you dislike, as it is better to have some of those nutrients than none at all.

5. **Hydration and Digestive Ease**: Smoothies are hydrating and easy to digest, which is beneficial during detoxification when the digestive system may be sensitive.

There are so many recipes for smoothies, I could just do a book on them alone but below are some simple ideas for making smoothies that can be beneficial for people who have stopped drinking alcohol.

Rehydrating Green Smoothie	**Liver Support Smoothie**
- 1 cup spinach or kale - 1 banana - 1/2 cup coconut water - 1/2 cup pineapple chunks - 1 tbsp chia seeds - Ice as needed	- 1 beet - 1 apple - 1/2 avocado - 1 tbsp ground flax seeds - 1 cup unsweetened almond milk - 1 inch fresh ginger - Squeeze of lemon
This smoothie is packed with hydrating ingredients and electrolytes to help combat dehydration often experienced during alcohol withdrawal.	Beets and flax seeds support liver health, while ginger can help with nausea.

B-Vitamin Boost Smoothie	**Antioxidant Recovery Smoothie**
- 1 cup mixed berries - 1/2 cup Greek yogurt - 1 tbsp almond butter - 1/2 cup oats - 1 cup unsweetened almond milk - 1 tsp honey (optional)	- 1 cup mixed berries (blueberries, strawberries, raspberries) - 1 banana - 1 tbsp chia seeds - 1 cup coconut water - Handful of spinach
This is rich in B vitamins, which are often depleted by alcohol consumption.	This is high in antioxidants, which can help repair cellular damage caused by alcohol.

When making these smoothies, blend all ingredients until smooth. Adjust liquid content for desired consistency. Remember to focus on whole, nutrient-dense ingredients that support overall health and recovery. Make some of your own with what you enjoy, but remember to pay a little attention to adding some of those vital vitamins and minerals that the body really needs. Google your ingredients to discover the benefits you are giving to your body. Here are a couple:

Spinach is a superfood, rich in antioxidants, supports eye health, helps regulate blood pressure, and boosts the immune system, contributing to strong bones with its calcium, magnesium, and vitamin K content. Kale is similarly packed with antioxidants, supports cardiovascular health by lowering cholesterol and blood pressure, and has anti-inflammatory properties. Both are excellent for digestive health due to their high fibre content and support overall well-being by providing essential vitamins and minerals. Incorporating these into your diet can enhance your nutritional intake and support a healthier lifestyle.

Bananas have essential nutrients like potassium, fibre, vitamins, and antioxidants. A medium banana contains about 89 calories, high water content (75%), and very little fat (0.3 grams). They are a good source of dietary fibre and are rich in vitamins B6 & C, potassium, and manganese. Potassium helps regulate blood pressure and supports heart health. They act as a prebiotic, supporting gut bacteria and promoting regular bowel movements. Bananas also provide instant yet sustained energy and contain tryptophan, which converts to serotonin, potentially supporting mood stability.

I love coconut water and drink it a lot. It's an excellent source of nutrients and electrolytes, which help maintain fluid balance and support hydration, especially after exercise or in hot weather. The high potassium content in coconut water can help manage blood pressure and reduce the risk of heart disease. It can act as a mild laxative due to its potassium content, potentially aiding in preventing constipation, plus it is a low-calorie, low-sugar alternative to sugary beverages, making it suitable for those managing weight or blood sugar levels.

Activity 2. Write a 6-word story

Writing therapy is an accessible, low-cost technique that helps individuals process emotions, manage anxiety, and gain mental clarity by transforming abstract thoughts into actionable insights without judgment. The simplicity of writing just six words makes this exercise especially approachable, distilling complex feelings into a concise form while encouraging deep self-reflection and emotional release. Many people, including those in recovery, find that expressing their inner world through writing frees up mental energy, lowers stress, and fosters a sense of empowerment. Sharing poetry or brief stories not only releases heavy emotions but can also boost self-esteem and highlight inner resilience.

One of the most powerful elements of this practice is reframing—actively changing the narrative of negative or limiting beliefs into more constructive, hopeful perspectives.

For example:

- **Negative:** "I'll never be able to stay sober; I've failed so many times before."
  Reframed: "I've had setbacks, but also successes. I can learn from my past and use it to strengthen my recovery."
- **Negative:** "I need to drink to relax and have fun."
  Reframed: "I can find healthier ways to relax and enjoy myself, such as exercise or spending time with supportive friends."
- **Negative:** "I'm a failure because I relapsed."
  Reframed: "Relapse is a part of the recovery process for many people. It doesn't define my worth or my ability to achieve long-term sobriety."

Effective writing therapy can use free-form journaling, guided prompts, or structured formats like the six-word story. Consistent practice (15–20 minutes daily) and emotional honesty amplify its benefits, but those with severe mental health concerns should consult a professional before beginning.

Tips for Creating a Six-Word Story

- **Focus on Conflict or Change:** Highlight a turning point in your journey. Examples: "Found strength in darkest moments." / "Relapse taught me resilience."
- **Use Strong Nouns and Verbs:** This brings imagery and emotion to life. Examples: "Shattered chains freed my soul." / "Healing began with one step."
- **Imply a Larger Narrative:** Suggest stories beyond what's written to engage the reader's imagination. Examples: "Last drink, first sunrise." / "Sobriety found in silence."
- **Avoid Excessive Adjectives:** Stick to impactful, clear language. Examples: "Sobriety blooms in gardens." / "Recovery walks the long road."

- **Create Tension or Contrast:** This can reflect inner struggles or social challenges.
  Examples: "Cravings war with newfound peace." / "Stigma hides behind smiles."

More Examples of Six-Word Recovery Stories
- "From darkness to morning light."
- "Addiction lost, life regained slowly."
- "Sobriety blooms in every sunrise."
- "Healing found in broken pieces."
- "Recovery is my new home."

Getting Started

Draw from personal experience or inspiration from others' stories. Try different formats (headlines, dialogue, first-person) and always keep the focus on simplicity and meaning. Whether used for daily self-check-ins or milestone reflections, writing six-word stories becomes a tool for empowerment and healing. Consider practising regularly and keep a dedicated journal to track your growth.

Other classic examples:

- "For sale: baby shoes, never worn." — Ernest Hemingway
- "Found true love. Married someone else." — David Eggers
- "Brought roses home. Keys didn't fit."
- "Alone, in silence, gazing and enlightened."
- "Preserving dignity throughout life, into death."

Remember: Practice is key. Challenge yourself to write multiple six-word stories—over time, this brief format will reveal significant insights and help foster emotional resilience.

Activity 3. Perform a plank challenge

I suffer with a lot of back pain, since I injured it whilst working as a Prison Officer which brought my career to an abrupt halt. Because I am so flexible the doctors said there was nothing wrong with me as I could touch my toes, although I could not lift a kettle and was in agony if I stood still more than 15-20 seconds, my back would lock. Over the course of a year with no treatment, my muscles set all twisted until I saw a new chiropractor opened up in my town and thought 'I have nothing to lose by trying it'. Sure thing, he had me back working in 3 sessions, but the damage was done, and my core was shot. I must work on my back a lot now.

A study on the effectiveness of plank exercises for low back pain found that planks can significantly improve trunk strength, decrease low back disability, and reduce pain experienced. The research also showed that plank exercises can bring about proper alignment and posture along with strength to alleviate pain and improve quality of life, so if you suffer any back pain, this is an ideal challenge.

As well as being good for back pain, planks are highly effective for strengthening all your core muscles, including the rectus abdominis, transverse abdominis, and obliques (or abs!), as well as the shoulders, back, glutes, and quads. This full-body workout can help boost your metabolic rate and improve overall muscle definition. This improved core strength leads to better stability and balance in everyday movements and athletic activities.

Engaging in a plank challenge can have positive effects on your mental well-being. The exercise releases endorphins, which can elevate mood and reduce stress. Additionally, the challenge aspect can boost motivation and self-confidence as you progress and improve your plank duration.

Bonuses are that you need no equipment, it is a low impact exercise so reducing the pressure on the knees and on your neck compared to exercises like running, sit-ups or crunches.

To perform a simple plank position, follow these steps:

1. Start by lying face down on the floor or a mat.
2. Place your forearms on the ground, with your elbows directly beneath your shoulders. Your forearms should be parallel to each other (for forearm planks).
3. Extend your legs behind you, resting on the balls of your feet. Your feet should be about hip width apart.
4. Engage your core muscles by drawing your navel towards your spine.
5. Lift your body off the ground, creating a straight line from your head to your heels. Your body should form a rigid plank-like position.

6. Keep your neck neutral by looking at a spot on the floor about a foot in front of your hands. This helps maintain proper alignment of your head and spine.
7. Squeeze your glutes and quadriceps to help stabilise your body.
8. Hold this position while breathing steadily. Aim to maintain the plank for 20-30 seconds to start, gradually increasing the duration as you build strength.

Remember to maintain proper form throughout the exercise:

- Keep your back flat and avoid letting your hips sag or rise too high
- Don't let your head drop; keep it in line with your spine
- Breathe normally and don't hold your breath

Modifications:

Too Challenging - Dropping to your knees while maintaining a straight line from your head to your knees.

Next Level - Push up onto hands directly beneath your shoulders (for high planks).

Dynamic movements - Add plank rocks or hip dips to challenge yourself.

Listen to your body: If you experience pain or discomfort, especially in your lower back, take a rest day or modify the exercise.

When you have mastered the technique, turn it into a challenge.

1. Choose a duration: Start with a 30-day challenge, as this timeframe allows for noticeable improvements in core strength and stability.
2. Set a daily goal: Begin with a manageable duration, such as 30-60 seconds, and gradually increase the time as you progress.
3. Track your progress: Keep a log of your daily plank times to monitor improvements.
4. Complement with other exercises: Include additional core-strengthening exercises to maximise benefits.

Remember that consistency is key. While daily planks can be beneficial, it's essential to allow for rest and recovery. Consider incorporating planks 4-5 times a week instead of every day to prevent overtraining and maintain motivation throughout the challenge.

Activity 4. Practice facial exercises

I am sure if you haven't pulled faces in the mirror, then I am almost sure you have for a selfie. But did you know there are benefits to doing this, mentally and physically!! I know, crazy right lol. Practicing facial exercises offers several potential benefits:

Physical Benefits	Additional Potential Benefits
➢ Improved facial muscle tone and strength ➢ Enhanced skin elasticity and firmness ➢ Reduced appearance of fine lines and wrinkles ➢ Improved blood circulation to the face ➢ Possible reduction in facial puffiness and sagging	➢ Alleviation of tension headaches ➢ Improved symptoms of temporomandibular joint (TMJ) disorders ➢ Enhanced lymphatic drainage in the face
Mental and Emotional Benefits	**Aesthetic Benefits**
➢ Increased relaxation and stress relief ➢ Improved mood and self-confidence ➢ Enhanced awareness of facial muscles and expressions	➢ A more youthful appearance ➢ Improved facial symmetry ➢ Enhanced cheek fullness and definition ➢ Lifted appearance of facial features

While more research is needed to fully validate these benefits, studies have shown promising results. For example, one study found that participants looked about three years younger after following a 20-week facial exercise program. However, it's important to note that results can vary, and consistent practice over time is typically necessary to see noticeable improvements.

Here are simple instructions to practice facial exercises:

1. **The Cheek Lifter**
    - Smile as wide as you can with your mouth closed
    - Lift your cheek muscles up towards your eyes
    - Hold for 5 seconds, then relax
    - Repeat 10-15 times

2. **The Forehead Smoother**
    - Place both hands on your forehead
    - Gently sweep your fingers outward from the centre to the temples

3. **The Eye Opener**
   - Open your eyes as wide as possible
   - Hold for 5 seconds
   - Relax and repeat 5-10 times

4. **The Neck Tightener**
   - Tilt your head back and look at the ceiling
   - Press your tongue to the roof of your mouth
   - Hold for 10 seconds, then relax
   - Repeat 5 times

5. **The Lip Plumper**
   - Purse your lips tightly
   - Hold for 5 seconds
   - Relax and repeat 10-15 times

- Apply light pressure to smooth out wrinkles
- Repeat 10 times

Perform these exercises daily for best results. Remember to be gentle and stop if you feel any discomfort. Consistency is key for seeing potential improvements in facial muscle tone.

Have some fun with it and if you do this in a mirror and end up laughing at yourself, then go with it and laugh, and then laugh some more. Laughing at yourself triggers the release of endorphins, which are natural feel-good chemicals in the brain. This helps to reduce stress hormones and alleviate moderate stress levels, improving your mood and even temporarily relieving pain.

Self-deprecating humour builds psychological resilience, enabling you to bounce back from setbacks more easily. By laughing at your own mistakes, you learn not to dwell on past mishaps and approach new challenges with increased optimism and can also make you appear more approachable, relatable, and likable to others. It signals that you're comfortable in your own skin and can help forge authentic relationships by creating an environment of trust and camaraderie.

Laughing at your own quirks and imperfections fosters self-acceptance and self-compassion, allowing you to embrace your authentic self, reducing the need for perfectionism and promoting a more relaxed, positive outlook on life, with greater levels of emotional well-being and sociability.

By cultivating the ability to laugh at yourself, you can enhance your emotional intelligence, boost your resilience, and maintain a more positive perspective on life's challenges, so GO FOR IT!

Activity 5. Do a quick face mask

DIY face masks are an easy and natural way to care for your skin using ingredients commonly found in your kitchen, so potentially are not really costing anything extra for some well-deserved pampering.

As if we all need a reason to pamper ourselves and practice self-care, here are 7 reasons why creating and using a DIY face mask offers several wellbeing benefits:

1. **Stress reduction**: The process of making and applying a face mask can be a relaxing, mindful activity that helps reduce stress and promote calm.

2. **Boost in self-confidence**: Taking time for self-care sends a message that you value yourself, which can enhance self-esteem and confidence.

3. **Emotional resilience**: Establishing a regular face mask ritual can provide a sense of stability and comfort, helping to build emotional resilience.

4. **Relaxation**: The act of applying a mask and taking time for yourself can be incredibly relaxing, offering a break from daily stressors.

5. **Mindfulness practice**: Making and using a face mask encourages being present in the moment, fostering a deeper connection with yourself.

6. **Sense of accomplishment**: Creating your own skincare product can give you a feeling of achievement and creativity.

7. **Natural ingredients benefits**: Using natural ingredients from your kitchen can provide skin benefits without harsh chemicals, potentially reducing skin irritation.

These well-being benefits, combined with the potential skin improvements, make DIY face masks a holistic self-care practice that nurtures both mind and body.

Here are several effective homemade face mask recipes for different skin concerns:

Moisturising Face Mask for Dry Skin	Hyperpigmentation and Brightening Mask
Avocado Honey Mask: - 1/2 avocado - 1 tablespoon honey - Handful of oats Benefits: This mask hydrates and nourishes dry skin. Honey acts as a humectant, helping skin retain moisture, while oats soothe and calm the skin. Avocado's oils leave skin silky smooth.	Turmeric Lemon Mask: - 1 tablespoon turmeric powder - 1 tablespoon fresh lemon juice - 1 tablespoon honey (optional) - Splash of water This mask targets uneven skin tone and reduces pigmentation. Turmeric is clinically proven to address hyperpigmentation and reduce skin irritation. Use twice a week for five weeks for best results.
Sensitive Skin Soothing Mask	Glow-Enhancing Mask
Yogurt Cocoa Mask: - 1 tablespoon yogurt - 1 teaspoon cocoa powder - 1 teaspoon honey Ideal for sensitive skin, this mask contains probiotics and proteins that soothe redness. Cocoa's flavanols calm irritation, while honey tightens the skin.	Banana Glow Mask: - 1/2 banana - 1 tablespoon orange juice - 1 tablespoon honey This mask works for all skin types, moisturising the skin and providing a natural glow. It's particularly effective when used before your regular moisturiser.

Application Tips:

- Mix ingredients until smooth
- Apply evenly to face
- Leave on for 10-20 minutes
- Rinse with warm water
- Gently pat dry

Remember to patch test new ingredients and consult a dermatologist if you have sensitive skin or allergies.

The best ingredients for face masks targeting acne-prone skin include:

Salicylic Acid: This beta-hydroxy acid exfoliates the skin, unclogs pores, and reduces oil production.

Bentonite Clay: Known for its powerful oil-absorbing properties, it helps unclog pores and control shine.

Tea Tree Oil: With antibacterial and anti-inflammatory properties, it combats acne-causing bacteria and reduces inflammation.

Charcoal: Activated charcoal attracts and absorbs impurities, toxins, and excess oil from the skin.

- **Kaolin Clay**: Another effective clay for absorbing excess oil and purifying the skin.

- **Sulfur**: Known for its ability to fight acne-causing bacteria and reduce inflammation.

- **Niacinamide**: Helps regulate oil production and reduce inflammation.

Alpha-Hydroxy Acids (AHAs): Such as glycolic acid or lactic acid, these exfoliate the skin and promote cell turnover.

Turmeric: Contains anti-inflammatory and antimicrobial properties that can help reduce acne flare-ups.

- **Honey**: A natural antibacterial and anti-inflammatory ingredient.

When choosing or making a face mask for acne-prone skin, it's important to consider your specific skin type and concerns. Combining ingredients can provide maximum benefits but always patch test new products to avoid potential irritation.

Activity 6. Give yourself a hand massage

I went for a massage last week for my birthday. I said to the therapist 'Why do we treat ourselves to massage's they should be part of our normal self-care routine!', and she completely agreed. She said that she had a bad knee and had a massage each single day for 11 days and as well as aiding the pain, it actually helped to tone her legs (I think I would need one every day for 11 years!!), but my point is there are so many benefits to massages throughout the body and they should be a part of our wellbeing routine. Here are just some of the reasons why:

The physical benefits, specifically for hand massages, they can alleviate pain associated with conditions like arthritis, carpal tunnel syndrome, and neuropathy by improving circulation and reducing inflammation. Regular hand massages may also help to increase flexibility and mobility in the wrists and fingers, which is particularly beneficial for people with arthritis or those recovering from sports injuries and decrease any swelling by promoting fluid drainage and improving circulation. Consistent hand massages can enhance grip strength, making daily tasks easier to perform.

The mental and emotional benefits include reducing stress and anxiety by promoting relaxation and releasing tension. This is achieved through the stimulation of pressure points that affect the nervous system. The calming effect of a hand massage can lead to an improved mood by releasing endorphins, the body's natural feel-good hormones.

By reducing tension and promoting relaxation, hand massages can improve sleep quality, helping you fall asleep more easily and enjoy deeper rest.

They produce overall health benefits by increasing the blood flow, delivering oxygen and nutrients to tissues more efficiently, which supports healing and overall health. Stimulating certain pressure points in the hands can help relieve headaches by enhancing blood flow and reducing muscle tension. Incorporating then regularly into your self-care routine can provide these benefits, supporting both your physical health and mental well-being. It's a simple yet effective practice that can be done daily to maintain hand health and promote relaxation.

Follow this step-by-step guide on how to give yourself a relaxing and beneficial hand massage:

Preparation

1. Find a comfortable, quiet place to sit, or pop on some of your favourite music.
2. Apply a small amount of lotion or oil to your hands.
3. Rub your palms together to warm up your hands and distribute the product.

Massage Techniques

Palm Massage
- Use your thumb to make small circles on your opposite palm.
- Apply firm pressure and cover the entire surface.
- Spend 1-2 minutes on each hand.

Finger Massage
- Start at the base of each finger and work towards the tip.
- Gently squeeze and release to alleviate tension.
- Rotate each finger to improve joint mobility.

Thumb Stretch
- Hold your thumb with the opposite hand.
- Gently pull it away from your palm to stretch the base joint.
- Hold for 5-10 seconds and repeat on the other hand.

Wrist Massage
- Apply gentle circular motions around your wrist.
- This helps release tension from repetitive movements.

Pressure Points
- Focus on the area between your thumb and index finger (Hoku point).
- Apply gentle pressure to help alleviate stress.

Additional Techniques
- Stroke your forearm from wrist to elbow using your palm.
- Use your thumb and fingers to apply circular or back-and-forth motions up your hand and forearm.
- Gently but firmly pinch the skin on your forearm, moving from wrist to elbow and back.

Finish the massage by stretching your fingers wide apart and gently shake your hands to release any remaining tension.

For best results, try to massage your hands daily for at least 15 minutes, using moderate pressure. This practice can help reduce hand pain, improve grip strength, and promote relaxation.

Activity 7. Paint rocks with inspiring words

Painting rocks with inspiring words is a valuable addiction recovery exercise due to its multifaceted benefits. This activity offers therapeutic stress relief and emotional expression while promoting mindfulness and focus. The act of creating positive affirmations on rocks reinforces recovery goals and boosts self-esteem, providing a tangible sense of accomplishment. Socially, it can foster connections within recovery groups and the wider community. The accessibility and portability of painted rocks make them practical tools for ongoing motivation. By combining art therapy with positive reinforcement, this simple yet powerful exercise supports individuals in expressing themselves creatively, maintaining their commitment to sobriety, and finding moments of inspiration throughout their recovery journey.

Painting rocks with inspiring words is a fun and creative activity. Put them in your garden, house plants, doorstep, workplace, anywhere to remind you and make you smile. Plus going outside and finding the stones is also get with your health and mental wellbeing!

Here are some ideas and instructions to get you started:

Materials Needed

- Smooth, clean rocks
- Acrylic paints or paint pens or even nail varnish, that's what I used!
- Paintbrushes (various sizes)
- Palette or paper plate for mixing paints
- Water cup for rinsing brushes
- Paper towels or cloth for drying brushes
- Sealant (optional, for outdoor use) or topcoat nail varnish.

Step-by-Step Instructions

1. **Prepare the Rocks**
   - Wash and dry your rocks to remove any dirt or debris.
   - If desired, apply a base coat of paint to create a background colour. Let it dry completely.

2. **"Choose Your Words Carefully"**
   - Select inspiring words or phrases you want to paint on the rocks, such as "Hope," "Love," "Courage," or "Believe."

3. **Plan Your Design**
   - Lightly sketch your design on the rock with a pencil if needed. Consider the size and shape of the rock when planning your layout.

4. **Paint the Words**
   - Use fine-tipped brushes or paint pens to carefully paint the words onto the rock.
   - Start with a light colour for the letters and go over them again if needed for better coverage.

5. **Add Decorative Elements**
   - Enhance your design with decorative elements like hearts, stars, flowers, or abstract patterns around the words.
   - Use contrasting colours to make these elements stand out.

6. **Let It Dry**
   - Allow the paint to dry completely before handling the rocks further.

7. **Seal the Design (Optional)**
   - If you plan to place the rocks outdoors, apply a clear sealant to protect the paint from weathering. I use clear nail varnish.

8. **Display or Share**
   - Place your painted rocks in your garden, around your home, or share them with friends and family as uplifting gifts.

By following these steps, you can create beautiful, inspiring rock art that spreads positivity and creativity. Enjoy the process and have fun experimenting with different designs and colours!

Activity 8. Try a new herbal tea

Different herbal tea flavours offer a variety of health benefits. As well as being caffeine free and being a great flavour addition towards your daily water count, keeping well hydrated, each type of tea has different benefits. You can get tea to help you sleep, to calm you down, to help detox, slim, digestion.... The list goes on and on.

Herbal tea, if you are not used to it, can be an acquired taste. The first time I tried it, I was not impressed and said 'No way I am drinking that stuff!', but 20 odd years later I love it. I preserved for a few days and ended up having a few a day as a substitute to my caffeine intake, because my caffeine intake was and still can be unhealthy, also milk has given my stomach a lot of trouble and I knew I had to make a change. So please give it a chance for a few days before you decide, as mental and physically it feels completely different to that large cappuccino or americano. Here's an overview of some popular herbal teas and their potential effects:

Chamomile Tea - Promotes sleep and relaxation - Soothes digestive issues - Has anti-inflammatory properties - Reduces anxiety - May help with skin health	*Peppermint Tea* - Aids digestion and relieves stomach discomfort - May help with headaches which can help with withdrawals - Boosts energy and mental alertness - Soothes cold symptoms
Ginger Tea - Relieves nausea and motion sickness - Has anti-inflammatory effects - May help with pain relief - Supports immune function	*Hibiscus Tea* - Rich in antioxidants - May help lower blood pressure - Good source of vitamin C - Supports metabolism
Rooibos Tea - High in antioxidants - Supports heart health - May help with weight management - Caffeine-free alternative to black tea	*Lavender Tea* - Promotes relaxation and stress relief - May improve sleep quality - Has calming effects
Echinacea Tea - Supports immune system function - May help with cold and flu symptoms	*Turmeric Tea* - Powerful anti-inflammatory properties - May help with joint pain - Supports overall well-being

If you have somewhere such as a Holland & Barrett or Neals Yard, you can get different herbs and (loose) teas to help with different symptoms.

Remember that while herbal teas can offer various health benefits, it's always best to consult with a healthcare professional before using them for medicinal purposes, especially if you have existing health conditions or are pregnant.

When giving up alcohol, certain herbal teas may be particularly helpful in managing cravings and supporting overall health. Based on the available information, here are some of the best herbal tea options:

Kudzu Tea, which I haven't heard of before appears to be one of the most promising herbal teas for those giving up alcohol. It is made directly from the root of the kudzu plant and is known for its calming properties.

- It may help reduce alcohol cravings and consumption.

- Studies have shown it can decrease alcohol intake by 20-57% in some cases.

- It works by inhibiting the breakdown of acetaldehyde, a toxic byproduct of alcohol metabolism.

- This may create an aversion to alcohol and reduce cravings

However, it's important to note that more research is needed, and finding standardised, high-quality kudzu supplements can be challenging.

Activity 9. Do a 6-minute HIIT workout

A HIIT workout is similar to circuit training, where you complete a short burst of energetic exercises followed by a period of recovery before starting again with a different exercise. Personally for me, I prefer this type of training, firstly to get it over and done with, but also because my stamina isn't great. I have great strength, but little stamina so this is a good form of exercise for me.

A 6-minute HIIT workout can be particularly beneficial for wellbeing and people in recovery for several reasons.

Neurochemical Benefits

HIIT workouts trigger the release of neurotransmitters that can help in addiction recovery:

> - Dopamine regulation: HIIT influences dopamine release in the brain, similar to addictive substances, but in a healthier way. This can help restore a more balanced neurotransmitter system, potentially reducing cravings for drugs or alcohol.

> - Endorphin release: The intense nature of HIIT promotes the release of endorphins, which can improve mood and act as a natural "high".

Mental Health Improvements

HIIT can positively impact mental health, which is crucial during addiction recovery:

> - Stress reduction: Both low and high-intensity exercises, including HIIT, help reduce stress, anxiety, and depression - common triggers for relapse.

> - Improved self-esteem: Overcoming the challenges of a HIIT workout can boost confidence and self-efficacy, important factors in maintaining sobriety.

Physical Health Benefits

HIIT helps counteract the physical toll of substance abuse:

> - Cardiovascular health: HIIT is particularly effective at improving cardiovascular function, which may have been compromised by substance abuse.

> - Metabolic improvements: HIIT can help regulate blood sugar and lipid levels, contributing to overall health improvement.

Practical Advantages

The short duration of a 6-minute HIIT workout offers unique benefits:

- Time efficiency: The brief nature of HIIT makes it easier to incorporate into daily routines, providing structure and purpose - crucial elements in recovery.

- Increased adherence: The short time commitment may improve exercise adherence, which is often challenging for individuals in recovery.

Craving Reduction

Research suggests that HIIT can be effective in reducing drug cravings:

- Direct impact on cravings: Studies have shown that HIIT can significantly reduce cue-induced cravings in individuals with substance use disorders.#

- Physiological similarity: The intense bursts in HIIT are physiologically similar to what people experience during addiction regulation, potentially helping to rewire the brain's reward system.

In conclusion, a 6-minute HIIT workout offers a potent combination of neurochemical, psychological, and physical benefits that align well with the needs of individuals in addiction recovery. Its time-efficiency and effectiveness in reducing cravings make it a valuable tool in supporting long-term sobriety and overall health improvement.

Here's a simple and effective 6-minute HIIT workout that you can do without any equipment:

This workout consists of 6 exercises performed for 30 seconds each, with 10 seconds of rest between exercises. You'll complete two rounds for a total of 6 minutes.

Exercises

1. Jumping Jacks: Start with your feet together and arms at your sides. Jump your feet out while raising your arms above your head, then jump back to the starting position.
2. Mountain Climbers: Begin in a high plank position. Alternate bringing each knee towards your chest in a running motion.
3. Squats: Stand with feet shoulder-width apart. Lower your body as if sitting back into a chair, then return to standing.
4. Push-Ups: Perform standard push-ups or modify by doing them from your knees.

5. Alternating Lunges: Step forward with one leg, lowering your hips until both knees are bent at about 90 degrees. Alternate legs with each rep.
6. Burpees: Start standing, drop into a squat, place your hands on the floor, kick your legs back into a plank, do a push-up, jump your feet back to your hands, and explode up with a jump.

How to Perform

1. Warm up for 3-5 minutes with light cardio and dynamic stretches.
2. Set a timer for 30 seconds of work and 10 seconds of rest.
3. Perform each exercise at maximum effort for 30 seconds, followed by 10 seconds of rest.
4. Move immediately to the next exercise after the rest period.
5. Complete all 6 exercises, then repeat the circuit for a second round.
6. Cool down with light stretching for 2-3 minutes.

Remember to maintain proper form throughout the workout, even as you fatigue, to prevent injury and maximise results. Stay hydrated and listen to your body, modifying exercises if needed.

This high-intensity workout is designed to boost your metabolism, improve cardiovascular health, and burn fat efficiently in just 6 minutes.

If you have joint issues, you can still enjoy the benefits of High-Intensity Interval Training (HIIT) by modifying your workout to be low-impact. Here's how you can adapt your HIIT routine to be gentler on your joints:

Low-Impact Alternatives

Replace high-impact exercises with joint-friendly options:

1. Instead of jumping jacks, try standing side leg lifts with jumping-jack arms.
2. Swap burpees for elevated squat thrusts using a step or bench.
3. Replace running or sprinting with power walking on an inclined treadmill.

Activity 10. Make energy balls

Energy balls are an excellent snack option as they provide balanced nutrition and sustained energy. Make some and keep them for when you are tempted to reach for the sugar or if you are struggling with your appetite, these can help. Here's a simple recipe:

Basic Recipe

- 1 cup rolled oats
- 1/2 cup nut butter (e.g., peanut, almond, or cashew)
- 1/3 cup honey or maple syrup
- 1/4 cup ground flaxseed
- 1/4 cup mini dark chocolate chips (optional)
- 1 teaspoon vanilla extract

Instructions

1. Mix Ingredients in a large bowl, combine all ingredients until well mixed.
2. Chill the mixture in the fridge for about 30 minutes to make it easier to handle.
3. Roll the mixture into small balls, about 1 inch in diameter.
4. Keep the energy balls in an airtight container in the refrigerator for up to a week.

Recovery-Supporting Add-ins and additional flavours:

- Chia seeds: Rich in omega-3 fatty acids and fibre
- Pumpkin seeds: High in zinc, which can be depleted during addiction
- Dried cranberries: Provide antioxidants and natural sweetness
- Coconut flakes: Offer healthy fats and flavour
- Cacao powder: Rich in magnesium and antioxidants

Benefits for Recovery

- Provides balanced nutrition with complex carbohydrates, protein, and healthy fats
- Offers a quick energy boost without sugar crashes
- Easy to prepare in advance for convenient, healthy snacking
- Can help stabilise blood sugar levels, potentially reducing cravings

Remember, while these energy balls are nutritious, they should be consumed as part of a balanced diet. Always consult with a healthcare professional or nutritionist for personalised dietary advice during recovery.

Activity 11. Try dry brushing

Now I must admit, I use a brush every now and then in the shower, but don't think about dry brushing as part of my routine. There are said to be several benefits, although, please note that some claims lack robust scientific evidence, so I will be saying, 'may help' or 'could improve' and please be careful if you have sensitive or broken skin.

So the main reason that people think of when it comes to dry brushing, is to remove dead skin cells, leaving skin softer, smoother, and more radiant. This exfoliation process unclogs pores and may improve skin texture over time. The brushing motion stimulates blood flow to the skin's surface, potentially enhancing oxygen and nutrient delivery to skin cells. This increased circulation can give the skin a healthy glow.

Whilst more research is needed, dry brushing is believed to stimulate the lymphatic system, which may aid in detoxification and support immune function. The gentle pressure and movement may help encourage lymph flow throughout the body.

Some people report a temporary improvement in the appearance of cellulite due to increased blood flow and plumping of the skin. However, this effect is likely short-lived and not a permanent solution. As a young person feeling like I should look like magazine covers, I can vouch that this never worked and I just had very red legs. Now I complain but accept my body for the protection and heat it maintains for me.

The repetitive, gentle motions of dry brushing can have a calming effect on the nervous system, potentially reducing stress and promoting relaxation. This I would very much agree with as in massage motions, if you do not press too hard. For this reason, it can be incorporated as a mindful self-care ritual, encouraging present-moment awareness and providing an opportunity for meditation.

Many people report feeling invigorated and energised after dry brushing, possibly due to the stimulation of nerve endings in the skin. Some find it more effective than coffee for waking up in the morning.

The practice encourages a deeper connection with your body, promoting overall body awareness and potentially boosting self-esteem. I personally would agree with this too.

While dry brushing shows promise for both physical and mental well-being, it's important to approach it gently and consult with a healthcare professional if you have sensitive skin or specific health concerns. Remember that many of these benefits are based on anecdotal evidence and personal experiences, and more scientific research is needed to fully validate some of the claims.

Here's a simple guide on how to do dry brushing, ensuring you purchase an appropriate dry body brush:

1. Start with dry skin before showering
2. Use a natural bristle brush with a long handle
3. Begin at your feet and work upwards towards your heart
4. Use firm, circular motions on your skin
5. Brush each area several times
6. Use lighter pressure on sensitive areas
7. Brush your arms towards your armpits
8. Brush your stomach and chest in a clockwise direction
9. Avoid brushing over broken skin, rashes, or wounds
10. Spend about 3-5 minutes total brushing your whole body
11. Follow with a shower to rinse off dead skin cells
12. Apply moisturiser after showering

Remember to clean your brush regularly with soap and water, and allow it to dry completely between uses. For best results, try to dry brush a few times a week as part of your routine.

Why not give it try!

Activity 12. Do a quick aromatherapy session

Aromatherapy offers multiple benefits by leveraging the therapeutic properties of plant-derived essential oils. These benefits span psychological, physical, and immune health, supported by both historical use and emerging research. Here's some key advantages:

Psychological Benefits

- Reduces stress and anxiety: Inhaling essential oils like lavender or bergamot activates the brain's limbic system, which regulates emotions. This interaction triggers the release of serotonin and endorphins, promoting relaxation and reducing stress.

- Improves mood: Scents such as citrus (lemon, orange) and floral oils (jasmine, rose) can uplift mood by evoking positive memories and emotional responses.

- Enhances sleep quality: Lavender oil is particularly effective in improving sleep duration and quality, especially in clinical settings like hospitals.

Physical Benefits

- Pain relief: Aromatherapy massage (with eucalyptus/peppermint) alleviates pain from conditions such as arthritis, headaches, and muscle soreness. Studies show reduced reliance on pain medications in some cases.

- Supports immune function: Aromatherapy massage has been linked to increased lymphocyte levels, which play a role in immune response.

- Aids digestion and reduces nausea: Oils like ginger and peppermint are used to ease stomach discomfort and chemotherapy-induced nausea.

Mechanisms of Action

- Olfactory stimulation: Essential oil molecules bind to nasal receptors, sending signals to the limbic system to regulate emotions.

- Topical absorption: When diluted and applied to the skin, oils like chamomile or sandalwood can reduce inflammation and soothe localized pain.

- Hormonal influence: Aromatherapy prompts the release of hormones like serotonin and dopamine, which improve mood and stress resilience.

Conditions Supported by Evidence

> ➤ Chronic health issues (e.g., dementia, psoriasis).
> ➤ Post-surgical recovery and dialysis-related discomfort.
> ➤ Menopausal symptoms and mild respiratory inflammation.

Safety Considerations

> ➤ Dilution is critical: Undiluted oils can irritate skin or mucous membranes. Always use carrier oils like almond or jojoba.
> ➤ Avoid ingestion: Consuming oils can harm kidneys or liver.
> ➤ Consult professionals: Work with an aromatherapist or doctor, especially for those with allergies, asthma, or pregnancy.

While research continues to explore its full potential, aromatherapy remains a versatile, non-invasive complement to traditional treatments, offering holistic benefits for both mind and body. Here are simple instructions for a quick aromatherapy session:

Choose Your Essential Oil - Select an essential oil based on your desired effect

Prepare Your Space – Somewhere quiet, comfortable area and ensure good ventilation.

Application Methods - Choose one of these quick methods:

Inhalation
1. Add 2-3 drops of essential oil to a tissue.
2. Hold the tissue near your nose.
3. Take 5-10 deep breaths.

Diffuser
1. Add water to your diffuser.
2. Add 3-5 drops of essential oil.
3. Turn on the diffuser for 15-20 minutes.

Palm Inhalation
1. Put 1-2 drops of oil in your palms and rub them together.
2. Cup hands over your nose and mouth and inhale deeply for 30 seconds.

Mindful Breathing

1. Close your eyes and take slow, deep breaths.
2. Focus on the aroma and its effects for around 5-10 minutes for a quick boost.

Remember to use high-quality, pure essential oils and discontinue use if you experience any adverse reactions.

Other advantages:

Mental and Emotional Health

- Reduces stress and anxiety through aromatherapy (e.g., lavender, bergamot, orange).
- Improves mood by stimulating neurotransmitters linked to emotional well-being.
- Enhances relaxation and sleep quality, particularly with lavender oil.
- Boosts cognitive function, including memory/focus (e.g., rosemary, lemon).

Physical Health

- Antimicrobial and antiviral properties combat infections (e.g., tea tree, oregano).
- Anti-inflammatory effects alleviate pain from arthritis and muscle soreness.
- Supports digestion by easing indigestion, nausea, and IBS symptoms (e.g., ginger, peppermint).
- Strengthens immunity through antioxidant-rich oils (lemon, frankincense, clove).
- Relieves respiratory issues (e.g., eucalyptus clears congestion, peppermint opens airways).

Skin and Hair Care

- Treats acne, fungal infections, and skin irritation (tea tree, lavender, geranium).
- Promotes hair growth and scalp health (rosemary, peppermint).
- Reduces signs of aging with antioxidant properties (frankincense, rose).

Hormonal and Metabolic Support

- Balances hormones (clary sage, geranium) to manage PMS, menopause, and PCOS.
- Regulates blood sugar levels (lemongrass).
- Boosts energy and athletic performance (peppermint, grapefruit).

Activity 13. Practice speed reading techniques

Learning new skills significantly enhances personal and professional growth. A new skill like speed reading techniques can enhance growth in many different ways:

It allows you to process information more quickly, saving valuable time and increasing productivity. By reading faster, you can cover more material in less time, freeing up hours for other important tasks or activities, great for studying and picking out the important parts needed and great for your career, as it can give you a competitive edge, allowing you to stay up-to-date with industry trends, prepare for presentations more efficiently, and take on additional responsibilities.

Contrary to popular belief, effective speed-reading techniques can enhance focus and comprehension. By training your brain to process information rapidly, you develop better concentration skills and improve your ability to understand and retain what you read.

It can also boost your memory and cognitive abilities. As you train your brain to absorb information quickly, you may notice improvements in your overall memory performance and logical thinking skills.

While it's important to note that some claims about speed reading may be exaggerated, developing techniques to read more efficiently can still provide valuable benefits in our information-rich world.

To learn speed reading techniques, follow these steps:

1. **Start with basic exercises**
   - Practice eye movements by focusing on the second word of each line and the second-to-last word, reducing unnecessary eye fixations.
   - Use a pen or finger as a guide to prevent rereading and maintain a steady pace.

2. **Implement advanced techniques**
   - Chunking: Read groups of words instead of individual words to reduce eye stops and increase speed.
   - Scanning and previewing: Quickly identify key information like headings, lists, and graphs before detailed reading.
   - Eliminate subvocalisation (the practice of reducing or stopping the internal voice that pronounces words in your head as you read silently) by counting in your head while reading or gently biting your tongue.

3. **Develop supportive habits**
   - Set specific reading goals and track your progress.
   - Take notes and summarise to improve comprehension and retention.

- Expand your vocabulary to recognize words faster.

4. **Practice regularly**
   - Dedicate 15-30 minutes daily to reading and speed reading exercises.
   - Use online tools and software programs designed for speed reading practice.

5. **Monitor your progress**
   - Regularly test your reading speed and comprehension to gauge improvement.
   - Adjust your techniques as needed to maintain a balance between speed and understanding.

Remember, consistent practice is key to developing and maintaining speed reading skills. There are several free online software options available for learning speed reading:

Web-Based Tools

1. **Spreeder**: A popular free online speed-reading tool that uses Rapid Serial Visual Presentation (RSVP) technology. It allows you to paste any text and practice reading at increased speeds.
2. **Readsy**: This simple, free web-based tool utilizes Spritz technology. You can input text, upload a PDF, or paste a URL to practice speed reading.
3. **SwiftRead**: A browser extension that helps you speed read articles, emails, and online documents using RSVP technique. It's free to use and can significantly increase your reading speed.

Open Source Applications

1. **Gritz**: An open-source file reader for Linux, Windows, and MacOS that displays words one at a time to reduce regression.
2. **Spray Speed-Reader**: A JavaScript-based open-source speed reading application.
3. **Sprits-it!**: An open-source web application that enables speed reading of web pages.

Mobile Apps

1. **Comfort Reader**: An open-source speed reading app available for Android users. It can be downloaded from F-droid and Google Play stores.
2. **ReadSpeeder**: While primarily known for its paid version, ReadSpeeder offers a free option aimed at doubling your reading speed while improving comprehension.

These free tools provide a good starting point for anyone interested in learning speed reading techniques without financial investment.

Activity 14. Delete & unsubscribe from unwanted emails (and trust me, if you are like me it will take much longer than 6 mins!)

I need to be in the mood for this as it is always a big job for me. I keep on top of them as much as possible, although I get over 500 a day. I always feel a great relief and psychologically I feel better when I see deleting 6000 emails from my trash bin!

For deleting old emails, I have a few tips:

- I sometimes list them in alphabetical order, this can help if you scroll through and see 'Amazon Subscribe & Save', you can select and delete in bulk, as I know I do not need to keep on of these, they are in my Amazon account.

- Other times I type in 'Easter' or 'takeaway' if I am having a quick clear up. The emails you want to delete might not be so obvious, but it means you probably pick up all the Easter sales or spam takeaway emails that you don't need.

- Or just type in 'Me' (as I often send emails to myself, as reminds) or 'Asda' and I can delete these in bulk.

The benefit of typing random words like 'CV', is that it will bring up emails from jobs I have applied for along with all the follow-ups, job sites I no longer need, companies that have offered to rewrite my CV etc. If I do not need to look for a job anymore, I can just unsubscribe before deleting them all.

I do find it so satisfying!

The benefits of doing this are that you reduce clutter and noise in your inbox, free up space (especially if you only have a certain volume allowed) and time for more important emails.

You may well come across subscriptions you forgot you had, allowing you to cancel and unsubscribe.

When you are deleting emails, you may come across emails that regularly go into spam that should be in your inbox, so you can mark these as 'Not Spam' making them easier to find.

When you unsubscribe, it will often ask you why you are unsubscribing, this can be really helpful to the business you are unsubscribing from, This can provide invaluable information for small businesses. Anything from 'products not affordable', 'now use a company who provide payment plans', 'content not relevant', 'receiving too many emails' etc. can help them to help other people (including maybe you) in the future.

There are several shortcuts and efficient methods to unsubscribe from unwanted emails. Many email providers offer built-in unsubscribe options:

- Gmail: Look for the "Unsubscribe" link next to the sender's name at the top of the email.

- Outlook: Check for a message saying "Getting too much email? Unsubscribe" at the top of promotional emails.

- Apple Mail: Look for an "Unsubscribe" banner at the top of emails from mailing lists.

Several third-party tools can streamline the unsubscribe process:

- **Unroll.me**: Allows you to unsubscribe from multiple emails at once.
- Clean Email: Offers an "Unsubscriber" feature to manage subscriptions efficiently.
- **Leave Me Alone**: Provides a one-click unsubscribe option for multiple email accounts.
- **Mailstrom**: Starting from $9/month for one email account, with a free trial available. Allows one-click unsubscribing if an unsubscribe address is available. It also offers features to delete messages in bulk and block senders

Some email clients offer additional shortcuts:

- Spike: Allows one-click unsubscribing directly from the email thread.
- Edison Mail: Displays a large "Unsubscribe" button at the top of applicable messages.

Tips for Faster Unsubscribing

➢ Look for unsubscribe links at the bottom of emails.
➢ Use your email client's search function to find all emails from a particular sender.
➢ Consider using email filters to automatically sort or delete unwanted emails.

Remember, while these methods can save time, always be cautious when interacting with unfamiliar links or granting access to third-party services.

Activity 15. Press Flowers

This activity reminds me of being young, but I have done it many times in my adulthood. Flower pressing is a therapeutic activity that allows you to engage in your creative process, which can reduce stress and anxiety through the calming, methodical nature of the task, distracting the mind from worries and promotes mindfulness. The act of collecting and pressing flowers also fosters a connection with nature, enhancing mood and overall mental health. The creative expression involved in arranging pressed flowers can boost self-esteem and stimulate problem-solving skills, providing a sense of accomplishment and fulfilment. This hobby encourages patience and perseverance as well, valuable skills that can be applied to other areas of life. Overall, flower pressing combines the soothing effects of nature with the therapeutic benefits of art, making it an excellent activity for promoting mental wellbeing.

Pressing flowers is a wonderful way to preserve their beauty and create lasting memories. Here's an easy method to press flowers using common household items:

1. Choose your flowers: Select flowers that are not too thick and preferably with a single layer of petals, such as daisies, pansies, or wild roses.
2. Prepare a book: Open a large, heavy book and place a sheet of parchment paper or absorbent paper on one page. If you do not have a big heavy book, try placing bricks or other heavy objects such as weights on top of the flowers to apply pressure. Ensure the weight is evenly distributed to avoid damaging the flowers. Alternatively, purchase a wooden flower press. Just ensure they are stable and evenly distributed.
3. Arrange the flowers: Place the flowers face down on the paper, ensuring they don't overlap.
4. Cover and close: Place another sheet of paper on top of the flowers and carefully close the book.
5. Add weight: Put additional heavy books or objects on top of the closed book to apply even pressure.
6. Wait patiently: Leave the flowers to press for about 2-4 weeks.
7. Check and remove: After the waiting period, carefully open the book and gently remove your pressed flowers.

Tips for Better Results

➢ Press flowers as soon as possible after picking for best colour retention.
➢ Remove any excess moisture from the flowers before pressing.
➢ For thicker flowers, consider pressing petals separately.
➢ Change the parchment paper once or twice a week to prevent browning.

Pressed flowers offer endless creative possibilities for home décor, gifts, and personalised crafts. Here's a list of projects to transform your pressed blooms into stunning creations:

- Framed art: Arrange pressed flowers in photo frames or shadow boxes for timeless wall art. Experiment with dark backgrounds (e.g., navy paper) to make colours pop.
- Lanterns: Adhere flowers to glass jars or vases and add flameless candles.
- Coasters: Seal pressed flowers onto wooden rounds with epoxy resin or Mod Podge for durable, nature-inspired coasters.
- Lampshades: Decorate plain lampshades with pressed blooms for a whimsical lighting accent.
- Bookmarks: Laminate flowers between clear adhesive sheets or embed them in acrylic for elegant, functional bookmarks.
- Greeting cards: Add to handmade cards for weddings, birthdays, or Mother's Day.
- Resin jewellery: Create pendants, earrings, or rings by embedding flowers in resin moulds.
- Holiday ornaments: Make pressed-flower Christmas baubles or Halloween ghost suncatchers with daisy petals.
- Tic-tac-toe rocks: Glue small blooms onto flat stones for a portable nature game.
- Wax seals: Incorporate tiny pressed flowers into melted wax seals for letters or invitations.
- Phone cases: Adhere flowers to plain cases and seal with epoxy resin.
- Tea trays: Transform a simple tray into a floral showpiece with resin-coated blooms.
- Botanical candles: Press flowers onto candle surfaces using heat-safe glue.

Tips for Success

- Use tweezers for precise placement of delicate petals.
- Preserve colour by pressing flowers quickly after picking (single-petal varieties work best).
- Frame projects with mats or shadow boxes to prevent petals from touching glass.

From minimalist wall art to resin-coated functional items, pressed flowers let you bring nature's beauty indoors while crafting meaningful, handmade pieces. Experiment with layering techniques or mix blooms with ferns for dynamic compositions.

Activity 16. Do a wall sit for as long as possible

I really like this exercise because it supports my bad back and I can really feel it working! It targets and strengthens the quadriceps, hamstrings, glutes, calves and most importantly for me the core muscles. This isometric exercise helps build muscular endurance and tone these areas effectively.

When your core muscles are strong, it helps with so many different weakness issues:

1. **Lower Back Pain**: A weak core often leads to chronic lower back pain due to the lack of support for the spine.
2. **Poor Posture**: Weak core muscles can cause poor posture, characterised by slouching or an arched lower back, which may lead to neck strain and spinal misalignment.
3. **Reduced Balance and Stability**: A strong core is essential for balance and stability. Weakness in this area increases the risk of falls and injuries, especially as we age.
4. **Digestive Issues**: Although less commonly discussed, a weak core can contribute to digestive problems due to compromised abdominal muscle function, affecting intra-abdominal pressure regulation.
5. **Sacroiliac Joint Pain**: This type of pain is often linked to core weakness or muscle imbalances, particularly in women. It can be exacerbated by pregnancy and childbirth.

Therefore, doing regular wall sits offers numerous benefits for your body and overall fitness improved posture and balance, increased lower body endurance and stamina for walking, hiking and climbing stairs, improved concentration, focus and perseverance and it offers cardiovascular benefits despite being a static exercise, it can Increase your heart rate, Improve cardiovascular endurance over time and help burn calories, contributing to weight loss efforts.

This exercise convenient, needs no equipment (well it needs a wall!) is suitable for people of various fitness levels. By incorporating wall sits into your regular fitness routine, you can enjoy these diverse benefits and improve your overall physical and mental well-being.

To hold a wall sit for as long as possible, follow these tips and techniques:

Proper Form

1. Stand with your back flat against a wall, feet shoulder-width apart.
2. Slide down the wall until your thighs are parallel to the ground, forming a 90-degree angle at your knees.
3. Keep your entire back pressed against the wall.

4. Ensure your ankles are directly below your knees.

Technique Tips

1. Engage your core muscles to maintain stability.
2. Keep your chest open and shoulders relaxed.
3. Distribute your weight evenly between both feet.
4. Focus on breathing steadily throughout the hold.

Mental Strategies

1. Distract yourself from discomfort by thinking of a "happy place".
2. Use your phone, read a magazine, or perform another task to combat boredom.
3. Set small time goals and gradually increase them.

Progressive Training

1. Start with shorter holds (10-20 seconds for beginners) and gradually increase duration.
2. Aim for 5 repetitions with 30 seconds rest between each.
3. Practice regularly to build endurance, aiming for daily wall sits.

Advanced Variations

Once you've mastered the basic wall sit, try these variations to increase difficulty:

1. Single-leg wall sit: Raise one foot off the ground.
2. Add weight: Hold a dumbbell or plate while performing the wall sit.
3. Decrease the angle: Bring your feet slightly closer to the wall for a more intense hold.

Remember, proper form is crucial for maximizing the benefits and avoiding injury. As you progress, aim to hold the position for longer periods, working up to 60 seconds or more for advanced practitioners.

Record your progress, challenge friends to keep each other accountable or set yourself a 30-day challenge.

Activity 17. Create a small mosaic

Mosaic art is versatile and forgiving, so you don't have to worry about perfectionism. Perfectionism isn't healthy and leads to failure, which perfectionists fear the most, as well as giving you unrealistic expectations and additional unneeded stress and anxiety. The beauty of a mosaic often lies in its unique, handcrafted appearance. With practice, you'll develop your own style and techniques for creating stunning mosaic pieces. Creating a small mosaic is an enjoyable and rewarding craft project that can be accomplished with a few simple steps. Here's a guide to help you get started.

Materials Needed

- Base material (e.g., wooden board, MDF blank, or acrylic tray)
- Mosaic tiles (glass, ceramic, or pre-cut)
- Tile adhesive or PVA glue
- Grout (optional)
- Pencil and paper
- Mosaic cutters or glass cutter (for larger pieces, but you do not need to buy some)
- Sponge or cloth
- Protective gloves

Step-by-Step Process

- Design Your Mosaic - Start by sketching your design on paper. For beginners, it's best to keep the pattern simple. You can then transfer this design onto your chosen base using a pencil or marker.
- Prepare Your Base - If using a wooden base, seal it with a mixture of PVA glue and water (1:1) to prevent warping. Other materials, ensure the surface is clean and dry.
- Arrange your tiles on the base according to your design before gluing. This allows you to make adjustments and ensure you have enough pieces.
- Adhere the Tiles - Apply a thin layer of adhesive or PVA glue to the base and start placing your tiles. Keep the pieces close together for neater grout lines. For a simple project, you can use pre-cut tiles to avoid the need for cutting.
- Allow to dry completely, which usually takes about 24 hours.
- Grouting (Optional) - If desired, apply grout between the tiles using a float or craft stick. Press firmly to fill all gaps. After about 20 minutes, wipe off excess grout with a damp sponge.
- Final Touches - Once the grout is dry, polish the tiles with a dry cloth to restore their shine. You may also apply a sealer for added protection.

Tips for Beginners
- Start with a small project, like a coaster or picture frame.
- Use a variety of colours and shapes to add interest to your design.
- For a grout-free option, consider using Mod Podge Ultra to adhere and seal your mosaic.
- Safety first: Wear gloves and eye protection when handling and cutting tiles.

Some Ideas
- Ceramic Leaf Serving Tray: Decorate a serving tray with ceramic leaf shapes for a nature-inspired look.
- Mosaic Tea Lights: Embellish plain tea light holders with small mosaic pieces for a cozy ambiance.
- Flowery Forest: Create a vibrant forest scene using small, coloured glass pieces on an acrylic tray. This grout-free design allows the colours to shine.
- Broken China Mosaic Flowerpots: Transform plain flower pots by covering them with broken plate pieces and grout.
- Mason Jar Mosaic Backsplash: Create a unique kitchen backsplash using broken tinted mason jars.
- Fancy Mosaic Mirror: Embellish a mirror frame with mosaic tiles and shells for an elegant look.
- Eggshell Vase Mosaic: Use dyed and broken eggshells to create a distinctive vase mosaic.
- Mosaic House Number: Design a personalised house number plaque using mosaic techniques.
- Aim Big! Mosaic Garden Stones: Repurpose broken China cups to make beautiful stepping stones for your garden using concrete instead of grout.

You can adapt these ideas to suit your style and skill level, experimenting with different materials, colours, and patterns to create unique pieces for your home or as gifts.

Remember to properly prepare your chosen materials before using them. They may need to be cleaned, sanded, or treated to ensure they adhere properly and withstand the test of time. Some more mosaic pieces you could use:

- Plates, cups, teapots, jars
- Broken mirrors, CDs, picture frames, jewellery
- Left over craft supplies, cork, shells,
- Old keys, bottle tops, buttons, beads, jigsaw pieces

The charity shop is your best friend; you could buy some China and release your stress by smashing them! Please be careful of splinters and please do not smash any mirrors! Just have fun.

Activity 18. Prepare overnight oats

I love porridge but cold oats for breakfast, I wasn't a fan of how they sounded until I tried them with the ingredients that I enjoy and there are so many scrummy recipes that you can do easily. Overnight oats are an excellent, nutritious breakfast option for people in especially if your body is in some kind of recovery. Here's a simple guide to preparing overnight oat:

Basic Recipe

- 1/2 cup rolled oats
- 1/2 cup milk (dairy, almond, or oat milk)
- 1/4 cup Greek yogurt
- 1 tablespoon chia seeds
- 1 tablespoon honey or maple syrup (optional)

Instructions

1. Mix all ingredients in a jar or container
2. Cover and refrigerate overnight (or at least 4 hours)
3. In the morning, stir and add toppings as desired

Recovery-Supporting Add-ins

- Banana slices: Rich in B6 and potassium, which may be depleted during recovery
- Blueberries: High in antioxidants to support overall health
- Almonds or walnuts: Provide healthy fats and protein
- Pumpkin seeds: Rich in zinc, which can be low in recovering individuals
- Cinnamon: May help regulate blood sugar

Tips for Success

- Prepare multiple jars at once for easy grab-and-go breakfasts
- Experiment with flavours to keep meals interesting and prevent boredom
- Adjust liquid amounts to achieve desired consistency

Remember, a balanced diet is crucial in recovery. Overnight oats provide complex carbohydrates, protein, and fibre, which can help stabilise mood and energy levels throughout the day.

Overnight oats can be made fun and different in several ways with different flavour combinations, colours and textures:

- Try peanut butter and jelly overnight oats with layers of peanut butter, strawberry jelly, fresh strawberries, and crushed peanuts.
- Make tiramisu overnight oats for a coffee-flavoured dessert-like breakfast.
- Enjoy birthday cake overnight oats with rainbow sprinkles and cake flavour.
- Apple pie overnight oats with chopped apples, pecans, maple syrup, and cinnamon for a fall treat.
- Pumpkin pie overnight oats using pumpkin, pumpkin pie spice, and vanilla extract.
- Make "carrot cake" oats with shredded carrots, cinnamon, and optional raisins or walnuts.
- Layer ingredients in clear jars to create visually appealing parfaits.
- Use vibrant fruits like blueberries or strawberries to add natural colour.
- Add chocolate chips, coconut flakes, or cacao nibs for extra texture and flavour.
- Top with homemade granola for a crunchy contrast.

By experimenting with flavours, presentations, and interactive elements, you can transform overnight oats into a fun and exciting breakfast experience.

Activity 19. Organise a junk drawer

Who is with me?! That drawer in the kitchen, your office, next to your bed or all of them... the plasters are with the lightbulbs that you don't think work, but will keep 'just in case', the instruction manual for the George Foreman you haven't had for 10 years is hiding a tangled mess of 40 odd cables, that you don't know what they fit or if you need them! For these very reasons organising a junk drawer can have several wellbeing benefits, both mentally and emotionally. It reduces stress, improves focus, boosts your mood and enhances productivity! Yeap, it really does!

Cluttered spaces can increase stress levels by creating a sense of unfinished work. Organising a junk drawer helps reduce this stress by removing visual clutter and creating a more organised environment. A cluttered environment can be distracting, making it harder to focus. By organising, you can create a clearer space that helps improve concentration and mental clarity and help you become more productive by reducing time spent searching for items and increasing efficiency in daily tasks.

Decluttering and organising can release, what we are ultimately after, a dopamine release, which is associated with feelings of satisfaction and happiness. This can lead to an improved mood and overall sense of well-being.

Successfully organising a junk drawer can give you a tangible sense of accomplishment, which can boost confidence and motivate you to tackle other areas of your life. Decluttering can help you let go of emotional baggage associated with cluttered items, allowing you to move forward and create space for new experiences.

Organising your environment can give you a greater sense of control over your life, which is beneficial for emotional well-being.

Specific Considerations for ADHD

For individuals with ADHD, a junk drawer can serve as a functional space if managed intentionally. It can act as a designated drop-off point for frequently used items, helping maintain consistency and reducing visible clutter that might distract from important tasks. However, it's important to ensure that the junk drawer doesn't become a repository for unnecessary items, which can lead to stress and disorganisation.

I need checklists/to-do lists to motivate me, so don't be offended. Here is an effective strategy to follow:

1. Empty the drawer completely, removing all items and place them on a clean, flat surface.
2. Clean the drawer, wiping down the inside of the drawer with a damp cloth.

3. Sort items: Group similar items together (e.g., office supplies, tools, electronics) and create piles for "keep," "relocate," and "discard."
4. Purge unnecessary items: Throw away broken or useless items and relocate items that belong elsewhere.
6. Invest in drawer organisers using small containers, dividers, or an organiser tray.
7. Arrange items strategically: Place frequently used items in easily accessible spots or group similar items together in designated sections.
8. Label compartments using a label maker or tape to clearly mark each section.
9. Implement a system: Create a "one in, one out" rule to maintain organisation, plus regularly review and declutter (e.g., every 3-6 months, popping it on your calendar).
10. Consider functionality, keeping only items that are genuinely useful in this drawer, then take a few minutes each week to ensure items are in their proper place.

Extra Tips

- Use these steps, to transform your junk drawer into an organised, functional space and add some creative ways to use dividers in a junk drawer:
- Repurpose everyday items, using cereal boxes, small cardboard boxes, or aluminium cans (be careful!) cut to size as DIY dividers.
- Use adjustable/interlock dividers to create sections that perfectly fit your needs.
- Use vertical dividers to store taller items like pens, scissors, or small tools upright.
- Use mini jars, plastic containers, or repurposed packaging to hold tiny items within larger compartments.
- Utilise drawer depth: For deeper drawers, stack dividers or use tiered organisers to maximise vertical space.
- Create a modular system: Use removable dividers that can be rearranged as your storage needs change over time.
- Add clear labels on dividers to ensure items are returned to their proper place and maintain organisation.

Mix and match materials, combining different types of dividers like bamboo, plastic, and fabric for a unique look and varied functionality. Think about using decorative paper or fabric. While not a structural material, you can use decorative paper or fabric to cover cardboard or foam board dividers for a personalised touch. Get artistic, get having fun and get organised!

Activity 20. Identify different bird species in your yard

Right, well I am no birdwatcher, but after the rabbit hole of research I did for this topic, I feel like an expert! I know all the terms and let me just say, as long as no one calls you a 'stringer', the worst insult in birding, then you are doing alright! But honestly from my research, and this all makes sense, bird watching in your own yard, garden or local area offers numerous mental and physical benefits:

- Observing birds can lower cortisol levels (stress) and decrease feelings of anxiety for up to eight hours
- Birdwatching has been shown to boost positive emotions, self-esteem, in-turn improving your mood
- The activity can restore cognitive energy, improve focus, and boost memory
- Identifying birds encourages present-moment awareness, similar to meditation practices
- Observing birds can make you feel more connected to nature and less isolated
- Birdwatching often involves walking and moving around, which can improve cardiovascular health
- Spending time outdoors while birdwatching allows for natural vitamin D absorption
- Time spent in nature observing birds can help reduce blood pressure
- Regular birdwatching can contribute to lowering the risk of chronic diseases like arthritis, heart disease, and diabetes

Identifying birds in your yard is an accessible way to engage with nature, providing both mental relaxation and gentle physical activity. It's a hobby that can be enjoyed by people of all ages and fitness levels, offering a sustainable approach to improving overall well-being.

I went to Cardiff last week as I was running an International Women's Event and I was stressed beyond belief. My hotel was in the Bay and it was beautiful. I went outside for a stroll and came across a sign pointing out the local birds. I read it and spent a really lovely, peaceful 20 minutes just looking at the birds. To be fair all I saw were seagulls and pigeons, none of the beautiful birds on the sign, but I treasure those times, in my own world with no worries, no phone buzzing. I was looking at nature and not the endless scroll of 'news' feeds on my phone. There is a lot to be said for that! There obviously won't be a sign in your garden or randomly on the street, so try having a look at one of the apps which you can download and people won't even know what you are doing.

1. Merlin Bird ID - a free app which offers multiple ways to identify birds:
- Answer questions about the bird's appearance and behaviour
- Upload a photo for AI-powered identification
- Record bird sounds for automatic recognition

- Explore birds in your region

2. Smart Bird ID - covers over 1000 bird species from the UK and Europe:
- Identify birds using your camera or microphone
- Add observations to a personal journal
- Listen to bird calls and songs
- Improve skills with quizzes

3. BirdTrack - a citizen science project for recording bird observations:
- Log sightings with precise locations using GPS
- Contribute to conservation efforts
- Maintain personal lists and records

4. eBird - a global platform for finding and recording birds:
- Search local hotspots for recent sightings
- Submit your own checklists
- Track personal life and year lists

5. Seek - while not exclusively for birds, this app can help with general wildlife:
- Photo-based identification for various taxa
- Gamified experience with challenges and achievements

A great site that I found gives great descriptions, colour pictures, times of year usually spotted etc. is: https://birdfact.com/articles/garden-birds-in-the-uk

Some key tips & ways of identifying birds:

- Focus on the size and shape, colour patterns, behaviour, habitat and distinctive markings
- Listen to bird calls, as many birds are easier to identify by sound rather than by sight. Use apps like Merlin Bird ID or ChirpOMatic to record and identify bird songs and calls.
- Use binoculars, so you do not scare them away
- Maintain a record/journal of the birds you see, including the date and time of sighting, weather conditions, the bird behaviour and activity
- Set Up a Feeding Station to attract a variety of birds to your yard for easier observation offering different types of food (seeds, suet, fruits), provide water sources like bird baths and install various feeder types to attract different species
- If you really get into it, participate in local birding events or join a birding club to learn from experienced birders and improve your identification skills.

By combining these methods, you'll become more proficient at identifying the bird species visiting your yard.

Activity 21. Leave positive reviews for local businesses

Some people are so quick to leave a negative review, even before they have found out the reason why something had gone wrong, sort replacements or a chance for the people to put wrongs right or blame the wrong people i.e. the retailer instead of the delivery company. We often forget to write reviews when we receive a good service, something special or just for our local businesses which we may take a bit for granted.

The first time I tried a Chinese takeaway near me, the food containers arrived with lovely messages on 'enjoy, your evening', 'May this weekend bring you love & laughter' and just things to make me smile. I always use this Chinese now and not just because of the messages but the food is great. They take the effort to handwrite these on every container, every time. I wrote a review! I also write one every few months because they deserve recognition and it keeps the reviews fresh if other people are not adding one. If I receive one bad meal, I am not going to go all out to write a bad review, because that is not my general experience with them and it is not my nature. Plus my bad takeaway could have been 'spot-on' for someone else.

Anyway, do you have a local shop you often use? I do, they know my name, they know what I like, we chat about the weather, the rugby, the boy racers, point me in the right direction if I need a plumber. They deserve a review! If it is a local shop we think everyone knows the place, but what about the people that don't. The people that move to the area or need a place to collect parcels from, where they will feel safe and looked after. Do they need their opening hours updating to help other customers or some details of what you can purchase there?

The small things we take for granted can mean so much to small businesses and trades people, especially in today's age where advertising costs a fortune and there are so many places that want to charge for the pleasure. FB and other social media, local papers, yell.com, traders expert websites, just to name a few, even to put a postcard up in a shop if they will even let you.

Writing positive reviews you both good for you and the businesses, they allow you to express gratitude and focus on positive experiences. This practice of gratitude can improve your overall mood and well-being.

- By leaving helpful reviews, you contribute to your community and support local businesses. This can provide a sense of purpose and fulfilment.
- Writing about positive experiences helps you process and relive those moments, potentially extending the positive emotions associated with them.
- Expressive writing, such as composing reviews, has been linked to reduced stress levels for those who do it regularly.
- Reflecting on and writing about positive experiences can lead to improved mood and increased happiness.

- Regular expressive writing has been associated with improved overall well-being.
- Providing feedback gives you a sense of empowerment, knowing that your voice can make a difference for both businesses and other consumers.
- Writing reviews can help you feel more connected to your local community, fostering a sense of belonging.

By taking the time to leave positive reviews for local businesses, you not only support those businesses but also engage in an activity that can benefit your own mental health and well-being.

Have a think or google of local tradespeople or businesses and help make their day, as well as yours.

Activity 22. Engage in a quick social media interaction

I am not advocating social media, and if you are having a difficult time with it, please do not engage. Social media definitely has its positives as well as negatives, it is about using it wisely and knowing your limits. I know many people in recovery who have set up new profiles that are under nick names or aliases so their 'old circle' of friends are not aware of their presence, as ensuring your profile is set to private can provide you with more protection against unwanted attention. Heavy social media use has been linked to an increased risk of depression, anxiety, and psychological distress. The constant exposure to curated content can lead to feelings of inadequacy and low self-esteem, particularly among adolescents. Do not let FOMO, the "Fear of Missing Out" catch you out, social media isn't always what it seems.

Social media platforms are designed to be addictive, activating the brain's reward centre by releasing dopamine. This can lead to compulsive checking and scrolling, disrupting daily activities and sleep patterns. I hear that TikTok is the worst for this, hence why I am not on it.

To address these concerns, experts recommend:

1. Limiting social media use to 30 minutes per day, which has been shown to reduce symptoms of loneliness and depression.
2. Practicing mindful usage by being aware of time spent and emotional responses to social media.
3. Prioritising real-world connections and face-to-face interactions.
4. Curating social media feeds to focus on positive and supportive content.
5. Taking regular breaks from social media, including "digital detoxes".

By being aware of these pitfalls and taking proactive steps to manage social media use, individuals can work towards a healthier relationship with these platforms and protect their overall wellbeing.

Ok, for the positives! Engaging in quick social media interactions i.e. not spending hours scrolling, can offer several wellbeing benefits:

Social media interactions can provide rapid access to social support, especially during times of stress or hardship. A quick interaction can help users feel more connected to their friends' lives and provide a sense of having a support network. Participating in online communities or groups, even briefly, can foster a sense of belonging and connection to like-minded individuals. Social media can provide safe spaces for individuals to express themselves and affirm their identities, particularly for marginalised groups like LGBTQ+ youth.

You can connect with my group for ongoing support:
https://www.facebook.com/groups/happiermoreresilientyou

Social media platforms serve as channels for mental health Organisations to share resources, tips, and information about available services. Open discussions about mental health on social media can help reduce stigma and foster empathy and understanding. This can also help decrease feelings of loneliness, particularly for individuals with underlying mental health issues. These interactions offer opportunities to maintain existing social networks and feel more connected to others.

It can lead to short-term positive emotions. Engaging with feel-good and motivational content can promote mental well-being by introducing positivity into one's day and provide a brief escape from daily stressors, offering a moment of distraction or entertainment that can help alleviate stress. Social media can be a tool for making new friends based on shared hobbies, interests, or identities. Platforms like Facebook and Instagram can be used to engage with new people who may develop into real-life friends.

Social media provides an outlet for self-expression, allowing users to share their thoughts, experiences, or creative content quickly. This can contribute to a sense of personal growth and identity development.

Activity 23. Practise & Hold Power Poses

I am hearing about this more and more. I won't lie, I did feel a bit daft at first, but something does shift within you when you practise these poses! A new confidence, a solid foundation, rooted to the ground, I am not 100% sure how to describe it, you will just have to try it.

Power posing is a technique where individuals adopt expansive, open body postures associated with confidence and dominance for a short period of time, typically 1-2 minutes. The concept was popularised by social psychologist Amy Cuddy in a 2012 TED Talk that has since garnered over 70 million views.

Power posing studies have reported that 86% of participants who adopted power poses felt more confident in subsequent tasks. Some found a 25% decrease in cortisol (a stress hormone) levels after power posing. A 2020 meta-analysis of 73 studies found that open poses, compared to closed poses, had significant effects on mood.

Power poses may help individuals feel more grounded and attentive in social situations. The confidence boost from power posing might lead to better performance in tasks like public speaking or job interviews.

While the physical health benefits are less established, although initial studies suggested power posing could increase testosterone levels and decrease cortisol, though these findings have been debated. Practicing power poses may contribute to better overall posture, potentially alleviating issues like back pain and headaches, which I have found myself. Good posture associated with power poses may improve circulation and increase energy levels. Some research suggests that reducing stress through techniques like power posing might benefit immunity.

It's important to note that while many people report feeling more confident after power posing, the scientific community remains divided on some of the claimed physiological effects. The most consistent finding across studies is that power posing can make individuals feel more powerful and confident, which may have positive impacts on mental well-being and performance in various situations.

Power posing can be particularly useful in certain contexts:

- Use as a quick mood booster
- Before important events: Practicing power poses for about two minutes before interviews, presentations, or challenging meetings may help boost confidence.
- In professional settings: Especially for women, adopting high power poses can help exude confidence and assertiveness in work environments.

While the effectiveness of power poses can vary from person to person, several specific poses are frequently cited as being particularly impactful:

1. The Wonder Woman Pose

This is arguably the most well-known and popular power pose:
- Stand with feet apart
- Hands on hips
- Chest lifted and head held high
- Lean slightly forward

2. The Victory/Starfish Pose

Also known as the "Performer" pose:
- Stand with arms stretched up in a V shape
- Spread fingers wide
- Imagine celebrating a victory

3. The CEO Pose

Designed to convey authority and relaxation:
- Sit in a chair with feet up on a desk
- Hands behind head
- Lean back slightly

Additional Effective Poses

4. The Salutation
- Plant feet firmly
- Lift chest and head
- Outstretch both arms with palms facing up
- Face lifted towards the sky

5. The LBJ (Loomer)

Named after President Lyndon B. Johnson:
- Lean slightly forward onto a desk or chair back
- Place hands on the surface
- Useful for commanding attention in business scenarios

While these poses are often cited as effective, it's important to note that the scientific community remains divided on some of the claimed physiological effects of power posing. However, many people report feeling more confident after practicing these poses, which may contribute to improved performance and well-being.

Activity 24. Upcycle an old t-shirt into a reusable bag

Now this is right up my street! A bit of art and another bag, you can never have too many bags! Get rig of old clothes to make room for something new, made by your fair hands. I have made loads of tie-dye totes before, using lots of elastic bands and also water repelling clothes spray, but these were a new level for me. By the way, I can not sew for toffee, but mine came out pretty good and you do not need to sew!

This is a great way to upcycling exercise and anything artistic will help you to be in the present moment. There is great satisfaction in being able to use something you have made yourself and be proud of it, enter into a conversation when someone asks 'Where did you get that bag from?'. Here's a simple method to create your own reusable shopping bag:

1. Prepare the t-shirt by turning it inside out and lay it flat on a surface.
2. Remove the sleeves cutting along the seams where the sleeves meet the body of the shirt, this will create the bag's handles.
3. Cut the neckline:
    o Cut a wider, deeper neckline to create a larger opening for your bag.
    o You can make it U-shaped or oval, removing about 2-3 inches from the original neckline.
4. Reinforce the bottom (optional but recommended for heavier items):
    o If using a sewing machine, sew a straight stitch across the bottom of the shirt about 1-2 inches from the edge.
    o For extra strength, sew a second line of stitches just above the first.
5. Create a flat bottom (optional):
    o While the shirt is still inside out, flatten one corner of the bottom.
    o Sew a diagonal line across the corner, about 2 inches from the point.
    o Repeat for the other corner.
    o Trim off the excess fabric beyond the stitching.
6. No-sew alternative for the bottom:
    o If you don't have a sewing machine, you can create a fringed bottom.
    o Cut slits about 3/4 inch apart and 3 inches deep along the bottom edge.
    o Tie the corresponding front and back fringe pieces together to close the bottom.
7. Finish by turning the bag right side out and trim any loose threads.

Your t-shirt is now transformed into a reusable shopping bag! This bag is washable, making it easy to clean and reuse multiple times. It's perfect for groceries, beach items, or as an everyday tote, but please test it first if you plan to put breakables in such as eggs, glass etc.

Besides tote bags, you can repurpose old t-shirts into several other types of bags:

Drawstring Bags - Create a simple drawstring bag by sewing the bottom of the t-shirt closed and using the existing hem at the top to thread a drawstring through. These are great for gym clothes, shoes, or as gift bags.

Backpacks – This is a bit too adventurous for me, but worth a Google! - Transform a larger t-shirt into a backpack by adding straps and creating a closure at the top. This can be done with some basic sewing skills and is perfect for casual day trips or beach outings.

Clutch or Zipper Pouch - Cut the t-shirt into smaller pieces and sew them together to create a clutch or zipper pouch. These are great for organizing small items in your larger bags or as standalone accessories.

Crossbody Bags - Cut the t-shirt strategically and add a long strap to create a casual crossbody bag. This style is perfect for everyday use or as a lightweight travel bag.

Remember that while t-shirts are great for small bags, they may not be suitable for weight-bearing due to the fabric's stretch and potential lack of durability, for these, choose thicker t-shirts (polo shirt?) or reinforce the fabric for a sturdier bag.

Here are some creative designs you can use for fabric painting on your t-shirt bag:

- **Floral Patterns**: Paint vibrant flowers or botanical illustrations. You could create a field of wildflowers or a single large bloom.
- **Abstract Nature**: Create swirling patterns reminiscent of leaves, waves, or clouds for a more artistic interpretation of nature.
- **Tropical Motifs**: Paint colourful toucans, palm leaves, or other tropical elements.
- **Ombre Effect**: Create a gradient effect using different shades of one colour for a simple yet striking look.
- **Pop Art**: Draw inspiration from pop artists to create bold, eye-catching designs.
- **Monograms**: Paint your initials or name in a stylised font.
- **Favourite Quotes**: Write an inspiring quote or lyrics from your favourite song.
- **Pet Portraits**: Paint a portrait of your furry friend or their paw prints.
- **Bookish Designs**: Create a design inspired by your favourite book or literary character.
- **Tie-Dye Effects**: Create interesting patterns using tie-dye techniques like hearts, polka dots, or kaleidoscope designs.
- **Texture Play**: Use different brushes, sponges, or even a blow dryer to create unique textures in your design.
- **Glow-in-the-Dark**: Incorporate glow-in-the-dark paint for a fun, luminescent effect.

Remember to choose fabric paints that work well with the colour of your t-shirt bag and place a piece of cardboard inside the bag while painting to prevent bleed-through.

Don't forget to heat-set your design with an iron when it's completely dry to ensure durability.

To make a waterproof t-shirt bag, apply a waterproofing spray designed for fabrics and for added protection, consider lining the inside of the bag with a waterproof material like PUL (Polyurethane Laminate) fabric or a repurposed shower curtain.

Activity 25. Make a DIY Natural Air Freshener

As you may have guessed by now, I absolutely love making things, any things. Knowing what the ingredients are, knowing I have made the effort to make something safe and smelling great. I have tried to make the ingredients in things as simple as possible and easy to get your hands on, without costing much if you have to purchase it. Making your own products can be much more cost effective than buying commercial products.

Making your own DIY natural air avoids synthetic chemicals and volatile organic compounds (VOCs) found in many commercial air fresheners which reduces the risk of allergic reactions, respiratory issues, and other health concerns, making them safe for you, kids and pets. You know what you are putting in the product, so it allows for personalised scents by mixing different essential oils and you can easily make the scent stronger or add different scents if wanted.

Essential oils used in natural air fresheners can offer therapeutic benefits like relaxation or invigoration and naturally purify the air, whereas some ingredients, such as baking soda, can even absorb odours while freshening the air. To make a DIY Natural Air Freshener without alcohol, follow this simple recipe:

Ingredients:
- 1 cup distilled water
- 20-30 drops of essential oils (your choice of scents)
- 1 tablespoon witch hazel (as a substitute for alcohol)

Instructions:
1. Fill a clean spray bottle with 1 cup of distilled water.
2. Add 20-30 drops of your preferred essential oils (see below)
3. Add 1 tablespoon of witch hazel to help the oils and water combine.
4. Shake the bottle well before each use to mix the ingredients.

This alcohol-free air freshener is natural, non-toxic, and customisable to your preferred scents. Adjust the number of essential oil drops to make the fragrance stronger or milder.

Alternative Methods:

1. Baking Soda Freshener: Mix baking soda with several drops of essential oils in an open container. This absorbs odours and releases a pleasant scent.
2. Stovetop Simmer: For an immediate freshening effect, simmer water with natural ingredients like cinnamon sticks, citrus slices, or herb sprigs on your stovetop.
3. Salt Diffuser: Mix crushed sea salt with essential oils and place in a decorative dish to naturally diffuse fragrance.

4. Remember to use caution when spraying around delicate fabrics or surfaces, and always shake the bottle before use to ensure the ingredients are well-mixed.

Coffee is highly effective as a natural air freshener, as it:

- **Absorbs odours:** coffee grounds contain nitrogen, which helps absorb and neutralise unpleasant odours.
- **Has a pleasant aroma:** the rich aroma of coffee can quickly fill a room, masking unwanted odours while providing a pleasant scent. Coffee's unique fragrance contains over 800 aromatic compounds, more than wine, with about 11 of these smelling like chocolate.
- **Is a mood enhancer:** coffee fragrance inhalation has been shown to enhance cognitive parameters, including continuity of attention, quality of memory, and speed of memory. It also increases alertness.
- **Is versatile:** it can be used as an air freshener in various ways:
  - Placing dried coffee grounds in a cloth bag in refrigerators or cars
  - Simmering coffee grounds with water on the stove
  - Using coffee beans in a room or car
- **Is natural and eco-friendly:** unlike chemical air fresheners, coffee is a natural and environmentally friendly option, free from harsh chemicals.

Essential oils suggestions for natural air fresheners:
- **Vanilla extract:** Real vanilla extract can serve as both an alcohol base and add a pleasant scent to your air freshener
- **Citrus Oils**
  - Lemon: Refreshing and bright, it helps neutralise odours
  - Orange: Sweet and uplifting
  - Bergamot: Citrusy with floral notes, great for energising blends
- **Herbal Oils**
  - Lavender: Calming and versatile, perfect for bedrooms
  - Peppermint: Invigorating and helps improve focus
  - Eucalyptus: Refreshing and great for clearing sinuses
- **Woody Oils**
  - Tea Tree: Strong antibacterial properties, use sparingly
  - Cedarwood: Warm and grounding
- **Floral Oils**
  - Geranium: Balancing and uplifting
  - Ylang Ylang: Sweet and exotic, good for focus blends
- **Spicy Oils**
  - Cinnamon: Warm and inviting, perfect for holiday blends
  - Clove: Spicy and comforting

These oils can be combined to create custom blends, such as for a popular energising blend use 5 drops bergamot, 4 drops grapefruit, & 3 drops lemongrass and for a calming blend, try 10 drops lavender, 5 drops chamomile, and 5 drops sweet orange.

Activity 26. Make flavoured water

Drinking water plays a crucial role in the day-to-day functioning and recovery of the body. When reducing or have stopped consuming alcohol, starting to drink water is so vitally important. Addiction aside here are just some of the things that can cause dehydration in day-to-day life:

1. Excessive sweating from exercise or physical labour	16. Certain medical conditions (e.g., kidney disease, cystic fibrosis)
2. Hot and humid weather conditions	17. Intense heat exposure (saunas, hot tubs)
3. High altitude environments	18. Strenuous outdoor activities
4. Not drinking enough water throughout the day	19. Skipping meals
5. Consuming caffeinated beverages (coffee, tea, energy drinks)	20. Smoking
6. Pollution	21. High-protein diets
7. Diuretic medications	22. Certain medications (e.g., some blood pressure medications)
8. Fever	23. Pregnancy and breastfeeding
9. Diarrhoea	24. Menstruation
10. Vomiting	25. Illness
11. Excessive urination (e.g., due to diabetes or certain medications)	26. Fasting or restrictive diets
12. Burns or skin injuries	27. Prolonged exposure to air conditioning
13. Severe sunburn	28. Certain occupations (e.g., firefighters, construction workers)
14. Prolonged air travel	29. Endurance sports
15. Eating a diet low in water-rich foods	30. Chronic stress

Remember, staying hydrated is crucial for overall health and well-being. It's important to be aware of these factors and ensure adequate fluid intake, especially when engaging in activities or experiencing conditions that may increase the risk of dehydration.

Need more reasons why it's so important?

Combating Dehydration - Alcohol is a diuretic that causes excessive urine production, leading to dehydration. When you stop drinking alcohol, your body needs to rehydrate and recover from this chronic dehydration. Proper hydration is essential for various bodily functions, including Nutrient transport, Temperature regulation and Waste elimination.

By increasing water intake during recovery from any illness, you support your body's efforts to heal and function optimally.
Supporting Detoxification of any kind - During a detox, your body works overtime to eliminate toxins accumulated from substance use whether alcohol, medication, excess

salt, sugar caffeine. Adequate hydration aids this process by helping the kidneys filter toxins more efficiently, supporting liver function in processing and removing alcohol-related toxins and facilitating waste removal through urine, sweat, and bowel movements

Alleviating Withdrawal Symptoms - Proper hydration can help mitigate some withdrawal symptoms, such as headaches, nausea, fatigue and dizziness. Have you ever had a caffeine withdrawal headache? I found this worse than a hangover headache!! By staying well-hydrated, you may experience less severe symptoms and a smoother recovery process.

Improving Cognitive Function and Mood - Dehydration can negatively impact brain function and emotional stability. Adequate water intake during recovery supports better cognitive function, including improved focus and decision-making and enhanced mood regulation, which is crucial for managing the emotional challenges of recovery.

Reducing Cravings - Dehydration can sometimes be mistaken for substance cravings. By maintaining proper hydration, you may experience fewer sugar cravings that could be confused with alcohol cravings and reduced overall cravings for substances.

Enhancing Physical Recovery - As your body heals from the effects of alcohol abuse, proper hydration supports improved skin and hair health, better joint lubrication and tissue repair, enhanced energy levels and more efficient nutrient absorption.

So you can see just how easily we can get dehydrated and how important it is to keep hydrated. If you struggle with water or need to twist, using natural ingredients can assist in helping you stay motivated and drink more water. My absolute favourite is cucumber and mint, but I like a strong flavour, so I infuse it for longer and add more ingredients.

Here are simple instructions to make flavoured water:

1. Choose your flavours, selecting fresh ingredients like citrus fruits, berries, cucumber, mint, or ginger. Use organic produce when possible for the best flavour and to avoid pesticides.

2. Prepare the ingredients by washing all produce thoroughly, then slicing fruits and vegetables thinly for maximum flavour infusion.

3. Combine the ingredients and cold water in a pitcher or large water bottle.

4. Allow to infuse in the refrigerator for at least 1-2 hours, or overnight for stronger flavour.

5. Strain and serve, removing the fruits/herbs or strain the water if desired and serve chilled, optionally over ice. I do not strain my flavoured water.

Remember to replace the fruits/herbs every 24-48 hours to keep fresh and flavourful.

Have a try of some of these flavour combinations or experiment with your own:

- Cucumber and basil
- Strawberry and lime
- Watermelon and basil
- Peach and Vanilla: Sliced peaches with a vanilla bean
- Blackberry and Sage: Fresh blackberries with sage leaves
- Fig and Thyme: Sliced figs with fresh thyme sprigs
- Cantaloupe and Lavender: Cubed cantaloupe with lavender buds
- Pear and Cinnamon: Sliced pears with a cinnamon stick
- Dragon Fruit and Lemongrass: Cubed dragon fruit with lemongrass stalks
- Apricot and Rosemary: Sliced apricots with rosemary sprigs

Activity 27. Set up a digital calendar

I must admit, I have a digital calendar, a wall planner, a physical calendar, a diary and a life planner. I know, I'm a bit mad, and I am a sucker for a new planner, but my digital calendar is the most valuable to me, for many reasons:

- I have colour coding to easily see if I have the gym that day, going out to an event, a study day, a podcast etc
- I can easily move dates and times without big scribbles in my diary
- I don't lose my digital calendar and don't forget it as it's on my phone and laptop
- I can block out days, like this weekend for the rugby or my holidays so people can't book into my calendar for appointments or podcasts, without me spending time going through my diary to find a spot for them. I do not even have to get involved, they can just book without having to speak with me, saving so much time!
- I can automatically post entries to occur daily (habit reminders), weekly (aqua aerobics), monthly (webinar events), annually (birthdays).
- I can save Zoom links and emails to the entry, saves me going through emails to try and find it on the day I need it.
- I can share the calendar with people if needed with a couple of clicks.

It has made my life so much easier and saved a lot of time for both me and my clients. Setting up a digital calendar is a straightforward process that can help you stay organised and manage your time effectively. Here's how to set up a digital calendar using Google Calendar:

1. Sign in to your Google Account and navigate to the Google Calendar page.
2. On the left side of the screen, scroll down to "Other calendars" and click the + button.
3. Select "Create new calendar" from the options.
4. Enter a name for your new calendar and an optional description.
5. Choose the appropriate time zone for your events.
6. Click "Create calendar" to finish.

After creating your calendar, you can personalise it:
1. Hover over the calendar name in the "My Calendars" list.
2. Click the three horizontal dots that appear.
3. Choose a colour to differentiate this calendar's events from others.

To add an event:
1. Click on the desired date and time slot in your calendar.
2. Enter the event details, such as title, time, and location.
3. Select the appropriate calendar if you have multiple ones.
4. Click "Save" to add the event.

Once you've set up your Google Calendar on a web browser, it will automatically sync with the Google Calendar app on your mobile devices, allowing you to access and manage your schedule on the go.

If I haven't given you enough reasons to set up a digital calendar, then make one of your own, or make one for someone else with quotes or pictures on it.

1. Select a calendar format that suits your needs, such as Wall calendar, Desk calendar, Planner/agenda book or Monthly/weekly/daily pages in a binder

2. Consider size, layout, and extra features like note sections or goal-setting pages.

3. Gather your Supplies, such as Coloured pens or markers, highlighters, sticky notes and stickers (optional for marking special events and they make events stand out more)

4. Write in recurring events such as birthdays and anniversaries, regular meetings or classes and bill due dates

5. Add important dates such as holidays, social events, appointments and school or work deadlines

6. Use colour-coding by assigning colours to different types of activities (e.g., blue for work, green for personal) and use a highlighter to emphasise important events

Maintain Your Calendar

1. Keep it in a visible, easily accessible place.
2. Review it daily, preferably in the morning or evening.
3. Update regularly, crossing off completed tasks and adding new events.
4. Use sticky notes for tentative plans or reminders.

By following these steps, you can create a simple, effective paper calendar system to help you stay organised and manage your time efficiently.

Activity 28. Practice portrait photography

This is a great thing to do to show how far you've come in recovery, use as a diary and use these photos for a recovery collage or in some of the other challenges in this book.

Practicing portrait photography at home can be beneficial for mental health, as it requires concentration and attention to detail, which can act as a form of mindfulness. This focus on the present moment can help reduce stress and anxiety by distracting from negative thoughts. The act of engaging in a hobby like photography can be a form of stress relief, providing a break from daily worries and allowing you to enter a state of flow.

It allows for creative self-expression, which can be therapeutic. It provides an outlet for emotions and can help process feelings that may be difficult to put into words. This all helps to boost self-esteem and confidence. Self-portraits, in particular, can be a powerful tool for self-exploration and improving self-image. They can help you recognise your strengths and increase self-esteem.

Sharing your photos and receiving positive feedback can further enhance your sense of accomplishment. You can involve family members or roommates as subjects, fostering positive interactions and strengthening relationships. To practice portrait photography at home, you can follow these steps:

Set Up Your Space

1. Find a room with good natural light, preferably near a large window
2. Choose a simple background, like a blank wall or a plain backdrop
3. Clear the area of clutter to keep the focus on your subject

Lighting Techniques

1. Position your subject at a 45-degree angle to the window for flattering light
2. Use reflectors or white boards to bounce light and fill in shadows
3. Experiment with different times of day to capture various lighting moods

Posing and Composition

1. Practice the 45-degree rule: turn the subject's body slightly away from the camera
2. Try different head tilts and shoulder positions
3. Experiment with various compositions, including close-ups and full-body shots

Subject Ideas

1. Self-portraits using a tripod or remote shutter

2. Family members or roommates
3. Pets
4. Still life objects for practicing lighting and composition

Additional Tips

1. Take regular breaks to keep your subject relaxed and natural
2. Shoot in RAW format for more flexibility in post-processing
3. Practice different facial expressions and emotions with your subjects
4. Experiment with props or clothing changes to add variety to your shots

Remember, the key to improving your portrait photography is consistent practice and experimentation. Don't be afraid to try new techniques and learn from your mistakes.

Some other tips:

Experiment with different angles and perspectives to add visual interest to your selfies. Try shooting from below to create a sense of power, or from above for a more vulnerable look. Consider using the rule of thirds to create a balanced composition.

Lighting is crucial for artistic selfies. Natural light from windows can create beautiful, soft effects. For a more dramatic look, experiment with side lighting to create interesting shadows and highlights on your face. You can also use artificial light sources like lamps or even your phone's flashlight to create unique lighting effects.

Incorporate props that reflect your personality or tell a story. This could be anything from your favourite book to a musical instrument. Choose interesting backgrounds or locations that complement your artistic vision.

Use reflective surfaces creatively. Mirrors are classic, but consider other reflective objects like windows, metal surfaces, or even puddles of water for unique effects.

Activity 29. Try a walking meditation

A walking meditation is a mindfulness practice that combines the physical act of walking with meditative techniques. It's an excellent way to incorporate mindfulness into daily activities and can be particularly beneficial for those who find it challenging to sit still during traditional meditation.

Why do it? Well, I am just going to list a load of benefits both physical and mental, as I feel they need no further explanation:

- **Reduces Sedentary Behaviour**: Increases physical activity and daily steps, contributing to overall fitness.
- **Improves Balance**: Enhances balance by focusing on foot placement, particularly beneficial for older adults.
- **Supports Brain Health**: Linked to healthier brain aging and improved cognition.
- **Weight Management**: Can aid in weight loss through increased metabolism and improved digestion.
- **Reduces Risk of Chronic Diseases**: Helps lower the risk of heart disease, cancer, and other conditions by promoting regular physical activity.
- **Reduces Stress and Anxiety**: Triggers the parasympathetic nervous system, leading to relaxation and reduced stress hormones.
- **Improves Mood**: Enhances mood by releasing endorphins and reducing symptoms of depression.
- **Enhances Mindfulness**: Cultivates mindfulness by encouraging presence and awareness of surroundings.
- **Improves Concentration and Focus**: Develops mental discipline, improving concentration and focus.
- **Promotes Emotional Regulation**: Helps manage emotions by observing them without judgment.
- **Improves Sleep Quality**: Associated with better sleep and coping with mood disorders.
- **Supports Mental Well-being**: Offers symptom relief for mental health conditions like anxiety and depression.
- **Connection with Nature**: Provides an opportunity to connect with nature, which can further enhance mental well-being.
- **Flexibility and Accessibility**: Can be practiced anywhere, making it suitable for busy lifestyles.

Here's how to try a walking meditation:

1. Choose a quiet, safe path or area where you can walk for 10-15 minutes without interruption. This can be done inside as well but try to find a relatively flat and free from obstacles area. Ensure you're wearing comfortable shoes and consider using cushioned insoles. Get creative with spaces at home, outdoor tracks,

parks, or even large store aisles. For indoor practice, use a long hallway or a quiet room in your home.

2. Stand still and take a few deep breaths to centre yourself. Choose a focus for your meditation (e.g., breath, body sensations, or surroundings)

3. Begin walking at a slow, natural pace. Take small, deliberate steps

4. Focus your attention on the sensations of walking:
   - Feel your feet making contact with the ground
   - Notice the movement of your legs, the lifting, moving, and placing of each foot
   - Be aware of your body's balance and posture

5. Coordinate your breathing with your steps if it feels natural. For example, inhale for two steps, exhale for three

6. When your mind wanders, gently bring your focus back to the physical sensations of walking and your chosen focus.

7. Maintain an open awareness of your surroundings without fixating on any one thing.

8. End Mindfully by gradually come to a stop. Stand still for a moment and notice how you feel. Take a few deep breaths before resuming normal activities.

Remind yourself that most people are too focused on themselves to notice (and this advice goes for everything you do in life!) and <u>remember</u>, the goal is not to reach a destination but to be fully present, in the act of walking consistency is key. Try to practice regularly, even if it's just for a few minutes each day, to develop your walking meditation skills.

Activity 30. Make a mini volcano (or use your head!)

Did you ever do this in school, or given it as homework? My stepdad was a bit crazy, well he still is! He made homemade rockets with gas cylinders and plastic bottles, sandpits tied to the back of his motorbike in the snow, and he just said 'Don't mention the bonfire'. But the one thing we did that I am happy to say was safe, without his alterations, was making a volcano.

Whether you enjoyed science or not in school, this is a fun activity, that can incorporate artistic skills and meditation, along with several well-being benefits, through its educational and sensory aspects. If you have children, then even better, it is exciting to teach them about how real volcanoes work and the different types of eruptions, as well as chemical reactions, specifically the acid-base reaction between baking soda and vinegar, which produces carbon dioxide gas and simulates a volcanic eruption.

It demonstrates the principles of pressure and force as the gas buildup causes the eruption and isn't this how we work?!! We can tolerate and tolerate until we explode, unless we do something to neutralise the vinegar! If you struggle with a volcano, make it a model of your head so you can watch the chemical reaction overflow!
Building a model volcano or 'your head' using baking soda and vinegar to create an "eruption", is more than chemistry. Think about making a colourful model out of papier-mâché, adding trees, little houses and even stick people. Use food colouring to produce a rainbow of colours. Just please do not do this over your carpet!

To make a volcano erupt at home, you can follow these simple steps:

1. Create the volcano base, using a plastic bottle or cup as the core. Then build the volcano shape around it using materials like modelling clay, papier-mâché, or even dirt

2. Prepare the eruption ingredients:
   - 3-4 tablespoons of baking soda
   - 1/2 cup to 1 cup of vinegar
   - A few drops of red food colouring (optional)
   - 1 teaspoon of dish soap (optional, for extra foam)
   - Warm water

3. Trigger the eruption:
   - Pour the baking soda into the bottle/cup
   - Add a few drops of food colouring and dish soap if desired
   - Quickly pour in the vinegar and step back

The chemical reaction between the baking soda and vinegar will create carbon dioxide gas, causing the "lava" to erupt from your volcano. For best results and easy cleanup, perform this experiment outdoors or in an area that's easy to clean.

You can adjust the amounts of baking soda and vinegar to create different eruption intensities. Warm water can also be added to accelerate the reaction.

Even if you leave the eruption up to the kids or someone else, take time to make a great model. To make your volcano look more realistic, consider these techniques:

- Use texture: Add sand, gravel, or small rocks to the surface of your volcano to create a rough, natural texture.
- Paint strategically: Use a mix of earthy colours like browns, greys, and blacks for the base. Add streaks of red, orange, or yellow near the crater to simulate lava flows.
- Create erosion features: Sculpt gullies and channels down the sides of the volcano to mimic natural erosion patterns.
- Add vegetation: Use green paint or small twigs and grass to represent trees and plants on the lower slopes of the volcano.
- Incorporate ash effects: Use grey or black paint to create ash deposits around the volcano's base and on its slopes.
- Model the crater: Shape the top of the volcano to have a realistic, irregular crater opening.
- Include surrounding landscape: Create a base that represents the area around the volcano, including hills, valleys, or even a small village for scale.
- Use realistic materials: If possible, incorporate actual volcanic rocks or sand into your model for authenticity.
- Add details: Include small features like steam vents or lava tubes to enhance realism.

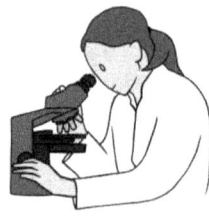

Activity 31. Observe plant growth

I have always killed every plant I have owned. You know they say, get a plant and if that survives get a fish, then a cat etc.. Well if my plants were anything to go by, my cats should have no chance. I have just always been that one person who can not keep a plant alive. Now I have about 10 in my house, one is over watered, but I still can't throw it yet and the others have good and bad days, but I quite enjoy it now.

The main plants that need my TLC are in my study/office, as I enjoy the mindfulness and pleasure they bring. Observing plant growth can be a highly mindful activity, offering numerous benefits for mental well-being and fostering a deeper connection with nature. When you observe plant growth, you naturally focus on the present moment. This practice encourages you to pay close attention to subtle changes in leaves, stems, and flowers. All also notice the intricate details of plant structures and become aware of the plant's current state without judgment.

This intense focus on the present helps quiet the mind and reduce stress, aligning with core principles of mindfulness. We begin to appreciate the slow, incremental changes, to develop patience as they wait for seeds to sprout or buds to bloom and learn to find joy in the process rather than fixating on the end result. This patience cultivated through observing plants can translate to other areas of life, promoting a more mindful approach to daily challenges.

Observing engages multiple senses, enhancing the mindfulness experience:

- Visual: Noticing colours, shapes, and textures of plants
- Tactile: Feeling the texture of leaves or soil
- Olfactory: Experiencing the scents of flowers or herbs
- Auditory: Listening to rustling leaves or buzzing pollinators

This multi-sensory engagement grounds you in the present moment, a fundamental aspect of mindfulness practices. Caring for and observing plants can foster a sense of responsibility and nurturing towards living things, increased empathy and compassion as you tend to the needs of plants and a deeper connection to the natural world and its cycles, this compassionate mindset is an essential component of many mindfulness traditions.

By regularly observing plant growth with intention and awareness, you can cultivate a more mindful approach to life, reducing stress and increasing overall well-being. This practice serves as a natural and accessible way to incorporate mindfulness into daily routines, especially for those who may find traditional meditation challenging.

Activity 32. Do a set of burpees

Hate these? Me too!!! Although, I do prefer these too lunges or squats, but they give me a bit of PTSD from the Prison Officer Physical days against the clock! All those hours of training and still had no stamina.

Doing a set of burpees is incredibly beneficial for both physical and mental wellbeing. Physically, burpees are a full-body exercise that strengthens major muscle groups, boosts cardiovascular fitness, and burns calories efficiently. They improve coordination, balance, and mobility by engaging multiple muscle groups simultaneously. Mentally, burpees help build resilience and mental toughness, as pushing through the challenging movements enhances discipline and stamina.

Additionally, the intense physical activity involved in burpees can reduce stress levels and improve mood by stimulating neurohormones that enhance cognition and mood. Overall, incorporating burpees into your workout routine can lead to improved physical fitness and enhanced mental wellbeing.

To do a set of burpees:

1. Start in a standing position with your feet shoulder-width apart.
2. Lower your body into a squat position, placing your hands on the floor in front of you.
3. Kick your feet back into a plank position. Perform a push-up, lowering your chest to the ground and then pushing back up.
4. Jump your feet forward, returning to the squat position.
5. Stand up and jump with your arms raised overhead.
6. Land softly and immediately begin the next repetition.

For beginners, aim to do 5-10 burpees in a set. As you build strength and endurance, you can increase the number of repetitions. Remember to focus on proper form rather than speed, especially when starting out.

Key tips:
- Engage your core throughout the movement
- Land softly on the balls of your feet when jumping
- Keep your back straight during the plank and push-up portions
- Take breaks if needed to maintain good form

If full burpees are too challenging, you can modify by:
- Stepping back to plank position instead of jumping
- Omitting the push-up
- Removing the jump at the end

Start with 1-3 sets, resting 30-60 seconds between sets. As your fitness improves, you can increase the number of repetitions and sets.

Remember to do a proper warm-up (pg....) before starting burpees to prepare your body and avoid performing burpees first thing in the morning or after long periods of sitting without warming up. Keep your core tight throughout the entire movement and remember to breathe consistently during the exercise, do not hold your breath.

Lastly know when to rest or modify to maintain proper form and prevent injury. Lack of intensity, or too much intensity will compromise your form, find a balance.

Activity 33. Learn a traditional dance move

Learning traditional dance moves offers numerous benefits, both culturally and personally. Traditional dances are deeply rooted in the culture and history of their communities. Learning these dances helps you understand and appreciate the cultural significance and traditions behind them. By learning traditional dances, you contribute to the preservation of cultural heritage and help pass down stories and traditions to future generations. Traditional dances serve as a universal language, facilitating communication and understanding between different cultures.

Dance obviously involves physical movement, which can improve cardiovascular health, flexibility, and muscle strength depending on the dance type or style. It can reduce stress and anxiety, improve mood, and enhance cognitive functions like memory and concentration. Consider participating in traditional dances involving group activities, fostering social skills, community bonding, and a sense of belonging.

Traditional dances provide a unique form of artistic expression, allowing dancers to convey emotions and tell stories through movement. Overall, learning traditional dance moves enriches both the individual and the community by promoting cultural understanding, physical and mental well-being, and artistic expression.

Here are some suggestions for learning traditional dance moves from around the world:

1. Flamenco (Spain): Practice the basic arm movements and hand clapping. Start with the "floreo," a graceful circular hand movement.
2. Irish Step Dance: Try the basic "1-2-3" step, keeping your upper body still while moving your feet.
3. Bhangra (India): Learn the "shoulder shrug" move, where you rhythmically raise and lower your shoulders to the beat.
4. Hula (Hawaii): Practice the basic hip sway and hand gestures that tell a story.
5. Capoeira (Brazil): Start with the "ginga," the basic rocking step that forms the foundation of this dance-like martial art.
6. Waltz (Austria): Learn the basic box step, moving in a square pattern with a partner.
7. Tinikling (Philippines): Practice the basic foot movements, stepping in and out between two bamboo poles (or imaginary ones).
8. African Dance: Try the "African shuffle," a basic step involving alternating foot movements and arm swings.

Remember, these are just starting points. To truly learn these dances, it's best to take classes or watch detailed tutorials. Many of these dances have deep cultural significance, so approach learning them with respect and appreciation for their origins.

Google different places in the world and their traditional dances. Have fun with it.

Activity 34. Set SMART goals

SMART goals are a structured approach to goal setting that can significantly improve your wellbeing. They are used a lot in therapy because they are:

Specific: Clearly defined objectives that spell out exactly what you aim to achieve.
Measurable: Quantifiable goals that allow you to track your progress.
Attainable: Goals that are challenging yet achievable.
Relevant: Objectives that align with your broader aims and values.
Time-bound: Goals that have a specific deadline or timeframe.

SMART goals are helpful for wellbeing in several ways:

By setting specific and relevant goals, you gain clarity on what you want to achieve, providing a clear sense of direction for your wellbeing efforts.

Measurable and time-bound goals allow you to track progress, celebrate small wins, and stay accountable to your objectives. This can boost motivation and commitment to your wellbeing journey.

Having a clear, achievable plan reduces uncertainty and anxiety. SMART goals provide a structured approach to improving your wellbeing, which can lead to reduced stress levels and better overall mental health.

As you achieve your SMART goals, you build confidence in your ability to make positive changes in your life. This increased self-efficacy can have a ripple effect on other areas of your wellbeing.

Time-bound goals encourage you to prioritise your wellbeing activities and use your time more effectively, leading to a better work-life balance.

By incorporating SMART goals into your wellbeing strategy, you create a framework for sustainable, positive change that can significantly improve your overall quality of life. To set your own SMART wellbeing goal, follow these steps:

Choose a clear, well-defined objective for your wellbeing. For example, instead of a vague goal like "get healthier," specify something like "practice mindfulness meditation for stress reduction."

Establish concrete criteria to track your progress. For instance, "meditate for 10 minutes every morning" is more measurable than simply "meditate regularly."

Set a goal that's challenging yet realistic given your current circumstances. If you're new to meditation, starting with 30 minutes daily might be too ambitious, but 5-10 minutes could be achievable.

Your goal should align with your broader wellbeing objectives and values. Ask yourself why this goal matters to you and how it will impact your life.

Define a specific timeframe for achieving your goal. This creates urgency and helps you stay focused. For example, "Practice 10-minute daily meditation for the next 30 days."

Create some of your own, ensuring you write them down, put them somewhere you can see to be reminded daily and keep a record of your progress and previous wins.

Here are some examples to get you started:

"To reduce my stress levels, I will practice mindfulness meditation for 10 minutes every morning for the next 30 days, using a meditation app to track my progress."

This goal is:
- Specific: Focuses on mindfulness meditation for stress reduction
- Measurable: 10 minutes daily, tracked via an app
- Attainable: A reasonable time commitment for most people
- Relevant: Addresses stress reduction, a common wellbeing concern
- Time-bound: Set for a 30-day period

- Walk 10,000 steps daily for the next month to improve cardiovascular health.
- Include at least two servings of vegetables in your diet daily for the next three weeks.
- Sleep for at least 7 hours each night for the next month, using a sleep-tracking app to monitor duration and quality.
- Engage in 30 minutes of moderate-intensity physical activity (brisk walking, swimming) five days a week for two months to reduce anxiety and improve mood.
- Practice 10 minutes of mindfulness meditation daily for the next 45 days to manage stress levels, using a meditation app to track progress.
- Journal for 10 minutes each day for the next month to understand emotional patterns better and improve self-awareness.
- Spend 10 minutes each day having meaningful conversations with a loved one for the next two weeks to improve relationships.
- Attend one social event or group activity related to your interests each week for the next month to build new connections.
- Limit daily leisure screen time to a maximum of two hours over the next two months, using device settings to monitor usage.

Activity 35. Practice positive affirmations

Incorporating positive affirmations into your daily routine can have a profound impact on both mental and physical well-being. By repeating empowering statements, you can rewire your brain to focus on positive thoughts, reducing stress and anxiety while enhancing self-confidence and resilience. Positive affirmations can also improve mood by increasing feelings of self-worth and motivation, helping to manage emotional responses to stress. Regular practice can lead to healthier lifestyle choices and a more optimistic outlook, contributing to overall well-being and improved mental health. By making affirmations a daily habit, you can cultivate a more positive mindset and foster a stronger sense of self, leading to a more fulfilling life. Lowering cortisol levels, improving sleep, improved cardiovascular health, with potential reduced risk of stroke and heart attacks, decreased negative self-talk and increased resilience to challenging situations are just a few more positive reasons to practice daily.

Positive affirmations rewire the brain by leveraging neuroplasticity, the brain's ability to form new neural connections. Repeatedly practicing affirmations strengthens pathways associated with positive thoughts and behaviours, making it easier for the brain to default to these patterns. This process involves key brain regions like the prefrontal cortex, which enhances decision-making, and the ventral striatum, which boosts motivation. Affirmations also influence neurotransmitters and hormones, increasing dopamine and serotonin to improve mood and motivation, while reducing cortisol to decrease stress. By focusing on core values, affirmations help maintain a positive self-view, leading to improved mental health, enhanced self-confidence, and healthier behaviours.

By consistently practicing positive affirmations, we can rewire our thought patterns, leading to improved overall health and well-being. However, it's important to note that while affirmations can be a powerful tool for self-improvement, they should be used in conjunction with other forms of self-care and professional help when needed for optimal results.

Here are some powerful affirmations and particularly useful for people in addiction recovery:

Self-Worth and Forgiveness

- I am worthy of love and respect.
- I forgive myself for past mistakes.
- I am not defined by my past.
- I deserve happiness and peace.

Strength and Resilience
- I am stronger than my addiction.
- I have the power to overcome challenges.
- I am proud of my progress, no matter how small.
- I am a survivor, not a victim.

Commitment to Recovery
- I choose to live a sober and fulfilling life.
- I am committed to my recovery journey.
- I trust myself to make healthy choices.
- I am capable of achieving my goals.

Positivity and Growth
- Every day, I make small improvements in my life.
- I am open to new and positive experiences.
- I am becoming the person I want to be.
- I have everything I need for happiness within myself.

Support and Gratitude
- I am surrounded by supportive and caring people.
- I am grateful for my strength and resilience.
- I allow myself time to process my emotions compassionately.
- I prioritise relationships that support my recovery.

Remember to repeat these affirmations regularly, ideally daily, to reinforce positive thinking patterns and support your recovery journey. You can say them aloud, write them down, or meditate on them during quiet moments.

Activity 36. Do a stress-relief colouring page

Colouring is known to significantly reduce stress and anxiety levels. The repetitive motion of colouring can calm the amygdala, the part of the brain responsible for the fear response, leading to a meditative state similar to that achieved through mindfulness practices. Studies have shown that even just 20 minutes of colouring can lower anxiety levels and promote relaxation by allowing individuals to focus solely on the task at hand, thus diverting attention from stressors and negative thoughts. making it a popular activity among adults seeking relaxation and mental clarity.

The act of colouring requires concentration, which activates the frontal lobe of the brain—responsible for organising and problem-solving. This engagement helps improve overall focus and attention span, as individuals become absorbed in the intricate details of their colouring pages. By shifting focus away from overwhelming thoughts, colouring can enhance cognitive function and allow for a clearer mind when returning to other tasks.

It can induce a meditative state by encouraging individuals to be present in the moment. This focus on a singular activity helps quiet intrusive thoughts, similar to traditional meditation techniques. As a result, individuals may experience improved emotional regulation and reduced mental clutter, fostering a sense of inner peace.

Colouring engages both hemispheres of the brain: the left side, responsible for logic (staying within lines), and the right side, which governs creativity (choosing colours). This dual engagement can enhance cognitive flexibility and problem-solving abilities while providing a comprehensive workout for the brain.

It also has benefits for the body in different ways, the calming effects of colouring extend beyond mental health; they also promote physical relaxation. By reducing stress levels, colouring can alleviate physical symptoms associated with anxiety, such as muscle tension and elevated heart rates. This relaxation response can lead to better overall health outcomes, including lower blood pressure and improved immune function.

Colouring involves precise hand movements that enhance fine motor skills. This activity requires coordination between hand-eye movements, which can be particularly beneficial for older adults or those recovering from injuries that affect dexterity. Regular practice may help maintain or improve these skills over time.

Incorporating colouring into your evening routine can improve sleep quality by providing a calming activity that does not involve screens. Unlike electronic devices that emit blue light (which can disrupt melatonin production), colouring helps prepare your body for restful sleep by promoting relaxation before bedtime.

Colouring is more than just a nostalgic pastime; this practice offers a variety of long-term benefits that extend beyond mere enjoyment. This activity has gained popularity among adults not only as a creative outlet but also an effective tool for enhancing mental health and well-being.

You can colour animals, affirmations, patterns, people, you name it, you can probably buy it. I have a swear word colouring book which can really help take out and then forget my stress. I choose the appropriate word for the situation and melt it away with colours!

These are some places to find stress relief colouring books, but really you can find them anywhere are shop, you may even want a child's colouring book some days when you do not want the intricacy of some adult colouring books.

Online Retailers such as Amazon (of course!), Etsy, eBay and Books2Door, to name but a few. Physical Stores – have a look in craft stores, bookstores, charity shops, Poundland and The Works. There are also some specialty shops for art and adult colouring supplies such as Crafter's Companion and David S Sales.

These resources provide a wide array of options for anyone looking to engage in stress relief through colouring, whether you prefer shopping online or visiting physical stores.

Activity 37. Try acupressure points for stress

Acupressure is a therapeutic technique rooted in Traditional Chinese Medicine (TCM) that involves applying pressure to specific points on the body, known as acupoints. This practice is believed to promote relaxation and alleviate stress, contributing to overall wellbeing.

In TCM, it is believed that the body contains pathways called meridians through which vital energy, or 'qi' (pronounced "chee"), flows. Stress and emotional disturbances can block or disrupt this flow, leading to physical and mental imbalances. Acupressure aims to restore the balance of *qi* by stimulating specific acupoints along these meridians, thus helping to relieve stress and promote emotional stability. For instance, points such as Heart 7 (Shenmen) are specifically noted for their ability to calm emotional distress and normalise heart rate during stressful situations.

Applying pressure to these acupoints can also activate the body's nervous system, triggering the release of endorphins—natural pain-relieving and mood-enhancing chemicals. This response can help reduce anxiety, induce a state of calmness and reduce pain making acupressure an effective tool for managing stress. Acupressure helps relieve muscle tension often associated with stress. Points located in the neck, shoulders, and back can be particularly beneficial for releasing physical stress manifestations.

Its ability to stimulate the body's natural healing processes through targeted pressure applications makes it an accessible option for many seeking relief from stress-related symptoms. While it may not replace conventional treatments for severe anxiety or stress disorders, it offers a complementary approach that can be easily integrated into daily self-care routines.

To effectively use acupressure points for stress relief on yourself, follow these steps and techniques targeting specific acupoints known for their calming effects.

1. **Heart 7 (Shenmen)**
   - Location: On the wrist, at the crease on the little finger side.
   - Technique: Apply firm pressure with your thumb for about 2-3 minutes. This point is known to calm emotional stress and reduce anxiety.

2. **Large Intestine 4 (He Gu)**
   - Location: In the webbing between your thumb and index finger.
   - Technique: Use your opposite thumb to apply pressure for 1-3 minutes. This point is effective for relieving stress and tension headaches.

3. **Spleen 6 (San Yin Jiao)**
   - Location: About three finger widths above the inner ankle bone.
   - Technique: Apply firm pressure for 1-3 minutes. This point helps with emotional balance and relaxation.

4. **Yin Tang (Third Eye Point)**
   - Location: Between the eyebrows.
   - Technique: Gently massage this point in small circular motions for 1-2 minutes to promote relaxation and relieve anxiety.

5. **Gall Bladder 21 (Shoulder Well)**
   - Location: At the highest point of the shoulder, midway between the spine and the outer shoulder.
   - Technique: Apply firm pressure with your fingers or a massage tool for about 1-2 minutes to release tension in the upper body.

6. **Du 20 (Bai Hui)**
   - Location: At the top of the head.
   - Technique: Use your fingertips to apply gentle pressure in small circles for about 1 minute. This point can help uplift energy and relieve mental fatigue.

7. **Liver 3 (Tai Chong)**
   - Location: On the top of your foot, between the first and second toes.
   - Technique: Apply moderate pressure for 1-2 minutes to help alleviate stress and irritability.

- Use firm but gentle pressure; avoid causing pain. You should feel a sensation but not discomfort.
- Hold each point for about 30 seconds to 3 minutes, depending on your comfort level.
- Breathe deeply while applying pressure to enhance relaxation. Focus on inhaling through your nose and exhaling through your mouth.
- You can perform acupressure multiple times a day as needed, especially during stressful moments.
- Create a calm environment by dimming lights or using soothing music or essential oils like lavender to enhance relaxation.

Experiment with different points to find which ones work best for you and consider combining them with deep breathing exercises or gentle stretching for enhanced relaxation benefits.

Acupressure is generally considered a safe practice, but like any therapeutic technique, it does come with certain risks and precautions that should be taken into account:

Some individuals may experience soreness or bruising at the acupressure points after a session. This is generally mild and temporary but can occur, particularly if excessive pressure is applied.

A few people report feeling lightheaded during or after an acupressure session. This can be due to various factors, including the body's response to relaxation or changes in circulation.

There are specific conditions under which acupressure should be **<u>avoided</u>**:

- **Cancer:** Avoid applying pressure over areas with cancerous tumours or where cancer has spread to bones.
- **Pregnancy**: Certain acupressure points may induce contractions, so it is advisable for pregnant individuals to avoid these areas.
- **Chronic Conditions**: Individuals with conditions such as rheumatoid arthritis, spinal injuries, or bone diseases should consult a healthcare provider before undergoing acupressure, as physical manipulation could exacerbate their condition.
- **Open Wounds and Varicose Veins:** Acupressure should not be performed over open wounds, bruises, or varicose veins, as this could lead to further complications.

Remember: it is important to seek treatment from professionally certified acupressure practitioners if seeking treatment.

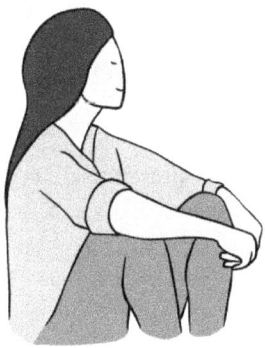

Activity 38. Do a quick journaling session

I know some people really do struggle with journalling! So please do not skip this, have a look at some of the ideas and give it a try. It doesn't have to be writing, typing or even drawing all about your deep darkest feelings and emotions. It can be light-hearted and fun. An opportunity to imagine and release whatever comes to mind. Don't overthink your entries; write or draw whatever comes to mind. Be playful with this, it does not have to be serious.

To engage in a quick journaling session, consider the following suggestions that can help you reflect, express your thoughts, and cultivate mindfulness in just a few minutes.

1. **Free Writing (10 Minutes)**
Set a timer for 10 minutes and write continuously about whatever comes to mind. This stream-of-consciousness technique can help clear your mind and spark creativity.

2. **Mood Check-In**
Spend a minute describing your current mood in one word, followed by two words that express what you need right now. This can help you gain insight into your emotional state and needs.

3. **Gratitude List (5 Minutes)**
Take a few minutes to list three things you are grateful for today. This practice can shift your focus to positive aspects of your life and enhance your overall well-being.

4. **One-Line Journal**
Write a single line summarising the best part of your day or an achievement you're proud of. This method is quick and encourages daily reflection without feeling overwhelming. I have a 5-year, one line journal, it really helps when I am not in the right state of mind to write much but can get it our on paper.

5. **Reflection on the Day (5 Minutes)**
Reflect on your day by answering questions like: What was the highlight? What challenges did I face? What did I learn? This can help consolidate your experiences and insights.

Journaling Prompts

Here are some prompts to inspire your writing:

- Describe a moment when you felt truly proud of yourself. What made it significant, and how did it impact your life?
- Write about a place you've never visited but would love to explore. What draws you to this location, and what do you hope to experience there?

- What is one challenge you've overcome recently? Reflect on what you learned about yourself during this process.
- Sketch and describe your dream home. What features make it special, and how does it reflect your personality?
- Make a list of things you're grateful for today. Explain why each item is important to you.
- Write a letter to your future self. What advice or encouragement would you give?
- Describe a perfect day. What activities would you do, and why would it be perfect?
- What does happiness mean to you? How do you create more happiness in your life?
- Write about someone who inspires you. What qualities do they possess that you admire, and how can you apply those qualities in your life?
- Document an interesting dream you recently had. What symbols or themes appeared, and what do you think they might mean?

These prompts are designed to bring humour and creativity into your journaling practice while encouraging reflection and storytelling.

- If you could have any completely useless superpower, what would it be and how would you use it?
- Write about a time when a DIY project or a cooking attempt went hilariously wrong. What happened, and what did you learn from it?
- Imagine your pet could speak for a day. What funny things would they say about you or their life?
- Create a ridiculous national holiday. What traditions or activities would this day involve?
- What's something you believed as a child that seems funny now? Write about why it was so convincing back then.
- If you could be invisible for a day, what would you do, and why?
- Write about a silly or strange talent or skill that you possess. How did you develop it?
- Share a funny autocorrect mistake from a text message or email. What was the intended message, and how did autocorrect change it?
- If your life was a sitcom, what would be the plot of the pilot episode? Include humorous moments and characters.
- Tell a tale of a camping trip gone humorously wrong. What unexpected challenges did you face, and how did you overcome them?

Activity 39. Try EFT tapping

EFT tapping, or Emotional Freedom Techniques, is a holistic approach that combines elements of psychology and traditional Chinese medicine to alleviate stress, emotional distress and pain. One of the most significant advantages of EFT tapping is its accessibility. It is a self-help technique that can be performed anywhere, without the need for special equipment or extensive training. Individuals can learn to use EFT on their own or with the guidance of a therapist, making it a convenient option for stress relief.

EFT tapping has been shown to significantly lower stress levels by calming the body's fight-or-flight response. Studies indicate that it can lead to substantial decreases in cortisol levels, a primary stress hormone, and promote relaxation and a sense of calmness. This technique helps individuals manage anxiety effectively.

By focusing on specific emotional issues while tapping on acupressure points, EFT allows individuals to confront and process their feelings. This practice can help neutralise negative emotions and foster a more positive mindset. Research has shown that participants often report increased happiness and improved self-esteem following EFT sessions.

EFT tapping not only addresses emotional distress but also has been linked to physical health benefits. It has been used to alleviate symptoms associated with chronic pain, headaches, and even conditions like PTSD. A review of studies found that EFT is moderately to largely effective in managing various psychological and physiological conditions, contributing to overall well-being.

To try EFT (Emotional Freedom Techniques) tapping on your own, follow this structured approach that combines elements of acupressure and psychological techniques. Here's a step-by-step guide to help you through the process:

Steps to Perform EFT Tapping

1. Identify the Issue:
Begin by pinpointing the specific emotional or physical issue you want to address. It's crucial to focus on one problem at a time to enhance the effectiveness of the tapping process.

2. Test the Initial Intensity:
Rate the intensity of your issue on a scale from 0 to 10, where 0 means no distress and 10 represents the highest level of distress. This initial rating will help you assess progress after tapping.

3. The Setup Statement:
Create a setup statement that acknowledges your issue and includes a self-acceptance affirmation. A common format is: "Even though I have this [issue], I deeply and completely accept myself." While stating this, tap gently on the side of your hand (the karate chop point) three times.

4. The Tapping Sequence:
Tap on the following nine acupoints in sequence, using your fingertips. Tap each point gently seven to nine times while repeating a reminder phrase related to your issue.

Here are the points and their order:

- Side of Hand (Karate Chop)
- Top of Head
- Beginning of Eyebrows
- Side of Eyes
- Under the Eyes
- Under the Nose
- Chin
- Beginning of Collarbone
- Under the Arm

As you tap each point, continue to focus on your issue and repeat variations of your setup statement or a reminder phrase like, "This stress I feel" or "The anxiety I am experiencing".

5. Test the Final Intensity:
After completing the tapping sequence, reassess your distress level using the same 0 to 10 scale. Note any changes in intensity; ideally, you should see a reduction in distress.

Additional Tips

- Emotional releases can lead to feelings of dehydration or thirst, keep hydrated and drink plenty of water
- Repeat as Needed: If your distress level has not decreased significantly, consider repeating the tapping sequence several times until you feel relief.
- Stay Focused: It's important to maintain focus on your feelings while tapping, as this helps release emotional blockages more effectively.
- Practice Regularly: For best results, practice EFT tapping regularly, especially during stressful situations or when facing specific emotional challenges.

Potential Risks and Side Effects of EFT Tapping

- While many people experience positive outcomes from EFT tapping, there are some common physical and emotional reactions that can occur during or after sessions:
- Yawning: A common response indicating a release of tension.
- Coughing or Sighing: These may occur as the body releases pent-up emotions.
- Tears: Crying can be a natural reaction to emotional release, often referred to as "trauma tears."
- Physical Sensations: Some individuals report feelings such as butterflies in the stomach, a lump in the throat, or even vibrations throughout the body.
- Fatigue: Feeling tired or sleepy after tapping sessions is not uncommon due to the emotional work involved.
- Tingling or Numbness: Some may experience unusual sensations in their bodies as they tap through emotions.
- Resistance: Initial sessions might provoke feelings of resistance as old patterns and beliefs are challenged.
- Intense Emotions: For individuals with significant trauma histories, tapping can sometimes evoke powerful emotions that may feel overwhelming.

Activity 40. Create a dialogue exchange

A dialogue exchange refers to the back-and-forth conversation between two or more characters, typically involving spoken words. This can be really powerful and a version of this is used in therapy, when feeling stuck for an answer or to figure out what you should do in a situation. It involves detaching yourself from the situation and in this version, you are writing a 'script' of 2 characters who will have a conversation about it. You can just write a dialogue of whatever comes to mind and create a story, or you can write it with finding the solution to a problem of yours or a friend. Examples of Dialogue Exchanges:

1. **Casual Conversation**:
   - Character A: "Did you see the game last night?"
   - Character B: "I did! I can't believe they won in the last minute!"

2. **Conflict**:
   - Character A: "You never listen to me!"
   - Character B: "That's not true! I just have my own opinions!"

3. **Revealing Backstory**:
   - Character A: "Remember when we used to sneak out at night?"
   - Character B: "How could I forget? That was the summer everything changed."

A dialogue exchange is an essential element of storytelling that facilitates character interaction, reveals personality traits, and propels the narrative forward. It allows readers to engage with characters on a deeper level while providing insight into their relationships and conflicts. Starting a dialogue exchange effectively can set the tone for the interaction and engage readers right from the beginning, whether you are using this skill for an audience or for yourself.

Begin with a Strong Statement or Question: Starting with a direct question or a bold statement can immediately capture attention and establish the stakes of the conversation.

Using dialogue exchanges effectively can be particularly beneficial for individuals in recovery, as it fosters communication, builds trust, and enhances emotional support. Here are some examples and scenarios where writing dialogue exchanges can be impactful for people in recovery:

Sharing Experiences:
A: "I remember my first week sober; I felt so lost. Did you feel that way too?"
B: "Absolutely. It was like stepping into a fog. But talking about it helps, doesn't it?"

Expressing Emotions:
A: "Sometimes I still feel the urge to use when I'm stressed."
B: "I get that. When I feel overwhelmed, I try to call someone instead of isolating myself."

Offering Support:
A: "I'm really struggling today. I don't think I can handle this alone."
B: "You're not alone. Let's talk it through together. What's on your mind?"

Discussing Triggers:
A: "I realised that being around certain friends makes me want to drink again."
B: "It's tough to set boundaries, but it's important for your recovery. Have you thought about how to approach them?"

Celebrating Progress:
A: "I hit my six-month mark yesterday!"
B: "That's amazing! How do you feel about it?"
A: "Proud, but also nervous about what comes next."

Navigating Conflict:
A*: "I felt hurt when you didn't check in on me last week."
B*: "I didn't realise you needed that. I'm sorry; I'll do better. Can we talk about how to support each other more?"

Rebuilding Relationships:
A: "I know I messed up before, but I'm trying to be better now."
B: "It's a process. Just keep being honest with me, and we'll figure this out together."

Expressing Understanding:
A: "I've been feeling so overwhelmed lately. Sometimes it feels like I'm drowning in my thoughts."
B: "I get that. It's completely normal to feel that way. Just remember, you're not alone in this."

Offering Encouragement:
A: "I don't know if I can keep going. What if I relapse?"
B: "It's okay to feel scared. Just take it one day at a time. You've come so far already, and I believe in you."

Sharing Personal Experience:
Character A: "I feel so ashamed of my past. I can't believe I let it get this far."
Character B: "I understand that shame. I felt the same way when I started my journey. But remember, your past doesn't define you; it's what you do now that matters."

Benefits of Dialogue Exchanges in Recovery

- Encourages Openness: Dialogue allows individuals to express their feelings and experiences, fostering an environment where they can share vulnerabilities without fear of judgment.
- Builds Trust: Honest conversations help rebuild trust between individuals and their support networks, which is crucial for recovery.
- Facilitates Problem-Solving: Discussing challenges openly enables individuals to brainstorm solutions together, reinforcing the idea that they are not alone in their struggles.
- Promotes Emotional Support: Engaging in meaningful conversations can provide emotional validation and support, helping individuals feel understood and less isolated.
- Enhances Communication Skills: Practicing dialogue exchanges helps individuals improve their communication skills, which are essential for building healthy relationships outside of recovery.

By incorporating these examples and focusing on effective dialogue exchanges, individuals in recovery can enhance their communication skills, foster deeper connections with others, and navigate the complexities of their journey toward sobriety more effectively.

Activity 41. Sketch a quick self-portrait

Creating a self-portrait can be a rewarding artistic exercise., as well as providing a unique opportunity for self-exploration and personal growth. It allows you to explore your identity and express yourself in a visual form. This process can lead to increased self-awareness as you observe and represent various aspects of your appearance and personality. Through this artistic endeavour, you can externalise your inner experiences, potentially uncovering hidden emotions or thoughts.

I can struggle with a mirror sometimes, I forever criticise my face, but more than that, my mother found it difficult to look at me as I look so much like my dad, the love of her life, who died when I was 3 and she was about 22. As I can't remember him and only have a couple of photos, I struggle to see him in me. Plus, the older I get the more and more I see my mum in me and this both scares me and makes me laugh. Mum died age 57 of liver cancer, so I have days thinking I only have a few years left before I die, then I give myself a kick up the arse and shake out of it, but also, I feel like I am losing the part of my dad that all my family see in me. Complicated but I work on it all the time, and this is a good way of dealing with it.

Engaging in the creative process of sketching can actually be a form of stress relief. The act of drawing can lower cortisol levels, reducing stress and anxiety. As you focus on the artistic process, racing thoughts may quiet down, providing a sense of calm and relaxation. It can boost your mood and combat depression. The sense of accomplishment that comes from completing a creative work can elevate your self-esteem and overall sense of well-being. This artistic expression, as all drawing can be, serves as an outlet for processing difficult emotions and experiences that may be difficult to verbalise.

As you become more comfortable with observing and representing yourself, you may develop a greater appreciation for your unique features and characteristics, as we are all unique and gorgeous! This process can help in overcoming self-criticism and fostering self-acceptance. The focused attention required for sketching can induce a state of mindfulness, bringing your awareness to the present moment. This can help in disconnecting from daily stressors and technology, offering a meditative-like experience.

By engaging in the practice of sketching quick self-portraits, you can tap into these emotional benefits, fostering personal growth, self-acceptance, and improved mental well-being.

You only need a pencil, paper, mirror and eraser, then:

1. Set Up Your Space, positioning your mirror so you can comfortably see your face. Spend more time observing your face than drawing it.

2. Outline the Head Shape, by sketching the overall shape of your head, considering the proportions of your face and the contour of your head.

3. Divide the Face
    - Lightly draw a vertical line down the centre of your face to help keep features symmetrical.
    - Divide the area from the hairline to the chin into three equal parts:
    - Hairline to eyebrows
    - Eyebrows to base of nose
    - Base of nose to chin.

4. Place Facial Features
    - Draw horizontal lines through these divisions to guide where features will be placed:
    - Eyes: Located in the middle section, with the distance between them approximately one eye-width apart.
    - Nose: Base aligns with the bottom of the second section.
    - Mouth: Positioned halfway between the base of the nose and chin.

5. Add Details
    - Sketch eyebrows above the eyes, following their natural arch.
    - Draw ears level with the eyes and nose.
    - Outline lips using small circles to form their shape, then connect them with curves.

6. Refine and Add Shadows
    - Add details like pupils, eyelids, and refine facial contours.
    - Use shading to add depth, focusing on areas like under the eyebrows, sides of the nose, and below the lips.

7. Finish with Hair and Neck
    - Sketch your hairline and style, ensuring it fits naturally with your head shape.
    - Draw your neck extending from below your ears.

8. Review and Adjust
    - Compare your sketch with your reflection frequently to ensure accuracy.
    - Make any necessary adjustments to capture unique features.

By following these steps, you can create a self-portrait that captures your likeness while practicing fundamental drawing skills. Remember, this is a process that improves with practice, so don't worry about perfection!

Activity 42. Prepare a healthy snack

Making your own healthy snacks offers numerous benefits for your overall well-being. By preparing snacks at home, you have full control over the ingredients, allowing you to choose nutritious options that support your health goals. Homemade snacks can help stabilise blood sugar levels, boost metabolism, and provide essential nutrients throughout the day. They also contribute to better portion control, reducing the likelihood of overeating and supporting weight management. Additionally, creating your own snacks can be cost-effective, saving you money compared to store-bought alternatives. Perhaps most importantly, homemade healthy snacks can be tailored to your personal tastes and dietary needs, making it easier to maintain a balanced diet and avoid potential allergens or sensitivities.

Make it fun if you can and implement things that will help choose a healthy snack instead of something in the junk food drawer.

Choose Your Base, selecting nutritious foundation like fresh fruits, vegetables, whole grains, or lean proteins.

Wash and prep your chosen ingredients, opting for items like apple slices, carrot sticks, whole grain crackers, or Greek yogurt.

Combine Flavors and Textures, pairing complementary items for a satisfying snack. For example, apple slices with peanut butter or carrot sticks with hummus.

Use small bowls or containers to manage serving sizes, aiming for a snack around 100-200 calories. For portable options, pack in a small container or resealable bag.

Enjoy Mindfully (See PG..) Eat your snack slowly, savouring the flavours and textures, paying attention to your hunger and fullness cues.

By following these steps, you can create a variety of healthy snacks that are both nutritious and satisfying. Some easy ideas include Greek yogurt with berries, vegetable sticks with hummus, or a small handful of nuts with dried fruit.

Make a mini menu of snacks you can prepare for the week or choose items that are quick to make to encourage healthy snacking. Although more expensive, it may maybe worth buy carrot batons instead of cutting them yourself to encourage grabbing them instead of a Twix or packet of crisps.

Activity 43. Practice desk stretching

Whether you are working, studying, playing computer games or completing paperwork at the dining room table. I love a good cat stretch! Movement is so important, to ensure you don't get stiff, lock joints and to correct a poor posture. By stretching often throughout the day, we can improve our physical and mental well-being.

Physical Benefits

It increases flexibility and range of motion in your joints, allowing for more freedom of movement and improved performance in physical activities. This can also help delay the reduced mobility that often comes with aging. It can reduce the risk of muscle strains and joint injuries by keeping muscles flexible and prepared for physical exertion. It can also help heal and prevent back pain by stretching tight muscles that may lead to strain.

Stretching specific muscle groups can reduce musculoskeletal pain and encourage proper alignment, which may improve your posture, as well as, increasing blood flow to your muscles, which can shorten recovery time, reduce muscle soreness, and improve the delivery of nutrients and oxygen to muscles and joints.

Mental and Emotional Benefits

Stretching can help relieve physical and emotional stress by releasing tension in your muscles, particularly in areas where you tend to hold stress, such as your neck, shoulders, and upper back. By participating in a regular stretching program you can calm your mind, providing an opportunity to focus on mindfulness and meditation exercises. It may help reduce the tension you feel from headaches, complementing other remedies like proper a diet, hydration, and rest.

Performance and Daily Life Benefits

Dynamic stretching before physical activities can help prepare your muscles for exertion and may improve your performance in athletic events or exercises, even before going for a walk or housework. Better flexibility allows you to perform everyday tasks with greater ease and comfort, improving your overall quality of life.

By incorporating regular stretching into your routine, you can enjoy these diverse benefits, contributing to better overall health and well-being.

Here are some quick and effective stretches you can do at your desk or the table to alleviate tension and improve your well-being:

Upper Body Stretches

Neck and Shoulder Relief
- Shoulder shrugs: Gently raise your shoulders towards your ears, hold for a few seconds, then release.
- Neck rotations: Keeping your head straight, gently turn it from side to side, trying to move beyond your shoulder.
- Shoulder rolls: Roll your shoulders up, back, and down in a circular motion.

Arm and Wrist Stretches
- Wrist stretch: Extend your arm with your palm up, then gently bend your wrist downward with your other hand. Repeat with your palm down.
- Upper arm stretch: Raise your arms in front of you with bent elbows and palms facing up. Separate your arms to form a W shape, then extend them to the sides.

Back and Core Stretches

Seated Spinal Movements
- Seated spinal rotation: Cross your arms over your chest, hold your shoulders, and gently rotate your upper body from left to right.
- Seated twist: Hold the back of your chair with both hands, inhale, and slowly turn towards one side, twisting from the hips.

Lower Back Relief
- Sitting back extension: Place your palms on the small of your back and gently lean back over your hands.

Lower Body Stretches

Hip and Leg Stretches
- Seated hip opener: While sitting, cross one ankle over the opposite knee and gently lean forward.

Remember to perform these stretches gently and within your comfort level at intervals during the day. Incorporating these quick desk stretches into your daily routine can help reduce stiffness, improve posture, and alleviate the negative effects of prolonged sitting.

Activity 44. Do a quick facial massage

Giving yourself a facial massage offers numerous benefits for your skin health and overall well-being. Give yourself a quick boost and rejuvenate for some great results, as a regular facial massage:

- Improves blood circulation as it stimulates blood flow to the skin's surface, delivering oxygen and essential nutrients to skin cells. This enhanced circulation promotes skin cell regeneration and leaves you with a fresh, youthful glow.
- It can stimulate collagen production, which is crucial for maintaining skin elasticity.
- Facilitates better absorption of skincare products, helping them penetrate deeper and work more effectively.
- Helps toxin removal from the skin by promoting lymphatic drainage, which can help reduce puffiness, especially around the eyes and cheeks.
- Can tone and lift facial muscles, as well as relax facial muscles, reducing tension and promoting a sense of overall relaxation. Relaxation and reduced stress levels can lead to fewer breakouts and less skin redness.
- Can enhance your mood, as the calming effect of facial massage releasing endorphins.
- May help reduce the appearance of wrinkles and fine lines.
- Can help alleviate sinus discomfort, congestion, and pressure.

By incorporating facial massage into your skincare routine, you can enjoy these benefits and promote healthier, more radiant skin. Here is a very brief guide to the best carrier oils & essential oils to use:

Carrier Oils	Essential Oils
• Jojoba Oil - Suitable for all skin types, including sensitive skin • Argan Oil (Also great for the Hair) - Deeply nourishing and moisturising, suitable for most skin types • Macadamia Oil - Ultra-rich and luxurious, ideal for dry skin • Oat Oil - Excellent for sensitive skin • Rosehip Oil - Helps smooth fine lines and wrinkles	• Tea Tree Oil - Excellent for oily and acne-prone skin • Lavender Oil - Soothes and calms the skin • Frankincense Oil - Reduces the appearance of scars, wrinkles, and fine lines • Eucalyptus Oil - Has a cooling and soothing effect on inflamed skin • Rosemary Oil - Stimulates collagen production • Ylang Ylang Oil - Antibacterial and anti-inflammatory properties

Experiment by blending different carrier & essential oils, using a 1% dilution, which is 1 tablespoon (15 ml) of carrier oil, to about 3-4.5 drops of essential oil. For 2 tablespoons (30 ml), use about 6-9 drops. Never put essential oil directly onto the skin without a carrier oil, unless you are aware of the contraindications and have received advice.

Once you have blended your oil prepare the skin by cleansing your face and hands thoroughly and then apply a small amount of your mixed blend, facial oil or moisturiser to your skin.

For each of the following massage techniques, repeat 5 times before moving onto the next area and pay special attention to areas of tension.

1. **Start with your forehead**:
   - Place your knuckles between your eyebrows
   - Move them up towards your hairline in smooth strokes

2. **Eye area**:
   - Use your ring fingers to gently massage around your eyes
   - Use light, rolling movements

3. **Cheeks**:
   - Rest your knuckles on your cheeks near your nose
   - Swipe them across your cheeks towards your ears

4. **Jawline and chin**:
   - Use your palms to massage from your chin towards your ears
   - Apply gentle pressure along your jawline

5. **Neck**:
   - Use upward strokes from your collarbone to your jawline
   - Massage in vertical motions

Tips

- Use gentle pressure throughout the massage
- Perform each movement slowly and deliberately
- Focus on areas of tension, such as the temples or jaw

When using essential oils on the face, it's important to dilute them properly with a carrier oil such as jojoba oil to prevent skin irritation. Always perform a patch test before applying any new essential oil to your face and consult with a skincare professional if you have sensitive skin or specific skin concerns.

Activity 45. Read a chapter of a book

No word of a lie, I have over 100 books here to here at the moment, that is without the ones on my Kindle and Kobo. I have books that I save for holiday, books for my Degree, books for research, books for personal development, books written by people I have interviewed for my podcast, books that I love and my favourite authors. I really enjoy reading, especially in the bath and once I pick up a good book, I find it hard to put down. It helps me to fall asleep and I should do this more instead of my night time routine of my husband and I catching up on our favourite YouTube shows!

Just taking some time out and reading a chapter of a book can be highly beneficial for people in recovery as well as everyone's wellbeing.

As mentioned, reading before bed can promote better sleep, which is essential for overall well-being. It helps calm the mind and redirect thoughts away from cravings or negative emotions.

Reading helps relax the body, lower heart rate, and ease muscle tension. This can be particularly helpful in managing withdrawal symptoms and reducing stress associated with recovery. It also provides a healthy form of escapism, allowing individuals to temporarily distance themselves from their challenges and anxieties. I think this is one of my favourite things about reading, I go there, and I am part of the scene in a good book. I can see the characters and all their fine details, clothes, hair, accents, height, the way they walk.

Books offer new perspectives and experiences, helping readers develop empathy and compassion for themselves and others. This can be crucial in overcoming feelings of shame often associated with addiction.

Reading engages multiple cognitive functions simultaneously, improving brain activity and strengthening decision-making abilities. This can help individuals in recovery process information better and make healthier choices. Whilst improving focus, concentration, and emotional regulation.

If you're struggling to concentrate on reading a chapter of a book, try these strategies:

Create an Optimal Reading Environment
- Choose a quiet, comfortable reading spot (although, I always need sound, so I can read with the tv or music on, I struggle without noise)
- Eliminate distractions by turning off your phone and other devices
- Use noise-cancelling headphones or play white noise if needed

Use Active Reading Techniques for Studying or Personal Development
- Take notes or underline key phrases as you read
- Summarise what you've read after each section
- Engage with the material by asking questions about the content

Manage Your Reading Sessions
- Use the Pomodoro Technique: Read for 25 minutes, then take a 5-minute break
- Set specific goals for each reading session
- Break the chapter into smaller, manageable sections

Improve Your Focus
- Practice mindfulness techniques, like taking deep breaths before reading
- Use a pointer (e.g., your finger or a pen) to guide your eyes along the text
- Ensure you're well-rested and have had proper nutrition

Adjust Your Approach
- Try reading aloud or using text-to-speech technology
- Change your reading position or location if you're feeling restless
- Take short breaks to stretch or move around if you're feeling fatigued

By implementing these strategies, you can improve your concentration and make your reading sessions more productive and enjoyable.

Activity 46. Update your device's software

We can forget these things and most devices nowadays will flash up when an update is ready to be installed. I know I can dismiss it and forget all about it, although if it gives you the option, choose a time at night when you are asleep. It is important to keep software up to date and I have been caught out by going to use Zoom or WhatsApp and it will not allow me as the software is outdated. This is not good when you are about to start a meeting! Apart from being frustrating and not popular with out of date software, there are many great reasons to keep on top of this, so please take some time to update tablets, phones, apps on your phone, laptops, oh and my PlayStation takes ages to update. I do not play it often (a couple of days a year) but when I want to play I have to wait about 30 minutes arrgghh!

Software updates often include critical security patches that protect your device from vulnerabilities and potential cyber threats. Keeping your software up-to-date helps safeguard your personal data and prevents hackers from exploiting known weaknesses. Updates frequently include bug fixes (especially games and apps on your phone) and performance enhancements that can make your device run more smoothly and efficiently. This can lead to faster operation, better battery life, and an overall improved user experience.

Software updates often introduce new functionalities and features that can enhance your device's capabilities, so staying current with software updates ensures your device remains compatible with the latest apps and services.

As for safety and data loss - software updates from official sources are generally safe. However, it's crucial to:
- Download updates only from trusted sources, such as official app stores or manufacturer websites.
- Read release notes to understand what the update includes.
- Scan for malware before installing, if possible. I have McAfee that does this for me automatically.

In most cases, you won't lose data when updating your device's software. However, it's always wise to back up your data before performing any update, just as a precaution. Most devices offer built-in backup options to cloud services or local storage.

To ensure a smooth update process, double check your device has sufficient battery life or is plugged in, that you are connected to a stable Wi-Fi network, don't do it in Starbucks and avoid interrupting the update process once it begins.

By following these precautions and regularly updating your device's software, you can enjoy improved security, performance, and features while minimising the risk of data loss.

Activity 47. Clean up your social media friends list

Periodically cleaning up your social media friends list can be highly beneficial for your mental health, especially during addiction recovery. This practice, often referred to as a "social media cleanse" or "friend purge," offers several advantages that can positively impact your well-being and support your recovery journey. Remember to include groups in your 'purge' as well. If you are not drinking alcohol anymore, there is not much benefit being in a 'The Best Gin Flavours Group' or 'Tested Beers around the World' anymore.

By also removing connections that trigger negative self-comparisons, you can boost your self-esteem and confidence. This is particularly important in addiction recovery, where maintaining a positive self-image is crucial. I am going on holiday soon and pictures of gorgeous bikinis bodies aren't making me feel holiday ready at the moment, so I need to decide if whether seeing these are going to motivate me to exercise or influence me ending up feeling ashamed to my body. I love my body by the way but still have down days

Unfriending or unfollowing accounts that post content related to substance use or whatever is on your mind currently, can help reduce exposure to potential triggers, supporting your sobriety efforts. If you don't want to unfollow, consider muting notifications for some time so it is not promoting you to check that group/person all of the time.

Limiting your friends list to people you genuinely know and trust creates a safer, more private online environment. This can reduce anxiety about who has access to your personal information and recovery journey. By doing this you can build more meaningful connections, focusing on relationships that truly matter, you create space for more authentic and supportive interactions.

Your social media feed becomes more relevant and enjoyable when it's filled with updates from people you care about, rather than acquaintances or strangers, or of your old enabling group that posting drunken videos or hangover photos every weekend. This minimises exposure to negative influences and potential triggers.

How to Approach a Social Media Cleanse

1. Evaluate Connections Regularly: Set aside time every few months to review your friend list and assess whether each connection still aligns with your current values and recovery goals.

2. Use Privacy Settings: Adjust your privacy settings to control who can see your posts and personal information.

3. Consider Muting or Unfollowing: If unfriending seems too drastic, consider muting or unfollowing accounts that don't positively contribute to your mental health.

4. Focus on Positive Content: Follow accounts that share uplifting, recovery-oriented content to create a more supportive online environment.

By regularly cleaning up your social media friends list, you can create a more positive digital space that supports your mental health and addiction recovery. Remember, it's not about the quantity of connections, but the quality of interactions and the impact they have on your well-being.

Please do not feel guilty or awkward about unfriending. Recovery is about a fresh start and receiving love and support. If you feel someone is a negative influence or could trigger you, then you do not need a reason to click that button and keep yourself as safe as possible. If someone does try to question it, you can always say, you are having a bit of a break from social media, but at the end of the day if they are not supportive, why are they on your friends list?

Ask yourself the question:
> "Am I keeping them as a backup by keeping them as a connection?"

Please join my private Facebook group full of meaningful connections that will support and positively encourage, as well as answering any burning questions.

www.facebook.com/EvolveRecoveryTogether/

Activity 48. Make a bird feeder

Why make a birdfeeder? Well why not, it has benefits for you and the environment!

Environmental Benefits
- Birds attracted by birdhouses help control garden pests like aphids, mosquitoes, and spiders, reducing the need for pesticides.
- Certain bird species, contribute to pollination by feeding on nectar and consume weed seeds, aiding in weed management. Bird droppings, also act as a natural fertilizer, improving soil health.
- Ultimately, birdhouses provide safe habitats for birds, supporting biodiversity and helping endangered species.

Personal Benefits
- Watching birds can be calming and therapeutic, offering mental health benefits.
- Creating a birdfeeder can lead to new hobbies like birdwatching, photography, or crafting.
- Birdfeeders add colour and sound to outdoor spaces, enhancing their beauty.
- Building birdhouses can foster community involvement in environmental projects.

Overall, making a birdfeeder is a simple yet effective way to support local wildlife while enjoying personal and community benefits.

Here are simple instructions for making a basic birdhouse:

What's Needed:
- 1x6 cedar board (at least 60" long)
- 4D galvanized finish nails
- Exterior wood screws
- Screw hook for hanging
- Hand saw or miter saw
- Hammer
- Drill with 1/16" and 1-1/4" bits
- Measuring tape
- Pencil

Steps (decide on the size and decorate for your pleasure!):

1. Cut the board into the following pieces:
   - Front and back: Two 7-1/2" pieces
   - Sides: Two 4-3/4" x 4-1/2" pieces
   - Bottom: One 8" piece

- Roof: One 8" x 5-1/2" piece and one 8" x 5-1/4" piece

2. Mark the centre of the front piece and drill a 1-1/4" entrance hole.

3. Pre-drill nail holes along the edges of the front and back pieces.

4. Assemble the four walls by nailing the sides to the front and back.

5. Attach the bottom piece with screws, leaving it slightly recessed for drainage.

6. Attach the roof pieces, overlapping the longer piece over the shorter one.

7. Install the screw hook on top for hanging.

8. Optional: Paint or stain the exterior for weather protection.

Tips

- Place the birdhouse 5-10 feet high in a sheltered location, away from cats.
- Clean out the birdhouse each year after nesting season.

By following these steps, you can create a simple and functional birdhouse to attract nesting birds to your yard.

Activity 49. Identify constellations

Looking at nighttime constellations can contribute positively to your wellbeing for many reasons. For me, I don't know where this comes from, but I believe my dad sits on Orion's belt and I talk to him whenever I see him, especially in March which is both of our birthdays, and I share what has been going on in my life. It brings me comfort, plus I just love looking at the stars and wondering what is out there, another piece of pure, beautiful nature! So, my research made perfect sense to me:

Stargazing has been shown to be a stress reliever, helping to calm the mind and body by providing a sense of awe and perspective. It can help individuals cope with depression and loneliness by fostering a sense of connection to something larger than themselves. The act of gazing at the stars encourages mindfulness, allowing individuals to be fully present, focused on the moment and can inspire creativity and make individuals more empathetic and kinder. Plus being outdoors and engaging in stargazing can improve sleep quality by promoting relaxation and reducing exposure to artificial light.

Find a dark location, away from the city lights is important. Allow your eyes to adjust to the dark and start your exploration of the sky.

Identifying constellations can be a fun and rewarding experience. Here are some ideas to help you get started:

1. **Use Familiar Constellations as Guides**

    - **The Plough (Big Dipper):** This is one of the most recognisable patterns in the northern hemisphere. It's circumpolar, meaning it's visible all year round from the UK. Look for a large "saucepan" shape in the northern sky.
    - Use The Plough to locate **Polaris (North Star)** by following the line from the two stars at the edge of the "bowl".
    - **Cassiopeia:** Known for its W or M shape, this constellation is also circumpolar and can help locate Polaris if the Plough is obscured.
    - **Orion:** Find three bright stars in a row (Orion's Belt) with four bright stars forming a large rectangle around them.
    - Follow Orion's Belt to find **Sirius**, the brightest star in the night sky.

2. **Follow Patterns to Other Constellations**

    - **From the Plough to Arcturus:** Follow the arc of the Plough's "handle" to find the bright red giant star Arcturus in Boötes.
    - **From Cassiopeia to Andromeda Galaxy:** Use Cassiopeia's W shape to locate the Andromeda Galaxy by extending a line from the bottom point of the right "V" shape.

3. **Use Technology and Resources**

    - **Star Maps and Apps:** Tools like AstroViewer, Starmap, or SkyView Lite can provide customised maps based on your location and time, helping you identify constellations.
    - **Online Guides:** Websites like CPRE and UK Astronomy offer step-by-step guides for beginners.

4. **Observe Seasonal Changes**

    - Different constellations are visible at different times of the year. For example, Orion is prominent in winter, while the Summer Triangle (Vega, Deneb, Altair) is visible in late summer and autumn.

5. **Practice and Record Observations**

    - Keep a journal of your observations to track progress and note changes in the sky over time.
    - Sketch constellations to improve your observational skills.

6. **Minimise Light Pollution**

    - Find a location with minimal light pollution for better visibility of fainter stars and constellations.

By following these steps, you can become proficient in identifying constellations and enjoy the beauty of the night sky.

Remember, patience and practice are the key to becoming proficient at identifying constellations.

Activity 50. Create a nature scavenger hunt list

Creating a nature scavenger hunt list is a fun and engaging way to encourage outdoor exploration for children and adults alike. Doing this as a group or solo encourages getting into nature, being in the moment and all of your senses.

My favourite way of doing this is with made up bingo cards, so easy to make if you are on your own or part of a group and more competitive than just a list of items. Consider adding a competitive element, such as a time limit or point system.

Start by selecting a theme for your scavenger hunt, it can be as basic or challenging as you wish. The theme could be a location (e.g., backyard, park, beach, forest), season (spring, winter), colours, textures or a specific type of nature (e.g., leaves, flowers, insects)

Create your list including at least 15-20 items for a balanced hunt, at ground and sky level, if using a bingo card, use 9, 16, 25 or 36 items. Incorporate items that engage multiple senses (sight, sound, touch, smell) and mix some easy finds with more challenging ones (grass, centipede). It's a good idea to laminate the list for reusability and protection. Here are some examples of items, create your list and get one with nature.

• Pinecone • Feather • Acorn or Other Nut • Wildflower • Bird's Nest • Butterfly or Moth • Smooth/Shiny Rock • Fern • Moss • Animal Tracks • Seeds or Seed Pod • Piece of Bark • Spider Web • Small Pebble • Y-Shaped Twig • Pine Needles • Fungus on a Tree • Stream or Creek • Dew on a Leaf • Tree Sap	• Small Branch with Thorns • Flat Rock • Caterpillar • Ant Hill • Purple Flower • Piece of Driftwood • Orange or Yellow Leaf • Stream or Brook • Dragonfly • Frog or Toad • Small Shell • Stick with Moss Growing on It • Blue Berry • Hollow Log • Small Waterfall • Chirp of a bird • Aromatic Herb	• Small Piece of Coal • Gnarled Root • Small Patch of Clover • Animal shaped Cloud • Small Boulder • Wild Strawberries • Stick with a Knot • Small Patch of Ivy • Feather • Rustling Leaves • Smell of Pine • Buzzing Insect • Small Piece of Slate • Small Patch of Thistle • Stick with a Natural "S" Shape

Activity 51. Create a bookmark - Personalise for you or your favourite book

Why a bookmark? Well, if you are following the different activities in this book then you may need a few bookmarks to keep track of your short stories, pages of writing, key pages in this book etc... Make different bookmarks for different topics, moods or days of the week for a diary. This activity helps you to be in the moment and you're your life a little easier! Here are several ideas for making different bookmarks to get your creative juices flowing.

These methods offer a range of options from simple to more complex, allowing you to create unique bookmarks that reflect your personal style or the theme of the book you're reading. They make great personal reading accessories or thoughtful handmade gifts for book lovers.

Fabric/Felt Bookmarks: Cut felt into animal shapes like birds or unicorns or any shape you desire and attach to paperclips

Leaf Rubbing Bookmarks: Place leaves under paper and rub with crayons to create leaf impressions on bookmark-sized strips.

Ribbon Bookmarks: Cut lengths of ribbon and add beads or charms to one end

Button Bookmarks: Glue colourful buttons onto strips of cardstock or felt.

Origami Butterfly Bookmarks: Fold colourful paper into butterfly shapes that clip onto page corners.

Pressed Flower Bookmarks: Preserve flowers from your garden between laminated sheets for a natural look.

Print out bookmark-sized colouring pages and colour them in with pencils or markers.

Corner Bookmarks: Cut squares of colourful paper and fold them into triangular corner bookmarks. Decorate with markers or stickers

Tear Art Bookmarks
- Cut cardboard into a rectangle, punch a hole at the top & cover with glue
- Tear small bits of paper (e.g., scrapbook paper, old books, junk mail, newspaper) and stick them on
- Trim excess paper and seal with Mod Podge or glue (I love saying Mod Podge, what a brilliant product name!) and add a ribbon or yarn through the hole

Activity 52. Grow crystals

Ok so these might not grow you those gorgeous amethysts, but they are still beautiful, unique and amazing to watch grow! As you set up your crystal-growing experiment, you need to focus on the present task, measuring ingredients carefully and following steps precisely. This attention to the present moment is a key aspect of mindfulness practice. It requires you to engage multiple senses: Visual by observing the formation and growth of crystal structures, Tactile by feeling the texture of materials and finished crystals and Olfactory by noticing any scents from the solutions used

It takes time, often days or weeks, which cultivates patience - an important mindfulness skill. As you watch your crystals form and grow, you practice non-judgmental observation, simply noticing changes without attaching expectations or frustrations to the process. The act of creating something beautiful and watching it develop over time can be both relaxing and rewarding, promoting a sense of well-being.

Growing crystals allows you to witness and appreciate the natural processes of molecular organisation and growth. This can foster a sense of wonder and connection to the natural world, which aligns with the mindful attitude of openness and curiosity.

In the UK, you can buy several substances to form crystals. Here are some common options:

1. **Epsom Salt (Magnesium Sulphate)**: Widely available at pharmacies and gardening stores, Epsom salt is easy to use for growing crystals. It forms transparent crystals quickly and is a popular choice for beginners.
2. **Alum (Potassium Aluminium Sulphate)**: Alum is another common compound used for crystal growth. It is available from chemical suppliers and some craft stores, though it might not be as readily available as Epsom salt due to its classification and use restrictions.
3. **Copper Sulphate**: Often used as a gardening fungicide, copper sulphate can be found in gardening stores. It grows blue crystals and is suitable for older children or adults due to its toxicity.
4. **Sugar and Salt**: While more challenging, you can grow crystals using sugar or salt. Sugar crystals can form quickly, but growing single crystals of salt requires patience and precise conditions.
5. **Citric Acid and Baking Soda**: These household items can be used to create sodium citrate crystals, offering a fun and accessible way to grow crystals at home.

For a more structured experience, you can also purchase crystal growing kits, which usually include safe and easy-to-use materials along with instructions.

The fundamental process for growing crystals involves creating a supersaturated solution and allowing it to cool slowly. As the solution cools, crystals form and grow. All you need is a crystal-forming substance such as alum, salt, or sugar, some water, a container (jar or glass), some string or pipe cleaner and a pencil or stick.

1. Dissolve the chosen substance in hot water until it's saturated (some undissolved material remains at the bottom).
2. Pour the solution into a clean container.
3. Tie a string or pipe cleaner to a pencil and suspend it in the solution.
4. Cover the container loosely and place it in an undisturbed location.
5. Wait for crystals to form and grow over several days or weeks.

Sugar Crystals (Rock Candy)
1. Mix 2 cups of sugar with 1 cup of water.
2. Heat and stir until fully dissolved.
3. Pour into a jar and suspend a string or stick.
4. Wait about a week for crystals to form.

Salt Crystals
1. Mix 1/2 cup salt with 1/2 cup water.
2. Heat and stir until saturated.
3. Pour into a container and suspend a seed crystal or string.
4. Allow to evaporate slowly for crystal formation.

Tips for Better Crystal Growth

1. Use distilled water to avoid impurities.
2. Keep the growing area free from vibrations and temperature fluctuations.
3. For larger crystals, use the slow evaporation method.
4. Add food colouring to the solution for coloured crystals.
5. Experiment with different substances like copper sulphate for blue crystals or potassium alum for clear octahedral crystals.

For more advanced crystal growing:

1. Try growing monoammonium phosphate (MAP) crystals, which can form large, impressive structures.
2. Experiment with adding small amounts of alum to MAP crystals to alter their shape and structure.
3. Attempt to grow single, large crystals by carefully controlling temperature and using seed crystals.

Growing crystals at home is not only a fun activity but also an excellent way to learn about chemistry, crystallisation, and the scientific method. With patience and experimentation, you can create beautiful crystal formations right in your own home.

Activity 53. Perform squats and lunges

My knees are absolutely shot, thanks to teenage girls and hockey sticks! But I only do what I can as I know these are beneficial and I do not force myself to the point of pain, well knee pain anyway! Both squats and lunges can contribute to mental wellbeing as the physical exercise triggers the release of endorphins, which can improve mood and reduce stress, as well as achieving fitness goals through these exercises can boost self-esteem and body confidence.

Incorporating squats and lunges into your workout routine can lead to a stronger, healthier body and improved mental resilience. Both squats and lunges are powerful exercises that offer numerous benefits for overall fitness and health. Here are some of the key advantages of incorporating these exercises into your workout routine:

- **Strengthens Lower Body Muscles:** Squats target the quadriceps, hamstrings, glutes, and calves, enhancing lower body strength and endurance.
- **Improves Core Strength:** Engages core muscles for balance and stability, contributing to better posture and reduced back pain.
- **Enhances Mobility and Balance:** Regular squatting improves flexibility, range of motion and balance, crucial for maintaining mobility as you age.
- **Supports Joint Health:** Promotes joint lubrication and nourishment, reducing pain and stiffness.
- **Boosts Bone Density:** Stimulates bone tissue formation, reducing the risk of osteoporosis and reducing the risk of fractures.
- **Injury Prevention:** Strengthens muscles and joints, making them less prone to injury.
- **Promotes Symmetry:** Helps address muscle imbalances by working each leg separately.
- **Cardiovascular Benefits:** Can be part of HIIT workouts, providing cardiovascular benefits.

Both exercises are versatile and can be modified to suit different fitness levels, making them excellent additions to any workout routine.

Here's a step-by-step guide on how to perform these exercises correctly:

Squats
1. **Starting Position:** Stand with your feet shoulder-width apart, toes slightly pointed outwards. Maintain a mid-foot balance throughout the movement
2. **Engage Core:** Keep your core muscles engaged and your back straight throughout the movement.
3. **Lower Down:** Lower your body by bending your knees and hips simultaneously. Ensure your knees track over your toes without extending beyond them.

4. **Depth:** Lower until your thighs are parallel to the ground or slightly lower if possible.
5. **Push Up:** Push through your heels to return to the starting position.

Common Mistakes to Avoid:
- **Rounding Back:** Keep your back straight.
- **Collapsing Knees:** Ensure knees track over toes.
- **Not Engaging Core:** Engage core muscles throughout the movement.

Lunges

1. **Starting Position:** Stand with your feet hip-width apart.
2. **Step Forward:** Step forward with one foot, keeping it flat on the ground.
3. **Bend Knees:** Lower your body until both legs form 90-degree angles. Keep your front knee aligned with your toes.
4. **Upright Torso:** Maintain an upright torso with your chest up.
5. **Return:** Push through your front foot to return to the starting position.

Common Mistakes to Avoid:
- **Front Knee Collapsing:** Keep your front knee in line with your toes.
- **Weight Distribution:** Keep most of your weight in your front leg.
- **Front Heel Lifting:** Ensure your front heel remains grounded.

Variations:
- **Reverse Lunges:** Step backward instead of forward.
- **Side Lunges:** Step to the side and bend the leg.
- **Weighted Lunges:** Add weights for increased challenge.

To perform bodyweight squats and lunges more safely, consider the following techniques:

1. Keep chest up and maintain a neutral spine. Initiate the movement by pushing your hips back, as if sitting in a chair and keep your knees in line with your toes, avoiding inward bowing. Lower yourself only as far as comfortable without losing balance or heel contact.
2. Activate your core muscles throughout the movement, timing your exhale with the upward motion, combining it with a strong core contraction.
3. For beginners or those with balance issues, use a chair or wall for stability

Safer Lunges

1. Opt for reverse lunges, instead of forward lunges to reduce knee strain. Step backward, maintaining a "train track" stance rather than a narrow line
2. Keep your front knee above your ankle, not extending past your toes and take a sufficiently large step back to avoid excessive forward knee movement

3. Keep your chest up and core engaged and ensure your knees track in line with your toes
4. If needed, perform supported lunges using a chair or wall for balance

REMEMBER TO BREATHE!

Activity 54. Take photos for a colour challenge

This challenge can be beneficial for individuals in addiction recovery or those suffering stress and anxiety for so many reasons:

1. **Mindfulness and Focus:** Engaging in photography requires being present in the moment, focusing on capturing specific colours or scenes. This mindfulness can help individuals stay grounded and focused, which is particularly beneficial for those dealing with anxiety or racing thoughts.
2. **Creative Expression:** Photography offers a creative outlet, allowing individuals to express themselves non-verbally. This form of expression can help process emotions and experiences, similar to other forms of art therapy.
3. **Community Building:** Participating in a colour challenge can connect individuals with others who share similar interests, fostering a sense of community and support. This social aspect is crucial for recovery, as it helps reduce feelings of isolation and promotes mutual support.
4. **New Hobbies and Coping Mechanisms:** Engaging in photography can serve as a healthy coping mechanism, replacing negative habits with positive activities. Finding new hobbies is essential for recovery, as it helps individuals manage cravings and difficult emotions.
5. **Emotional Healing and Reflection:** The process of capturing specific colours can prompt reflection on the emotional significance of those colours. For example, colours like turquoise and purple are associated with addiction recovery, symbolising hope and resilience. This reflection can aid in emotional healing and personal growth.

To take photos for a colour challenge:

- Choose your colour theme, a specific colour as your focus (e.g., red, blue, yellow).

- Make a list of objects or scenes featuring your chosen colour, then scout locations that offer opportunities to capture your colour theme

- Use the colour as the main subject or as an accent in your photos, experiment with different compositions to highlight the colour effectively. Also consider using colour blocking for minimalist, eye-catching images.

- Shoot during golden hour for warm, rich colours. Try harsh lighting to create intense colours and shadows. Experiment with different times of day.

- Adjust white balance on your camera or phone to accurately represent colours, using a low ISO for better colour quality, then experiment with aperture to control depth of field and colour emphasis.

- Edit your pictures to fine-tune the colours but avoid over-saturation.

Here are some creative suggestions for your colour challenge:

Red	Blue
- A field of poppies or tulips	- A clear summer sky
- Vibrant autumn leaves	- Ocean waves or a serene lake
- A classic red car	- Blue hydrangea flowers
- Fresh strawberries or cherries	- A peacock's feathers
- A bright red door on a building	- Weathered blue jeans
Yellow	Green
- Sunflowers in bloom	- Lush forest canopy
- A lemon slice close-up	- Close-up of a leaf's veins
- Yellow taxis in a city	- A vibrant chameleon
- Autumn leaves	- Rows of lettuce in a garden
- A field of canola flowers	- Moss-covered rocks
Purple	Orange
- Lavender fields	- A monarch butterfly
- A bunch of grapes	- Pumpkins in a patch
- Jacaranda trees in bloom	- A blazing sunset
- Amethyst crystals	- Citrus fruit close-ups
- A sunset with purple hues	- Fall foliage
White	Brown
- Fresh snow on tree branches	- Chocolate cake
- Cotton bolls in a field	- Tree bark
- Clouds in a bright sky	- Coffee beans
- White sand beaches	- Leather items
- Delicate white flowers	- Wooden furniture

Remember to consider different textures, lighting conditions, and compositions to make your colour-themed photos more interesting and dynamic.

Activity 55. Practice a body scan meditation

Body scan meditation is a great excuse (not that you should need one) for a lie down and have 15-20 minutes to yourself. I find it really useful for pain and for a mid-day boost or reset. It helps with so many things, such as significantly reducing stress and anxiety by shifting focus away from racing thoughts to physical sensations, activating the parasympathetic nervous system, promoting relaxation and helping to identify and release areas of tension in the body. This practice enhances interoception (awareness of internal bodily sensations) fostering a stronger mind-body connection.

Regular body scan meditations can improve sleep quality by relaxing the mind and body before bedtime, reducing racing thoughts that often interfere with sleep and by promoting overall relaxation and calmness. This is also a popular way to start meditating, as you are focusing on parts of the body, instead of closing your eyes and wandering what you should be doing, hence your mind goes beserk.

For those dealing with chronic pain, body scan meditation can help by altering the experience of pain through mindful observation, reducing emotional reactivity to physical discomfort and potentially decreasing the intensity of pain sensations.

This practice supports emotional well-being by increasing self-awareness of the connection between physical sensations and emotions, promoting acceptance of present-moment experiences and developing greater emotional resilience.

Regular practice can lead to increased ability to sustain attention, enhanced mindfulness in daily activities and greater overall mental clarity. By incorporating body scan meditation into a regular routine, you can experience these benefits and develop a more balanced, mindful approach to your physical and emotional well-being.

To practice a body scan meditation, follow these steps:

1. Find a comfortable position, either lying down or sitting.

2. Close your eyes and take a few deep breaths to relax.

3. Begin at either your head or toes and slowly move your attention through your body.

5. As you focus on each body part, notice any sensations present without trying to change them. These may include tingling, tightness, temperature, or discomfort.

6. If your mind wanders, gently bring your focus back to the body part you were scanning.

7. Move systematically through your entire body, spending about 20-30 seconds on each area.

8. When you finish scanning your whole body, take a moment to notice how you feel overall.

9. Slowly open your eyes and move gently, as periods of stillness may cause a drop in blood pressure.

For beginners, aim to practice for at least 15 minutes and gradually increase the duration over time. To encourage body scan meditations as a habit, try meditating first thing in the morning, in a consistent location ensuring you are comfortable and setting a time limit for your session.

I use a guided mediation, as I like the music and it keeps me on track while working down the body if my mind wanders. There are so many on YouTube or free apps you can use.

Remember, it's normal for your mind to wander, especially when starting out. With regular practice, you'll likely find it easier to maintain focus and experience the benefits of this mindfulness technique.

Activity 56. Create a dream catcher

Dream catchers are traditional Native American talismans, primarily originating from the Ojibwe tribe, designed to protect sleepers from bad dreams and negative energies. They are typically hung above beds or cradles to filter out bad dreams while allowing good ones to pass through.

Key Components and Their Meanings

- **Hoop (Circle):** Represents the circle of life, symbolising unity and the endless cycle of life. It is often associated with the sun and moon.
- **Web:** Patterned after a spider's web, it is meant to catch bad dreams or negative energies. The web is usually made from threads or yarn.
- **Feathers:** Attached to the dream catcher, feathers symbolise breath or air and serve as a gentle path for good dreams to reach the sleeper.
- **Beads:** Often represent the spider or the captured dreams. They can also symbolise good dreams that have been caught.

Purpose and Use

Dream catchers are used to:
- **Protect Sleepers:** They are believed to safeguard against bad dreams, nightmares, and evil spirits.
- **Filter Dreams:** The web catches bad dreams, which are then destroyed by the morning sunlight, while good dreams pass through and slide down the feathers to the sleeper.
- **Promote Positive Energies:** Dream catchers are thought to attract positive energies and dreams, enhancing the quality of sleep and promoting harmony.

Dream catchers have deep cultural and spiritual significance, originating from the legend of the "Spider Woman" (Asibikaashi), who protected Ojibwe children. As the tribe grew and dispersed, mothers and grandmothers created dream catchers to continue this protection. Today, dream catchers are used not only for their original purpose but also as decorative items and symbols of hope and healing.

Create your own dream catcher choosing one of the meanings above. It is yours to decorate how ever you want, to put wherever you want, so have fun and make it unique to bring positivity and banish bad dreams.

Materials Needed:
- Hoop (metal, wooden, or plastic)
- Sinew, string, or thin leather cord
- Beads
- Feathers

- Scissors
- Decorative elements (optional)

1. If using a wooden hoop, wrap it with leather or fabric strips for a more traditional look.

2. Create the web:
    - Tie the end of your string to the hoop.
    - Loop the string around the hoop, moving about an inch each time.
    - As you go, pull the string across the centre to create a web pattern.
    - Continue until you have a complete web with a small hole in the centre.

3. Thread beads onto the string as you create the web for decoration.

4. Secure the web by tying off the end of the string when your web is complete.

5. Attach feathers and decorations:
    - Cut several lengths of string.
    - Tie feathers and beads to these strings.
    - Attach these decorated strings to the bottom of the hoop.

6. Add any additional decorative elements as desired.

7. Create a hanging loop: Tie a string to the top of the hoop for hanging.

Remember, dream catchers are deeply significant in Native American culture. If you're not part of this culture, approach the craft with respect and consider learning about its origins and meaning.

You can create a simple dream catcher using items commonly found around the house.

6. For the hoop use a plastic lid and cut out the centre with a knife (please be careful) or alternatively, use an old bangle bracelet or embroidery hoop

7. For the web use string, yarn, wool or twine

8. For decorations use old earrings or necklaces for beads and feathers. Repurpose buttons or cut strips of fabric or ribbon for hanging elements.

Activity 57. Try calligraphy

Calligraphy is an excellent mindfulness exercise because it combines focus, creativity, and deliberate movement, allowing you to be fully present in the moment. The slow and precise strokes required in calligraphy foster a meditative state, similar to yoga or meditation, by engaging multiple senses and promoting a strong mind-body connection. This practice encourages patience, concentration, and self-expression, helping individuals disconnect from distractions and reduce stress. Additionally, the rhythmic alignment of breath with each stroke enhances relaxation and inner calm, making calligraphy a therapeutic outlet for mental wellness. For the record, I am awful at calligraphy, but each time I try, I believe it will be brilliant, much more practice is needed by me!

Really, all you need is a pencil, eraser, calligraphy pen (I had a felt one in school, but you can also get a gel or fountain ink pen) and paper, although you can invest in a pen holder, ink pot, nibs and calligraphy paper if you are really serious about this. Utilise free online resources such as free practice sheets, tutorial videos or join an online calligraphy communities for support and inspiration.

Creating or printing guidelines helps to maintain straight baselines, consistent letter heights and even spacing.

Begin with practicing these fundamental strokes:
- Curved zig-zags: Master transitions between upstrokes and downstrokes
- Loops: Essential for many letter forms
- Combined zig-zags and loops: Practice letter transitions
- "Crazy 8's": Improve fluid movements and control

Once you feel comfortable with basic strokes, move on to forming individual letters and eventually whole words. Remember, calligraphy requires patience and consistent practice. Start with these basics, and gradually develop your skills and personal style.

There are several styles that are particularly well-suited for beginners, give them a Google and practice till your heart flows like your calligraphy:

Modern Calligraphy - This style is popular among beginners due to its flexibility and forgiving nature. It uses a pointed pen or brush pen and focuses on creating thin upstrokes and thick downstrokes.

Foundational Hand - According to Edward Johnston, this is considered the best script for beginners. It's a clean, upright style written with a broad-edge pen, focusing on rounded shapes and balanced strokes.

Faux Calligraphy - This style allows beginners to create calligraphy-like effects using any writing tool by thickening downstrokes. It's an excellent way to learn letter forms before transitioning to Specialised tools.

Monoline Calligraphy - Also known as basic handwriting or hand lettering, this style uses a regular pen or pencil. It's ideal for learning letter structure and serves as a foundation for other calligraphy styles.

Brush Pen Calligraphy - This accessible style uses tapered markers or brush pens. It combines elements of pointed pen and broad edge calligraphy, making it versatile for beginners.

Italic - A slanted script that's relatively easy for beginners to learn with a broad-edge pen.

Copperplate - While more challenging, some beginners start with this elegant, slanted style using a pointed nib and ink.

Remember, the key to success in calligraphy is consistent practice, starting with basic strokes and exercises before moving on to full letters and words. Take your time when writing. Calligraphy requires patience and deliberate strokes. Improving your handwriting as a great stepping stone to calligraphy is an excellent approach.

Activity 58. Make a DIY cleaning product

Making your own DIY cleaning products offers several compelling benefits that cater to health, budget, and environmental concerns. Plus the satisfaction of making the products yourself giving an amazing clean, your own accomplishment. For some stubborn marks commercial cleaners may be required, as they target specific areas.

The Health Benefits

Many commercial cleaning products contain harsh chemicals that can trigger allergies or respiratory issues. By making your own cleaners, you can avoid these substances and use safer, natural ingredients. Homemade cleaners typically have fewer volatile organic compounds (VOCs) than their store-bought counterparts, leading to better air quality in your home. They lower the risk of skin irritations, and long-term organ damage. In turn, making them safer for children, pets, and individuals with pre-existing health conditions.

The Cost-Effectiveness

DIY cleaning solutions are often significantly cheaper than commercial products. Basic ingredients like vinegar and baking soda are inexpensive and can be used in various recipes, making it a cost-effective choice for maintaining cleanliness. By creating your own products, you can select ingredients that meet your specific needs or preferences, avoiding potentially harmful additives.

The Environmental Impact

Making your own cleaners helps minimise plastic waste associated with commercial products. You can reuse old spray bottles and containers, promoting a more sustainable lifestyle and homemade cleaners often use biodegradable materials that are less harmful to the environment compared to many commercial options.

The Effectiveness

Many DIY cleaning solutions are just as effective as store-bought ones for everyday cleaning tasks. Ingredients like vinegar and baking soda are well-known for their cleaning properties and can tackle common household messes effectively. You can tailor your cleaning products to suit specific tasks or preferences—adding essential oils not only enhances fragrance but also provides additional antibacterial properties.

This is a simple recipe for a DIY all-purpose cleaning product that you can easily make at home: mix 1/2 cup white vinegar, 1/4 cup baking soda and 2 litres of hot water in a clean spray bottle. Shake extra well to combine and use for general household cleaning. For tougher cleaning jobs, you can increase the concentration of vinegar or baking soda, but ensure you test on a small, inconspicuous area first to ensure compatibility with the surface you're cleaning.

This simple DIY cleaner is an excellent starting point for those looking to make their own cleaning products. As you become more comfortable, you can experiment with adding essential oils for fragrance or trying other natural ingredients to customise your cleaning solutions.

Here are some of the most common and versatile eco-friendly ingredients:

1. Baking Soda (Bicarbonate of Soda)
    - Acts as a natural deodoriser and gentle abrasive.
    - Effective for cleaning sinks, toilets, and surfaces.
    - Can be used alone or mixed with other ingredients for various cleaning solutions

2. White Vinegar
    - A powerful natural disinfectant that helps remove stains and odours.
    - Effective for cleaning glass, countertops, and appliances.
    - Works well in combination with baking soda for tougher cleaning tasks

3. Castile Soap
    - A plant-based soap that is versatile for various cleaning needs.
    - Can be used for making all-purpose cleaners, dish soap, and laundry detergent.
    - Gentle on the skin and the environment.

4. Lemon Juice
    - Contains natural antibacterial properties and a pleasant scent.
    - Effective for cutting through grease and removing stains.
    - Use in combination with vinegar or baking soda for enhanced cleaning power.

5. Hydrogen Peroxide
    - A mild bleach alternative that acts as a disinfectant and stain remover.
    - Breaks down into harmless water and oxygen, making it eco-friendly.

6. Salt
    - Acts as a scrubbing agent and can help with stain removal.
    - Useful in combination with other ingredients for enhanced cleaning effects.

Others include:
- Soda Crystals: Effective for laundry and heavy-duty cleaning tasks.
- Olive Oil: Can be used to create furniture polish when mixed with essential oils.
- Citric Acid: Useful for descaling appliances and removing hard water stains.

Please Note: Lemon juice works well for cleaning glass/mirrors, deodorising the refrigerator/garbage disposal, removing limescale, polishing stainless steel surfaces and cleaning cutting boards and kitchen utensils. But please be aware that while it is versatile, there are some limitations:

- It is not a disinfectant, so does not have the same power as bleach or vinegar.
- Avoid using lemon juice on natural stone surfaces (like granite or marble) and brass items, as it can cause corrosion or damage.
- Lemon juice can leave a sticky residue when it dries, which may attract dirt or pests if not rinsed properly.

Several essential oils are effective natural disinfectants due to their antimicrobial properties. Add them to homemade cleaners for scent and effectiveness:

- Tea Tree Oil: It has powerful antibacterial, antiviral, and antifungal properties, making it an ideal choice for homemade disinfectants.
- Peppermint Oil: Known for its antimicrobial and antifungal properties, peppermint oil is effective for disinfecting surfaces and repelling pests.
- Eucalyptus Oil: A powerful antiseptic that's great for cutting through grease and destroying germs on surfaces.
- Clove Oil: Highly effective against various bacteria due to its high eugenol content.
- Lavender Oil: Possesses antimicrobial properties and can kill bacteria, viruses, and fungi, particularly useful in bathrooms and kitchens.

These essential oils can be diluted with water and used in homemade cleaning solutions for various purposes around the home. They not only disinfect but also leave a pleasant, natural fragrance.

Activity 59. Create eco-friendly gift wrap

Creating eco-friendly gift wrap is a sustainable approach to gifting that minimises waste and reduces environmental impact. There are so many different ideas to not only enhance the aesthetic of your gifts but also allow for personal expression while being environmentally conscious. Note: Brown paper is an excellent canvas for creativity and we get sent loads of it!

Here are some simple and creative ways to create eco-friendly gift wrap:

- Brown Kraft Paper: Use recycled brown kraft paper as a straightforward and compostable alternative to traditional wrapping paper. It's versatile for various gift shapes and can be decorated with natural crayons, stamps (potato stamps) or splatter paint (white paint for snow) for a personal touch.

- Repurpose Household Papers: Old newspapers, magazines, or even pages from unused books can serve as unique wrapping materials. This not only recycles these items but also adds a distinctive flair to your gifts.

- Furoshiki (Fabric Wrapping): Embrace the Japanese art of Furoshiki by wrapping gifts in fabric. You can use old clothes, scarves, or fabric scraps, which can be reused multiple times, thus reducing waste significantly and are often machine-washable.

- Natural Decorations: Enhance your gift wrap with natural elements such as leaves, pine cones, or dried fruits, flowers and herbs. This not only beautifies the presentation with an elegant touch, but also connects your gift to nature.

- Twine or Yarn Instead of Plastic Ribbons: Replace plastic ribbons with twine, yarn, or fabric ribbons that can be reused year after year. These materials are biodegradable and add a rustic charm to your gifts.

- DIY Gift Bags: Create reusable gift bags from old fabric or even paper bags that you decorate yourself. This approach is not only sustainable but also allows for creativity in your gift-giving.

- Upcycled Containers: Use glass jars or other containers to hold small gifts. This method is practical and encourages recycling while providing a unique presentation.

- Buttons and Confetti: Attach buttons or sprinkle confetti on the wrapped gift for a playful touch. This can be particularly charming for children's gifts.

- Thematic Toppers: Create themed gift toppers using items like mini wreaths, stars made from straws, or even small ornaments that reflect the occasion.

- Layering Techniques: Layer different textures by combining brown paper with other materials like fabric scraps, creating a multidimensional look.

- Seasonal Themes: For Christmas, consider wrapping gifts in brown paper decorated with stencilled snowflakes, reindeer prints, or even hand-drawn winter scenes for a whimsical touch.

- Seed-Infused Paper: This unique option allows the wrapping to grow into plants when buried in soil, combining the gift with an environmentally friendly experience. I've just thrown some away, this would have been a brilliant idea for my step-dad, Doh!

- Repurposed Boxes: Use old boxes or shipping materials to wrap gifts securely, which also reduces waste from packaging materials.

- Map Gift Boxes: Instead of traditional wrapping, cover a sturdy box with map sections. This allows the box to be reused for future gifts, adding an element of sustainability. Wrap gifts in maps of cities they love or places they dream of visiting

What will you design?

Activity 60. Try Cold Water Therapy (CWT)

CWT, which includes practices like cold showers, ice baths, and cold water immersion, offers several benefits for both physical and mental health. Also known as cold hydrotherapy or cryotherapy, involves exposing your body to cold water to stimulate various physiological responses that can help reduce stress, improve circulation, and boost your immune system.

It has been explored as a complementary tool in addiction recovery, offering several potential benefits. While it is not a standalone treatment for addiction, it can be integrated into comprehensive recovery programs to support both physical and mental health. Here are some ways CWT may help in addiction recovery:

Benefits of CWT in Addiction Recovery

1. **Endorphin and Dopamine Release**: Cold water exposure triggers the release of endorphins and dopamine, which are natural mood elevators. This can help alleviate withdrawal symptoms and cravings by providing a healthy alternative to substance-induced pleasure. It may decrease cortisol levels, enhancing resilience to stress and improving overall mental well-being.
2. **Stress Response Management**: Cold water immersion helps train the body's stress response system, enabling individuals to better manage stress and triggers associated with addiction.
3. **Mental Clarity and Resilience**: The intense sensory experience of cold water can interrupt compulsive thought patterns and provide mental clarity, helping individuals develop emotional resilience.
4. **Anxiety and Depression Reduction**: CWT has been reported to reduce symptoms of anxiety and depression, which are common co-occurring conditions with addiction.

Physical Benefits

1. **Improved Circulation**: Cold water causes blood vessels to constrict, directing blood to the core, and upon warming up, they dilate, improving circulation and delivering oxygenated blood to tissues.
2. **Reduced Muscle Soreness**: Cold water immersion helps reduce inflammation and muscle soreness after exercise by constricting blood vessels and flushing out waste products like lactic acid.
3. **Boosted Metabolism**: The body expends energy to maintain its core temperature in cold water, potentially increasing metabolism.
4. **Immune System Support**: Some evidence suggests that CWT can stimulate the immune system, helping to fight off infections.

Additional Benefits

1. **Weight Loss**: Regular cold water immersion can increase your metabolic rate loss.
2. **Improved Cardiovascular Health**: CWT may help improve cardiovascular circulation and reduce risk factors for heart disease.

Here's a simple way to incorporate CWT into your routine at home:

CWT Session at Home

Preparation
1. **Temperature**: The ideal temperature for CWT is between 50°F (10°C) and 55°F (13°C). If you don't have a thermometer, you can start with cold tap water and adjust as needed.
2. **Duration**: Begin with short sessions of 30 seconds to 1 minute and gradually increase the time as you acclimate.
3. **Safety**: Ensure you have a safe place to stand or sit, and consider having a towel nearby to dry off quickly.

Methods for CWT at Home

1. Cold Shower
    - **Start Warm**: Begin your shower with warm water to relax your muscles.
    - **Gradually Cool Down**: Reduce the temperature to cold and stand under the water for 30 seconds to 1 minute.
    - **Focus on Breathing**: Take deep breaths to help manage any discomfort.

2. Cold Water Immersion (Foot or Hand)
    - **Fill a Basin**: Use a large bowl or basin and fill it with cold water.
    - **Immerse Your Feet or Hands**: Place your feet or hands in the water for 30 seconds to 1 minute.
    - **Breathe Deeply**: Focus on your breathing to relax.

3. Cold Water Dripping
    - **Use a Cup**: Fill a cup with cold water.
    - **Drip on Wrists**: Gently drip cold water onto your wrists. This can be a quick and refreshing way to stimulate circulation.

After the Session Remember to quickly dry yourself with a towel to prevent chilling, and if needed, take a warm shower or use a warm towel to gradually warm up. Take a few minutes to relax and enjoy the invigorating feeling.

Tips and Precautions

- **Consult a Doctor:** If you have any health conditions, consult with a healthcare professional before starting CWT.
- **Gradual Acclimation:** Gradually increase the duration and intensity of your sessions.
- **Listen to Your Body:** If you experience discomfort or pain, stop the session.

I went on a business retreat and it had a cold water swimming lake, I really wanted to go in as I know the benefits of CWT, although I had reports that there are problems with the left side of my heart, so I did not attempt it at that time until my heart had been checked out by the hospital.

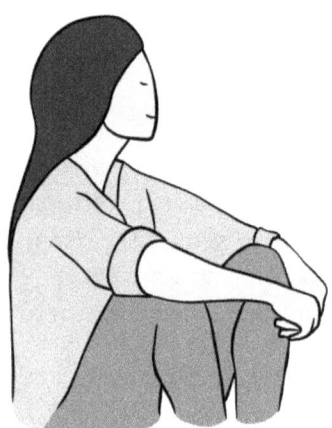

Activity 61. Create a Memory Jar

Creating a Memory Jar for addiction recovery can be a powerful tool to reflect on progress and celebrate milestones, anyone can make them for any reason; Great grandparents' memory Jar, Newborn Nephew Memory Jar, Last year's holiday Memory Jar & so on, you get the idea. So, although recovery suggestions are made, you can easily adapt for whatever type of memory Jar you decide to create. I have a (well numerous) memory boxes, but you beauty of the jar, is if you leave gaps in the decorating, then you can see inside as a present reminder, rather than going to get the box out. I look at my boxes whenever I am feeling sentimental or need a boost. Here are some suggestions for your own Memory Jar:

1. **Choose a Jar**: Select a jar that resonates with you, such as a decorative glass jar, a simple mason jar or one of those massive pickled eggs jars you see in the chippy!
2. **Decorate the Jar**: Personalise the jar with paint, stickers, or ribbons to make it meaningful.
3. **Gather Items**: Collect items that represent positive memories or milestones in your recovery journey.

Items to Include in the Memory Jar

- **Tickets or Brochures**: From events or meetings that were significant in your recovery.
- **Notes from Loved Ones**: Messages of support or encouragement. I have a card with the serenity prayer on it from my mum, she has passed now.
- **Small Mementos**: Tokens from places you've visited during recovery, like a beach stone or a coin from a foreign country.
- **Recovery Milestones**: Write down dates of milestones, such as the day you started recovery or completed a challenging program. I do not record dates so much, so I use first holiday sober, sober Christmas etc.
- **Inspirational Quotes**: Print out quotes that motivate you to stay on track.
- **Photos**: Of people who have supported you or places that hold positive memories.

Using the Memory Jar

1. **Daily Reflections**: Write down something positive that happened each day and put it in the jar.
2. **Milestone Celebrations**: Add items to the jar when you reach significant milestones, like completing a treatment program.
3. **Reflection Time**: Set aside time to read through the items in the jar, reflecting on your progress and growth.

Benefits of the Memory Jar

- **Encourages Gratitude**: Focusing on positive memories helps cultivate gratitude.
- **Motivates Progress**: Seeing your progress can motivate you to continue on your recovery path.
- **Provides Comfort**: During challenging times, reviewing the jar's contents can offer comfort and reassurance.

Here are some other ideas you could include in a memory jar:

- **Hand-Drawn Art**: Simple doodles/drawings that represent your feelings or progress.
- **Poetry or Lyrics**: Write down poems/lyrics that resonate with your recovery journey.
- **Personal Mantras**: Create personalised mantras to remind you of your strength.
- **Stones or Pebbles**: Painted stones with motivational messages or symbols.
- **Dried Flowers**: Representing growth and renewal.
- **Small Jewellery**: Items like a sobriety coin or a charm that symbolises your journey.
- **Challenges Overcome**: Write about difficult situations you've navigated successfully.
- **Lessons Learned**: Reflect on important lessons or insights gained during recovery.
- **Goals for the Future**: Include notes about goals you're working towards.

Involving others in creating memories for a recovery memory jar can be a meaningful way to build connections and foster a sense of community. Do one for your family, or for your sobriety family as a collective.

1. **Shared Memory Writing**: Ask family/friends to write down their favourite memories or moments of support during your recovery journey. T
2. **Photo Contributions**: Encourage loved ones to contribute photos of special moments you've shared together.
3. **Joint Crafting Session**: Host a crafting session where everyone can decorate the jar together or create items to include in it.
4. **Recovery Group Contributions**: If you're part of a recovery group, ask members to share inspiring stories or quotes that can be added to the jar.
5. **Community Events**: Organize or participate in community events where people can share their experiences and add them to the jar.
6. **Memory Prompts**: Use prompts like "A time when [Name] supported me" or "My favourite memory with [Name]" to encourage others to contribute stories.
7. **Gratitude Sharing**: Host a gratitude circle where everyone shares something they're thankful for, and these can be written down and added to the jar.

8. **Virtual Memory Jar**: Create a digital version of the memory jar where people can send messages or photos via email or social media, which you can then print and add.
9. **Online Sharing**: Encourage others to share their memories or messages on social media using a specific hashtag, and then print these out to include in the jar.

By involving others in the process, you can create a rich tapestry of memories and experiences that celebrate your journey and the support you've received.

Activity 62. Do a proprioception activity

If you have never heard to this, do not worry, as I hadn't either until recently, but I bet you have done most of them before. Proprioception activities are exercises designed to enhance your body's ability to sense its position and movement in space. This sense, often referred to as "body awareness," is crucial for maintaining balance and coordinating movements effectively. Proprioception involves specialised sensors in the muscles, tendons, and joints that send information to the brain about body positioning, which helps prevent injuries and improve athletic performance.

These activities help you become more aware of your body's movements and positions without needing to look at them. The enhance your ability to maintain balance on various surfaces and during different activities and can help to reduce the risk of falls and injuries, particularly in sports or physical activities. A study found an 81% reduction in ankle sprains observed in basketball players who participated in a proprioceptive training program.

There are many benefits of engaging in proprioceptive training, including:

- Enhanced Coordination: Improved body awareness translates into better coordination during physical activities.
- Greater Balance: Regular practice helps you maintain balance in various situations, reducing the likelihood of falls.
- Improved Athletic Performance: Athletes often see enhanced performance due to better control over their movements and body positioning.

Here are some effective proprioception activities you can incorporate into your fitness routine whilst having fun (remember to laugh!). You can even do many in front of the TV:

1. Heel-to-Toe Walk
Instructions: While standing, walk in place by placing one foot directly in front of the other, heel to toe, as if walking a tightrope. You can do this while watching TV to enhance focus and stability.
Duration: Continue for 1-2 minutes.
Benefits: Promotes balance and coordination.

2. Bean Bag Balance
Instructions: Place a lightweight bean bag or similar object on your head. Walk forward in a straight line while keeping your head upright to avoid dropping the bean bag.
Challenge: Try walking backward or zig-zagging to increase the difficulty.
Benefits: Develops balance and stability while adding an element of fun.

3. Rock the Boat

Instructions: Stand with feet hip-width apart and shift your weight onto one foot, lifting the opposite foot off the ground. Hold this position for up to 30 seconds before switching sides.
Challenge: Close your eyes or try moving your arms to make it more challenging.
Benefits: Improves balance while engaging core muscles.

4. Musical Statues

Instructions: Play music and dance around. When the music stops, freeze in place and hold a challenging position that requires balance.
Challenge: Encourage participants to strike unusual poses that test their stability.
Benefits: Combines movement with balance training, making it enjoyable for groups or families.

5. One-Legged Balance with Arm Movements

Instructions: Stand on one leg and extend your arms out to the sides. While maintaining your balance, perform various arm movements (e.g., circles, reaching overhead).
Challenge: Change the position of your standing leg (bent knee, straight) or close your eyes while doing this.
Benefits: Challenges proprioception while engaging the core and improving coordination.

6. Obstacle Course

Instructions: Set up a mini obstacle course using household items (cushions, chairs, etc.). Navigate through the course by balancing on one leg, crawling under tables, or stepping over obstacles.
Challenge: Time yourself or compete with family members for added excitement.
Benefits: Creating an obstacle course enhances proprioceptive skills through varied movements and challenges.

7. Yoga Poses

Instructions: Incorporate yoga poses that focus on balance, such as Tree Pose or Warrior III. Hold each pose for 20-30 seconds while focusing on breathing and stability.
Challenge: Try transitioning between poses without losing balance.
Benefits: Improves proprioception but also promotes relaxation and mindfulness.

8. Sideways Walking

Instructions: Stand with feet together and step sideways in a controlled manner, moving one foot to the side first and then bringing the other foot to join it.
Challenge: Increase speed, add arm movements for coordination or place a resistance band around your legs just above the knees and take sideways steps.
Benefits: Engages lateral muscles and enhances body awareness in different planes of movement.

- Make these activities fun by incorporating games or challenges that motivate you to keep practicing.
- If you're new to these activities, have a wall or sturdy chair nearby for support until you feel more confident.
- Consistency is key for improving proprioception; try to incorporate these activities into your daily routine.

By integrating these enjoyable proprioception activities into your home workout routine, you can enhance your balance and body awareness while having fun!

While proprioception activities offer significant benefits for balance, coordination, injury prevention, and athletic performance, it's essential to consider contraindications related to health conditions, age, and physical capabilities before starting these exercises. Consulting with a healthcare professional or physical therapist can help tailor a safe and effective proprioceptive training program.

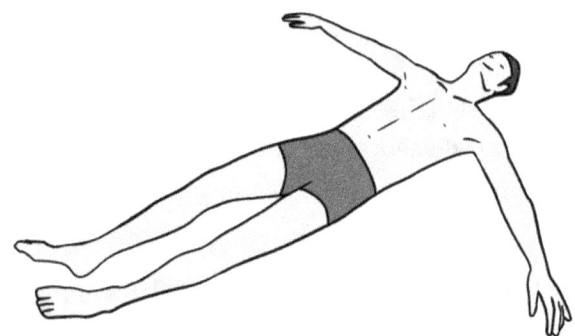

Activity 63. Do a jigsaw puzzle

Doing a jigsaw puzzle for just 6 minutes is a great way to distract yourself and 6 minutes easily turns into 6 hours. You do not have to start at 1000 pieces, if you haven't done one before 100 to 250 would be plenty. They are great for stress relief and relaxation (until you get to the end, and you've lost a piece lol!), lowering the heart rate, blood pressure, and breathing rate, even for a short session, as they shift the brain into a more meditative state. The activity shifts the brain from a "Beta" (wakeful) state to an "Alpha" state.

Completing puzzle pieces releases dopamine, the "feel-good" hormone, providing a sense of accomplishment and satisfaction, offering a break from your daily stressors. Plus dopamine is released with every successful piece placement, providing quick mood boosts even in short sessions. While longer puzzle sessions may provide more pronounced benefits, even a short 6-minute engagement can serve as a quick mental reset and mood booster, making it a valuable tool for managing stress and promoting wellbeing throughout the day.

A quick puzzle session engages both sides of the brain, enhancing cognitive function, improving your focus and concentration and is great for your problem-solving skills, I think this is why I love them so much.

I love Wasgijs, they can become an expensive habit, although they can be found in charity shops, eBay, the works etc. so it makes it much cheaper. Another way if you struggle with space is buy a jigsaw board or rolling mat. I have a board which I can close and put behind my wardrobe without the pieces being disrupted, they are a great idea, although when I open it to do my jigsaws, the cats decide it is the purrfect place to sleep!!

You can also do jigsaws online from sites such as: Jigidi.com, I'm a Puzzle, jigsawscapes.com. Or www.dailyjigsawpuzzles.net. Just give it a Google or look for games on your phone.

With online jigsaw puzzles you can adjustable difficulty levels, easily find different themes and categories, do not need to download or installation and play on computers, tablets, and smartphones, there are apps available also.

Personal I prefer a physical puzzle, as I do a physical book, as I need to keep my hands busy, so this is also something to consider along with getting away from the screen, give your eyes a rest. Now-a-days you can buy any type of jigsaw, 3D buildings, the earth, a plate of baked beans, peaky blinders, 50th Coronation Street edition, whatever takes your fancy, so look for something you enjoy, get down those charity shops and give it a go.

Activity 64. Water your plants

Having plants in your house can provide health benefits that are both physical and psychological. If you haven't got any plants, please invest, you can even get one for a pound or two from Home Bargains or your local newsagent. Here are the why's!

Houseplants can help purify the air, improving air quality by absorbing carbon dioxide and releasing oxygen, reducing dust levels by up to 20% and removing harmful volatile organic compounds (VOCs) like formaldehyde and benzene. Don't be alarmed formaldehyde and benzene could be in the home due to tobacco smoke, it is in some personal care or household items and some building materials. While the extent of air purification may vary, plants like peace lilies, spider plants, and Boston ferns are known for their air-cleaning properties.

Psychologically, plants can positively impact mental health, reducing stress and anxiety levels, improving mood/overall well-being, increasing productivity and creativity, plus enhancing focus and attention span. Studies have shown that people in rooms with plants experience lower stress levels, decreased blood pressure, and improved mood.

Physically, indoor plants may contribute to better physical health by lowering blood pressure, reducing fatigue and headaches, speeding up recovery from illness or surgery and decreasing post-operative pain in hospital settings. Although flowers are not allowed in hospitals in the UK, previous research indicates that patients in rooms with plants reported less pain and had shorter hospital stays. So, imagine what they can do for your home. Some plants (gerbera daisies), continue to release oxygen at night, which may improve sleep quality.

Horticultural therapy is even being used in some medical settings to support mental health treatment, I did courses when I was in rehab, I was so proud of my first radishes, easy to grow and delicious to eat, very satisfying that I grew them. So, caring for plants can have the therapeutic benefits of reducing symptoms of depression and anxiety, improving self-esteem and life satisfaction and fostering a sense of purpose and accomplishment.

Please remember to water them, give them some plant feed in accordance to the directions and have a little research of if they thrive in sunlight, shade, keep away from drafts etc, take some time to stroke them (Yes that is a thing! And talk to them, as plants respond to vibrations, which are essentially sound waves). I have purchased some drip water feeds in the shapes of birds and tulips so when I go away, I do not have to worry or relay on someone else to water them, as my husband can't be trusted to do it lol!! By incorporating a variety of indoor plants into your living space, you can create a healthier, more relaxing environment that supports both your physical and mental well-being.

Activity 65. Create a playlist

Music plays a significant role in addiction recovery, although it is vital you acknowledge your state of mind and whether the music you choose is going to influence you to feel sad when you need a boost or feel triggered. For this reason, playlists can be an excellent thing to prepare, so you are not hit by unexpected wave of emotion that you were not prepared for, especially in early recovery. I have numerous playlists and if I am feeling particularly vulnerable, then I avoid any playlist that has the music that my mum and I shared together.

That being said, music helps people in recovery manage their emotions, reduce stress, and promote relaxation. It provides a safe outlet for expressing and processing complex feelings such as guilt, anxiety, depression, and anger that often arise during recovery. Music helps individuals develop healthy coping mechanisms to manage stress, triggers, and future challenges in recovery. Don't forget the fun side of music, it can uplift spirits, alleviate boredom, and provide moments of joy and connection, supporting overall well-being during the recovery process. Think about concerts or parties, if you are at that stage, music and live events help dispel the myth that sobriety means a life devoid of pleasure.

As I mentioned I have many playlists and they are mainly on YouTube, as I enjoy the visual aspect, they are great for lyrics and I love reminiscing to the old videos. I went to school in the 90's, so I have my 90s School playlist. Everything from Soul Asylum – run away train to East17. Yes I was a huge East17 fan and I still am, I saw Terry at a Butlins weekend playing my old favourites with Artful Dodger and my husband just left me to it as I ran to the stage singing and dancing like it was 1994 again! Yes I was sober! Another, is just of songs I hear and add because I enjoy them, another a dance one, relaxing one, a meditation one etc. So I can easily choose and change to suit my mood, or feelings and emotions I want to feel.

To begin putting your favourite playlist together, think of a playlist theme/mood, actually think of a couple so you have lists ready to put songs into. This could be based on a specific genre, an activity or occasion, a particular emotion/vibe and/or empowering songs that remind you of rehab or nostalgic trip.

Then choose your music streaming service to create your playlist, such as Spotify, Apple Music, YouTube Music, Amazon Music and Deezer. Each platform has its own features and user interface, so pick one that you're comfortable with and that offers the music you want to include. As I said I choose YouTube so I can easily see the videos &/or lyrics on the big screen.

Begin by adding a few essential songs that perfectly capture the essence of your playlist. These could be your absolute favourite tracks, songs that strongly represent the theme or tracks with personal significance

Once you have your core songs, expand your playlist by including a variety of artists and sub-genres within your theme. Add both popular and lesser-known tracks and consider the flow and energy levels between songs

Pay attention to the order of your songs to create a smooth listening experience. So start with a strong, attention-grabbing track and gradually build or change the energy throughout the playlist. Consider factors like tempo, key, and mood when arranging songs

Listen to your playlist from start to finish and make adjustments. Remove songs that don't fit well and add new ones (I do this if being overplayed on the radio or now have a different meaning than to when originally added) and ensure the playlist maintains a consistent vibe throughout (do you want Nirvana after The Men's Welsh Choir!?)

Give your playlist a catchy or descriptive title that reflects its theme. If your chosen platform allows, add custom artwork to make it visually appealing. Remember, creating a great playlist is an art form that takes practice. Don't be afraid to experiment and refine your playlist over time as you discover new music and get feedback from others. Here are a few more ideas to get you started and ready for dance, relaxation, TLC, meditation or nostalgia night!

- Comforting Sad: Melancholic tracks that provide solace during difficult times
- Nightdrive: Atmospheric tracks perfect for late-night cruising
- Productivity Boost: Energising songs to enhance focus and motivation while working
- Rainy Day Relaxation: Soothing melodies to accompany a cozy day indoors
- TimeTravel: Compile from different decades simulating a journey through time
- London Calling: Showcase artists from a UK city or songs about London
- Global Beats: Feature music from countries or cultures around the world
- Seaside Serenade: Compile tracks that evoke the atmosphere of coastal towns
- One-Hit Wonders: Celebrate artists known for a single popular track
- Alphabet Adventure: Each song title starts with a different letter of the alphabet
- Classical Reimagined: Feature modern interpretations or remixes of classical compositions (Perfect Symphony by Andrea Bocelli and Ed Sheeran - Amazing!!)
- "Epic Battle Beats" - Intense orchestral pieces for climatic fight scenes
- "Rom-Com" - Sweet, uplifting songs for romantic comedy first encounters
- "Hogwarts House Party" - Modern party tracks sorted into Harry Potter houses
- "Panem's Underground Radio" - Rebellious songs that might be banned in The Hunger Games' dystopia
- "Director's Cut" - Songs mentioned by famous directors as inspirations

Activity 66. Do a quick-self-acupressure session

Ever pressed a point on your neck and it just feels so good! You don't know what you have pressed but you feel relief, a pain that feels satisfying and a bit of a head rush. Well, it's similar to acupressure. Doing a quick self-acupressure session can offer both physical and mental benefits. I was actually suffering from a continuous fizzy, headachy, crappy head feeling for months which I could not shake, and I had heard about an ear piercing that can help. I asked in a piercing place and the lady told me it was called the Daith (and she told me I had a very nice Daith, which I do not hear every day, so I snapped up that compliment!) and since having it pierced, I have noticed a big positive difference. Here are some other benefits, bearing in mind they all require different acupressure points:

- Help release muscle knots and tension, particularly in areas like the neck, shoulders, and back.
- Alleviate various types of pain, including headaches, menstrual cramps, and lower back pain.
- Enhance blood flow throughout the body, promoting overall health and vitality.
- May boost the immune system, helping the body fight off illnesses more effectively.
- Help relax the body and mind, potentially improving sleep quality and duration.
- Known to activate the parasympathetic nervous system, promoting relaxation and reducing stress levels.
- Regular practice can help alleviate symptoms of anxiety by calming the mind and promoting a sense of well-being.
- Help balance emotions and elevate mood, potentially alleviating symptoms of depression.
- Can help clear mental fog, improve focus, and boost cognitive function.
- Practicing regularly can enhance your connection with your body, leading to better overall self-awareness.

By incorporating quick self-acupressure sessions into your daily routine, you can experience these physical and mental benefits, contributing to improved overall well-being and quality of life.

Here's a quick self-acupressure session you can perform for stress relief and relaxation:

1. Yintang (Hall of Impression)
- Located between your eyebrows.
- Gently press or make small circles with your index finger for 1-2 minutes.
- This point helps calm the mind and reduce stress.

2. Heart 7 (Shenmen or Spirit Gate)
- Found on the inner wrist crease, on the pinky side.
- Apply moderate pressure with your thumb for 1-2 minutes.
- This point helps relieve emotional stress and calm the heart.

3. Du 20 (Baihui or Hundred Convergences)
- Located at the top of your head.
- Use your fingertips to apply moderate pressure for 1-2 minutes.
- This point helps uplift energy and clear the mind.

4. GB-21 (Shoulder Well)
- Found at the highest point of your shoulder.
- Squeeze and massage this area for 1-2 minutes.
- This point helps release shoulder tension associated with stress.

5. Liver 3 (Taichong)
- Located on the top of the foot, between the big toe and second toe.
- Press firmly and massage for about 1 minute.
- This point helps ground energy and restore emotional balance.

To enhance the effectiveness of your session:

1. Find a comfortable position, either sitting or lying down.
2. Take deep, slow breaths throughout the session.
3. Focus on each point as you apply pressure, allowing yourself to relax.
4. Spend about 1-2 minutes on each point, or longer if desired.

Remember to use firm but comfortable pressure and listen to your body's cues when performing these self-acupressure techniques. You can practice these exercises throughout the day as needed to manage stress and promote relaxation. It's advisable to consult a healthcare professional before starting acupressure, especially if you have underlying health conditions. Here are some common problems and their corresponding acupressure points for alleviation. Please do your own research if I haven't mentioned where some acupressure points are located as there are so many:

- Menstrual Cramps: Spleen 6 (SP6) – Sanyinjiao, Liver 3 (LV3) – Taichong, Large Intestine 4 (LI4) – Hegu and Spleen 8 (SP8) - Diji.
- Headaches: Union Valley (LI4 or Hegu), Gates of Consciousness (GB20 or Feng Chi), Drilling Bamboo (BL2 or Zanzhu), Third Eye (Yin Tang or GV24.5), Ear Gate (SJ21 or Ermen) and Daith (flap of ear above the entrance of the earhole).
- Back Pain: CV6 (Conception Vessel 6), BL23 and BL47, GB30 and B48
- Nausea and Vomiting: PC6 (Nei Guan)
- Fatigue: ST36 (Zusanli)
- Digestive Issues: Inner Gate (PC6)

Activity 67. Clean out your wallet or purse

Now I always have about 4 handbags on the go, ok I lied about 6 or 7 handbags! I always have bags and purses to clear out and ALWAYS find something I have been looking for or forgot I had. I find this a really satisfying activity and it offers several important benefits:

- Reduces clutter and makes it easier to find essential items quickly
- Helps you carry only what you truly need on a daily basis
- Streamlines your belongings, saving time and reducing frustration
- Allows you to better track your spending by removing unnecessary cards and receipts
- Helps you be more mindful of your finances by carrying only essential cards
- Reduces the risk of overspending or impulse purchases
- Minimises the risk of identity theft by carrying fewer sensitive documents
- Reduces the potential loss if your wallet or purse is stolen or misplaced
- Makes it easier to notice if important items go missing
- Lightens the load you carry, potentially reducing back and shoulder strain
- Creates a sense of order and control, reducing stress and anxiety
- Promotes a feeling of accomplishment and fresh start (my favourite thing apart from finding money)
- Removes accumulated dirt, crumbs, tissues and bacteria

If you believe it, applying feng shui principles to clean your wallet can offer several benefits:

Improved Financial Energy Flow: Decluttering and organising your wallet helps promote smooth financial energy flow. Removing old receipts, expired cards, and unnecessary items allows wealth energy to circulate freely, potentially attracting more abundance into your life.

Enhanced Financial Awareness: A clean, organised wallet encourages better money management and financial mindfulness. By regularly sorting through, you become more aware of your spending habits and financial status.

Increased Prosperity: Feng shui wallet practices are believed to attract wealth and abundance. Some specific tips includes keeping cash neatly arranged and unfolded, using wallet colours like black or green to attract wealth and adding symbols of prosperity, such as a small jade stone.

Reduced Stress and Anxiety: An organised wallet can lead to reduced stress and anxiety related to finances. Knowing exactly what's in your wallet and being able to find things easily can provide a sense of control and peace of mind.

Better Overall Energy: In feng shui, a cluttered wallet is seen as a reflection of a cluttered mind. By maintaining a clean and organised wallet, you may experience improved mental clarity and positive energy in other areas of your life.

To maintain optimal financial energy according to feng shui principles, you should clean and organise your wallet regularly with these tips:

Daily Quick Clean by removing any trash like gum wrappers or used tissues, deal with receipts or items that need to be put away, straighten bills and organise them neatly.

Weekly Deep Clean by emptying out the entire contents of your wallet. Wipe down the wallet with a slightly damp cloth and sort through all items and discard unnecessary ones. Organise remaining items neatly back into the wallet

Periodic Overhaul by evaluating if you need a new wallet (replace every 3 years or 1,000 days). Remove and shred expired cards or unused loyalty cards and reorganise all compartments for optimal use

Here are some effective ways to minimise clutter in your wallet:

- Start by emptying your wallet completely and sorting through the contents. Discard or relocate items you don't need to carry daily, such as old receipts, expired coupons/gift cards, unnecessary loyalty cards and spare keys (consider using a keychain instead).

- Use smartphone apps where possible to store information digitally by scanning and save receipts using an app or onto your computer, store loyalty and membership cards in apps like Keyring (I think this is just US), mobile-pocket, WalletPasses or Stocard and use mobile payment options like Apple Pay or Google Pay to reduce the need for physical cards.

- Limit yourself to carrying only the most essential cards, one or two credit/debit cards
- and your driver's license or ID. Only carry the amount of cash you need for daily expenses and opt for a slim, minimalist wallet design that encourages you to carry less. This suggestion, the same as my handbags, just doesn't work for me, I just end up buying more bags and purses, so think about this one, although I do not need a handbag that can easily fit at least 3 bottles of wine in it anymore! & on that note, if you have a stash handbag that you used to disguise old behaviours, say goodbye to it!

Activity 68. Do a quick health check

Regular health checks are vital for overall wellbeing and for spotting potential health issues early. Even if there are no obvious symptoms, simple at-home checks can alert you to changes worth discussing with a doctor. Set aside just six minutes for a basic self-assessment—you'll build awareness, track your own health trends, and empower yourself to make informed lifestyle choices.

Why Do Health Checks?

- **Early Detection:** Catch problems before they get serious (e.g., high blood pressure has no symptoms but increases stroke/heart risk).
- **Tracking Changes:** Know your usual numbers so you can spot unusual results and advocate for yourself.
- **Peace of Mind:** Regular checks help you feel more in control and reduce anxiety about unknowns.

What to Check

1. **Heart Rate/Pulse**
   - Sit quietly for 5–10 minutes.
   - Place index and middle finger on your inner wrist (base of thumb).
   - Count beats for 60 seconds (or 30 seconds and multiply by 2).
   - Normal adult resting rate: **60–100 bpm**.

2. **Blood Pressure**
   - Use a home monitor, if available—machines are affordable (from £20).
   - Hypertension is often silent—knowing your numbers helps prevent long-term risks.

3. **BMI & Waist-to-Height Ratio (WHtR)**
   - Use your weight and height to check BMI (NHS/BMI online calculators).
   - For WHtR:
     (a) Find the midpoint between your lowest rib and hip bone (usually above the belly button).
     (b) Stand relaxed, measure waist at midpoint, then measure height (no shoes).
     (c) Divide waist by height (in the same units):
        - WHtR ≤ 0.5: healthy
        - 0.5–0.59: increased risk
        - ≥ 0.6: high risk
        - Example: Waist 80 cm, Height 160 cm → 80/160=0.580/160 = 0.580/160=0.5

4. **Skin Check**
   - Inspect for new lumps, moles, or changes—early sign of skin cancer.

5. **Breast/Testicular Self-Examination**
   - Women: Check breasts regularly for lumps or changes.
   - Men: Examine testicles for lumps or differences.

6. **Diet & Hydration**
   - Track daily food and water.
   - Aim for balanced nutrition and plenty of fluid.

7. **Physical Activity**
   - Review weekly exercise.
   - Set a small, realistic goal to increase activity if needed.

8. **Mood & Stress**
   - Take note of stress/anxiety levels.
   - Use simple NHS questionnaires or mood diaries; wellbeing is as much mental as physical.

Tips for Your Self-Check

- Record your results in a diary or calendar—you'll spot trends and remember to review monthly.
- Don't worry if everything isn't "perfect"—these checks are for awareness, not judgment.
- DIY checks are not substitutes for regular doctor appointments.
  - If you notice worrying changes or symptoms, always consult a healthcare professional.

Take six minutes to check in now and make your health a regular priority!

Activity 69. Play with bubbles

Did you do this as a kid? When did you last blow bubbles? They are popular at the beach, wedding parties, summers in the park and playing with your pets. Ok, if you have been reading the book from the start, 'Pop quiz hotshot' (What film was that?), what physical and wellbeing health benefits do you think this activity has?

Did you cheat and look down? Lol, well when you read these think yourself and others, if you have a baby or young family members, like my ickle baby nephew Benji, any pets that you will play with, anyone....

- Fine motor skills: Improves dexterity and hand-eye coordination.
- Gross motor skills: Enhances large body muscle movements and balance.
- Oral motor skills: Strengthens mouth muscles, aiding speech and eating abilities.
- Visual tracking: Develops the ability to follow moving objects with eyes.
- Respiratory health: Blowing bubbles can help expand and oxygenate lungs.
- Sensory processing: Engages multiple senses, enhancing cognitive development.
- Spatial awareness: Improves understanding of directional concepts and body movement.
- Cause and effect: Teaches basic cognitive concepts through bubble popping.
- Motor planning: Enhances problem-solving skills related to movement.
- Stress relief: Acts as a calming activity, reducing stress and anxiety.
- Emotional regulation: Helps soothe anxious or overstimulated children.
- Social interaction: Encourages communication and cooperation during play.
- Mood enhancement: Releases endorphins, promoting overall well-being.
- Creativity: Stimulates imagination and divergent thinking.
- Persistence: Teaches frustration control and determination.

Playing with bubbles is not only enjoyable but also provides a holistic approach to health and development, benefiting physical, cognitive, and emotional well-being.

To make a bubble solution, use 1 cup (240ml) water and then add 2 tablespoons (30ml) dish soap (Dawn or Fairy brands work well) and 1 tablespoon (15ml) glycerine or light corn syrup.

Instructions: Pour the water into a clean container and slowly add the dish soap to the water, stirring gently to avoid creating foam. 3. Add the glycerine or corn syrup and mix carefully, then let the solution sit for a few hours or overnight for best results.

Tips for Better Bubbles
- Use distilled or filtered water for stronger bubbles.
- Avoid shaking the mixture, as this creates unwanted foam.
- Let the solution rest before use to improve bubble quality.

- Experiment with the amount of glycerine to find the perfect balance.
- Remember, the key to great bubbles is using quality ingredients and mixing them gently.

Making the bubble wand, by taking a pipe cleaner and form it into a circle or other shape. Twist the ends together to create a handle and you can decorate with beads if desired. Remember to dip your homemade wand into bubble solution and blow gently to create bubbles. Experiment with different shapes and sizes to see how they affect your bubbles. No pipe cleaners, no problem, check out all of these creative materials you can use to make bubble wands at home:

- Paperclips: Bend them into wand shapes or use as-is
- Straws: Use individually or tape multiple straws together
- Biscuit cutters: Various shapes create interesting bubbles
- Fly swatters: The mesh design produces multiple small bubbles
- Cookie cutters: Different shapes offer unique bubble-making possibilities
- Slotted spoons, Whisks, Colanders & Funnels
- Floral wire: Easily shaped into various wand designs
- Foam shapes: Cut holes in foam sheets for bubble-making
- Plastic water bottles: Cut off the bottom to create a bubble blower
- Plastic food tub lids: Cut holes in the centre
- Sides of plastic milk jugs: Cut into wand shapes
- Sticks: Use thin branches and wrap wire around them to form loops

Remember to experiment with different shapes and sizes to see how they affect your bubbles. The key is to create an opening that can hold the bubble solution and allow air to pass through. Cet creative and have fun exploring the fascinating properties of bubbles!

Here are some fun ways to play with making bubbles:

- Try blowing bubbles inside bubbles
- Create bubble snakes by blowing through a sock-covered bottle
- Make bubble paintings by blowing coloured bubbles onto paper
- Create bubble print butterflies or flowers
- Try bubble foam art using coloured bubble solution
- Do a bubble obstacle course, trying not to pop bubbles
- Experiment with different bubble solutions to make the biggest or strongest bubbles
- Try making square bubbles using cube-shaped wands
- Attempt to make bouncing bubbles that don't pop on contact
- Try glow-in-the-dark bubbles with non-toxic glow sticks
- Create scented bubbles using essential oil

Activity 70. Solve a Sudoku puzzle

I will never forget my first sudoku! One of those important milestones in life lol! Now I love numbers, I was sat in the Con Club in Chepstow and my mum said 'Em, check this new puzzle out, it's right up your street'. So was my first sudoku, but it was taking me forever, and it was only when mum explained to me that you need the numbers 1-9 in the 3x3 boxes, as well as each row and column that it then took me about 60 seconds to complete and my new love was born!

Even if you are not so much a numbers person, with the normal sudoku's there is no maths involved as such, it is about problem solving. You can get word sudoku's with 9 letter words, so you could easily replace the numbers 1 to 9 with symbols! Replace 1 with a circle, 2 with a square, 3 a star, 4 a +, you get the picture.

Sudoku requires intense concentration, which helps improve mental clarity and focus. One of my favourite sudoku's goes from 0-25 and A-Z, it's huge and takes some time but extremely satisfying when completed. Regular play can enhance your ability to concentrate on tasks for extended periods. The logical reasoning required to solve Sudoku puzzles sharpens problem-solving abilities, which can be applied to various real-life situations, and they can potentially improve overall memory function.

Engaging in Sudoku can provide a healthy distraction from daily stressors, helping to reduce anxiety and promote relaxation, completing a Sudoku puzzle gives a sense of achievement, which can boost mood and self-esteem. Focusing on the puzzle can help break cycles of negative thoughts and promote a more positive mindset, helping to alleviate symptoms of anxiety and stress by redirecting attention away from worries. Regular mental exercises like Sudoku may help build cognitive reserve, potentially reducing the risk or impact of conditions like Alzheimer's and dementia.

There are numerous websites where you can find and play Sudoku puzzles online. Here are some popular options:

Many newspapers offer sudoku puzzles, there are so many sudoku puzzle magazines and books that you can even pick-up in Poundland and Free Online Platforms including Sudoku.com, 247sudoku.com, websudoku.com and Sudoku9x9.com.

Most of the online platforms and apps offer additional features such as hints, time tracking, and the ability to save unfinished puzzles. Whether you're a beginner or an expert, you'll find suitable challenges across these various online Sudoku resources.

There are numerous variants of Sudoku that offer unique challenges and twists on the classic puzzle, to keep you engaged and motivated, my favourite being 'Killer'. Here are some of the most popular types:

Jigsaw Sudoku - Instead of the standard 3x3 boxes, this variant features irregularly shaped regions. The basic rules remain the same, but the unusual shapes add complexity.

Killer Sudoku - This combines elements of Sudoku and Kakuro. Cells are grouped with a given sum, adding a mathematical component to the puzzle.

Samurai Sudoku - This large puzzle consists of five overlapping 9x9 Sudoku grids, creating a more extensive and challenging solving experience.

Sub Doku - Smaller grids, such as 4x4 or 6x6, often considered easier and sometimes called "Children's Sudoku."

Super Doku - Larger grids, like 16x16 or 25x25, offering increased difficulty and complexity.

Sudoku X - The main diagonals must also contain unique digits 1-9.

Even-Odd Sudoku - Cells are marked to indicate whether they contain even or odd numbers.

Consecutive Sudoku - Adjacent cells with consecutive numbers are highlighted, adding another layer of logic.

Wordoku - Letters replace numbers, often forming a word when completed.

Argyle Sudoku - Features diamond-shaped patterns within the grid, adding visual and logical complexity.

Thermo Sudoku - Contains "thermometer" shapes where numbers must increase from the bulb to the top.

These variants offer diverse challenges for Sudoku enthusiasts, from subtle twists on the classic format to entirely new puzzle experiences. Each type requires different solving strategies and provides a fresh perspective on this popular logic game. If you are new, give one a try at the beginners' level and if you are a veteran, give a Super Doku a try or one with a new additional challenge. Search online or in your apps, to play and enjoy.

Activity 71. Do some vocal warm-ups

Vocal warm-ups are not just for singers - they can be beneficial for anyone who uses their voice regularly, including speakers, podcasters, teachers, actors, or anyone else who relies on their voice. I must say my voice can get croaky after a day of podcasting and when I go to see Stereophonics at the Millenium stadium in a couple of months, well I know I will be in pain and unable to use my voice for a week!! So, for me as well as you, here are some key reasons why vocal warm-ups can be so valuable.

Vocal warm-ups help prepare your vocal mechanism for extended use by increasing blood flow to the larynx, stretching and relaxing the muscles of the vocal folds and reducing tension in the throat and neck. This gradual engagement can help minimise strain and potential injury when you need to use your voice for long periods. The warm-up can enhance vocal output, improve the clarity and precision in speech and just enhancing overall vocal quality.

Studies have shown that even a brief warm-up of 5-10 minutes can lead to noticeable improvements. Regular warm-ups can contribute to long-term vocal health by reducing the risk of vocal fatigue and injury, help to maintain vocal stamina for extended speaking and promoting good vocal habits and techniques.

Warming up your voice can serve as a mental preparation tool too. It can boost your confidence, reduce speaking anxiety, increase your focus, signal to your brain that it's time to engage your vocal mechanism and help you assess how your voice is functioning on any given day.

While these exercises might differ from those used by singers, as I don't know how many of us are planning on a Whitney Houston ballad tonight?! These simple exercises can help prepare your voice for optimal performance and long-term health. Even if you are not doing a speaking engagement today, give these exercises a try. Memorise a couple of them, as you never know when you might need them.

1. **Relaxation and Breathing**
    - Do spinal rolls to relax your whole body and open your breath
    - Focus on breathing deeply from your diaphragm to support your voice and reduce strain on your vocal cords

2. **Vocal Cord Engagement**
    - Lip flutters or trills to engage your voice and connect it to your breath
    - Humming exercises to loosen up your vocal cords

3. **Articulation**
   - Do some jaw and facial muscle exercises (see pg....) to enhance vowel formation and consonant clarity
   - Repeat some tongue twisters to improve clarity and precision in speech, as they challenge the coordination between the brain, tongue, and vocal muscles, thereby enhancing pronunciation and speech control, like these:
   -
     a) **Peter Piper Picked a Peck of Pickled Peppers**
        i. Breakdown: Focuses on plosive 'P' sounds.
        ii. Benefits: Excellent for practicing plosive sounds, speed, and rhythm.
        iii. Tips: Start slow, emphasising each 'P' sound, then increase speed.
     b) **Six Slippery Snails Slid Silently**
        i. Breakdown: Alliteration of 'S' and 'SL' sounds.
        ii. Benefits: Enhances smooth transitions and alliteration.
        iii. Tips: Maintain a steady pace and focus on smoothness.
     c) **Fred Fed Ted Bread, and Ted Fed Fred Bread**
        i. Breakdown: Mix of 'F,' 'T,' 'D,' and 'B' sounds.
        ii. Benefits: Excellent for practicing consonant transitions and vocal dexterity.
        iii. Tips: Focus on quick shifts between sounds for crisp articulation.
     d) **Any Noise Annoys an Oyster**
        i. Breakdown: Focuses on 'OY' sounds.
        ii. Benefits: Helps with pronunciation of specific phonemes.
        iii. Tips: Repeat several times to improve muscle memory.

4. **Resonance**
   - Exercises exploring how to speak with your whole body. Speaking with your whole body involves engaging not just your mouth and throat but also your posture, gestures, and emotional connection. Here are some exercises examples:
     - Practice speaking while moving your body naturally, using gestures and posture to emphasise your message.
     - Record yourself to observe how your body language enhances your speech.
     - Maintain an upright posture to open up your vocal tract and enhance resonance.
     - Practice mindfulness to connect your emotions with your body movements while speaking.
     - Use movement to express passion and authenticity in your speech.

- Seek feedback from others to improve your non-verbal communication.

Other Tips:

- Aim for a 10-20 minute warm-up session before important speaking engagements or singing
- If time is limited, even a 5-minute routine can be beneficial
- Incorporate warm-ups into your daily routine for long-term vocal improvement
- Take regular breaks during practice to avoid overexertion
- Stay hydrated and avoid alcohol and smoking, which can dehydrate and irritate your vocal cords
- Practice proper vocal technique to minimise strain and maximise endurance

By consistently practicing these vocal warm-ups, you can enhance your speaking voice's clarity, strength, and overall quality, leading to more effective and confident communication in various settings, from public speeches to everyday conversations.

Activity 72. Sculpt a tiny clay figure

Sculpting a tiny clay figure (or go big!) can be highly beneficial for both mental and physical well-being. Have you ever done this when bored at work with blu-tak? I have so many times, the kneading and shaping, kept me busy and entertained on both boring and stressful days.

Manipulating clay can be a calming and meditative experience. The tactile nature of working with clay helps release tension and reduce stress levels. The focused attention required when sculpting a tiny figure can quiet the mind, offering a respite from intrusive thoughts and daily worries.

Clay sculpting serves as a powerful outlet for emotional expression, especially for complex feelings that may be difficult to verbalise. The process of shaping clay allows individuals to externalise their inner world, providing a safe space for emotional release and healing. No matter how simple your design, this activity can provide a sense of accomplishment and pride. This boost in confidence can extend to other areas of life, encouraging resilience and a positive mindset.

As for physical benefits, working on a small scale with clay helps improve hand-eye coordination and fine motor skills. The precise movements required for detailing a tiny figure can be particularly beneficial for maintaining dexterity. The tactile experience of handling clay engages multiple senses, providing a rich sensory experience that can be both grounding and stimulating. The act of kneading and shaping clay can help release physical tension in the hands, arms, and even the whole body.

It is a handy hobby to have as working with small amounts of clay is a portable form of art therapy that can be done almost anywhere, making it an accessible tool for managing stress and anxiety in various situations. So by engaging in the simple act, individuals can experience a holistic blend of mental relaxation, emotional release, and physical engagement, contributing significantly to overall well-being.

I had a quick look at that huge online rainforest, and you can get air dry clay at a really reasonable price for white clay, it goes up steeply in proportion if you opt for the coloured clay. DAS White Air Hardening Modelling Clay, Non-Bake, Ready To Use, Ideal for Professionals & Hobbyists £3.99 for 1kg (weight of a bag of sugar), whereas;

Air Dry Clay 27 Colours, £9.99 for 330g (or 76 colours – 1kg - £19.99). There are positives for both as the white clay you can decorate yourself, paint etc, which could be another spend (or make a snowman and put a tiny, knitted scarf on him!) whereas the coloured clays will probably need little further decoration after modelling your piece. I have just put some suggestions for you to run with, but be creative, if a bowl takes your fancy to display your fruit, then go for it or if you want to make the world's longest clay snake, then you can aim for the Guiness Book of Records! Just have fun!

Mushroom - Rolling a cylinder for the stem - Adding a flattened half-sphere for the cap - Creating texture on the cap with small indentations	**Duck** - Forming a teardrop shape for the body - Adding a smaller ball for the head - Creating a bill with a small piece of clay - Shaping wings by pinching clay into curved shapes
Caterpillar - Rolling small balls of clay - Connecting them in a line - Adding simple features like eyes and antennae	**Tiny House** - Shaping a small rectangular base - Adding a triangular roof - Creating windows and a door with small clay pieces
Pinch Pots: Create small pinch pots using any type of clay. They are easy to shape and can be used for small plants or as decorative items.	**Cupcake** - Making a cup-shaped base - Adding a rounded top for frosting - Decorating with small clay pieces for sprinkles
DIY Vases: Make a vase using air dry clay and add a textured effect for a unique look.	**Ring Holder:** Create a simple ring holder using air dry clay and decorate with paint.
Beads: Make beads using air dry or polymer clay. They are great for jewellery-making and can be painted for added colour.	**Spoon Rest:** Use clay to make a simple spoon rest, which is a great beginner project for hand-building skills.

These simple clay figures are perfect for beginners and can be made with basic techniques like rolling, pinching, and shaping clay. As you practice, you'll develop your skills and be able to create more complex sculptures. Remember to have fun and let your creativity guide you!

Activity 73. Speed clean a room

Here we go a speed challenge. Speed, as in motion ok! Again, I don't want to teach you, how to suck eggs. I work best from lists and prompts, also you might read some tips that make your life a little easier. Also, this is your little challenge so either; set a stopwatch on your phone to time how long it takes and see if you can beat it next time as you work out little shortcuts or set a timer for 10-15 minutes with the aim of completing as much as you can in that time. For this reason, which ever challenge time type you have chosen, hopefully the list will help!

Prepare
- Set a timer for 10-15 minutes to stay focused or get your stopwatch ready
- Gather all necessary cleaning tools in a caddy or bucket
- Put on comfortable shoes for mobility

Declutter Quickly
- Scan the room and remove items that don't belong
- Use a basket to collect misplaced items for later sorting
- Make the bed if it's a bedroom, or straighten the main furniture piece as it instantly improves appearance

Clean Top to Bottom
- Start dusting surfaces with a microfiber cloth or duster
- Wipe down furniture, tables, and other surfaces with a damp cloth
- Focus on high-traffic areas and visible spots

Floor Cleaning
- Sweep or vacuum the floor, moving quickly but thoroughly
- For hard floors, use a dry mop or spot clean as needed
- Move furniture only if absolutely necessary

Empty the trash
- Replace the bag for a fresh look and smell

Final Touches
- Arrange pillows and straighten items on surfaces
- Do a quick mirror and glass wipe-down if necessary
- Finish with a room spray or open a window, giving a clean, fresh scent to the room

Remember to keep moving and avoid getting caught up in details. The goal is to make the room presentable quickly, not to deep clean. With practice, you'll become more efficient and can clean a room effectively in just 10-15 minutes.

When speed cleaning, it's important to avoid these common mistakes:

Rushing Too Much: While the goal is to clean quickly, it's crucial to strike a balance between speed and thoroughness. Rushing can lead to missed spots or ineffective cleaning.

Not Prioritising Tasks: Failing to identify and focus on the most critical cleaning tasks first can result in wasted time on less important areas.

Using Too Much Product: Overusing cleaning products can create more work, leading to streaks and longer drying times. Use just enough product to be effective.

Neglecting to Declutter First: Attempting to clean around clutter is inefficient. Take a moment to quickly tidy up and remove items that don't belong before starting to clean.

Cleaning in the Wrong Order: Cleaning from bottom to top or in a random order can undo your work. Always clean from top to bottom to avoid re-cleaning areas.

Forgetting to Ventilate: Not opening windows or doors while cleaning can lead to poor air quality and lingering chemical odours.

Using the Wrong Tools: Relying on ineffective tools like dry cloths or feather dusters for dusting only spreads particles around instead of removing them.

Neglecting to Clean Cleaning Tools: Forgetting to clean your cleaning equipment, such as vacuums or mops, can reduce their effectiveness and spread dirt around.

By avoiding these mistakes, you can make your speed cleaning sessions more efficient and effective, achieving a cleaner home in less time. Plus you have done a workout! 2 stars for you!

Activity 74. Try body percussion exercises

Bet you weren't betting on doing this day! Don't panic this is not the classic 'one-man band', although if you do try strapping tambourines to your knees and a drum on your back, then please, please send me a photo!! Body percussion exercises can significantly enhance your overall wellbeing in several ways.

You should be used to all the benefits of these exercises by now, but if you are opening this book for the first time to this very page, then you are in luck with lots and lots of benefits.

Body percussion activities can reduce stress and anxiety, boost your mood and emotional well-being, enhance mindfulness and present-moment awareness and also improve cognitive functions like memory and attention.

It is also a fun, full-body workout, which helps to improve coordination and motor skills as well as your rhythm and timing, which can all change with age. Participating in body percussion can provide a form of emotional expression and boost self-esteem and confidence.

Start simple with basic sounds, experimenting with different parts of your body to discover unique sounds. For example a gentle thigh slap (or patting) sounds completely different to an upper arm slap. Also try changing the shape of your hands or feet, such as; clapping with cupped hands creates a nice, low sound. Begin by mastering fundamental body percussion sounds:

- Clapping
- Stomping
- Patting (chest, thighs, etc.)
- Snapping fingers
- Clicking tongue

Progress to More Complex Sequences, as you improve:

- Combining different sounds (e.g., clap-stomp-snap)
- Creating longer patterns
- Varying the tempo
- Listen to different musical genres and try to replicate rhythms
- Experiment with leaving out beats or incorporating rests to create more interesting rhythms.
- Use silence to improve your internal sense of timing and rhythm.

Then get funky by incorporating music, maybe use your favourite songs to:

- Keep a steady beat with body percussion

- Create rhythmic accompaniments

Some other techniques and sequences to try:

Rhythmic Breathing
- Inhale deeply for 4 counts while patting your chest
- Hold your breath for 4 counts while tapping your shoulders
- Exhale for 4 counts while rubbing your thighs
- Repeat this cycle, syncing your breath with the body movements

Heartbeat Simulation
- Place your hand over your heart and feel your heartbeat
- Use your other hand to tap out your heartbeat rhythm on your thigh
- Gradually slow down the tapping, encouraging your actual heartbeat to follow

Body Scan Percussion
- Start at your feet, tapping or patting gently
- Slowly move up your body, creating soft percussion on each body part
- Focus on the sensations and sounds as you progress

Emotional Release Drumming
- Identify an emotion you want to release
- Choose a body part to represent that emotion
- Create a rhythm expressing the feeling, then gradually transform it into a calmer pattern

Copycat Challenge
- In a group, have one person create a short body percussion pattern
- Others in the group copy the pattern
- Take turns leading, fostering connection and reducing social anxiety

Rhythmic Declarations
- As a group, create a simple body percussion beat
- Take turns saying positive affirmations or stress-relief mantras in rhythm with the beat

Remember, the key to using body percussion for stress relief is to focus on the present moment, the physical sensations, and the rhythms you're creating. Start with simple patterns and gradually increase complexity as you become more comfortable. Regular practice can help reduce stress levels, improve mood, and enhance overall well-being. Focus on enjoying the process and staying present in the moment to maximise the wellbeing benefits of body percussion exercises, no one can see you, if you do not want them too.

Activity 75. Learn a magic trick

Now, I am not a massive fan of magic, maybe because I know it is not real, or is it?! But learning simple magic tricks offers a wide array of mental health benefits that can positively impact various aspects of someone's life. Yes, really!

On the cognitive front, it enhances problem-solving skills, improves focus and concentration, and boosts creativity. Psychologically, mastering magic tricks can significantly increase self-esteem, reduce anxiety, and contribute to overall emotional wellbeing. Socially, it provides a unique way to connect with others, improving interpersonal skills and potentially elevating one's social status, especially among children. Moreover, the therapeutic applications of magic are gaining recognition in mental health settings, where it's being used to boost patients' self-esteem and as a component in cognitive behavioural therapy programs.

Learning and practicing magic tricks, especially those involving sleight of hand, can help improve your fine motor skills and hand-eye coordination and interestingly, witnessing or performing magic tricks has been used as a distraction technique to manage perceived pain and anxiety in medical settings. I can see how that would work. That short sentence that I discovered, could have me researching for hours, but I haven't got time for that, I need to get this book to you!

The combination of cognitive stimulation, psychological benefits, and social advantages makes learning magic tricks a surprisingly effective tool for promoting mental health and wellbeing. Here are just a few 'simple' tricks to start practising. If you find the words to difficult to follow, with these types of activities I need to see it to understand, please use your best research terminology and see what videos, guides you can find online.

The Vanishing Act - To make the coin disappear:

1. Hold the coin between your thumb and index finger of your dominant hand, with your palm facing up.
2. Slowly move your other hand over the coin, as if you're about to grab it.
3. As you close your hand around the coin, secretly drop it into your palm. This move is called the "French Drop".
4. Keep your hand closed as if holding the coin, and bring it up towards your head to misdirect the audience.
5. Discreetly drop the coin from your palm into your pocket or under a table.
6. Open both hands to show the coin has vanished.

The Reappearing Trick - To make the coin reappear:

1. After the vanish, keep the coin hidden in your dominant hand.
2. Make a magical gesture with your empty hand.

3. Reach into the air or behind someone's ear and produce the coin from hidden hand.
4. Show the coin to your audience, completing the illusion.

   - Practice the French Drop technique until it looks natural and smooth.
   - Use misdirection to draw attention away from the hand holding the coin
   - Keep your movements relaxed and confident to sell the illusion.
   - Start with a larger coin until you master the technique, then move to smaller coins.

Here are some more beginner-friendly magic tricks that use common household items:

The Jumping Rubber Band - This classic trick creates the illusion of a rubber band jumping between your fingers.

1. Place a rubber band around your first two fingers.
2. Secretly insert all four fingers into the band while closing your hand.
3. When you open your hand, the rubber band appears to jump to your last two fingers.

The Levitating Card - Create the illusion of a floating playing card with this simple trick.

1. Prepare a "trick" card by attaching a thin, clear thread or hair.
2. Hold the card horizontally between your thumb and index finger.
3. Move your other hand above the card, using subtle movements to make it appear to float.

The Spoon Bend Illusion - Create the illusion of bending a spoon with your mind.

1. Hold a spoon by the handle.
2. Press down on the spoon while sliding your hand along the handle.
3. This gives the illusion of the spoon bending.
4. Quickly straighten the spoon to show it's unbent.

Remember, the key to performing these tricks successfully is practice and presentation. Develop a confident, engaging style to enhance the illusion and captivate your audience. Magic tricks stimulate curiosity, which is linked to cognitive and emotional wellbeing. This curiosity can foster a love for learning that extends beyond magic.

For individuals with certain conditions, such as ADHD or emotional disturbances, learning magic tricks has been shown to have therapeutic benefits, including increased self-esteem. The structured nature of magic practice and the sense of control it provides can be particularly beneficial for those struggling with mental health issues.

Activity 76. Try a quick Pilates routine

Pilates is a holistic practice that offers a comprehensive approach to both physical and mental health, making it an excellent choice for enhancing overall wellbeing.

Physically, it improves flexibility, posture, and muscle strength, particularly in the core, while also aiding in injury prevention and rehabilitation. Mentally, Pilates fosters mindfulness through controlled breathing and movement, reducing stress and anxiety by promoting relaxation and mental clarity. It also enhances emotional resilience and boosts mood by increasing serotonin and endorphin levels, which can lead to better sleep quality and improved concentration. Additionally, Pilates provides a social benefit when practiced in group classes, helping to combat feelings of isolation.

Overall, Pilates offers a comprehensive wellness solution that integrates physical fitness with mental well-being.

Important Safety Note

Before starting any exercise routine, ensure you understand the correct form and technique. If you have not performed a Pilates routine before or if you are unsure, please consider researching online or using a free app that demonstrates the proper way to perform these moves.

This routine is designed to focus on core strength, flexibility, and mindfulness, which can be particularly beneficial during the recovery process.

Warm-Up (2-3 minutes)
- Begin with deep breathing exercises to calm your mind and prepare your body.
- Perform gentle neck and shoulder rolls to loosen tension.

Main Routine (15-20 minutes)
1. Cat-Cow Stretch (1 minute)
    - Start on hands and knees.
    - Alternate between arching and rounding your back, focusing on coordinating your breath with movement.

2. Pelvic Tilts (1 minute)
    - Lie on your back with knees bent.
    - Gently tilt your pelvis, pressing your lower back into the mat.

3. Bridge Pose (1 minute)
    - From the pelvic tilt position, lift your hips towards the ceiling.
    - Hold for a few breaths, then lower slowly.

4. Single Leg Circles (1 minute each leg)
   - Lie on your back and extend one leg to the ceiling.
   - Make small circles with your leg, keeping your core engaged.

5. The Hundred (2 minutes)
   - Lie on your back, lift your head and shoulders.
   - Pump your arms up and down while holding the position.

6. Roll-Up (1 minute)
   - Slowly roll up from lying to sitting position, focusing on articulating through your spine.

7. Spine Twist (1 minute)
   - Sit with legs extended, twist your upper body side to side.

8. Side Leg Lifts (1 minute each side)
   - Lie on your side, lift your top leg up and down.

9. Plank Hold (30 seconds to 1 minute)
   - Hold a forearm plank position, focusing on core engagement.

10. Child's Pose (1 minute)
    - Rest in child's pose, focusing on deep breathing.

Cool-Down (2-3 minutes)
- Perform gentle stretches to relax your muscles.
- End with final deep breathing exercises to calm your mind.

Benefits for Addiction Recovery

This routine incorporates key Pilates principles that can benefit those in addiction recovery. The focus on controlled breathing and mindful movement can help reduce stress and anxiety, while the core-strengthening exercises promote physical well-being. The mind-body connection fostered through Pilates can aid in developing self-awareness and emotional regulation, crucial for managing cravings and maintaining recovery.

Remember to listen to your body and modify exercises as needed. Consistency is key, so aim to practice this routine regularly to experience the full benefits of Pilates in supporting your recovery journey.

Activity 77. Write a letter to your future self

This is such a powerful exercise, and I recommend it to everyone! No matter how silly or unusual it feels, stick with it, as the benefits will really pay off.

I spoke with a woman this week and she told me that when she moved house, she was going through all of her old paperwork to downsize. She came across her old NVQ paperwork and just burst into tears. This serge of emotion came from an exercise she reluctantly had to complete for her qualification. She was unhappy with her life and had to write about what she had and what she wanted in life. This lady put exactly how she was feeling and how she felt she would never have her own home, would never pass her driving test, hated the job she was in and wanted to run her own business etc. She burst into tears, happy tears because upon reading this, she realised that she had achieved everything that she had written on that piece of paper and that on days when she is feeling ungrateful, she had forgotten just how far she had come in her life. Can you see why this exercise can be so powerful!?

If you are unhappy, let it all out! If you have nothing to worry about, write this down. If you want a 15-bed mansion, write this down. If you want to live on a desert island with only dogs for company, write this down.

Looking back, you will see what frame of mind you were in at the time and how far you've come. You might be in the same house but got married. You might have wanted 10 kids but now have a cattery. Look at what your life's journey says about you and the hidden strengths.

Writing a letter to your future self is a valuable practice that:
- Provides an opportunity to reflect on your thoughts, emotions, and experiences
- Helps you gain insight into your desires, fears, and motivations
- Allows you to articulate your vision for the future
- Increases commitment to your goals by writing them down
- Serves as a tool for tracking your progress over time
- Encourages you to make positive changes in your life
- Acts as a form of self-care and self-expression
- Can reduce stress and provide a sense of clarity and purpose
- Captures your current state of mind for future reflection
- Allows you to relive memories and experiences from your past self
- Provides an opportunity to send positivity and support to your future self
- Can serve as a source of motivation during challenging times
- By writing a letter to your future self, you create a unique connection between your present and future, fostering personal development and self-understanding.

Activity 78. Practice good posture exercises

Now this I feel I have little right to talk about, as my posture is absolutely diabolical. I try on and off over the years, although I feel I have spent so long in a protective position since my back injury, that my funny positions give me comfort. I sit on my feet or with my legs crossed in the ergonomic desk chair with my feet over the arm rests, really random positions. I would love to know if you sit in random positions? Or is it just me?

Practicing good posture exercises offers benefits for both physical and mental well-being reducing back pain by aligning the spine, reducing strain on muscles and joints, which can alleviate and prevent chronic back pain.

Proper alignment also allows the lungs to expand more fully, increasing lung capacity and making breathing easier and I do notice that I hold myself up straight when I am hosting my podcasts, allowing me to breathe and relax during the recording.

Maintaining good posture engages and strengthens core muscles, providing better support for the spine and reduces the risk of musculoskeletal injuries, particularly in the back, shoulders, arms, and wrists.

As well as the physical benefits, the mental and emotional benefits of a good, upright posture include reduced depressive feelings, improve mood, increase energy levels and has been linked to improved self-esteem and confidence in individual's thoughts and abilities. Productivity is enhanced due to the reduction in pain and fatigue, so good posture can lead to improved focus.

Proper alignment reduces abnormal wear and tear on joints, potentially decreasing the risk of osteoarthritis and contributes to better circulation, digestion, and overall bodily function.

Consistently good posture prevents the spine from becoming fixed in abnormal positions over time (like mine!).

By regularly practicing good posture exercises, you can develop greater body awareness, train your muscles to maintain proper alignment, and ultimately enjoy these numerous health benefits.

Here are some simple exercises to practice good posture:

Standing Posture Exercise

1. Stand with your feet shoulder-width apart
2. Keep your shoulders back and relaxed
3. Pull your stomach in slightly

4. Keep your head level, with your earlobes aligned with your shoulders
5. Let your arms hang naturally at your sides
6. Hold this position for 30 seconds, focusing on maintaining alignment

Seated Posture Exercise

1. Sit with your back straight and shoulders back
2. Keep your feet flat on the floor, shoulder-width apart
3. Avoid crossing your legs
4. Rest your forearms on the desk or table while keeping shoulders relaxed
5. Ensure your chin is parallel to the floor
6. Hold this position for 1 minute, being mindful of your alignment

Wall Slides

1. Stand with your back against a wall
2. Keep your head, upper back, and lower back flat against the wall
3. Slide your arms up and down the wall, keeping them in contact with the surface
4. Simultaneously perform chin tucks by gently tucking your chin towards your chest
5. Repeat for 10-15 repetitions

Plank (See the plank 30-day challenge Activity 3)

1. Start in a push-up position with your forearms on the ground
2. Keep your body in a straight line from head to heels
3. Engage your core and glutes
4. Hold this position for 30 seconds, focusing on maintaining a neutral spine

Cat-Cow Stretch

1. Start on your hands and knees
2. Inhale and arch your back, lifting your chest and tailbone (Cow pose)
3. Exhale and round your spine, tucking your chin to your chest (Cat pose)
4. Repeat this flowing movement for 10 cycles, focusing on spinal mobility

Remember to perform these exercises regularly and be mindful of your posture throughout the day to develop good habits.

Activity 79. Do a quick manicure

Now this is something I do regularly. We all have something about us don't we! We are known for our hair, jewellery collection or our perfumes, something we do regularly or people always comment on. Now mine is my nails! I have always been lucky with strong nails, but I do try my best to look after them. I use UV gels for added strength and love my nail art, it makes me feel good. Treat yourself and give your hard working hands some TLC.

Here's a guide to doing a manicure at home:

1. Remove old nail polish, I use pure acetone due to wearing UV gel, but this can really dry out your nails. Also, this may sound random, but if you or someone who has access to your polish remover may have an issue with drinking this type of alcohol, please use with caution. You may think I am crazy, but I know someone who would drink aftershave if they had no alcohol to get their fix.
2. Shape your nails choosing your preferred shape (square, round, oval). File from the edge to the centre of the nail and not back and forth, as this can break the nail.
3. Soak fingertips in warm water (2 mins) and gently push back cuticles with a cuticle stick.
4. Exfoliate with an equal mix of sugar and olive oil and gently scrub your hands and nails.
5. Apply cuticle oil and really massage your cuticles, as this brings the blood to the nail bed to help them strengthen and grow well. If you wish to tidy your cuticles further, use nail nippers, but be careful not to take too much away as they are likely to start bleeding.
6. Apply a thin layer of base coat to protect nails, otherwise nail polish can dye the nails.
7. Paint nails applying two thin coats of your chosen colour, waiting for each coat to dry before applying the next, or use UV gel and a nail lamp.
8. Remember to close the tip of the nail with your chosen varnish.
9. Finish with a clear topcoat for shine (or matte top coat) and protection. If you want to add some nail art, do this before adding the top coat.
10. Moisturise with hand cream and massage into hands, nails, and cuticles, take your time with this and pay attention to different parts of your hands, wrists and fingers. Massaging your cuticles really helps to bring the blood to the nail bed to help them strength and grow well.
11. Clean up using a small brush dipped in nail polish remover to clean edges

Activity 80. Experiment with food plating

Experimenting with food plating is an art form that chefs use to enhance the visual appeal and overall dining experience. This also works in the home for all the family. I will write relating to research and findings of diners and restaurants, but the same results can be obtained at home and cooking for friends and family. Food plating can significantly influence our perception of flavour in several ways:

1. **Visual Appeal:** Attractive plating makes food more appetising before it's tasted. Research by Professor Charles Spence found artistically plated meals are rated higher and seen as more valuable than plain presentations.

2. **Taste Perception:** Food on a beautiful plate is often perceived as tastier and healthier than the same food on a less attractive plate.

3. **Emotional Response:** Creative plating can evoke positive emotions, enhancing the overall flavour experience.

4. **Colour Contrast:** Using contrasting colours stimulates interest and may influence taste perception. The plate's colour can even affect how spicy or intense food seems, engaging multiple senses for a richer experience.

5. **Portion Placement:** Food placed in the centre of the plate is often judged tastier than the edges. This approach supports portion control and keeps plates visually satisfying.

6. **Texture and Height:** Combining varied textures and building height boosts visual appeal and makes flavours seem more complex.

7. **Portion Size:** Smaller, well-presented portions can taste more satisfying than larger, messier servings. Attractive plating can encourage better eating habits and nutritional intake, especially in healthcare settings.

Food plating provides an opportunity for creators to express their creativity and showcase their culinary skills. And for those who love to post pictures of their meals… it looks great on social media, and you can say, I did that! By carefully considering these factors in food presentation, restaurants and chefs can potentially enhance customers' perception of flavour, leading to increased satisfaction and enjoyment of the meal. Here are some simple experiments you can try with food plating:

Colour Contrast
- Pair complementary colours on the plate
- Example: Place green asparagus next to red tomatoes or orange carrots
- Pair beige foods (pasta, chicken) with dark plates
- Use vibrant leaves as a bed for salads

- Incorporate colourful vegetables or sauces

Height and Layers - Create different levels on the plate, use three different heights when plating to fill up space and make food look more substantial. For example; Stack proteins on starches (e.g., steak over mashed potatoes) and use vegetables or garnishes to add height

Combine different textures on one plate
- Combine smooth purees with crispy elements, such as crispy fried onions with creamy mashed potatoes and tender meat
- Add foams or sauces for contrast
- Use ingredients like fried leeks or vegetable chips as garnishes

Sauce Artistry
- Use sauces to create visual interest and add flavour
- Try drizzling, dotting, smearing, swirling or spreading sauces in patterns
- Example: Make a zigzag pattern with balsamic reduction across the plate

Plating methods:
- Free Form Plating: Create an abstract, artistic arrangement on the plate
- Landscape Plating: Arrange food in long, low placements across the plate
- Hide and Seek Plating: Layer elements to create surprise discoveries for diners
- Classic Plating: Use traditional arrangements with precise placement
- Clock Method: Arrange food items like a clock face, place protein at 6 o'clock, vegetables at 2 o'clock, and carbs at 11 o'clock

Think outside the box:
- Serve dishes in bowls instead of plates for a "super bowl" effect
- Use unique materials like glass, metal, or LED-lit plates for futuristic plating
- Deconstruct classic dishes to reimagine their components
- Garnish Creatively using edible flowers, herbs, or microgreens

Negative Space - Leave some areas of the plate empty, this can make the food stand out more. For example: Place a small portion of food off-centre on a large white plate

Remember, the goal is to make the food visually appealing while keeping it practical to eat, maintaining the integrity of the flavours and ingredients. Start with these simple techniques and have fun experimenting with your presentations.

Activity 81. Start a mini book review

Starting a mini book review is an excellent way to share your thoughts on books concisely while helping others decide if a book is right for them. It can be a fun and rewarding pass time for several reasons.

A mini book review allows you to express your thoughts and feelings about a book in your unique voice. You can convey your enthusiasm, humour, critique, or admiration in a way that reflects your personality, experimenting with language, tone, and style, making the review as formal or informal as you like. Reviews are a great way to practice and improve your writing skills. It helps you learn how to articulate your thoughts clearly and concisely.

Writing reviews encourage you to think critically about the book's themes, characters, and plot. This deeper analysis can enhance your appreciation of the work. Reflecting on characters and their journeys can create a personal connection to the story, making it more memorable.

If you're sharing your review online or in a blog, you can enhance it with images, quotes, or design elements that reflect the book's theme. All this can help others discover new books or authors they might not have considered. Sharing your insights can spark discussions and inspire fellow readers, encouraging connections with fellow book lovers, whether in person or online.

Finishing a mini book review gives you a sense of achievement, especially if you've read a challenging book or one that resonated deeply with you. Mini reviews serve as a record of what you've read and how you've felt about each book, allowing you to look back on your literary journey over time.

Research shows that reading for just 6 minutes a day lowers stress by up to 68%, more effectively than music or walks. Writing reviews reinforces this by providing a structured outlet for reflection, reducing heart rate, blood pressure, and muscle tension. A review-writing ritual can extend this calm, akin to mindfulness practices.

Studies have also linked regular reading to a 20% lower mortality risk over 12 years, attributed to cognitive preservation.

Spiritual books act as "medicine for the soul," nurturing self-awareness and connection to transcendent values. Reviewing such texts encourages intentional reflection on their lessons.

A mini book review habit not only leverages the innate benefits of reading but also transforms it into a purposeful practice that enhances mental clarity, physical relaxation, and spiritual depth.

Activity 82. Create a photo story in 6 images

Creating a photo story in six images can be a profoundly beneficial activity, an excellent way to convey a narrative visually. This visual narrative allows individuals to express complex emotions and experiences in a non-verbal manner, fostering self-awareness and emotional healing. By capturing moments and milestones, individuals can reflect on their journey, celebrate progress, and visualise future aspirations, which can enhance motivation and resilience. Photography also encourages mindfulness, helping individuals stay grounded in the present and focused on their recovery goals. Sharing these stories can further promote connection and empathy, reducing feelings of isolation and stigma associated with addiction. Overall, this creative process supports personal growth, empowerment, and a deeper understanding of your journey. Although it does not have to be about you, it could be about the weather, about a village, a sibling or even your pets. Whatever comes to mind. Here are some ideas to get you thinking and how to capture your vision:

1. **Plan Your Narrative** - Choose a clear theme or story you want to tell
   - Outline the key elements of your story
   - Decide on the beginning, middle, and end

2. **Storyboard Your Shots** - Sketch or list the 6 key moments you want to capture
   - Consider the following structure:
     1. Establishing shot (setting the scene)
     2. Introduction of characters or subject
     3. Rising action or conflict
     5. Climax or turning point
     6. Falling action
     7. Resolution or conclusion

3. **Compose Your Shots** - Use a variety of shot types (wide, medium, close-up)
   - Consider the rule of thirds for balanced compositions
   - Pay attention to lighting and colour consistency across images

4. **Capture Your Images** (or obviously you can use photos you have already taken)
   - Take multiple shots of each scene for options
   - Ensure each image can stand alone while contributing to the overall story
   - Pay attention to details that connect the images

5. **Edit and Sequence** - Select your best 6 images that tell the story effectively
   - Edit the photos for consistency in style and tone
   - Arrange the images in a logical sequence that flows naturally

6. **Review and Refine**
   - Ensure each image contributes to the narrative
   - Check that the story is clear and coherent

- Get feedback from others to see if your story comes across as intended

Remember, a successful photo story should engage the viewer and evoke emotion while clearly conveying your intended narrative. Here are some suggestions:

A Day in the Life - Begin with a morning routine, including waking up, getting ready, and a quick breakfast. Follow this with the commute and the work environment, whether at home or outside. Take a lunch break to recharge, then continue with afternoon tasks or activities. Evenings bring relaxation—perhaps a hobby, connecting with loved ones, or unwinding alone. End the day with a soothing bedtime ritual, preparing for restful sleep

The Changing Seasons - Capture one location as it transforms all year: winter brings snow, followed by spring's blossoms and nature's renewal. Summer arrives with full greenery, then gives way to vibrant fall foliage as leaves change. As temperatures drop, winter returns, and the cycle of change begins again.

From Farm to Table - Trace the journey of a meal: it starts with planting or harvesting ingredients, followed by transportation to markets or shops. At home, the ingredients are prepped and cooked, plated attractively, and finally enjoyed at the table, connecting everyone to the origins of their food.

Urban Transformation - Show how a city block or building evolves: an old structure or empty lot gives way to demolition or groundbreaking, shifting to construction. Near completion, anticipation builds for the space's grand opening, finally becoming a thriving hub of activity for its community.

Learning a New Skill - Learning begins with a first, sometimes awkward, attempt. Practice brings improvement, though it may include moments of frustration. With perseverance come breakthroughs and skilful refinement, leading finally to a satisfying and successful demonstration of the new skill.

A Local Event - Follow a community gathering from setup and preparation through the arrival of attendees. Experience the main activity or performance and catch behind-the-scenes moments. Enjoy the crowd's reaction before the event closes with cleanup and departure, leaving lasting memories.

Activity 83. Decorate a picture frame

This activity fits perfectly with the previous one, so if you have completed the 6-picture story, consider a frame decorated around your story's theme. Repurpose any frame for picture of your favourite people, travels, pets or sunsets and the ideal place to buy them if you haven't any spare frame are charity shops.

Engaging in DIY projects like upcycling frames encourages creativity, problem-solving, and a sense of accomplishment, which can enhance feelings of self-worth and confidence. Additionally, transforming old items into new ones supports sustainable practices, reducing waste and contributing to a sense of purpose and pride in contributing to environmental sustainability. The creative process involved in upcycling can also serve as a form of therapeutic activity, providing a calming and fulfilling experience that promotes mental well-being.

Are any ideas coming to mind? If not, check out some of these ideas and add buying an old map or beads onto that charity shopping list:

Paint and Embellish
- Use craft paint to give the frame a new colour
- Add texture with a stone or vintage tin effect using adhesive sheets
- Create a weathered look by distressing painted frames

Add Decorative Elements
- Glue on seashells, pebbles, or dried flowers for a nature-inspired frame
- Attach buttons, beads, or small charms for a personalised touch
- Use gold or copper leaf to add metallic accents

Upcycle and Repurpose
- Cover the frame with fabric, wallpaper, or decorative wrapping paper
- Transform an old window frame into a unique multi-photo display
- Use reclaimed wood or pallet boards to build a rustic frame

Create Themed Frames
- Make a travel-themed frame by adding maps or ticket stubs
- Design a beach-inspired frame with sand and small shells
- Craft a seasonal frame with artificial leaves or snowflakes

Functional Frames
- Replace the backing with cork to create a pinboard frame
- Use chalkboard paint on the back panel for a customisable message area
- Add a mirror instead of glass for a decorative and functional piece

Remember to choose a decoration style that complements your photo and home decor. Mix and match ideas to create unique, personalised picture frames.

Whilst at school doing my G.C.S.E Art, I created a collage out of all the old photographs that had been taken by mistake or were blurred or people we had no idea who they were!? Using small, roughly cut-up pieces, with all the different colours, shades and shapes, I produced a collage of myself out of my photographs, I was so proud of it. I lost it when I became street homeless. Never mind I have the memories and the 'A' grade qualification to remember it by.

Here are some other creative suggestions:

1. Use a map as the background: Cut a map from your travel destination to fit the frame and use it as a backdrop for your photos and mementos (or travel books from a charity shop).

2. Add 3D dimensional elements: Attach small souvenirs, ticket stubs, or pressed flowers.

3. Create a collage: Combine multiple photos, postcards, and other flat items.

4. Incorporate textures: Use fabric, buttons, or textured paper to add visual interest.

5. Paint and distress: Give a wooden frame a weathered look by painting it and then sanding parts of it for a vintage feel.

6. Add quotes or captions: Use letter stickers or hand-lettering to include meaningful text related to your memories.

7. Use washi tape: Decorate the frame with colourful washi tape patterns.

8. Create a themed design: Match the frame's decoration to the memory's theme (e.g., beach-themed with shells and sand for a vacation memory).

9. Incorporate personal mementos: Glue small items like foreign coins, dried flowers, or fabric scraps from the trip to the frame.

10. Use Mod Podge: Decoupage photos or paper for a unique, personalised look.

Remember to choose decorations that complement your photos and evoke the emotions tied to your memories. The goal is to create a frame that not only displays your photos but also tells a story about the special moments you're preserving.

Activity 84. Try a loving-kindness meditation

Loving-kindness meditation, also known as Metta meditation, is a practice that cultivates feelings of goodwill, kindness, and compassion towards oneself and others. But why send love & kindness to yourself, strangers or people who may be driving you around the bend?....

- **Reduces Self-Criticism and Increases Self-Acceptance**: Loving-kindness meditation helps reduce self-criticism by promoting self-acceptance and kindness towards oneself, leading to improved self-esteem.
- **Enhances Emotional Well-being**: It increases positive emotions such as joy, love, and gratitude, contributing to higher life satisfaction and overall well-being.
- **Improves Mental Health**: This practice has been shown to decrease symptoms of anxiety and depression by fostering a more compassionate mindset.
- **Fosters Empathy and Compassion**: Loving-kindness meditation strengthens empathy and compassion for others, enhancing social connections and relationships.
- **Reduces Stress and Anxiety**: By activating the parasympathetic nervous system, it helps manage stress and anxiety, which often arise from negative emotions towards others, promoting relaxation and calmness.
- **Physiological Benefits**: It offers relief from chronic pain and migraines by altering how the mind perceives pain.
- **Increases Happiness and Resilience**: Regular practice can increase feelings of happiness and resilience, helping individuals cope better with life's challenges.
- **Promotes Forgiveness and Self-Love**: Practicing loving-kindness towards difficult people can help you let go of resentment and cultivate self-love and forgiveness.
- **Encourages Mindfulness and Presence**: It encourages mindfulness by focusing on the present moment and the interconnectedness of all beings.
- **Broadens Perspective**: Including people you don't know or like in your loving-kindness practice helps broaden your perspective and understanding of others' experiences and emotions. Why are they the way they are in your opinion?
- **Reduces Aversion**: It helps reduce aversion and ill-will, promoting a more peaceful and compassionate mindset.
- **Fosters Interconnectedness**: Recognising that all beings share common desires for happiness and freedom from suffering can deepen your sense of interconnectedness with others.

Overall, practicing loving-kindness meditation towards people you don't know or like can lead to personal growth, improved mental health, and a more compassionate outlook on life.

Here's a guide to try a loving-kindness meditation:

Find a quiet, comfortable place to sit or lie down, close your eyes and take a few deep breaths to centre yourself, then set an intention to cultivate feelings of love and kindness.

1. Start with Self-Compassion. Direct loving-kindness towards yourself, repeating phrases like: "May I be happy. May I be healthy. May I be safe. May I live with ease."

2. Extend to a Loved One by visualising someone you care about deeply. Direct the same wishes towards them: "May you be happy. May you be healthy. May you be safe. May you live with ease."

3. Include a Neutral Person: Think of someone you neither like nor dislike (e.g., a cashier or neighbour). Extend the same loving-kindness to them.

4. Consider a Difficult Person: Bring to mind someone you have difficulties with. Try to extend the same wishes to them, acknowledging any resistance you feel.

5. Expand to All Beings: Gradually expand your circle of compassion to include all living beings: "May all beings be happy. May all beings be healthy. May all beings be safe. May all beings live with ease."

6. Close the Practice by taking a few deep breaths, feeling the warmth and positivity you've generated. Slowly open your eyes and carry this feeling with you into your day.

Remember to practice regularly and be patient with yourself. The goal is to cultivate genuine feelings of kindness and compassion, which may take time to develop fully.

Alternative Phrases:

- May I be filled with lovingkindness
- May I be safe from inner and outer dangers
- May I be well in body and mind
- May I be at ease and happy
- May I be peaceful
- May I be free from suffering
- May I live with joy
- May I be kind to myself
- May I accept myself as I am

It's important to note that these phrases can be adapted to direct kindness towards others by replacing "I" with "you" or "we" as the meditation progresses from self to others and eventually to all beings.

Activity 85. Learn basic coding concepts

As we journey through recovery, it's essential to explore activities that not only support our mental health but also provide a sense of purpose and fulfilment. Learning to code can be a highly rewarding endeavour, offering numerous benefits for those in recovery. Coding equips you with problem-solving and logical thinking skills, fosters creativity, and can be a fun and empowering hobby. In today's digital world, understanding how technology works can make you more capable and adaptable, whether for personal projects or professional growth.

How Coding Supports Mental Health

1. Cognitive Stimulation: Learning to code stimulates the brain, promoting cognitive health by triggering neuroplasticity. This can improve memory, increase cognitive flexibility, and reduce the risk of cognitive decline.
2. Boost in Confidence and Self-Esteem: Completing coding projects, even simple ones, can provide a significant boost to confidence and self-esteem. This sense of accomplishment is particularly beneficial for those struggling with anxiety or self-doubt.
3. Mindfulness and Focus: Coding naturally fosters mindfulness by requiring intense focus on the present task. This deep concentration can help practice patience and provide a mental break from everyday pressures.
4. Resilience Building: The process of debugging and fixing errors in code teaches valuable lessons in perseverance. This resilience can be applied to various aspects of life, helping individuals navigate stressful situations more effectively.
5. Creative Expression: Coding allows for creative expression in a digital format. It can serve as a form of digital art therapy, providing a healthy way to process emotions and reduce stress.
6. Social Connection: Joining coding communities increases social connection, reducing feelings of isolation and loneliness. The coding community is known for its inclusivity and willingness to help newcomers.

Getting Started with Coding

For those new to coding, starting with a beginner-friendly language is crucial. Python and JavaScript are excellent choices due to their versatility and gentle learning curves. Here are some tips to get you started:

- Begin with a Beginner-Friendly Language: Python or JavaScript are great options.
- Set Achievable Goals: Break down your learning process into small, manageable objectives.
- Join Coding Communities: Platforms like JetLearn offer support and guidance.
- Make It Fun and Stress-Free: Look for curricula that emphasize enjoyment.
- Take Regular Breaks: Prioritize self-care practices like exercise and meditation.

Coding can be a powerful tool for managing stress and anxiety during recovery. By engaging in coding activities, you can create a constructive outlet for channeling thoughts and emotions into problem-solving and innovation. Here are some ways to incorporate coding into your recovery journey.

Coding Activities for Stress Relief

1. Inducing a Flow State: Engage in coding projects that are challenging yet achievable. This can lead to a state of "flow," reducing anxiety and increasing concentration.
2. Creative Expression: Use coding as a form of digital art therapy by creating games, animations, or websites. This allows you to express yourself creatively, providing a healthy outlet for processing emotions.
3. Developing Self-Care Applications: Create tools specifically designed for self-care and stress management, such as a personal mood tracker or a meditation timer app. This combines coding skills with stress management techniques, providing personalized tools to support mental well-being.

Activity: Create a Personalized Self-Care App

Objective: Develop a simple app or tool that helps you manage stress or track your mood.

Steps:
1. Choose a Platform: Use a beginner-friendly language like Python or JavaScript.
2. Design Your App: Decide what features you want, such as mood tracking or reminders for self-care activities.
3. Build and Test: Use online resources or coding communities for guidance.
4. Reflect and Refine: Reflect on your experience and refine your app based on what you learn.

By integrating coding into your recovery routine, you can experience the dual benefits of learning a new skill and improving your mental health. Remember, the journey to recovery is unique to each individual, and finding activities that bring joy and fulfilment is key to long-term success. Here are some basic free online coding courses available in the UK:

1. FreeCodeCamp - https://www.freecodecamp.org/
    - Offers a comprehensive platform with tutorials and certifications. Learners can progress at their own pace and engage with a supportive community.
2. Code First Girls - https://www.codefirstgirls.org.uk/
    - Provides free, part-time coding courses for women, focusing on web development, Python, data science, and SQL.
3. Codecademy - https://www.codecademy.com/

    - o Offers a free 'Basic' plan with foundational coding courses in languages like HTML, CSS, JavaScript, and Python.
4. Coursera - https://www.coursera.org/
    - o Provides a wide range of free coding courses.

These platforms are excellent starting points for anyone looking to learn coding skills without financial commitment.

Activity 86. Try pronouncing words in a new language

Pronouncing words in a new language can be beneficial for your wellbeing by stimulating cognitive function and enhancing mental agility. The process of learning and practicing new sounds and intonations challenges your brain, which can help improve memory and concentration. Additionally, mastering a new language can boost confidence and self-esteem, providing a sense of accomplishment and pride in your abilities. This intellectual engagement can also serve as a stress-relieving activity, offering a mental escape and a sense of fulfilment.

Living in South Wales, I am surrounded by the rich cultural heritage of the Welsh language. Road signs proudly display Welsh phrases, and train station announcements are thoughtfully made in both English and Welsh. Despite these efforts, it's clear that Welsh is not spoken as widely as it once was, which is a concern for many. The government is actively working to implement initiatives that will help preserve this beautiful language, recognizing the immense cultural loss that would occur if it were to fade away. It would indeed be heartbreaking to see Welsh disappear, and I believe it's essential that we support these efforts to ensure its continued vitality.

Being able to say simple phrases like "hello," "good morning," or "thank you" in Welsh not only fills me with confidence but also significantly boosts my self-esteem. The act of showing consideration for the language by using it, even in small ways, is met with grateful responses, which reinforces my sense of pride and accomplishment. This ability to connect with others through their native tongue creates a profound sense of connection and appreciation, further enhancing my personal growth and sense of self-worth.

Whether you're embarking on a holiday, visiting family abroad, or dreaming of a destination you've always wanted to explore, learning a few words in the local language can be incredibly rewarding. Greeting people with a simple "hello," expressing gratitude with "thank you," and ordering a coffee can go a long way in showing respect for the culture and its people. Your efforts will be genuinely appreciated, and it's easier than you think. Websites like Google offer free resources to help you get started, and YouTube videos can guide you through the correct pronunciation of essential phrases. Take a few minutes to explore these tools, and you'll be well on your way to connecting with the locals and enhancing your travel experience.

Some effective ways to learn:

Listen and Repeat
1. Listen to native speakers pronouncing words and phrases
2. Try to mimic their pronunciation, focusing on individual sounds and intonation
3. Use language learning apps or websites that provide audio recordings of native speakers

Break Words Down
1. Divide words into syllables
2. Practice pronouncing each syllable separately
3. Gradually combine the syllables, paying attention to stress and rhythm

Use the International Phonetic Alphabet (IPA)
1. Learn the IPA symbols for the language you're studying
2. Use IPA transcriptions in dictionaries to understand the correct pronunciation
3. Practice pronouncing individual sounds represented by IPA symbols

Record Yourself
1. Record yourself saying words or phrases
2. Compare your pronunciation to that of native speakers
3. Identify areas for improvement and focus on those specific sounds

Utilise Technology
1. Use speech recognition software to check your pronunciation
2. Try apps with voice comparison tools to see how your pronunciation compares

Practice Tongue Twisters (this is brave!)
1. Find tongue twisters in your target language
2. Start slowly and gradually increase your speed
3. Focus on producing clear, accurate sounds

Engage with Native Speakers
1. Join language exchange platforms to practice with native speakers
2. Ask for feedback on your pronunciation
3. Listen carefully to how they pronounce words and try to replicate their sounds

Remember, improving pronunciation takes time and consistent practice. Be patient with yourself and celebrate small improvements along the way.

The Welsh word for "welcome" is "Croeso" (pronounced kroy-so). You see this on the sign as you travel over the Severn Bridge into Wales. Here are a few other words/phrases to practice, just in case you ever need them:

English	Welsh	Pronunciation
Good morning	Bore da	*bor-eh daah*
Thank you very much	Diolch yn fawr	*dee-olch uhn-va-oor*
How are you? (S. Wales)	shwmai?	*shoo-mai*

Activity 87. Practice time management techniques

Practicing time management techniques is crucial for improving productivity, reducing stress, and achieving personal and professional goals, so please remember when reading to apply at home and in the workplace. Also consider helping others who may be stressed and having difficulty prioritising by sharing some of these techniques.

Why Practice Time Management Techniques?

- Effective time management allows you to accomplish more in less time, leading to increased productivity in both work and personal life.
- By planning and prioritising tasks, you can reduce anxiety and stress associated with looming deadlines and overwhelming workloads, at home and in the workplace.
- Good time management skills help you allocate time for work, personal activities, and relaxation, leading to a more balanced lifestyle.
- With proper time management, you're more likely to realise your short-term and long-term goals by focusing on important tasks.
- When you manage your time well, you have more space to consider options thoroughly, leading to better decision-making.

Procrastination is one of the most significant obstacles to effective time management. People tend to delay important tasks due to many reasons including fear of failure, perfectionism, lack of motivation and unclear instructions or goals. It may well be worth spending a little time trying to get to the bottom of why you procrastinate. Ask where, when, what and why you procrastinate? Overcoming procrastination often requires breaking tasks into smaller, manageable chunks and setting clear deadlines for each step. Here is how to Practice Time Management:

1. **Assess Your Current Time Usage** - Start by tracking how you spend your time. Use a time log or app to record your activities in 15-minute intervals for a week or two. Toggl is an easy, free site to use and I have used it for many years.

2. **Set Clear Goals and Priorities (See SMART Goal Activity)** - Use the SMART method to set achievable goals. Prioritise tasks based on importance and urgency.

3. **Use Planning Tools** - Adopt a planning tool such as a planner, calendar, or app to schedule tasks and deadlines. Consistently use one tool that works best for you.

4. **Implement Time Management Techniques** - such as The Pomodoro Technique – which is focused on working in 25-minute intervals (pomodoros) followed by 5-minute breaks. After four pomodoros, take a longer 15–30-

minute break. For someone who procrastinates, this technique is often considered one of the most effective time management strategies. The short time frame helps create a sense of urgency, reducing the tendency to delay starting tasks and helps to prevent burnout and maintain focus. Completing just one Pomodoro can provide a sense of accomplishment, encouraging continued productivity and the technique can be adjusted to suit individual needs, making it easier to adopt and maintain.

5. **Time Blocking** - Allocate specific time periods for different tasks or types of work. This helps maintain focus and prevents multitasking. This can be planned out in your diary or a to-do-list.

6. **Eat That Frog** - Tackle your most important or challenging task first thing in the morning when your energy and focus are at their peak.

7. **Minimise Distractions** - in our hyper-connected world, distractions are abundant, such as digital notifications, social media, talkative colleagues and unplanned meetings. These interruptions can significantly disrupt focus and productivity. Implementing strategies like time blocking or using website blockers can help minimise distractions. Try using OneTab, which converts open tabs into a list, saving memory, reduces clutter and aids in the prevention of tab hopping.

8. **Take Regular Breaks** - schedule short breaks between tasks to clear your mind and maintain productivity throughout the day.

9. **Review and Adjust** - regularly evaluate your time management strategies and adjust as needed. Be flexible and willing to try different techniques until you find what works best for you.

Taking on too many tasks or projects is a common pitfall. This often stems from difficulty saying no, underestimating the time required for tasks and having a lack of clear boundaries. Learning to set realistic expectations and communicate limitations is crucial for managing workload effectively.

Adopting new time management techniques often requires changing ingrained habits, which can be difficult. People can resist learning new tools or systems, adjusting their daily routines or giving up familiar (but ineffective) work patterns. So, patience and persistence are key when implementing new time management strategies.

Activity 88. Tighten loose screws

My TV screen has been wobbling for weeks, a nagging reminder of my procrastination. I can almost imagine the scene: the 48-inch screen crashing to the floor, shattering into a hundred pieces. The irony would be crushing. "I should have tightened it ages ago!" I'd lament. But instead of dwelling on what could go wrong, I take a deep breath and decide to act. "Actually," I say to myself, "I'm going to take care of it right now. Back in five, I'm off to tighten that screw in the back of the TV!"

Now, I'm no longer procrastinating over something that should have been done weeks ago. While I won't delve into the well-being and physical benefits of this task, I can attest that completing it has brought me greater peace of mind. Not only have I prevented a costly mishap, but I can now focus on writing without distraction. This task will keep you occupied for a while today, but it will save you a significant amount of time in the long run. By addressing small issues, you can prevent larger problems, such as drawers completely breaking and their contents spilling onto the floor. It might seem simple or even trivial, but you might find yourself grateful when you discover a loose screw before it becomes a major issue.

You can either start writing a list of places/things that have screws that may need tighten or go from room to room looking.

1. Look for screws that are visibly loose or wobbling in their holes.

2. Remove any dirt or debris around the screw and in the screw hole.

3. Determine if the screw is simply loose or if the hole has become stripped or enlarged.

4. For slightly loose screws:
    - Use the appropriate screwdriver (matching the screw head type)
    - Turn the screw clockwise to tighten it
    - Be careful not to overtighten, which can strip the hole or damage the screw

5. For screws that won't tighten:
    - Remove the screw completely
    - Apply a thread stopper product like DAP's Tank Bond Thread Stopper Tape
    - Wrap the tape tightly around the screw threads, about 2 times
    - Reinsert the screw and tighten as normal

6. For severely stripped holes consider using one of the repair methods like inserting wooden dowels, toothpicks with wood glue, or oversized screws

Remember to use the correct tools and avoid using power drills as screwdrivers, as they can easily strip the screw head or overdrive the screw.

Here are several places to check for loose screws around your house that you might forget about:

- Outdoor furniture: Check porch swings, Adirondack chairs, and outdoor benches.

- Indoor furniture: Inspect chairs, stools, bed frames, and recliners.

- Cabinet and cupboard hardware: Look at knobs, pulls, and handles on kitchen and bathroom cabinets.

- Door hinges and doorknobs: Examine all doors in your home.

- Toilet seats: Check the bolts securing the seat to the toilet.

- Faucet handles: Inspect kitchen and bathroom sink faucets, as well as shower and bath fixtures.

- Yard tools: Check string trimmers, leaf blowers, snow blowers, and lawn mowers.

- Glasses and sunglasses: Look at the screws on arms and nose pieces.

- Exercise equipment: Inspect treadmills and other fitness machines.

- Fans: Check ceiling and standing fans for loose screws.

- Appliances: Check any appliances with moving parts or that experience frequent vibration.

Regularly inspecting these areas can help you identify and address loose screws before they become a bigger problem.

Activity 89. Set a Short-Term Savings Goal

I used to use the "save the change" feature with my old bank account that would round up each debit card purchase to the nearest pound, transferring the difference into a separate savings account. It was always a delightful surprise when I checked my balance and found I'd tucked away £8 here and there without even trying. I also collected every £2 coin I received in a metal money tin, that only a can opener could unlock. Over several months, those coins grew into a meaningful sum, showing how effortless, small steps can add up when consistent.

But, like many people, my relationship with "spare change" wasn't always positive. When drinking, it was easy to dip into coin jars, raid pockets, or even empty savings tins just to fund my next purchase. For years, I missed out on that sense of accomplishment that comes from watching small savings grow and seeing pennies turn into pounds. The UK average household spends nearly £1,000 a year on alcohol—a figure that made me smile wryly, considering how normal it seemed at the time! After I stopped drinking, I noticed that any "saved" money quickly seeped into other expenses: food, hobbies, coffee dates, or little treats. It's the same dilemma with quitting smoking; savings don't always stay put, unless you actively redirect them.

That's why setting a short-term savings goal can be truly powerful. Instead of letting money drift, try putting the daily or weekly amount once spent on alcohol directly into a savings account. You can use a jar, set up a "round up" feature, or automate transfers online. Over time, you're not just working towards financial health—you're giving yourself a visible, tangible reward for your new habits and reinforcing the changes you're making.

Why Short-Term Saving Works - Short-term goals create a sense of security and accomplishment. They help you build up an emergency fund, keep cash available for unexpected bills, and reduce anxiety and debt. Paying off high-interest credit cards or simply having a cushion to cover the washing machine when it breaks can make a huge difference. Beyond basics, your weekly savings could go towards future joys: a day trip, fresh furniture, new kitchen gadgets, a course or workshop, or even a dream holiday. Knowing you're saving for something specific helps you stay motivated and make smarter choices about your spending.

Practical Saving Strategies
- Use high-yield savings accounts or ISAs for better returns.
- Create separate accounts for different goals—easy access for day-to-day needs, longer-term for dreams.
- Set up weekly or monthly automatic transfers to make saving effortless. Time these for payday or right after your usual "spending" day.
- Use digital apps or bank round-up features to save extra pennies from every purchase.

For larger goals (3–5 years), look at safe, low-risk investments or NS&I accounts for extra growth. Personally, I use separate accounts for each purpose, so I can "forget" about serious savings until I actually need them, removing temptation! If you're thinking about investments, financial advice is always a good idea—I learned more from one honest conversation than months of internet searching.

Reward Yourself and Stay Motivated - Saving's not just about sacrifice; it's about celebrating progress. Challenge yourself with fun, achievable milestones, such as £2 a week for a massage, savings for a special outfit or gym membership. Try treating small savings as an investment in wellness: use student beauty colleges for low-cost pampering, or book a cooking class for a culinary adventure. Track your progress visually (savings jar, charts, vision boards), and don't forget to celebrate each step.

Inspiration for Savings Goals
- Weekend getaway to a new city or cozy B&B.
- Tickets for your favourite concert or sports event.
- Fresh paint or new furniture for your living space.
- A short course or workshop in a hobby you've always wanted to try.
- Outdoor adventures, upgraded exercise gear, or lessons in a creative skill.
- Special donations to charity or sponsorship for a cause close to your heart.

Challenge Ideas
- 52-week challenge: Save the number of pounds that matches the week.
- No-spend month: Save all the cash you would have spent in thirty days, just to see how much it amounts to.
- "Found Money Jar": Every time you discover unexpected money (a rebate, a forgotten note in a pocket), pop it in your fund.

Automating and Tracking
- Set up automatic transfers so saving isn't something you have to remember.
- Use visual tools or digital apps to track your progress.
- Adjust your budget using the 50/30/20 rule (needs/wants/savings) to boost your rate of saving.

Accountability and Motivation
- Share your savings goal with a supportive friend or in a recovery group.
- Celebrate big and small milestones—each achievement strengthens your confidence.
- Use positive reinforcement and small rewards to keep momentum going.

By turning saving into a practical, enjoyable challenge, you're not just building financial resilience, you're proving to yourself how positive decisions accumulate.

Activity 90. Have a 6-minute dance party

Now this is right up my street! When I was drinking, I would do this often! Put on my favourite playlist and dance, dance, dance the night away but why did I stop? A number of reasons! My husband would say 'sit down you're drunk', or I would play loud music dancing around the kitchen until silly o'clock and really piss my him off, then I would get up feeling ashamed. When sober these behaviours to my husband, were 'old behaviours'. Actually, dancing is something I love to do, and I don't care how I look, I just wasn't respecting others with my behaviour when drunk. It is good for me, it's movement, exercise, release of endorphins and makes me feel really happy!

A 6-minute dance party can offer several wellbeing and physical benefits for everyone including people in recovery, as long as it is not a trigger! Even a short dance session can trigger the release of endorphins and dopamine, the "feel-good" neurotransmitters. This can provide a quick boost to mood and create a natural high, offering a healthy alternative to substance use. It shifts the brain into a more relaxed state, similar to meditation. This can reduce stress and anxiety levels, allowing for non-verbal expression of emotions, which can be particularly beneficial for those who struggle to articulate their feelings verbally. This is why it can be an amazing therapy for some people.

Depending on your dance moves, it can be an effective cardiovascular workout, improving heart health and circulation, enhancing body awareness, coordination, and balance, engaging multiple muscle groups, providing a full-body workout in a short time frame. A brief boogey can help combat fatigue and increase energy levels, which is particularly beneficial for those dealing with post-acute withdrawal symptoms.

While a 6-minute dance party may not provide the same depth of benefits as longer dance therapy sessions, it can serve as a quick, accessible tool for managing cravings, improving mood, and promoting overall wellbeing during the recovery process. Incorporating such brief, enjoyable activities into daily routines can support long-term recovery by providing healthy coping mechanisms and moments of joy.

Dancing can boost several key neurotransmitters that play important roles in mood regulation and wellbeing:

Dopamine: Dancing stimulates the release of dopamine, the "feel-good" neurotransmitter. Dopamine is associated with pleasure, reward, and motivation. The physical activity and enjoyment of dance triggers its release, providing a natural high that can help replace the artificial high of substance use.

Serotonin: Engaging in dance activities increases serotonin levels in the brain. This helps regulate mood, sleep, appetite, and cognitive functions. Higher serotonin levels are linked to improved mood and reduced symptoms of depression and anxiety, which are common challenges in recovery.

Endorphins: Dancing, especially more vigorous forms, leads to the release of endorphins. These natural opioids produced by the body can reduce pain perception and induce feelings of euphoria, often described as a "runner's high." This natural endorphin boost can help manage cravings and provide a healthy alternative to seeking artificial highs.

Oxytocin: While not strictly a neurotransmitter, oxytocin is a hormone that acts as a neurotransmitter in the brain. Often called the "love hormone," oxytocin is released during social bonding activities. Group dance sessions or partner dances can stimulate oxytocin release, fostering feelings of connection and trust, which are crucial for building support networks in recovery.

By boosting these neurotransmitters, dance can provide a natural and healthy way to improve mood, reduce stress, and support the recovery process. The combination of physical activity, social interaction, and creative expression in dance makes it a particularly effective tool for promoting overall wellbeing during addiction recovery.

There is a very good reason why dance is a therapy (Dance Movement Therapy). It offers a unique approach to psychotherapy that complements traditional talk therapy.

So set the stage, choosing a space where you feel comfortable moving freely, like your bedroom or living room. Close the door to create a private dance floor. Ensure you have enough room to move without bumping into furniture.

Prepare Your Playlist – Activity 65 with 2-3 high-energy songs that get you moving. Choose music that makes you want to dance instantly.

Put on comfortable clothes that allow you to move easily. Pyjamas work great, and a bra is optional but recommended for comfort and safety. Turn up the volume on your speakers or put on headphones for an immersive experience.

Hit Play, Let Loose and Let Go of Inhibitions and dance like nobody's watching - because they aren't!

Activity 91. Learn basic First Aid

It goes without saying, this is for information and a reminder that it is so important that we are all aware how to carry out basic first aid. Please do your own research and check out the free UK first aid courses to ensure you are using the correct up-to-date methods of first aid. While there are no completely free UK first aid certified courses available that I have found, there are some options that offer free training or certification with certain conditions:

1. **St John Ambulance Cymru**: Offers free online first aid courses, but these do not provide a qualification. Upon completion, you can download a certificate of participation.
2. **Omnia Solutions**: Provides a free First Aid Appointed Person E-Learning Course with a certificate upon completion, but you need to use a specific coupon code.
3. **British Red Cross**: Offers free first aid workshops, both online and face-to-face, but these are unaccredited. They do provide a foundation in basic first aid skills.
4. **First Aid for Free**: Offers free online first aid, CPR, and AED courses with a downloadable certificate upon completion. However, these courses may not meet all UK certification standards for workplace first aid.

For fully certified first aid courses, you typically need to pay for accredited training, such as those provided by the British Red Cross or St John Ambulance. These courses are recognised by employers and meet HSE guidelines for workplace first aid. First aid knowledge can literally mean the difference between life and death. A Red Cross survey revealed that 59% of deaths from injuries could have been prevented if first aid had been administered before emergency services arrived.

First aid training enables you to respond quickly and effectively to emergencies, preventing medical situations from deteriorating. For instance, in the case of a deep cut, applying pressure using simple first aid techniques can prevent severe blood loss and stabilise the patient until further medical help arrives.

Early intervention with proper first aid can significantly impact a person's recovery:
- It can reduce the length of time a patient needs to stay in hospital.
- Proper first aid can mean the difference between short-term or permanent disability.
- By treating wounds immediately, healing can be improved, infection chances lessened, and patient deterioration prevented.

First aid training helps individuals become more conscious of safety, in the workplace and at home. This increased awareness can lead to:
- A reduction in the number of accidents and injuries.
- Better hazard identification and risk prevention.
- Improved overall safety culture in various environments.

Learning first aid provides individuals with:
- The confidence to act appropriately when an accident occurs.
- The ability to remain calm and think clearly in stressful situations.
- A sense of empowerment to help others in need, whether they are friends, family, colleagues, or strangers.

In conclusion, learning basic first aid is a vital skill that not only saves lives but also improves overall health outcomes, increases safety awareness, and empowers individuals to act confidently in emergency situations. It's an investment in personal and community well-being that can make a significant difference when it matters most.

Basic first aid skills can be lifesaving in emergency situations. Here are some fundamental first aid techniques to help you respond effectively:

The DRSABCD (Remember by saying 'the Doctors (DRS) ABCD') action plan is a crucial first aid method to remember:

Danger: Check for any dangers to yourself, bystanders, and the injured person.
Response: Are they conscious? Check by asking them or gently squeezing their shoulder.
Send for help: Call emergency services.
Airway: Ensure the person's airway is clear.
Breathing: Check if the person is breathing.
CPR: If the person is not breathing, begin cardiopulmonary resuscitation.
Defibrillation: Use an automated external defibrillator (AED) if available.

Recovery Position - For an unconscious but breathing person:
1. Place the person on their side.
2. Bend the top leg for stability.
3. Tilt the head back to keep the airway open, so not to choke if they vomit.

CPR (Cardiopulmonary Resuscitation) – This changes so please check the latest recommendations. If someone is unresponsive and not breathing:
1. Call emergency services immediately.
2. Begin chest compressions: Place the heel of your hand on the centre of the chest and compress at a rate of 100-120 compressions per minute. Remember the Vinnie Jones Advert, do compressions to the tune of 'Staying Alive'.
3. Give rescue breaths if trained and willing: Tilt the head back, lift the chin, and give two breaths after every 30 compressions.

Bleeding Control
For severe bleeding:
1. Apply direct pressure to the wound using a clean cloth or sterile dressing.
2. Elevate the injured area above the heart if possible.

3. If bleeding continues, add more dressings without removing the original one.

Burns Treatment
For burns:
1. Cool the burn under cool running water for at least 10 minutes.
2. Remove any jewellery or tight clothing near the burned area.
3. Cover the burn with a clean, dry dressing.

Remember, these are basic guidelines. Proper first aid training is essential for developing the confidence and skills needed to respond effectively in emergencies.

If someone is choking, follow these steps:
1. Encourage the person to cough if they can. This may naturally dislodge the obstruction.
2. If coughing doesn't work proceed with first aid.

Back Blows
1. Stand behind and slightly to the side of the person.
2. Support their chest with one hand and lean them forward.
3. Give up to 5 sharp blows between the shoulder blades with the heel of your hand.

Abdominal Thrusts - If back blows don't work:
1. Stand behind the person and wrap your arms around their waist.
2. Make a fist with one hand and place it just above their navel.
3. Grasp your fist with the other hand and pull sharply inwards and upwards.
4. Repeat up to 5 times.

Repeat and Call for Help
1. Alternate between 5 back blows and 5 abdominal thrusts.
2. Call 999 or your local emergency number if the obstruction doesn't clear.
3. Continue cycles until object is dislodged, they becomes unconscious, or help arrives.

If the Person Becomes Unconscious
1. Carefully lower them to the ground.
2. Begin CPR if you're trained.
3. Check the mouth for visible obstructions before giving rescue breaths.

Remember, these steps are for adults and children over 1 year old. Different techniques are used for infants under 1 year. Always seek professional medical attention after a choking incident, even if the obstruction is cleared.

Activity 92. Play a quick game of darts

I must admit, I've never been skilled at darts. As a pool enthusiast, I've always admired the game from afar, fascinated by its unique blend of strategy and skill. My mother and grandmother were both accomplished darts players, winning numerous trophies and participating in local teams. It seems I inherited my father's less-than-stellar aim, but that hasn't deterred me from appreciating the many benefits of playing darts.

Darts offers a wide range of advantages, making it an excellent hobby for anyone looking to enhance their mental and physical well-being. Not only is it engaging and accessible, but it also provides numerous solo games perfect for practicing and honing your skills before impressing your friends.

Engaging in darts can have a profound impact on the brain, offering a dynamic mental workout that sharpens cognitive skills and fosters neuroconnectivity. The game stimulates the prefrontal cortex, which is responsible for executive functions such as planning, problem-solving, and decision-making. This mental stimulation can help prevent cognitive decline and age-related memory loss.

Darts also enhances mathematical skills by requiring quick mental arithmetic for scorekeeping and strategizing the most efficient path to zero. It encourages strategic thinking, as players must plan several steps ahead.

Playing darts can serve as a cathartic release from daily stresses, offering a temporary escape and promoting mindfulness. The focused yet relaxed environment of a dart game allows players to immerse themselves in the present moment, providing a mental break from worries and anxieties.

Darts requires precision and focus, enhancing hand-eye coordination. The act of throwing darts engages muscles in the arms, shoulders, and core, providing a low-impact form of exercise that can contribute to improved muscle tone and overall physical well-being.

Darts fosters social connectivity and community bonding, providing an avenue for building relationships, making new friends, and strengthening existing bonds within communities. It's relatively inexpensive compared to other sports, which you can practice alone or with friends.

Trying darts can provide a well-rounded experience that benefits your mental acuity, physical coordination, social life, and personal growth. It's an enjoyable and rewarding activity that offers more than just entertainment – it's a gateway to improved cognitive function, stress relief, and social connection.

Before you start playing, ensure your dartboard is set up safely:
- **Secure the dartboard**: Attach it to a wall, not on the back of a door, and keep it away from foot traffic.

- **Position the board**: Place the board so the centre of the bullseye is 5 feet 8 inches from the ground.
- **Mark the throwing line (oche)**: 7 feet 9 inches from the front of the board.
- **Clear the area**: Remove any breakable items around the board.
- **Protect your walls**: Use a dartboard surround.
- **Consider soft-tip darts**: They offer added safety.
- **Never throw at people**: Always ensure no one is in the line of fire.
- **Stand behind the player**: When someone is throwing, stand behind them.
- **Avoid walking in front**: Never walk in front of the board when others are playing.
- **Keep darts out of reach**: Store darts safely away from small children.

Multiplayer Games
- **Knockout**: A fun game where the first player sets a score with three darts. Each subsequent player must beat the previous score. If a player fails to beat the score, they receive a mark. Three marks eliminate a player. The last player remaining wins.
- **Killer**: Players become "killers" by hitting their assigned number and then aim to eliminate others by hitting their numbers. With each player having a set number of lives, the last one standing wins.

Solo and Beginner-Friendly Games
- **Around the Clock**: Ideal for beginners, players aim to hit numbers 1 through 20 in order, often ending with a bullseye. It's a great way to improve accuracy and learn the board.
- **301**: A faster version of the classic 501, players start with 301 points and aim to reach exactly zero by subtracting their scores. The game typically requires a double to finish, adding an extra challenge.
- **Halve-It**: Players start with a set score (e.g., 301) and aim to halve their score by hitting specific targets in each round. Failing to hit the target can result in the score remaining unchanged or even doubling, adding excitement to the game.

These games offer a mix of skill development, strategy, and fun, making them excellent choices for quick dart sessions with friends or family.

Remember, consistent practice is key to improving your darts skills. Even just 10-15 minutes of mindful practice can be beneficial. As you get more comfortable, you can try more advanced solo games to challenge yourself further.

Activity 93. Make a keyring/chain

I have more keychains than pairs of knickers, socks and other essential items! I have no idea why?? Another addiction and something I have spent too much money on, but I love them, and they bring me pleasure, so I enjoy making them as well as buying them. My local Chinese ties a keychain in the knot of my prawn crackers, and it has a QR code on there for them, which I think is a brilliant idea!

Keychains are incredibly versatile and do not have to be just for keys, if you need an excuse for them, here are some other ways to use keychains:

- Use them as zipper pulls on jackets or hoodies for a decorative touch.
- Hang them on doorknobs, curtain tiebacks, or drawer pulls to add a whimsical touch to your home decor.
- Use them as wall decor by arranging them in a visually appealing pattern.
- Customise keychains with personalized designs or photos to make memorable gifts.
- Use them as party favours or commemorative items for special events.
- Incorporate keychains into scrapbooking, handmade cards, or jewellery-making projects for added visual interest.
- Combine keychains with practical tools like LED lights, mini bottle openers, or whistles to enhance their functionality.
- Create a personalised lanyard by mixing and matching keychains that reflect different aspects of your personality.
- Attach a keychain to your phone case or use it as a phone charm for a personalised touch.
- Attach keychains to the straps or handles of your handbag or backpack to personalise it and make it easier to identify.

Here are some creative suggestions for making your own keychain:

Resin keychains are made by pouring clear resin into a silicone mould, allowing endless custom shapes. Creative additions like glitter, dried flowers, or small charms can be embedded before curing. Once set, simply attach your design to a keyring for a personalized accessory.

A beaded keychain starts by threading colourful beads onto string or wire. Designs can include patterns or messages using letter beads. For extra flair, add a decorative tassel before securing to a keyring.

Photo keychains let cherished memories travel with you. Print a tiny photo and set it in resin inside a pendant, or shrink a drawing using "shrinky dinks" for a cute, one-of-a-kind piece.

Fabric keychains are soft and fun. Cut fabric into small shapes, sew them together, and add a bit of stuffing for plushness. Stitch a keyring to the top for a unique handmade touch.

Polymer clay keychains involve shaping clay into charms or figures. Once baked, you can paint your creations before adding a jump ring and keyring.

Button keychains are simple and quick: choose a sturdy button, thread string or wire through the holes, and attach to a keyring—add extra beads to decorate.

Macramé keychains use cord and knots for pretty patterns, with beads or tassels often added for personality.

Braided keychains involve braiding three strands of string, yarn, or fabric strips, tying off the ends, and securing to a keyring.

Bottle cap keychains are great souvenirs—clean the cap, punch a hole at the edge, and thread a keyring through. Decorate the inside with a photo or small design.

For wooden keychains, use small wooden shapes or discs, paint or wood burn designs onto the surface, seal if needed, and attach the hardware. Popsicle sticks also work for simple shapes.

Upcycled keychains repurpose objects like old jewellery, buttons, or bottle caps. Attach using strong jump rings or glue for a sustainable, creative option.

Paper clip keychains give a new twist to office supplies—bend a large clip into a shape, add beads for detail, and finish by attaching it to a keyring.

Activity 94. Identify Your Personal Values

Identifying personal values is a foundational step in understanding ourselves and navigating life's complexities. These values serve as guiding principles that shape our decisions, behaviours, and relationships. By knowing our core values, we gain a deeper understanding of who we are, what drives us, and how we can recover from challenging situations, leading to better relationships and a sense of purpose. It's important to remember that core values may not be immediately apparent and can evolve over time, so regular reflection is essential.

1. **Inner Compass**: Personal values act as an inner compass, providing clarity and direction in decision-making processes. They ensure that actions align with deeply held beliefs, fostering authenticity and ethical behaviour.
2. **Satisfying Life**: Living by your values leads to a more satisfying life, as it aligns your actions with what truly matters to you. This alignment enhances personal growth and development.
3. **Relationships**: Personal values influence how we interact with others. Sharing similar values with partners, friends, or colleagues can strengthen relationships and improve communication.
4. **Professional Success**: Integrating personal values into professional settings can enhance trustworthiness, build positive working relationships, and contribute to career success.
5. **Purpose and Meaning**: Personal values give life meaning and purpose. They help define who you are and what you stand for, guiding your goals and aspirations.

Reflecting on Personal Values
- **Self-Understanding**: Identifying personal values helps you understand yourself better, including what you believe in and what makes you happy.
- **Evolution of Values**: Values can evolve over time due to life experiences or personal growth, making it important to regularly reflect on them.
- **Goal Alignment**: Aligning goals with personal values ensures that pursuits are meaningful and fulfilling.

To uncover your core values, consider the following exercises:

1. **Brainstorming Questions**: -ask yourself these questions to identify potential values:
    - What matters most to me?
    - What do I strongly believe in?
    - What experiences spark joy within me?
    - What gives my life purpose?

2. **Peak Experiences and Suppressed Values:**
   - **Peak Experiences:** Reflect on meaningful moments in your life. What values were being honoured during these times?
   - **Suppressed Values:** Think about times when you felt angry or frustrated. What values were not being met? Flip those feelings to identify the suppressed values.

3. **Code of Conduct** - Consider what must be present in your life for you to feel fulfilled. This could include aspects like creativity, health, or adventure.

4. **They're Talking About Me:** - Imagine overhearing people talking about you. What would you like to hear them say? This can reveal values such as loyalty, positivity, or kindness.

5. **Value Selection from a List:**
   - Use a comprehensive list of values (available online) and select those that resonate with you. Don't overthink; just choose what feels right.
   - Then, group similar values together and narrow down to your top values.

6. **7-Step Personal Core Values Exercise:**
   - **Step 1:** Start with a beginner's mind, letting go of preconceived notions.
   - **Step 2:** Create an initial list of personal core values.
   - **Step 3:** Group related values together.
   - **Step 4:** Identify the central theme of each group.
   - **Step 5:** Determine your top values.
   - **Step 6:** Craft personal values statements.
   - **Step 7:** Test the ecology of each value.

7. **Reflecting on Life Areas** - Consider different areas of your life (e.g., family, relationships, health, career). What values are important in each area? How can you align your actions with these values?

When reflecting on your values, it's helpful to go deeper by asking "why?" For example, if you consider your wedding day as a meaningful moment, ask why it was important to you. Was it about family, commitment, or something else? Perhaps it was about being seen, having fun, or achieving status. Journaling these insights will help you keep a record and review your values over time.

Once you've identified your core values, apply them in real-life situations. When faced with a frustrating scenario, ask which value isn't being met. Use your values as a framework for viewing the world around you. Limit your list to 5-10 core values to maintain focus and practicality.

Activity 95. Create a vision board

The act of creating a vision board can be a therapeutic and empowering practice. It serves as a positive emotion booster, energising your brain and fostering a resilient mindset crucial for achieving your aspirations. They ae fun and powerful!

A **vision board** is a visual tool used to help individuals clarify, focus, and manifest their goals and desires. It typically consists of a board or poster where people place images, words, and other materials that represent their aspirations, dreams, and intentions.

The purpose of a vision board is to:

1. **Clarify Goals**: By selecting images and words that resonate with personal goals, individuals can better define what they want to achieve in various areas of life, such as career, relationships, health, or personal growth.
2. **Focus Intentions**: The visual representation helps to concentrate one's intentions and maintain focus on desired outcomes.
3. **Manifest Desires**: The belief is that by regularly viewing the vision board, individuals can align their thoughts and actions with their goals, potentially attracting opportunities and circumstances that help manifest these desires.
4. **Motivation and Inspiration**: Vision boards serve as a constant reminder of one's aspirations, providing motivation and inspiration to work towards achieving them.

A vision board is a powerful tool that serves as a visual reminder of one's goals and aspirations, playing a significant role in activating the brain's **Reticular Activating System (RAS)**. By regularly viewing a vision board, individuals reinforce their mental images and align their thoughts with their goals, which in turn activates the RAS to notice opportunities that might have otherwise gone unnoticed. This process involves clarifying goals, evoking positive emotions, and shifting one's mindset to seek out aligned possibilities. Vision boards help define and clarify goals, programming the RAS to be on high alert for relevant information. They also evoke emotions that increase determination and motivation to take action. Overall, vision boards complement the process of visualization by providing a constant reminder of one's goals and desires, enhancing the effectiveness of visualisation practices and activating the RAS to notice opportunities that align with one's objectives.

Before you begin, take some time to reflect on your goals, dreams, and aspirations. Consider different areas of your life such as career, relationships, health, personal growth, and hobbies. Clarify what you want to manifest or achieve through your vision board.

Decide whether you want to create a physical or digital board. For physical, you'll need a poster board, corkboard or for ease of changing easily a magnetic board. For digital, choose a platform like Canva, Pinterest, or a app such as Visuapp or Vision Board & Quote Maker.

Collect images, quotes, and words that resonate with your goals and evoke the feelings associated with your aspirations. Look through magazines, websites, or use online image libraries.

Experiment with different layouts until you're satisfied, customising your vision board with personal photos, handwritten affirmations, or small objects that make it uniquely yours.

Place your completed vision board where you'll see it regularly, such as on a wall in your bedroom or office. For digital boards, set it as your computer or phone wallpaper.

Take time each day or week to look at your vision board. Reflect on your goals and the progress you're making. Consider journaling about your vision board to deepen your connection with your aspirations and periodically review your vision board and make updates as your goals evolve. This keeps your board relevant and aligned with your current aspirations.

Remember, creating a vision board is a personal process. There's no right or wrong way to do it – the most important thing is that it resonates with you and inspires you to work towards your goals.

Some ideas:

- Design a custom phone lock screen featuring your vision board, ensuring you see it multiple times a day.
- Include personal photographs or mementos that hold special meaning to you.
- Add handwritten affirmations or goals to create a more intimate connection.
- Incorporate small trinkets, keychains, or other 3D objects that represent your goals.
- Create separate sections for different life areas, such as career, health, relationships.
- Design a "you-core" board that celebrates your unique personality and style.
- Develop a theme-based vision board, such as a travel-inspired or a wellness-focused.
- Use a consistent colour scheme that resonates with your personality and goals.
- Incorporate doodles, sketches, or paintings to represent your aspirations creatively.
- Experiment with different textures and materials, such as fabric swatches or textured paper, to add depth to your board.

Activity 96. Take a brisk walk around the block

I have to be careful with my back and walking, or more so standing for any period of time, but I know that incorporating physical activity into my daily routine can be as simple as taking a brisk walk around the block. This accessible form of exercise offers a multitude of benefits for both physical and mental health and I feel the benefit almost immediately. Brisk walking is defined as walking at a pace of about 3 miles per hour, where you can still talk but not sing. It is a moderate-intensity aerobic activity that requires minimal preparation or equipment, making it suitable for all fitness levels and ages.

Brisk walking is an effective way to improve cardiovascular fitness, reducing the risk of heart disease and strengthening heart muscles. It also helps lower blood pressure, aids in weight management, and tones the muscles in the lower body. Additionally, brisk walking enhances bone density, reducing the risk of osteoporosis, and strengthens muscles supporting joints, potentially alleviating arthritis pain. Regular brisk walking can also help maintain a healthy weight and improve overall physical fitness.

The mental health benefits of brisk walking are equally impressive. It boosts mood by triggering the release of endorphins, reduces symptoms of anxiety and depression, and improves sleep quality. Brisk walking enhances cognitive function, improving focus, concentration, and problem-solving skills. It also promotes mindfulness and stress reduction by lowering levels of stress hormones like cortisol.

Brisk walking enhances cognitive function through increased blood flow to the brain, boosting oxygen and nutrient delivery. It stimulates the release of brain-derived neurotrophic factor (BDNF), promoting neuron survival and growth. Regular brisk walking can improve executive functions such as attention, working memory, and inhibitory control, potentially reducing the risk of neurodegenerative diseases like dementia.

One of the most significant advantages of brisk walking is its accessibility. It is a low-cost activity that requires no special equipment or skill, making it easy to incorporate into daily routines. Brisk walking can be done outdoors, providing additional benefits from nature exposure, such as improved mood and reduced stress.

While high-intensity exercises like running or jogging may offer additional physical benefits, brisk walking provides comparable mental health benefits with a lower risk of injury. It is similar to meditation in improving mood and reducing fatigue, and comparable to Tai Chi in enhancing cognitive function.

To maximise the benefits of brisk walking, consider the following guidelines:

1. **Aim for 150 Minutes Per Week**: Break this down into shorter sessions, such as 10-minute walks several times a day.
2. **Take Frequent Short Walks**: Try to take a brief walk every 20-30 minutes throughout the day to regulate blood sugar levels and improve overall health.
3. **Increase Duration for Greater Benefits**: If your goal is weight loss or more significant health benefits, consider increasing your walking time to 300 minutes or more per week.
4. **Consistency is Key**: Regular short walks are more beneficial than occasional long walks.

By incorporating brisk walking into your daily routine, you can improve your physical and mental health, boost your mood, and reduce the risk of various chronic diseases.

Brisk walking for as little as 15 minutes can lead to measurable cognitive benefits, with consistent exercise over time yielding more substantial improvements in brain health and function. Plus significant mental health benefits that are comparable to other forms of exercise, while being more accessible and lower-impact.

Incorporating brisk walking into your daily routine can be easier than you think, here are some tips to help you make brisk walking a consistent part of your day:

1. Set Realistic Goals - Start slowly, such as walking for 10 to 15 minutes a day and gradually increase the duration and frequency over time. Make sure plan your walks in advance and treat them as non-negotiable appointments in your diary.

2. Incorporate Walking into Daily Activities – Such as walk your commute such as to work, local shop or school, opt for stairs instead of elevators or escalators or you could even park further away from your destination, so you get a short walk in.

3. Make It Convenient such as morning walks to start your day with a boost of energy and set a positive tone. Similarly, at lunch break, it can refresh your mind and body, and in the evening it can help to unwind.

4. Stay Motivated by finding a walking buddy, using fitness/walking apps and varying your route.

5. Be Consistent so to make it into a habit and do not let the weather be your excuse.

By incorporating these strategies into your daily routine, you can make brisk walking a sustainable and enjoyable part of your lifestyle.

Activity 97. Write down any fears you want to overcome and how to tackle them

Fears are an integral part of the human experience. Whether it's phobias, change, people, places, or things, we all have fears that can impact our lives. As the saying goes, "even Superman had kryptonite," highlighting that no one is immune to fear. The good news is that while we may learn fears, we can also unlearn them. Humans are born with only two innate fears:

1. **Fear of Falling**: This fear is crucial for survival, helping infants avoid falling and potential injuries. Experiments involving a "visual cliff" demonstrate this instinctual avoidance, as most infants do not step forward onto a transparent surface.
2. **Fear of Loud Noises**: This fear triggers a startle response, acting as a protective mechanism. When infants hear a loud noise, they react by being startled or ducking down, a natural defensive reaction to potential danger.

All other fears are acquired through experiences, social interactions, and cultural influences. Fear can lead to anxiety and prevent us from pursuing activities we truly desire. Confronting and documenting our fears can have significant benefits, providing clarity and helping us:

- Identify specific fears and their root causes
- Distinguish between rational and irrational fears
- Recognise patterns in thinking and behaviour
- Release pent-up emotions and reduce stress
- Lower cortisol levels, the stress hormone, through writing
- Create a safe space to express concerns without judgment
- Challenge and change thought patterns
- Gain new perspectives on fears
- Develop more balanced and realistic viewpoints
- Make fears seem less daunting when seen on paper
- Develop and document strategies to tackle each fear
- Promote problem-solving by thinking through solutions
- Reduce symptoms of anxiety and stress
- Become less reactive to negative situations with daily writing
- Aid in recovery from trauma and PTSD

Some of the most common fears include:

- **Social Phobia (Fear of Social Interactions)**: This phobia makes everyday interactions challenging and stressful for those affected.
- **Fear of Failure (Atychiphobia)**: This fear can prevent individuals from taking risks or pursuing opportunities.

- **Fear of Spiders (Arachnophobia)**: This common phobia can cause intense fear responses, even to images of spiders.
- **Fear of Public Speaking:** This common fear can limit career and personal growth.
- **Fear of Relapse:** returning to substance use after putting in hard work to achieve sobriety.
- **Fear of Facing Life Without Substances:** navigating life's challenges without the crutch of drugs or alcohol can be daunting. Many worry that life won't be enjoyable or manageable without substances.
- **Fear of Change:** Recovery involves significant lifestyle changes, which can be intimidating. This includes fear of the unknown and concerns about losing one's identity.
- **Fear of Rejection or Loss:** Many worry about being judged or abandoned by loved ones, or losing friends.

General Strategies for Addressing Fears

1. Face your fears gradually through exposure therapy
2. Practice relaxation techniques like deep breathing
3. Challenge unhelpful thoughts and replace them with more realistic ones
4. Seek support from friends, family, or a mental health professional
5. Consider cognitive behavioural therapy (CBT) for more severe phobias

Remember, overcoming fears takes time and patience. If a phobia significantly impacts your daily life, consider seeking help from a mental health professional for tailored treatment strategies.

Several effective techniques can help you journal about your fears:

Write a Letter to Your Fear

Address your fear directly by writing a letter to it. Begin with "Dear [Fear]," and explore:

- What you want it to know
- What it wants you to know (Really stop and listen to whatever comes to mind!)
- How it makes you feel
- How it's holding you back
- Where you feel it in your body

This technique creates distance from the emotion, allowing for a more objective perspective.

Use Structured Prompts

Try these prompts to explore your fears:
- Complete "I am afraid that..." five times
- Describe your earliest memory of this fear
- Explain what "facing your fears" means to you
- Detail your physical reactions to fear

Personify and Interview Your Fear

Imagine your fear as a person and describe their appearance. Then, interview your fear, asking questions like:

- What does your fear care most about?
- What does it hope to accomplish?
- How does it feel about you?
- What is your fear afraid of?

This approach can provide new insights into your fears.

Use the Fear Journaling Template

Follow this structured approach:

1. Fear: Write your specific fear in one sentence
2. Facts: List related facts, both supporting and contradicting the fear
3. Feelings: Describe emotions associated with the fear
4. Fixes: Brainstorm potential solutions or coping strategies

Explore Worst-Case Scenarios

Write about your worst-case scenarios to gain perspective:

- Define your fear clearly
- List ways to prevent the worst-case scenario
- Identify how you could repair any potential damage

By regularly journaling about your fears using these techniques, you can gain clarity, reduce anxiety, and develop more effective coping strategies.

Activity 98. Create a miniature origami animal

Ok this one is a bit difficult in a book without loads of step-by-step pictures, so I am suggesting ideas for you to find a YouTube video or website for detailed instructions, as it will make life sooo make easier! I have added some free online tutorial resources that I found.

A few tips before the tutorials:

- Use thin, crisp origami paper (kami) for best results. For miniature animals, start with a small square, around 3-5 cm and use double-sided paper to create contrasting colours for different parts of the animal, enhancing its visual appeal.
- Prepare your workspace: Find a quiet, well-lit area with a flat surface. Ensure you have enough space to work comfortably.
- For miniature origami, accuracy is crucial. Take your time to make sharp, clean folds. If you do not have a ruler, then your fingernails can serve as effective tools for effective folding.
- Be gentle: When working with small pieces of paper, apply less pressure to avoid tearing.
- Practice patience: Miniature origami requires extra care and attention to detail. Don't rush the process.
- Display your creation: Place your miniature origami animal in a safe spot where it won't be crushed or damaged.

Remember, creating miniature origami animals takes practice. Start with larger sizes and gradually work your way down to smaller dimensions as you improve your skills.

Online resources for learning origami through tutorials include Instructables - Origami for Everyone, Origami Fun, Craft Haven on YouTube, Origami.me and WWF Origami Patterns.

The simplest origami animal for beginners to start with is the fish, which is described as one of the easiest and quickest animals to fold, taking only a few folds and less than 5 minutes. Followed by the cat, dog, butterfly, rabbit, penguin and mouse head.

These animals are often recommended for children and beginners due to their simple folding techniques and quick completion time. Starting with these simpler designs can help build confidence and basic skills before moving on to more complex origami animals.

Activity 99. Do a water displacement experiment

Conducting a water displacement experiment is a surprisingly enjoyable activity for adults, blending nostalgia with intellectual curiosity. Many may recall similar experiments from their school days and revisiting them can evoke a sense of nostalgia while reigniting their curiosity. The hands-on nature of the experiment allows adults to actively engage with scientific principles, such as Archimedes' Principle, which explains how objects float or sink based on the volume of fluid they displace. Do you remember what Archimedes was doing and who he was working for when he discovered this principle? This experiment also provides an opportunity for creative application and problem-solving, as adults can explore how these principles apply to real-world scenarios, like understanding buoyancy in ships or measuring the volume of complex shapes. Furthermore, it can be a fun group activity, encouraging social interaction and discussion among participants.

To try it at home, simply gather these items:

- A large clear container (like a glass or plastic measuring cup)
- Water
- Food colouring (optional, for better visibility)
- Various objects of different sizes and shapes
- A marker or tape
- A ruler (optional)

Steps for the Experiment

1. Fill the container about halfway with water. If using food colouring, add a few drops to make the water level more visible.
2. Mark the initial water level on the outside of the container using a marker or tape.
3. Choose an object and predict whether it will sink or float.
4. Gently place the object in the water and observe what happens.
5. Mark the new water level on the container.
6. Measure the difference between the initial and new water levels. This difference represents the volume of water displaced by the object.
7. Repeat the process with different objects, comparing the amount of water displaced by each.

Explaining the Results and Variations

The experiment demonstrates Archimedes' principle: an object immersed in a fluid experiences a buoyant force equal to the weight of the fluid it displaces. Objects that sink displace their volume in water, while floating objects displace their weight in water. This simple experiment can help visualise abstract concepts like volume and density, making it an excellent educational activity for learners of all ages.

Variations and Extensions

- Use objects of similar mass but different shapes to demonstrate how shape affects buoyancy.
- Try objects that are hollow or have irregular shapes.
- For more precise measurements, use a graduated cylinder instead of a large container.

Fun Variations and Challenges

- **Object Variations**: Use different types of objects to compare displacement, such as Lego bricks, sweets (M&M, Jelly Beans), or small toys.

- **Challenge Activities**:
    - **Penny Boat Challenge**: Design foil boats to hold the most pennies before sinking.
    - **Floating vs. Sinking**: Compare displacement of floating and sinking objects.
    - **Target Displacement**: Try to displace an exact amount of water using various objects.

- **Themed Experiments**:
    - Recreate "The Crow and the Pitcher" fable using stones and a toy bird.
    - Conduct a "rescue mission" by raising a toy in water to a certain height.

These variations can make the water displacement experiment more engaging and allow for exploration of different scientific concepts while maintaining the core principle of displacement. So, dive in and enjoy the fun of learning!

Activity 100. Research traditional costumes

Traditional costumes are not just beautiful garments; they are carriers of cultural identity, history, and values. I have learnt so much about the world whilst researching traditional dress. By just Googling something different, it has led me down a rabbit hole of things I never knew, as such:

The **Dress Act of 1746** in Scotland, banned the wearing of traditional Highland dress, including kilts, as part of an effort to suppress Scottish culture following the Jacobite Risings. This act was a response to the Jacobite Uprisings, particularly the final rising in 1745 led by Charles Edward Stuart, also known as Bonnie Prince Charlie. The ban on kilts was an attempt to assimilate the Scottish Highlands into British culture and reduce the influence of clan identities.

Historical Context and Significance

- **Cultural Suppression**: The Dress Act was part of a broader strategy to suppress Scottish culture and identity. By outlawing traditional dress, the British government aimed to reduce the distinctiveness and pride associated with Scottish heritage.
- **Resilience and Revival**: Despite the ban, the kilt remained a symbol of Scottish identity and resilience. When the ban was lifted in 1782, the kilt experienced a revival, becoming an even more potent symbol of Scottish pride and defiance against cultural suppression.
- **Cultural Expression Today**: Today, kilts are worn proudly at formal events, parades, and weddings, symbolizing a strong connection to Scottish heritage and history. The study of traditional Scottish dress, particularly the kilt, highlights how clothing can reflect historical events and cultural resistance.

Did you know....
1. **Cultural Significance:**
   - Traditional costumes often symbolise a community's deep-rooted connection to its past, preserving customs and history in every stitch.
   - They are used to express identity, regional roots, or social status, fostering unity and pride among community members.
2. **Symbolism and Meaning:**
   - **Maasai Shúkà**: In Kenya, the Maasai people wear vibrant red shúkà to symbolize courage and unity. Blue represents the sky.
   - **Scottish Kilts**: The tartan patterns on Scottish kilts represent different clans and occasions, reflecting centuries of Gaelic customs.
3. **Cultural Adaptation:**
   - Traditional costumes are evolving, blending modernity with tradition to remain relevant. This evolution demonstrates that these garments are dynamic elements of cultural expression.

- In Bhutan, traditional clothing like the gho and kira is mandatory in public spaces to emphasise national identity.
4. **Artistic Expression:**
   - Traditional garments often reflect artistic ingenuity through techniques like embroidery, dyeing, and weaving, encoding local myths and legends into wearable art.
   - The kimono in Japan is a revered emblem of cultural values, with layered kimonos developed for comfort across seasons.
5. **Preservation and Revival:**
   - Efforts to preserve traditional costumes are crucial to honour cultural heritage and ensure these attires continue to tell stories for generations to come.
   - Younger generations and artisans are revitalising traditional costumes by infusing them into modern fashion.

These facts highlight the rich cultural significance and diversity of traditional costumes worldwide, showcasing their role in preserving history and expressing identity.

To research traditional costumes, you can follow some different steps:

1. Access digital collections and databases focused on costume history.

2. Visit or research online collections of costume museums, such as:
   - The Costume Institute at the Metropolitan Museum of Art
   - The Museum at the Fashion Institute of Technology (FIT)
   - Victoria and Albert Museum's fashion collection
   - Metropolitan Museum of Art Online Collection
   - Kyoto Costume Institute Digital Collection
   - Brooklyn Museum - Libraries and Archives: Fashion and Costume Sketch Collection

3. Study historical photographs, paintings, and illustrations depicting traditional dress. Examine period magazines and fashion plates for contemporary descriptions of costumes. Look into the symbolism, materials, and construction techniques used in different cultural dress traditions.

4. Go down a rabbit hole and see what you can find out about your local traditional customs or further afield.

Activity 101. Try the Method of Loci Technique

The Method of Loci, also known as the memory palace technique, is an ancient mnemonic strategy that dates back to Greek and Roman times. This powerful method enhances memory by associating information with specific locations (loci) within a familiar mental environment. Its versatility has made it invaluable across various domains. Students use it to anchor complex information—such as vocabulary, historical events, or scientific concepts—to mental spaces, improving both retention and comprehension. Public speakers and performers rely on it to memorise speeches or scripts by mentally navigating their "memory palace," enabling seamless recall without notes. Memory champions employ the technique to accomplish astonishing feats, like recalling long sequences of numbers or cards, by linking vivid mental images to specific loci. Even in everyday life, the Method of Loci proves practical for tasks like remembering grocery lists or to-do items through simple visualisation.

Beyond its practical applications, the Method of Loci offers profound cognitive benefits. By leveraging the brain's natural strength in spatial memory, it significantly enhances recall accuracy and learning efficiency. Studies suggest it helps organise information for deeper understanding and better academic performance. Regular use can also sharpen cognitive functions such as reasoning and comprehension while potentially mitigating age-related decline by keeping the mind active. Moreover, mastering this technique fosters confidence in memory skills, empowering individuals to excel in situations like exams or presentations. Whether for academic success, professional growth, or everyday convenience, the Method of Loci remains a timeless and transformative tool for unlocking the full potential of human memory.

1. Choose Your Memory Palace - Select a place you know well, such as your home, school, or a familiar route. This will serve as your "memory palace." Ideally, it should have distinct locations (loci) that you can visualise clearly.

3. Create a Mental Journey - Visualise a specific route through your memory palace. For example, you might start at your front door, move to the living room, then to the kitchen, and so on. Ensure that the path you choose is logical and straightforward, allowing for easy navigation in your mind.

4. Identify Key Locations - Pick specific spots along your route where you will place items or concepts you want to remember. For instance, the front door, living room couch, kitchen table, bathroom sink and bedroom bed. These spots will serve as anchors for the information.

5. Associate Information with Locations - Take the information you need to memorise and assign it to each location using vivid imagery. The more unusual or exaggerated the image, the better it will stick in your memory. For example, if you need to remember "milk," imagine a giant milk carton sitting on your

couch. Incorporate colours, sounds, and textures into your mental images to make them more memorable.

6. Practice Your Route - Mentally walk through your memory palace several times, stopping at each location to recall the associated item or concept. This practice helps reinforce the connections between the loci and the information.

7. Recall Information - When you need to retrieve the information, visualise walking through your memory palace again. As you reach each location, the associated item should come to mind easily.

Start small with a few items (e.g., a shopping list) before expanding to larger sets of information. Practice regularly and remember the more bizarre or humorous your mental images are, the more likely they are to stick in your mind.

Practical Examples of the Method of Loci

1. Memorising Speeches or Presentations

Imagine placing different sections or key points of your speech at various locations in a familiar room (e.g., your living room). Example: You could visualise the introduction on the couch, the first main point on the coffee table, and subsequent points on different pieces of furniture. As you mentally walk through the room, you recall each part sequentially.

2. Learning Languages

Use loci to memorize vocabulary or phrases by associating them with specific locations. Example: If learning Spanish, you might place words like "mesa" (table) on your kitchen table and "silla" (chair) on your chair. When you need to recall these words, you mentally walk through your home.

3. Studying for Exams

Organise information by subjects and chapters, placing key concepts in different rooms or areas. Example: For a biology exam, you could visualise different topics (e.g., cell structure, genetics) in specific rooms of a house, allowing for a structured mental review.

4. Remembering Grocery Lists

Create a memory palace using your route through a grocery store. Example: Imagine placing items like milk in the dairy section and apples in the produce aisle. As you mentally navigate the store, you can recall each item as you "pass" it. Visualise your kitchen and place each grocery item at different spots. For example, imagine a giant apple on your dining table and a loaf of bread in the pantry.

5. Memorising Historical Dates or Events

Associate significant dates or events with specific locations along a familiar route. Example: You could visualise important events from World War II placed at various landmarks along your route to school, recalling them as you pass each landmark.

6. Memorising Names and Faces

Use loci to remember names by associating them with distinct features or locations. Example: If meeting someone named "Rose," you might visualise a rose flower on their forehead as you mentally place them in your memory palace.

7. Preparing for Memory Competitions

Memory athletes often use this method to memorize long sequences of numbers or cards. Example: A competitor might visualise a long street and assign each number to a specific house along that street, allowing for quick retrieval during competitions.

Activity 102. Practice juggling

Juggling is more than just a fun activity; it can be a powerful tool for mental and physical well-being, particularly for individuals recovering from addiction. This skill combines focus, mindfulness, and physical coordination, offering numerous benefits that support the healing process.

It offers numerous mental benefits, making it a valuable tool for recovery. Its rhythmic motions and focus help relieve stress and anxiety, providing a healthy outlet for emotional challenges. The intense concentration required enhances focus, mindfulness, and present-moment awareness, breaking cycles of rumination about the past or future. Studies show that juggling promotes brain plasticity, increasing grey matter in areas tied to movement, memory, and visual processing, which supports cognitive recovery. Additionally, mastering this skill fosters a sense of achievement and boosts self-esteem, offering motivation for those rebuilding their self-worth. As a healthy coping mechanism, juggling provides a constructive way to fill time and redirect negative thoughts into positive action.

Juggling also offers valuable physical benefits, including improved hand-eye coordination and spatial awareness, which enhance overall motor skills. Though not strenuous, it provides light exercise that supports general fitness and physical well-being, making it a great addition to recovery routines. Interestingly, juggling also leads to measurable changes in brain structure. It enhances white matter connectivity between regions responsible for peripheral vision and motor skills while expanding grey matter in areas linked to visual motion processing, such as the mid-temporal area and posterior intraparietal sulcus. These brain changes persist even after practice ends, though regular juggling helps maintain them. The benefits arise from the learning process itself rather than mastery, showcasing the brain's remarkable capacity for adaptation at any age. Learning to juggle is accessible to anyone with patience and practice, here's how:

Gather your supplies. Use three juggling balls (beanbags are ideal for beginners), or alternatively, soft objects like rolled-up socks or small stuffed animals work well.

Master Basic Throws
1. Start with one ball.
2. Toss it from one hand to the other in an arc at eye level.
3. Aim for consistent throws while keeping your elbows close to your body.

Learn the Exchange
1. Hold two balls—one in each hand.
2. Toss the first ball in an arc.
3. When it reaches its peak, toss the second ball underneath.
4. Practice until you can consistently catch both balls.

Progress to Three Balls
1. Hold two balls in your dominant hand and one in your other hand.
2. Toss one ball from your dominant hand.
3. As it peaks, toss the ball from your other hand underneath.
4. Continue alternating throws while catching each ball.

Practice Tips
- Begin with short sessions (5–10 minutes).
- Practice over a soft surface like a bed to minimize chasing dropped balls.
- Focus on consistent throws rather than catching initially.
- Use a wall behind you to help control forward throws.

Remember: dropping is part of learning! With patience and persistence, you'll improve steadily. Expensive equipment isn't necessary, many household items can serve as excellent props for starting out!

1. Juggling Balls - Beanbags or soft balls are ideal because they don't roll away when dropped. Koosh balls or filled tennis balls (weighted with water) are beginner-friendly options.

2. Scarves or Handkerchiefs - Silk scarves fall slowly, giving beginners more time to react.

3. DIY Options - Rolled-up socks or small stuffed animals work well as juggling props.

4. Other Beginner-Friendly Props - Spinning plates or ribbon sticks provide alternative ways to practice coordination skills.

Considerations:
- Weight: Heavier balls offer better tactile feedback for beginners.
- Size: Balls with a diameter of 2–3 inches are comfortable for most learners.
- Material: Soft materials like beanbags are easier to handle and less likely to bounce away.

By incorporating juggling into daily routines, individuals recovering from addiction gain not only a fun hobby but also a multifaceted tool for improving mental focus, emotional resilience, physical health, and cognitive function—a step toward holistic recovery!

Activity 103. Upcycle an old item

Upcycling is the process of creatively repurposing waste materials or unwanted products into new items of higher quality, value, or environmental usefulness. Unlike traditional recycling, which often involves breaking down materials to create new products, upcycling focuses on transforming discarded items into functional or artistic creations. This sustainable practice has gained widespread popularity due to its numerous environmental, economic, and social benefits.

One of the most significant advantages of upcycling is its positive impact on the environment. By reducing waste, upcycling helps decrease the amount of discarded materials sent to landfills, alleviating the strain on these sites and preventing unnecessary accumulation. Additionally, upcycling conserves valuable natural resources such as water, energy, and raw materials by reusing existing items rather than relying on new production. This conservation effort protects ecosystems and biodiversity, promoting long-term sustainability. Furthermore, upcycling contributes to a lower carbon footprint by reducing greenhouse gas emissions associated with manufacturing new products. Since producing new goods often relies on energy from fossil fuels, upcycling minimises this demand and helps combat climate change.

Upcycling also offers notable economic benefits. It is a cost-effective way to create new items without purchasing raw materials, allowing individuals to save money while fostering creativity. Whether repurposing old furniture or crafting handmade accessories, upcycling empowers people to innovate while staying budget conscious. Moreover, this practice supports local economies by encouraging small businesses and artisans who specialise in creating unique products from repurposed materials. These businesses often offer one-of-a-kind items that appeal to environmentally conscious consumers, driving demand for sustainable goods and boosting local commerce.

Look around your house, charity shop and come up with some ideas and make something beautiful and unique. Here are some of the most creative upcycling ideas that stand out for their ingenuity and practicality to help generate that creative spark from within.

- Old Dressers: Convert an old dresser into a bookshelf by removing the drawers and adding shelves.
- Sweater Pillows: Transform old sweaters into cozy pillows by cutting to size, sewing the edges, and stuffing them.
- Old Windows: Repurpose old windows as picture frames by replacing the glass with photos.
- Vinyl Record Bowls: Heat vinyl records to shape them into bowls for storing small items.
- Bicycle Wheel Clocks: Create a unique wall clock using an old bicycle wheel by attaching clock hands and numbers.

- Old Tyres: Wrap an old tyre in rope to make an ottoman or use it as a planter in your garden.
- Old Ladder Bookshelves: Transform an old ladder into a stylish bookshelf, adding character to any room while providing functional storage.
- Chipped Plate Bird Bath: Instead of discarding broken dishes, repurpose them into a charming bird bath that enhances your garden.
- Magazine Garland: Create a colourful garland from old magazines, which can serve as decorative accents for parties or home decor.
- Aquarium from an Old TV: A more unconventional project involves converting an outdated television into a unique aquarium, providing a striking conversation piece.
- Tennis Racket Trellis: Upcycle old tennis rackets into garden trellises, combining functionality with a whimsical aesthetic for climbing plants.
- Stuffed Toy Doorstop: Repurpose unwanted stuffed toys by filling them with heavy materials like sand to create cute doorstops.
- Upcycled Baby Crib Storage: Convert an old baby crib into creative storage solutions for craft supplies or other household items, blending nostalgia with practicality.
- Rug from Old Sheets: Use old sheets or duvet covers to create a braided rug, offering both functionality and a pop of colour to your floors.
- T-shirts are amazing for a lot of different projects:
  - Make a memory blanket from old sentimental t-shirts. It is a wonderful way to preserve cherished memories, such as concerts, events, holidays.
  - Old t-shirts make excellent cleaning rags due to their absorbent nature. Cut them into squares and use them for various cleaning tasks around the house.
  - Repurpose t-shirts into dog toys by cutting them into strips, braiding them tightly, and tying knots at both ends. This creates a durable toy that your pet will love.
  - Old t-shirts can be cut and fashioned into stylish headbands or hair ties.
  - Create t-shirt yarn by cutting the fabric into continuous strips. This yarn can be used for crocheting or knitting projects, allowing for unique handmade items.

Activity 104. Make beeswax wraps

Beeswax wraps are a reusable, eco-friendly alternative to plastic wrap, designed for food storage. Made from cotton fabric coated with beeswax, tree resin, and oils like jojoba or coconut oil, they are pliable, tacky, and breathable. This allows them to mould around various shapes and create a seal for food items, keeping them fresh while reducing reliance on single-use plastics. Beeswax wraps are biodegradable and compostable, making them an excellent choice for anyone looking to live more sustainably.

The benefits that go beyond their environmental impact. They help preserve food by allowing air circulation, which prevents spoilage and keeps items like fruits, vegetables, bread, and cheese fresh for longer (mold them over bowls or wrap the food). Their antibacterial properties also protect food from bacteria growth. Additionally, they are cost-effective, lasting up to a year with proper care, as well as versatile enough to wrap sandwiches, cover bowls, or store leftovers. By replacing disposable plastic wrap with these, you save money while contributing to a healthier planet.

Crafting beeswax wraps is not just practical but also deeply therapeutic, especially for individuals in addiction recovery or those seeking emotional well-being. The process involves hands-on steps like cutting fabric, melting wax, and spreading it evenly—activities that promote mindfulness and focus. This immersive experience helps calm the mind and reduce stress by encouraging present-moment awareness. For people in recovery, this mindfulness can be a powerful tool to manage anxiety and redirect attention away from negative thoughts or cravings.

The creative aspect of designing beeswax wraps—choosing fabrics, colours, and patterns—stimulates creativity and provides a sense of accomplishment. Completing a project like this boosts self-esteem and reinforces feelings of capability and purpose. Additionally, crafting can lead to a "flow state," where individuals become fully absorbed in the activity, providing emotional relief and fostering positive mental health. For those rebuilding their lives after addiction, this sense of achievement can be incredibly empowering. Creating beeswax wraps at home is simple and rewarding. Here's how:

Materials Needed
- Cotton fabric (100% cotton is recommended)
- Beeswax pellets or grated beeswax
- Jojoba oil (optional for pliability)
- Pine resin (optional for added stickiness)
- Parchment paper
- Baking sheet
- Paintbrush

Instructions

1. Prepare the Fabric: Wash and dry the cotton fabric. Cut it into squares or rectangles of your desired size (e.g., 12"x12") using scissors or pinking shears to prevent fraying.
2. Preheat the Oven: Set your oven to a low temperature (around 170°F/77°C).
3. Assemble the Baking Sheet: Line a baking sheet with parchment paper and place the fabric on top.
5. Add Beeswax: Sprinkle an even layer of beeswax pellets over the fabric. Add small amounts of jojoba oil and pine resin if desired for enhanced properties.
6. Melt the Wax: Place the baking sheet in the oven for 3–8 minutes until the wax melts completely.
7. Spread the Wax: Remove the sheet from the oven and use a paintbrush to spread the melted wax evenly across the fabric while it's still warm.
8. Cool and Dry: Hang wrap using pegs or lay flat to cool and harden completely.

Care Instructions: Wash wraps with cool water and mild soap; avoid hot water as it can melt the wax coating and allow them to air dry before storing flat or rolled up.

With their flexibility, antimicrobial properties, and ability to reduce waste, beeswax wraps are an excellent addition to any sustainable lifestyle. From food preservation to creative household uses, they offer a practical and eco-friendly solution for everyday needs! Here are some of the most popular ways to use these reusable wraps:

Beyond Food Storage
- Bouquet Wrapping: Beeswax wraps can replace plastic and tape when wrapping flowers, offering a sustainable and beautiful presentation for gifts.
- Jar Lid Grip: Their tacky texture provides extra grip for opening stubborn jar lids, making them a handy tool in the kitchen.
- Bottle Covers: Use beeswax wraps to seal carafes or bottles during picnics or outdoor dining, preventing spills and keeping contents fresh.
- Deck of Cards Storage: Replace torn boxes by wrapping playing cards in beeswax wraps for easy storage.
- Herb Preservation: Rinse fresh herbs with cold water, dry them, and wrap them individually in beeswax wraps to keep them fresh longer.
- Fire Starter: When wraps lose their stickiness after extended use, they can be repurposed as biodegradable fire starters due to their natural wax content.

Activity 105. Create a comic strip

Creating a comic strip is a fun and creative way to express yourself and tell stories. This activity combines visual art with storytelling, allowing you to convey messages and themes in a unique and engaging way. For those in recovery, it can be a therapeutic outlet to explore emotions, experiences, and personal growth.

Creating a comic strip can be a therapeutic activity for several reasons:

Creative Expression: Comic strips offer a unique form of creative expression, allowing individuals to convey emotions, experiences, and stories through a combination of visual art and text. This creative outlet can be particularly therapeutic, providing a healthy way to process emotions and reduce stress.

Mindfulness and Focus: The process of creating a comic strip requires intense focus on the present task, similar to mindfulness practices. This deep concentration can help individuals practice patience and provide a mental break from everyday pressures.

Cognitive Stimulation: Developing a comic strip involves planning, storytelling, and problem-solving, which can stimulate the brain and promote cognitive health. This cognitive engagement can be beneficial for mental well-being, improving memory and cognitive flexibility.

Social Connection: Creating comic strips can also facilitate social connections, especially when shared with others or created collaboratively. This can help reduce feelings of isolation and loneliness, fostering a sense of belonging within a community of creatives.

Emotional Release: Through storytelling and visual representation, comic strips can serve as a form of emotional release. By expressing emotions and experiences in a creative format, individuals can process and manage their feelings more effectively.

Confidence Building: Completing a comic strip project can provide a significant boost to confidence and self-esteem, particularly for those struggling with anxiety or self-doubt. This sense of accomplishment is beneficial for mental health and personal growth.

In the context of recovery, creating comic strips can be an empowering activity that combines creativity with personal reflection, helping individuals navigate their experiences and emotions in a constructive and engaging way.

Brainstorm Ideas: Start by thinking about the story you want to tell. Consider the theme, message, and whether it will be humorous, adventurous, or dramatic. Jot down your ideas and think about how they can fit into a short, sequential format.

1. **Develop Characters**: Create unique and relatable characters for your comic strip. Give them distinct personalities, appearances, and backstories. Strong characters are crucial for engaging your audience.
2. **Outline the Plot**: Sketch a rough outline of your story, determining the beginning, middle, and end. Keep the story simple and focused due to the limited space.
3. **Choose Your Tools**: Decide whether to draw by hand using traditional materials (pen and paper) or use digital tools. There are online comic strip makers available.
4. **Plan the Layout**: Start with rough sketches of each panel. Determine how many panels you need and how they'll be arranged. 3-panels is a good starting point.
5. **Draw Your Characters and Scenes**: Begin with basic shapes to draw your characters. Sketch in the backgrounds and add details to bring your comic to life. Don't forget to include speech bubbles for dialogue.
6. **Add Text and Dialogue**: Write in your dialogue and any narration. Make sure the text is clear and easy to read. The size of your lettering can indicate whether a character is shouting or whispering.
7. **Finalise and Ink**: Once you're happy with your pencil sketches, go over them with ink to make the lines clean and bold, this step adds depth and clarity to your drawings.

Look at existing comic strips to understand them better, start with simple stories and gradually move to more complex ones. Draw your characters multiple times to maintain consistency and don't be afraid to revise and edit your work. The first draft is rarely perfect.

Brainstorming Ideas for Your Comic Strip

1. **Mind Mapping and Free Association**: Start with a central theme and branch out with related ideas. This technique allows you to explore various tangents and make unexpected connections.
2. **Draw Inspiration from Everyday Life**: Use interesting situations, conversations, or observations from your daily life as starting points for your comic strip ideas.
3. **Combine Unrelated Concepts**: Mash up two or more unrelated ideas to create something unique. For example, combine "superheroes" with "support group" to create a comic about a "Supervillain support group."
4. **Explore Different Perspectives**: Take a familiar situation and view it from an unusual angle. For example, instead of focusing on the hero, create a story about "The reluctant hero" who just wants a normal life but keeps getting pulled into action.
5. **Focus on a Theme or Message**: Begin with a theme or message you want to convey. This gives your comic strip a deeper meaning and purpose.
6. **Experiment with Different Styles**: Consider starting with a particular writing or art style. For example, the creators of "Blue in Green" used a jazz-inspired approach.

7. **Use the "What If" Technique:** Ask "What if" questions to generate unique scenarios - "What if retired superheroes formed a club to reminisce about their glory days?"
8. **Embrace the Absurd:** Don't be afraid to explore outlandish or campy ideas. Often, these unconventional concepts can lead to the most interesting and memorable.

Activity 106. Wipe down kitchen counters

Ok, at first glance, wiping down kitchen counters might seem like a mundane chore, but it can actually be a powerful tool for improving mental health, fostering mindfulness, and promoting overall well-being. For individuals in addiction recovery, this seemingly small act can serve as a grounding ritual that provides structure and a sense of accomplishment. With a little creativity, wiping down kitchen counters can become an enjoyable and meaningful activity for everyone.

Engaging in repetitive tasks like cleaning counters can have a calming effect on the mind. The rhythmic motions involved in wiping surfaces encourage mindfulness, allowing you to focus on the present moment and temporarily set aside stress or worries. For individuals in addiction recovery, this practice can help redirect thoughts away from triggers and provide a healthy outlet for nervous energy.

The act of cleaning also fosters a sense of control and accomplishment. Seeing the transformation from dirty to clean counters offers instant gratification, which can boost self-esteem and reinforce positive habits. This is particularly valuable for those rebuilding their lives after addiction, as small victories contribute to long-term progress.

Cleaning counters can be turned into light physical activity by incorporating exaggerated movements or exercises like lunges and squats. This adds an element of fitness to the task, promoting circulation and releasing endorphins—the body's natural mood boosters. Physical activity, even in small doses, is beneficial for overall health and can improve energy levels and mood.

Wiping down counters also provides an opportunity to engage your senses. Using pleasantly scented cleaners or adding essential oils to your cleaning solution can create a soothing sensory experience. Pairing this with upbeat music or a favourite podcast transforms the task into an enjoyable ritual that lifts your spirits.

For those in recovery, cleaning rituals like this offer structure and predictability—key factors in reducing anxiety and promoting emotional stability. Establishing routines helps create a sense of normalcy, which is essential during the healing process.

Even if cleaning isn't your favourite activity, we all have to do it and there are plenty of ways to make wiping down kitchen counters more engaging:

Turn It Into a Game
- Set a Timer: Challenge yourself to clean as much as possible before the timer goes off.
- Beat the Song: Pick an upbeat song and try to finish cleaning before it ends.
- Superhero Mode: Pretend you're a cleaning superhero dramatically "defeating" dirt.

Make It a Workout
- Use exaggerated arm movements to engage your muscles while wiping.
- Do lunges as you move along the counter.
- Incorporate squats when reaching low areas or corners.

Engage Your Senses
- Choose cleaners with pleasant scents or add essential oils to your solution.
- Listen to music, audiobooks, or podcasts while you clean.
- Focus on the satisfying visual transformation from dirty to sparkling clean counters.

Reward Yourself
- Plan a small treat for afterward, such as enjoying a cup of tea or relaxing for a few minutes.
- Track your cleaning streaks with stickers or an app to celebrate milestones.
- Take pride in admiring your clean kitchen—it's always rewarding to see your efforts.

For wellbeing in general, wiping down counters offers more than just cleanliness:

1. Mindfulness Practice: Cleaning encourages focus on the present moment, reducing stress and helping individuals stay grounded.
2. Sense of Accomplishment: Completing small tasks builds confidence and reinforces positive habits that are essential for recovery.
3. Structure and Routine: Establishing regular cleaning rituals creates stability, which is crucial during recovery.
4. Healthy Distraction: Cleaning redirects attention away from cravings or negative thoughts, offering a constructive outlet for energy.
5. Physical Activity: Incorporating movement into cleaning promotes physical health while boosting mood through endorphins.

Invite friends over for a "cleaning party" where everyone tackles chores together while chatting or listening to music. If you're in recovery, this type of social interaction can strengthen bonds while making tasks feel less isolating. Some people love cleaning and honestly they would be happy to help and keep you motivated, plus you have less work to do!

Activity 107. Groom a pet

Grooming your pet is more than just keeping them clean—it's a vital practice that contributes to their physical health, emotional well-being, and strengthens the bond between you. Whether you own a dog, cat, or another furry companion—or even borrow a friend's pet for the experience—grooming offers numerous benefits for both pets and their caretakers. Here's why grooming matters, how it can enhance mental health, and ideas for those without pets.

Regular grooming plays a crucial role in maintaining your pet's physical health. It allows you to inspect their skin, ears, and nails for signs of infections or abnormalities, helping prevent painful conditions caused by bacteria or yeast buildup. Grooming also aids in early detection of health issues such as lumps, rashes, or parasites, enabling timely treatment for better outcomes. Another key benefit is pest control. Grooming helps eliminate fleas and ticks while reducing the risk of infestations that can cause discomfort or transmit diseases. Brushing your pet's coat removes dead hair and debris, promoting healthier skin by allowing it to breathe. This process also reduces shedding around the home, keeping your living space cleaner.

Grooming is not just about hygiene—it's a calming ritual that can reduce anxiety and stress in pets. The gentle motions involved in brushing or bathing distribute natural oils across their coat, preventing matting and discomfort that could lead to anxiety. For older pets or those prone to stress, the predictability of regular grooming sessions provides comfort and reassurance. The act of grooming also strengthens the bond between you and your pet. Spending one-on-one time during grooming fosters trust and affection through gentle touch and verbal reassurance. This interaction deepens your connection with them, making them feel safe and loved. Additionally, a clean and well-groomed pet often displays improved behaviour—feeling more confident and comfortable in social situations.

Grooming your pet can be therapeutic for you as well. The repetitive motions involved in brushing or bathing have a calming effect that lowers cortisol levels—a key stress hormone—for both pets and owners. This shared experience creates a soothing environment that promotes relaxation. The bonding time during grooming enhances emotional connection, fostering feelings of trust and affection that boost mood, even if the pet is not your own. Physical touch releases oxytocin (the "bonding hormone"), which counteracts stress responses and improves overall emotional well-being. Additionally, the routine of grooming encourages mindfulness by focusing your attention on the present moment—a meditative practice that alleviates anxiety.

For individuals in addiction recovery or those seeking emotional stability, grooming pets can be especially beneficial. The nurturing act of caring for an animal builds self-esteem while providing structure and purpose—key elements for maintaining mental health.

Ideas for Those Without Pets

- Borrow a Friend's Pet: Offer to groom a friend's dog or cat. Many pet owners appreciate help with this task, especially if their schedules are busy.
- Volunteer at Animal Shelters: Shelters often need volunteers to groom animals awaiting adoption. This is a rewarding way to contribute while enjoying the therapeutic benefits.
- Pet Therapy Programs: Join organisations like Therapy Dogs Nationwide or Dogs for Health that use therapy pets to support communities. These programs often involve interacting with animals through grooming or other activities.
- Pretend Play with Kids: If you have children, set up a "pet grooming salon" using stuffed animals. This imaginative activity mimics the benefits of real pet care while fostering creativity.
- Visit Friends with Pets: Spend time with friends who own pets—helping with grooming can be a fun way to bond with both the animal and its owner.

Whether you own a pet or borrow one from a friend, regular grooming is an essential practice that promotes physical health, emotional well-being, and strengthens bonds. For those without pets, volunteering at shelters or engaging in therapy programs offers similar benefits while supporting animals in need. Grooming isn't just about keeping pets clean—it's about creating moments of connection that foster happiness for both humans and their furry companions.

Activity 108. Sort through old papers

I love this task at the beginning and at the end, halfway through it can be laborious and overwhelming, so organisation is key! Sorting through old paperwork might not seem exciting, but it can be surprisingly beneficial for your mental health and overall well-being. For mental health, this task offers a healthy distraction, fosters a sense of control, and provides an opportunity to create order in both physical and emotional spaces. By tackling this task step by step, you can declutter your environment, reduce stress, and even discover a sense of accomplishment. Here's how to get started and why it's so valuable.

For individuals with mental health, sorting paperwork can serve as a grounding activity. The process requires focus and decision-making, which helps redirect thoughts away from cravings or negative emotions. It also encourages mindfulness as you concentrate on categorising and organising each piece of paper. This kind of focused attention can reduce anxiety and promote a sense of calm.

The act of decluttering has psychological benefits for everyone. Studies show that a clutter-free environment can improve focus, reduce stress, and create a feeling of control over your surroundings. Completing this task provides a tangible sense of accomplishment, which is particularly empowering for those rebuilding their lives after addiction.

Sorting through old papers often brings up memories—some pleasant, some bittersweet. This process can help you reflect on the past while letting go of unnecessary baggage, both physical and emotional. For those in recovery, this symbolic act of clearing out the old to make room for the new aligns with their personal journey.

From a practical standpoint, organising paperwork ensures that important documents are easy to locate when needed. It also reduces the risk of losing critical items like birth certificates or tax records while freeing up physical space in your home.

To Start:

Step 1: Choose a Workspace
- Select a clear, well-lit area with plenty of space to spread out papers.
- Use a comfortable chair since this task may take some time.
- Create an environment that feels calming—play soft music or light a scented candle to make the process more enjoyable.

Step 2: Gather Supplies
- Prepare several boxes or bins labelled: Keep / Recycle / Shred / To File
- Have a shredder nearby for sensitive documents.
- Keep a recycling bin within reach to quickly dispose of non-sensitive papers.

Step 3: Start with Quick Decisions
Begin by making quick decisions about obvious categories:
- Junk mail, old newspapers, and expired vouchers (recycle).
- Outdated bills or statements (shred).
- Important documents like birth certificates or property deeds (keep).

As you sort through your paperwork, create clear categories for items you're keeping:

1. Financial Documents: Tax returns, investment statements, loan agreements.
2. Medical Records: Test results, vaccination records.
3. Personal Documents: Birth certificates, marriage licenses.
4. Work-Related Papers: Contracts, certifications.
6. Miscellaneous: Receipts for warranties or major purchases.

Sorting paperwork can feel overwhelming if you try to tackle it all at once. Break the task into manageable chunks, so work in focused sessions (30–60 minutes) to avoid burnout. Take breaks between sessions to recharge and celebrate small milestones—like finishing one box.

Consider digitising your paperwork:

1. Use a scanner or mobile scanning app like Adobe Scan or Microsoft Lens.
2. Save files in organised folders on your computer or cloud storage.
3. Use descriptive file names for easy searching (e.g., "2024_Tax_Return").
4. Back up digital files regularly to prevent data loss.

Once digitised, shred the physical copies unless they are original legal documents.

For individuals in recovery, sorting paperwork offers unique benefits:

1. Healthy Distraction: The focus required keeps your mind occupied, away from triggers.
2. Structure and Routine: Establishing regular decluttering sessions creates stability.
3. Symbolic Renewal: Letting go of unnecessary papers mirrors the emotional process of releasing past burdens.
5. Sense of Control: Organising your environment reinforces feelings of capability and responsibility, key elements in recovery.

To stay motivated, pair it with something fun like listen to music or an audiobook while you work, setting small goals. Don't forget to reward yourself after each session with something simple like a cup of tea or watching an episode of your favourite show.

Activity 109. Practice Laughter Yoga

You might think I am mad after this one, but please, please, please try this if you haven't before, no matter how you are feeling today please try this. Laughter yoga is an innovative and uplifting practice that combines intentional laughter with breathing exercises to promote physical, emotional, and mental health. For individuals in addiction recovery, laughter yoga offers a unique way to manage stress, improve mood, and build resilience. Beyond recovery, this practice can benefit anyone by fostering mindfulness, enhancing social connections, and boosting overall well-being. Here's why laughter yoga is so effective and how you can incorporate it into your daily life.

Laughter yoga significantly reduces stress by lowering cortisol levels—the body's primary stress hormone. It triggers the release of endorphins, serotonin, and dopamine, which are natural feel-good chemicals that promote relaxation and happiness. For those in recovery, this can be especially helpful in managing stress and anxiety—two major factors that contribute to addiction relapse. Engaging in laughter yoga helps build emotional strength and adaptability. By providing a healthy outlet for managing stress, it teaches individuals to respond to triggers more effectively. This increased resilience can lower the risk of relapse and support long-term recovery while enhancing overall emotional well-being.

Laughter yoga is often practiced in groups, creating a sense of camaraderie and belonging. These social connections are vital for reducing feelings of isolation and fostering support networks. Sharing laughter with others strengthens relationships and builds trust. The practice encourages participants to be present in the moment, enhancing mindfulness and mental clarity. Laughter yoga can improve cognitive functions such as positive thinking and emotional balance, helping individuals in recovery navigate challenges with greater ease. One of the most compelling benefits is its ability to naturally stimulate dopamine production. Dopamine is the brain's "reward chemical" often associated with addictive substances. Laughter provides a healthy way to satisfy cravings for pleasurable sensations without harmful side effects.

Laughter yoga isn't just good for the mind, it also benefits the body. It relaxes muscles, improves cardiovascular health, boosts immunity, and even provides temporary pain relief. These physical improvements support overall well-being, making it easier for individuals in recovery to focus on healing. Laughter yoga doesn't require special equipment or prior experience. You can try these simple exercises at home or with a group. Even if the laughter feels forced at first, your body doesn't differentiate between real or fake laughter, the benefits remain the same!

Warm-Up Exercises
- Clap your hands rhythmically while chanting "Ho Ho Ha Ha Ha."
- Take deep breaths, raising your arms as you inhale and lowering them as you exhale with laughter.

Playful Laughter Exercises
- Silent Laughter: Open your mouth wide and laugh without making any sound—it often leads to genuine giggles.
- Lion Laughter: Stick out your tongue, widen your eyes, stretch your hands like claws, and laugh heartily.
- Greeting Laughter: Pretend you're meeting people, shake imaginary hands, and laugh as you greet them.
- Gradient Laughter: Start with a smile, progress to a gentle chuckle, then build up to hearty laughter before returning to a smile.
- Childlike Laughter: Let your inner child take over—laugh freely for 30 seconds.

Calming Exercises
- Close your mouth and laugh while humming (Humming Laughter). I love doing this!
- Practice laughter meditation by starting with a soft smile that grows into laughter. **Remember** that your body doesn't know the difference between real or fake laughter, so fake it until you make it!

To make laughter yoga part of your routine and maximise its benefits try these practical strategies:

Morning Ritual - Start your day on a positive note:
- Begin with a smile as soon as you wake up (even if it feels forced).
- Take a "laughter shower" while getting ready, laugh intentionally as you lather up.
- Pair deep breathing exercises with gentle laughter to release tension.

Laughter Breaks - Include short bursts of laughter throughout your day:
- Laugh at red traffic lights instead of feeling frustrated.
- Take regular "laughter breaks" at work or home.
- Use deep breaths followed by playful chuckles whenever you feel stressed.

Social Activities - Strengthen connections through shared laughter:
- Organise group laughter yoga sessions with friends or support group members.
- Share funny stories during support group meetings or gatherings.
- Schedule regular "laughter meetups" where everyone participates.

Bedtime Routine - End your day with calming laughter:
- Keep a humour journal to record funny moments from your day, then review before bed.
- Practice gentle laughter combined with deep breathing to release tension from the day.
- Visualise amusing scenarios as you drift off to sleep.

Activity 110. Write & Reflect on your Personal Values

Values are the principles and beliefs that guide our decisions, shape our behaviours, and define what matters most to us in life. They act as an internal compass, helping us navigate challenges and make choices that align with our true selves. Identifying and reflecting on personal values is a powerful exercise that fosters self-awareness, emotional resilience, and purpose. It can also benefit everyone by promoting mental clarity, reducing stress, and enhancing overall well-being.

Values are deeply rooted ideals that influence how we think, feel, and act. They can encompass a wide range of concepts, such as honesty, compassion, creativity, family, freedom, or achievement. While values are unique to each person, they often reflect what we prioritise in life and how we define success and fulfilment.

Understanding your values provides clarity about who you are and what you stand for. This self-awareness is especially important during times of uncertainty or change, as it serves as a grounding force that helps you stay true to yourself. In addiction recovery, reconnecting with personal values can provide a sense of direction and motivation for building a healthier, more meaningful life.

Writing down personal values has been shown to lower cortisol levels—the body's primary stress hormone. By focusing on what truly matters to you, this exercise creates a sense of stability and calm that helps manage anxiety during stressful situations. Then reflecting on your values encourages introspection, allowing you to process emotions more effectively. This clarity helps you understand your reactions to challenges and identify healthier ways to cope.

Values act as a foundation for resilience by providing a sense of purpose during difficult times. When faced with adversity or temptation, revisiting your values can help you stay grounded and make decisions aligned with your long-term goals. Living in alignment with your values promotes authenticity, which is a key factor in life satisfaction. When your actions reflect your beliefs, it reinforces your sense of integrity and boosts self-esteem.

How to Do the Values Exercise

Step 1: Self-Reflection - Begin by reflecting on your experiences and emotions:
1. Analyse Meaningful Moments: Think about times when you felt truly fulfilled or motivated. What made those moments special? Consider peak experiences like achieving a goal or helping someone in need.
2. Examine Your Reactions: Identify situations that trigger strong emotions—both positive and negative. What makes you angry or frustrated? What energizes or excites you? Who do you admire and why?
3. Envision Your Ideal Life: Picture your ideal environment without limitations. What does it look like? What activities or relationships bring you joy?

Step 2: Practical Techniques: Use these methods to clarify your values:
1. Values Sorting:
    - Start with a comprehensive list of values (you can find examples online).
    - Highlight the ones that resonate with you.
    - Narrow down the list to your top 10 values and rank them in order of importance.
2. Flip Your Frustrations:
    - Write down things that frequently frustrate you.
    - For each frustration, identify the underlying goal or desire being thwarted.
    - Use this insight to uncover hidden values.
3. Use Assessment Tools - Take free online assessments like the VIA Character Strengths Survey or Personal Values Assessment for additional guidance.

Step 3: Create a Values Statement
Write a brief statement summarising your top values (200–250 words). This helps solidify your understanding and provides a reference point for future reflection.

Tips for Incorporating Values Into Daily Life

Once you've identified your core values, use them as a tool for decision-making and personal growth:

1. Set Goals Aligned With Your Values: Use your top values to guide short- and long-term goals that reflect what truly matters to you.
2. Revisit Your Values Regularly: Reflect on your values every six months to see how they evolve over time.
3. Use Values During Stressful Situations: When faced with difficult decisions or temptations, revisit your written values to help ground yourself.

Identifying personal values is more than just an exercise—it's an opportunity for self-discovery that fosters mental clarity, emotional resilience, and authenticity. For individuals in addiction recovery, this practice serves as a powerful tool for rebuilding life with purpose and intention. For everyone else, it's a chance to align actions with beliefs, reduce stress, and enhance overall well-being. By taking the time to reflect on what truly matters to you, you create a foundation for living a more meaningful and fulfilling life.

Activity 111. Create shadow art using household objects

Shadow art is a creative and engaging activity that uses light and everyday objects to produce captivating designs and scenes. This simple yet imaginative exercise can be a powerful tool for improving mental and physical well-being, especially for individuals in addiction recovery. It encourages mindfulness, boosts mood, and provides a healthy outlet for self-expression. Here's an explanation of what shadow art is, why it's beneficial, how to do it, and additional tips to enhance your experience.

Shadow art involves using a light source to cast shadows of objects onto a surface, such as a wall or cardboard base, and arranging them to create artistic designs or tell stories. We all did the butterfly or bird with our hands when we were kids right?! Or did your mind just go somewhere else? You know what I mean! By experimenting with the placement of objects and light angles, you can produce fascinating shapes, patterns, or even detailed scenes. This activity combines creativity with problem-solving as you manipulate objects to achieve your desired effects. For individuals in addiction recovery, shadow art can serve as a therapeutic activity that promotes mindfulness and emotional healing. It's also an excellent way for anyone to explore their artistic side while engaging in a calming and rewarding process.

Mental Health Benefits

1. Encourages Mindfulness: The process of arranging objects and adjusting light angles requires focus on the present moment. This mindfulness reduces stress and anxiety by grounding you in the creative process.
2. Boosts Mood: Engaging in creative activities like shadow art triggers the release of dopamine—the brain's "feel-good" chemical—which enhances mood and provides a sense of accomplishment.
3. Promotes Self-Expression: Shadow art allows you to express emotions or tell stories visually, which can be particularly therapeutic for individuals processing complex feelings during recovery.
4. Reduces Negative Thoughts: Concentrating on an artistic task can redirect attention away from cravings or negative emotions, offering a healthy distraction.

Physical Health Benefits

1. Improves Fine Motor Skills: Arranging objects, and sketching designs enhances hand-eye coordination and dexterity.
2. Encourages Movement: Setting up your workspace involves physical activity like bending, stretching, or reaching—helping you stay active while immersed in the task.
3. Relieves Tension: The calming nature of this activity relaxes muscles and reduces physical tension caused by stress.

To Create Shadow Art

Step 1: Gather Materials
You don't need fancy equipment—just items readily available at home:
- Light source (lamp, flashlight, or sunlight)
- Base (cardboard, Styrofoam, or wall)
- Household objects (kitchen utensils, toys, plants, etc.)
- Paper for sketching
- Adhesive (glue, tape, or wire)

Step 2: Set Up Your Space
1. Choose a flat wall or surface where shadows can be projected clearly.
2. Position your light source to cast distinct shadows—experiment with angles.
3. Place your base in front of the wall or surface.

Step 3: Create Your Design
1. Sketch your desired shadow shape or scene on paper.
2. Experiment with object placement until the shadows match your vision.
3. Secure objects on the base using adhesive materials like tape or glue.

Tips for Success
- Use objects with varied shapes and sizes for more dynamic shadows.
- Incorporate transparent items like glass bottles for unique effects.
- Adjust the distance between objects and the light source to change shadow sizes.
- Experiment with different angles to create distortions or layered shadows.

Creative Themes

1. Nature-Inspired Scenes:
   - Enchanted Forest: Use leaves, branches, and figurines to create woodland shadows.
   - Underwater World: Arrange seashells and toy fish for ocean-themed designs.
   - Floral Garden: Use flowers and plants to craft blooming shadow patterns.

2. Storytelling:
   - Fairy Tale Silhouettes: Use cutouts of characters to narrate classic tales.
   - Shadow Puppet Theatre: Create movable puppets to enact scenes on the wall.
   - Cityscape: Arrange small buildings and cars for an urban landscape.

3. Personal Themes:
   - Childhood Memories: Use toys from your past to create nostalgic scenes.
   - Self-Portrait: Arrange objects that represent aspects of your personality.
   - Dream Landscape: Combine unexpected items for surreal compositions.

To take your shadow art to the next level, try some advanced techniques:
- Use coloured lights or gels on your light to introduce vibrant hues into your shadows.
- Experiment with warm and cool tones for contrasting effects.
- Position multiple light sources at different angles to create layered shadows/depth.
- Use rotating platforms or sliding mechanisms to add motion to your shadow designs.

Activity 112. Do a quick foot rolling exercise for plantar fasciitis prevention

Plantar fasciitis is a common condition that causes pain in the heel and bottom of the foot. It occurs when the plantar fascia—a thick band of tissue connecting your heel to your toes—becomes inflamed or irritated. This condition can make everyday activities like walking or standing painful, but simple self-care measures, such as a foot rolling exercise, can help prevent or alleviate symptoms. This quick and easy exercise not only supports foot health but also offers mental and physical benefits that contribute to overall well-being.

Plantar fasciitis is characterised by sharp, stabbing pain near the heel, especially during the first steps in the morning. The pain may improve with activity but often returns after periods of rest. Common causes include overuse, poor foot mechanics (like flat feet or high arches), wearing unsupportive shoes, sudden increases in physical activity, or prolonged standing on hard surfaces. Risk factors include being overweight, tight calf muscles, and certain types of exercise like running or ballet. While plantar fasciitis is treatable with rest, ice, and stretching exercises, prevention is key. A quick foot rolling exercise is one of the simplest ways to maintain healthy feet and prevent inflammation of the plantar fascia.

Physical Health Benefits

1. Prevents Foot Pain: Regular foot rolling massages the plantar fascia, reducing tension and improving flexibility.
2. Improves Circulation: Rolling stimulates blood flow to the feet, promoting healing and reducing inflammation.
3. Relieves Muscle Tension: The pressure helps relax tight muscles in the feet/calves.
4. Cold Therapy Option: Using a frozen water bottle adds cold therapy to reduce swelling and soothe tired feet after a long day.

Mental Health Benefits

1. Stress Relief: The rhythm provides a calming effect, helping to reduce stress.
2. Mindfulness Practice: Focusing on the sensations in your feet encourages mindfulness, grounding you in the present moment.
3. Improved Mood: Relieving foot pain can enhance your overall sense of well-being, making it easier to stay active and positive.

For individuals in addiction recovery, this exercise offers an additional benefit as a healthy distraction from cravings or negative thoughts while promoting relaxation and self-care. This exercise is simple, requires minimal equipment, and can be done almost anywhere.

1. Set Up Your Space: Sit comfortably in a chair or stand near a stable surface for balance, ensuring you have enough room to move your foot back and forth.
2. Choose Your Tool: such as tennis ball for gentle pressure, golf type ball for more targeted intensity or try a frozen water bottle for added cold therapy.
3. Perform the Exercise:
   a. Place the ball or roller under your foot. Applying gentle pressure, roll it back and forth from the heel to the ball of the foot.
   b. Roll for 1–2 minutes per foot, focusing on areas where you feel tension.
4. Adjust Pressure as Needed, starting with light pressure and gradually increase as tolerated. Avoid pressing too hard to prevent irritation.
5. Repeat Daily: Perform this exercise 2–4 times daily for maximum benefit.

Additional Tips for Success
1. Experiment with Tools such as, a foam roller provides broader pressure for sensitive feet, a massage ball with knobs offers deeper stimulation of pressure points and a rolling pin is a convenient alternative if you don't have specialised tools.
2. Combine with Stretches: Pair this exercise with calf stretches or toe stretches to enhance flexibility and reduce tension further.
3. Use Cold Therapy After Activity: If you've been on your feet all day, use a frozen water bottle for added relief while rolling.
4. Incorporate into Your Routine: Add this exercise to your morning routine to loosen stiff feet or use it before bed to relax after a long day.

In addition to foot rolling, these exercises can help strengthen and stretch your feet:
1. Towel Curls: Place a towel on the floor and use your toes to scrunch it toward you. Repeat 10 times on each foot.
2. Calf Stretch: Stand facing a wall with one leg extended behind you. Lean forward until you feel a stretch in your calf muscle; hold for 30 seconds.
3. Plantar Fascia Stretch: While seated, cross one foot over your knee and pull your toes back toward your shin to stretch the arch of your foot.
4. Heel Raises: Stand with feet hip-width apart and lift your heels off the ground; hold briefly before lowering back down.

For individuals in addiction recovery, incorporating physical activities like this into their routine promotes self-care while offering mental health benefits such as stress relief and mindfulness. A quick foot rolling exercise is an easy yet effective way to prevent plantar fasciitis while promoting overall foot health. By massaging and stretching the plantar fascia regularly, you can reduce tension, improve circulation, and keep your feet feeling their best. Beyond physical benefits, this simple practice also provides mental health advantages by encouraging mindfulness and relieving stress—making it an excellent addition to anyone's daily routine. Whether you're recovering from addiction or just looking for ways to care for yourself better, this small step can lead to big improvements in both body and mind!

Activity 113. Make a Lava Lamp

Hands up, who had a lava lamp back in the late 90's or even 60s? I still remember mine; it was blue with luminous green lava. I found it very meditative and would just forget everything going on in the world and relax. Did you know that you can make your own?! Making an at-home lava lamp can be created using different methods:

1. Alka-Seltzer Method
- Clear plastic or glass bottle
- Vegetable oil
- Water
- Alka-Seltzer tablets
- Food colouring/dye

1. Fill the bottle about 1/4 full with water.
2. Add vegetable oil to fill the bottle, leaving some space at the top.
3. Add a few drops of food colouring.
4. Break an Alka-Seltzer tablet into pieces and drop them into the bottle.
5. Observe the colourful, bubbly effect as the Alka-Seltzer reacts with water to produce carbon dioxide bubbles.
6. Add photoluminescent pigment to the water for a glow-in-the-dark effect.

2. Baking Soda and Vinegar Method
- Tall empty jar or bottle
- Baking soda
- Water
- Food colouring
- Vegetable oil
- Vinegar

1. Place a few tablespoons of baking soda at the bottom of the jar and add water to fill about 1/4 of the jar.
2. Add 5-10 drops of food dye, mix and then fill the jar about 3/4 full with vegetable oil.
3. Slowly add vinegar one tablespoon at a time to create the lava effect.

3. Tonic Water Variation
- Clear jar or bottle
- Tonic water (contains quinine, which glows under UV light)
- Vegetable oil
- Alka-Seltzer tablets
- Food colouring

1. Fill the bottle with 1/4 full tonic water and then vegetable oil to fill the bottle.
2. Add a few drops of food colouring.
3. Break an Alka-Seltzer tablet into pieces and drop them into the bottle.
4. Use a UV light to enhance the glow effect.

Each method offers a unique twist on the classic lava lamp, allowing you to experiment with different materials and effects. Also consider experimenting with different oils, while vegetable oil is the most commonly used due to its effectiveness in creating large, colourful bubbles, other oils can also be used with varying effects:

- Baby Oil: This oil is clear and colourless, but it tends to produce smaller bubbles that move quickly through the oil, which can make the lava lamp effect less distinct.
- Mineral Oil: Similar to baby oil, it is clear and can be used as an alternative to vegetable oil.
- Coconut Oil: This oil can be used, but it might solidify at room temperature, affecting the lava lamp's performance.
- Canola Oil: Another option that can be used, though it may not provide the same visual effect as vegetable oil.

You can try mixing different oils to create a unique lava lamp effect as it can alter the size and movement of the bubbles in your lava lamp.

- Start by mixing a small amount of one oil with another to observe the effect. For example, you might mix 75% vegetable oil with 25% baby oil and adjust the proportions for the desired bubble size and movement speed.
- If you want a clear oil layer, use clear oils like baby oil or mineral oil.
- If you prefer a coloured oil layer, you can add a few drops of food colouring to the oil mixture.
- Keep in mind that some oils may separate over time, so you might need to shake the lamp occasionally.

Example Mixtures
- Vegetable Oil and Baby Oil: This mixture can create a combination of large and small bubbles, offering a varied visual effect.
- Vegetable Oil and Coconut Oil (melted): This blend can add a unique texture due to the coconut oil's properties, though it may require heating to maintain liquidity.
- Mineral Oil and Vegetable Oil: Similar to baby oil, mineral oil can help create smaller bubbles when mixed with vegetable oil.

Considerations
- Stability: Some oil mixtures might not be stable over time, leading to separation or changes in the lava lamp's behaviour.
- Chemical Compatibility: Ensure that the oils you mix are chemically compatible to avoid any adverse reactions.

By experimenting with different oil mixtures, you can create a lava lamp that is both visually appealing and unique.

Activity 114. Observe and record wildlife

Observing wildlife is a fulfilling way to connect with nature, support science, and build your mental and physical health. Whether you're spotting birds in the garden or documenting insects on a walk, this activity cultivates mindfulness, gentle movement, and a sense of purpose—especially supportive for those in addiction recovery.

This practice involves watching animals in their natural habitats and noting what you see—species, behaviour, location, and time. Your records add to valuable biodiversity data that helps researchers understand and protect wildlife. Here is why it's good for you:

Mental Health

- Reduces stress by lowering cortisol and promoting relaxation.
- Fosters mindfulness: focusing on the present eases anxiety and sharpens attention.
- Builds purpose and accomplishment—your observations matter.
- Stimulates curiosity; you'll keep learning and growing.
- Boosts mood with fresh air, gentle movement, and the joy of discovery.

Physical Health

- Encourages walking/moving outdoors, supporting a healthy heart.
- Sunshine increases vitamin D, and fresh air boosts immunity.
- Looking near and far works your eye muscles—resting your gaze from screens.
- Gentle movement in nature naturally eases physical tension.

How to Get Started

1. Gather Basic Tools
- Notebook or digital device for notes.
- Camera or binoculars (optional).
- Field guide or ID app for help with species.

2. Choose a Location
- Start nearby: your garden, local park, or nature reserve.
- Explore wetlands, woods, or even city green spaces.

3. Make Your Observations
- Be still and quiet: wildlife appear more easily.
- Record: what you see (species/description), where, when, and your name as observer.
- For extras: note numbers, behaviour, habitat, and life stage.

4. Record and Share
- Keep a personal nature journal.

- Submit sightings using apps like iNaturalist or iRecord.
- Join local nature groups or online citizen science projects.

Tips for Enriching the Experience
- Start small: Common birds, insects, or plants are great for beginners.
- Use photos to check species later or to share findings easily.
- Take part in group activities (bird counts, butterfly surveys), or follow themes (focus on birds one week, mammals the next).
- Sketch what you see, map animal tracks, or record sounds for a creative twist.
- Set challenges: "Spot five birds this weekend," or "Learn three new species this month."

Beginner-Friendly Wildlife Activities
- Start a bird list in your backyard—use a guide or app to identify species.
- Keep a nature journal: draw or write about your sightings, noting location, weather, and behaviour.
- Survey butterflies: note colours and patterns, plant flowers to attract more.
- Listen for animal calls at dusk—keep a sound log.
- Look for signs: tracks, feathers, nests—match them with species, make your own "wildlife map."
- Create a wildlife-friendly garden: bird feeders, water bowls, or wildflower patches encourage visits.

Connecting with wildlife isn't just nature study, it's healing time for mind and body. You'll experience more peace, move your body, and discover the purpose that comes from supporting a bigger mission. For individuals in recovery or anyone seeking solace, this activity provides personal healing while contributing to the world around you.

Activity 115. Do jumping jacks for 6 minutes

Jumping jacks are a classic, full-body exercise that's easy to do anywhere, requiring no special equipment and only a few minutes of time. This simple movement gets your heart pumping and uses your arms, legs, and core—all while boosting energy and helping manage stress. For individuals in recovery or anyone seeking quick mental and physical benefits, jumping jacks are an accessible way to add structure, positivity, and a sense of accomplishment to daily life.

Physical and Mental Health Benefits

- **Cardiovascular Boost:** Jumping jacks strengthen your heart and improve circulation.
- **Coordination and Strength:** They work multiple muscle groups, building strength and balance.
- **Calorie Burn:** The aerobic movement burns calories and can aid in managing weight.
- **Natural Mood-Lifter:** Exercise triggers the release of endorphins, reducing stress and boosting mood.
- **Quick Energy:** Just a few minutes of jumping jacks can shake off lethargy and sharpen focus.

Recovery-Specific Benefits

- **Healthy Distraction:** Jumping jacks offer a constructive way to redirect energy and attention when facing cravings or negative thoughts.
- **Routine and Empowerment:** A consistent, short exercise habit builds structure and motivation—key components of recovery success.
- **Craving Relief:** Physical movement helps reduce the urge for old habits by releasing "feel-good" chemicals in the brain.

How To Do Jumping Jacks Safely

1. **Prepare Your Space:** Choose an area where you can move freely. Wear comfortable clothes and supportive shoes.
2. **Warm Up:** Light marching or stretching for 1–2 minutes helps prevent injury.
3. **Perform:** Stand with feet together and arms at your sides. Jump, spread your legs outward while raising your arms overhead. Return to start position. Repeat rhythmically for up to 6 minutes.
4. **Adjust As Needed:** Start with shorter intervals and increase as you get stronger. Slow down or use low-impact options if needed (marching on the spot, side steps, or arm raises while seated).
5. **Cool Down:** End with gentle marching or stretching to relax muscles.

Extra Tips
- Start with a goal of two minutes and build up.
- Use music or set a timer to keep yourself motivated.
- Track your sessions in a journal or app.
- Mix jumping jacks with other light exercises for balance.

Low-impact options—such as step touches or seated arm raises—are great alternatives if jumping is too intense. All these choices make it easy to adapt your routine, whatever your fitness level.

By dedicating just a few minutes to jumping jacks each day, you'll boost your mood, improve cardiovascular health, and give yourself a practical, accessible tool for emotional resilience and daily wellbeing.

Activity 116. Clear your browser cache

My husband is obsessed with clearing his cache, I've just asked him why we should clear our cache and he simply said, 'more storage and more speed!' Clearing your cache is a straightforward yet often overlooked maintenance task that can improve the performance of your devices while offering indirect benefits for mental and physical health. While it might seem like a purely technical chore, the act of clearing cached data can reduce frustration, enhance privacy, and contribute to a sense of control over your digital environment.

Cache is made up of temporary files—images, scripts, and data—saved by browsers, apps, and devices to speed up loading. Over time, these files build up, hogging space and slowing performance. Clearing cache gives devices a fresh start, fixes glitches, speeds up browsing, and can help you feel more in control of digital clutter.

Mental Health

- **Less Frustration:** Quicker browsing and fewer glitches mean less stress and smoother online experiences.
- **Better Privacy:** Removes local records of visited sites—ideal for shared devices or privacy concerns.
- **Clarity and Calm:** Decluttering your device helps reduce overwhelm, just like tidying your physical space.
- **Sense of Control:** Completing small tech tasks fosters organisation and gives a confidence boost.

Physical Health

- **Reduced Screen Fatigue:** Less time troubleshooting means less strain and better focus.
- **Encourages Breaks:** Treat cache-clearing as a prompt to step away from screens and reset.

Step-by-Step Guide

On Most Web Browsers (Chrome, Safari, Firefox):
1. Go to browser "settings" or "preferences."
2. Find "Privacy," "History," or "Clear Browsing Data."
3. Select "Clear Cache" (choose a time range, e.g., last hour or all time).
4. Confirm to clear.

On Mobile:
- **iOS (Safari):** Settings > Safari > Clear History and Website Data.
- **Android (Chrome):** Chrome > Three dots > History > Clear Browsing Data.

On Apps/Other Devices:
- Many apps have a cache-clear option in their settings.
- Smart TVs, streaming devices, or even gaming consoles all benefit from regular cache clearing.

On Computers:
- **Windows:** Use Disk Cleanup.
- **Mac:** Finder > Go > Go to Folder > "~/Library/Caches" > Delete unnecessary files.

Tips for Digital Health

- **Regular Routine:** Clear your cache monthly to keep devices speedy and secure.
- **Declutter Together:** Delete unused apps/files while clearing cache for a deeper clean.
- **Privacy Settings:** Enable automatic cache clearing on browser closure.
- **Screen Breaks:** Combine cache clearing with stepping away for a brief rest.
- **Check Performance:** If issues remain after clearing cache, try restarting your device or tackling larger clean-ups.

Who Benefits?
- **Everyone:** Faster, smoother devices and enhanced privacy.
- **Professionals:** Save time and reduce frustration.
- **Families/Shared Devices:** Maintain privacy for all users.
- **Anyone in Recovery:** Digital decluttering is a mindful, confidence-building task that offers immediate rewards—a small step with positive ripple effects.

Taking a few minutes to clear your cache is a quick win for productivity, privacy, and peace of mind—proving that even tech chores can support emotional health and recovery routines.

Activity 117. Make a list of everything that makes you happy!

A happiness list, your very own "Happy List", is a personal collection of the moments, things, or rituals that never fail to lift your spirits. Think of it as your pocket toolkit for joy: something to turn to when you need a boost, a distraction from cravings, or just a reminder that pleasure can be simple and close at hand.

What's a Happiness List?

It's anything and everything that puts a smile on your face! Write, doodle, cut-and-paste, or snap photos: favourite places, foods, people, songs, smells, silly habits, magical memories...the works. Keep your list in a journal, on your fridge, on sticky notes, or even turn it into a bingo card. No rules—just good vibes.

Why Bother Making One?

Mental Health

- Instantly shifts focus from worries to wins.
- Acts as an easy pick-me-up when you feel low or bored.
- Practises daily gratitude and mindfulness, turning them into habits.
- Builds confidence—look how great you are at finding joy!

Physical Health

- Joyful activities (think dancing, walking, gardening) get you moving and boost those happy chemicals.
- Less stress leads to better sleep, looser muscles, and a stronger immune system.

How To Start

1. Reflect:
What made you laugh out loud this week? Are there tiny routines that bring comfort? Which song always gets you singing? Use your five senses for inspiration: sights, sounds, smells, tastes, and textures that feel good.

2. Explore Categories:
- **Personal Experiences:** Making art, stargazing, people-watching in a café.
- **Relationships:** Catching up with friends, a loving hug, surprise texts.
- **Self-Care:** Bubble baths, comfy pyjamas, meditation.
- **Sensory Pleasures:** Chocolate, rain tapping on windows, soft scarves.
- **Achievements:** Finishing a book, learning a new trick, nailing a recipe.
- **Simple Joys:** Sunset walks, funny animal videos, that old photo album.

3. Write It Down:
Go specific: not just "music," but "dancing to Queen in the kitchen"; not just "tea," but "peppermint tea in a sunny window."

4. Make It Visual:
Draw it, collage old magazines, set up a "Happiness Bingo," or fill a decorated jar with little slips recording happy moments as they happen.

Keep It Playful
- Update your list as tastes change or new discoveries roll in.
- Challenge yourself: try a new "happy" once a week.
- Compare lists with trusted pals or family—extra inspiration, no comparing allowed!
- Label items by time: "5-minute boosts," "rainy afternoon fun," "outdoor adventures."
- Use prompts: "What did I love as a child?" or "What's my weirdest happy?"

Creative Twists
- Pretend each day is a happiness scavenger hunt—can you spot something from your list?
- Make seasonal mini-lists: cocoa by the fire in winter, picnics in summer sun.
- Imagine a magical bag and list out everything you'd pack for instant comfort.

A happiness list isn't just fluff—it's a genuine self-care tool, a resource for recovery, and a nudge to seek joy in the little (and big) things. Life can be tough, but collecting and savouring sparks of happiness—one by one—makes everything lighter, brighter, and a bit more magical.

Activity 118. Create a quick salad

Salad can sound boring, but what things do you like? You don't have to just have lettuce and tomatoes. I love pickled red cabbage and would have it with everything! (Except puddings!!) So, I researched the health benefits and it turns out, it is good for a load of things. It is rich in antioxidants, it helps reduce inflammation and supports heart health. The pickling process introduces beneficial probiotics that aid digestion, while the vegetable's high fibre content promotes gut health. Pickled red cabbage is also a good source of vitamins C and K, and contains various minerals. What do you love to eat that will make more salads more interesting? Oh and I always have strawberries in my salad, they really enhance the flavour, try it they good perfectly!

Here are some simple ideas for creating quick salads that are particularly beneficial for people who have given up alcohol:

Detoxifying Green Salad	Protein-Packed Chickpea Salad
- Mixed leafy greens (spinach, kale, arugula) - Cucumber slices - Avocado chunks - Lemon juice dressing - Sprinkle of chia seeds This salad is rich in antioxidants and helps support liver function.	- Canned chickpeas, rinsed - Cherry tomatoes, halved - Diced red onion - Chopped parsley - Olive oil and lemon dressing High in protein and fibre, this salad helps stabilise blood sugar levels.
Hydrating Watermelon Feta Salad	B-Vitamin Boost Salad
- Cubed watermelon - Crumbled feta cheese - Fresh mint leaves - Balsamic glaze drizzle Watermelon is excellent for hydration, while the electrolytes in feta can help balance minerals.	- Quinoa, cooked and cooled - Roasted sweet potato cubes - Chopped walnuts - Baby spinach - Honey mustard dressing This salad is rich in B-vitamins, which are often depleted by alcohol consumption.

Here's a simple recipe for making olive oil and lemon dressing:

Ingredients

- 1/4 cup extra virgin olive oil
- 2 tablespoons fresh lemon juice
- 1 teaspoon Dijon mustard (optional)
- 1/2 teaspoon honey (optional)
- Salt and freshly ground black pepper to taste

Instructions

1. Combine Ingredients in a small bowl, whisk together the lemon juice, Dijon mustard (if using), and honey (if using).

2. Slowly drizzle in the olive oil while whisking constantly. This creates an emulsion, helping the dressing stay mixed.

3. Add salt and freshly ground black pepper to taste. Start with a pinch of each and adjust as needed.

4. Taste the dressing and adjust the flavours if necessary. You may want to add more lemon juice for acidity or honey for sweetness.

5. Use immediately or store in an airtight container in the refrigerator for up to a week.

This versatile dressing pairs well with a variety of salads and can also be used as a marinade for vegetables or proteins.

Activity 119. Plan a random act of kindness

A random act of kindness is an unexpected gesture performed to brighten someone's day without expecting anything in return. These acts can be as simple as holding the door open for someone or as thoughtful as sending flowers to a friend. They are rooted in generosity and compassion, aiming to spread positivity and joy. The beauty of such acts lies in their spontaneity and the ripple effect they create—encouraging others to pass on kindness. I am going on holiday next week and I have donated my HelloFresh box to someone who really needs it, as I will be fed well.

Random acts of kindness have profound benefits for both mental and physical health. Research shows that performing kind gestures releases feel-good chemicals like dopamine, serotonin, and oxytocin, which reduce stress, anxiety, and depression while boosting happiness levels. This phenomenon, often called the "helper's high," fosters a sense of purpose and connection, improving overall emotional wellbeing.

On a physical level, kindness can lower blood pressure and promote heart health by reducing cortisol (the stress hormone). Regularly engaging in kind acts has even been linked to increased physical activity and healthier lifestyle choices. Furthermore, witnessing or receiving kindness strengthens community bonds, creating an environment of trust and support.

Planning a random act of kindness involves four simple steps:

1. Choose Your Act
Select an act that resonates with you or aligns with your interests. Here are some ideas:
- For strangers: Pay for someone's coffee, leave positive sticky notes in public places, or help carry groceries.
- In your community: Volunteer at an animal shelter or donate books to a local library.
- At work or school: Write encouraging notes for colleagues or bring treats to share.
- For friends and family: Cook a meal for someone stressed or send a heartfelt letter expressing gratitude.

2. Prepare Materials (I have put this to give you ideas)
Gather the necessary items for your chosen act:
- Sticky notes and pens for leaving messages.
- Money or items for donations.
- Tools if helping with chores or yard work.

Preparation ensures your act goes smoothly and maximises its impact.

3. Pick a Time and Place
Decide where and when you'll perform your act:
- During routine activities like commuting or running errands.

- At work, school, or within your neighbourhood.

Timing is key—choose moments when your gesture will be most appreciated.

4. Execute Your Plan

Carry out your act with sincerity and enthusiasm. Whether it's helping someone shovel snow or surprising a colleague with coffee, approach it with genuine care. Remember, the goal is to spread positivity without seeking recognition.

Kindness doesn't just benefit the giver—it creates a ripple effect. Studies show that recipients of kind acts are more likely to pay it forward. This cycle builds stronger communities by fostering cooperation, trust, and goodwill.

Moreover, practicing kindness regularly can become habit-forming. Incorporate small gestures into your daily routine—complimenting strangers, volunteering time, or simply smiling at others—and watch how it transforms your outlook on life.

Planning random acts of kindness is more than just an altruistic endeavour; it's a powerful tool for enhancing mental and physical wellbeing. By spreading joy through thoughtful gestures, you not only uplift others but also cultivate happiness within yourself. So why not challenge yourself today? Start small—leave an encouraging note or help a neighbour—and embrace the transformative power of kindness in your life!

Activity 120. Start a compost bin - even without a garden

Composting is the process of recycling organic waste—such as food scraps and yard trimmings—into nutrient-rich soil that can be used to nourish plants. It's an eco-friendly practice that helps reduce landfill waste, cut greenhouse gas emissions, and create valuable compost for gardening or houseplants. Even if you don't have a garden, composting is still possible and beneficial, thanks to indoor methods like bokashi systems, worm farms, or small-scale bins. Composting offers surprising benefits for both mental and physical. Here's how:

Mental Wellbeing: Composting connects us to nature, fostering mindfulness and a sense of purpose. Watching food scraps transform into rich soil can be deeply rewarding, reminding us of the cycles of life and renewal. It's also a way to practice sustainability, which can boost feelings of accomplishment and environmental stewardship.

Physical Wellbeing: Handling compost materials often involves light physical activity, such as turning the pile or collecting scraps, which keeps you active. Composting also contributes to healthier living environments by reducing waste that would otherwise attract pests or produce unpleasant odours in landfills. Additionally, using compost for houseplants or community gardens can improve air quality and create greener spaces that promote relaxation.

Starting a compost bin is simple and adaptable to any living situation. Follow these steps:

1. **Choose Your Bin**
Select a bin based on your space:
    - For outdoor spaces: Enclosed plastic bins or tumbling bins are great for small yards, while open heaps work well for larger areas.
    - For apartments or small spaces: Bokashi buckets, worm farms, or indoor compost bins are ideal options.

2. **Select a Location**
Find the best spot for your bin:
    - Outdoors: Choose a flat, well-drained area that's semi-shaded to prevent drying out. Keep it accessible but away from your house or neighbour's fence.
    - Indoors: Place your bin in a convenient location like under the sink or on a balcony (if available). Ensure it's airtight to avoid odours.

3. **Set Up Your Bin**
Prepare your compost bin with these steps:
    - Start with a layer of twigs or straw at the bottom for drainage (if outdoors).
    - Add alternating layers of green (nitrogen-rich) and brown (carbon-rich) materials in a 2:1 ratio.

- Sprinkle water between layers to maintain moisture, your pile should feel like a damp sponge but not soggy.
- Top with soil or finished compost to activate decomposition by introducing microorganisms.

4. Add Compost Materials

Here's what you can add - Green materials: Fruit/vegetable scraps, coffee grounds, grass clippings, fresh plant trimmings. Avoid adding meat, dairy, oily foods, or synthetic materials unless using specialised systems like bokashi bins that can handle these items. Brown materials: Dry leaves, straw, shredded paper/cardboard, wood chips.

Even without outdoor space, you can still compost effectively using indoor methods:

Bokashi Composting

Bokashi is an anaerobic fermentation method ideal for apartments:
1. Use an airtight bokashi bucket or make one with two sealed containers.
2. Add food scraps (incl meat/dairy) in layers, sprinkling bokashi bran after each addition.
3. Seal the bucket tightly and let it ferment for two weeks. Drain the liquid regularly—it makes an excellent fertilizer for houseplants or cleaner for drains!
4. After fermentation, bury the pre-composted waste in soil-filled containers for further decomposition.

Indoor Compost Bin

1. Create a small-scale compost bin at home:
2. Use a plastic container with a lid as your bin. Line the bottom with shredded paper or cardboard for aeration.
3. Add food scraps and cover with soil/wood chips after each addition to minimise odours.
4. Stir or shake the mixture every few days to aerate it.
5. In about four weeks, you'll have nutrient-rich compost for houseplants.

Compost Pick-Up Services

Many cities offer residential compost pick-up programs:
1. Collect food scraps in an airtight countertop container.
2. Schedule regular pick-ups through local services (weekly or bi-weekly). This option is convenient but may involve fees.

If home composting isn't feasible, look into community options like community gardens, or municipal drop-off locations often accept food scraps.

Starting a compost bin—whether outdoors or indoors—is an empowering way to reduce waste while contributing to sustainability and personal wellbeing. By turning organic waste into valuable compost, you're helping the planet while enjoying mental clarity and physical activity in the process! Whether you have a sprawling garden or live in an apartment, there's always a way to compost—and every effort makes a difference!

Activity 121. Try Pointillism art

Pointillism is an artistic technique that involves creating images using small, distinct dots of pure colour. Developed in the late 19th century by Georges Seurat and Paul Signac, this method is rooted in Neo-Impressionism and relies on the science of optical blending—where the viewer's eye merges individual dots into cohesive shapes and colours when viewed from a distance. Unlike traditional painting, where colours are mixed on a palette, pointillism uses juxtaposed dots to achieve vibrant tones and subtle gradients directly on the canvas. Ione of my tattoos is actually pointillism art and I absolutely love it! Engaging in pointillism offers therapeutic benefits for both mental and physical health:

Mental Wellbeing

- The repetitive process of applying dots promotes mindfulness and relaxation.
- It activates the parasympathetic nervous system, reducing stress, anxiety, and intrusive thoughts.
- The meditative nature of pointillism encourages focus, helping individuals find calm and achieve a state of creative flow.

Physical Wellbeing

- Creating pointillist art involves fine motor skills, which can improve hand-eye coordination.
- The slow, deliberate movements required for this technique also foster patience and concentration, contributing to overall cognitive health.

Moreover, completing a pointillist artwork can boost self-esteem and provide a sense of accomplishment, making it particularly beneficial for those struggling with emotional distress or low confidence.

To begin your journey into pointillism, gather the following supplies:
- Canvas or paper
- Acrylic or oil paints (acrylics are recommended for beginners due to faster drying times)
- Fine-tipped round brushes or tools like Q-tips, toothpicks, or markers
- Palette for mixing colours
- Optional: Easel and good lighting to enhance your workspace.

Step-by-Step Guide

1. Choose Your Subject
Select a simple subject for your first attempt—such as fruit, flowers, or basic landscapes. Lightly sketch it on your canvas to serve as a guide.

2. Plan Your Colour Palette
Start with primary colours (red, blue, yellow) and white. Use complementary colours (e.g., red and green) to create vibrant contrasts through optical blending.

3. Apply Initial Dots - Begin with one colour at a time:
- Use fine-tipped brushes or tools to place small dots on your canvas.
- Dots should be denser in areas of intense colour and spaced in transitional zones.

4. Layer Colours for Depth - Build up layers by adding dots of different colours:
- Combine yellow and blue dots to create green, or red and yellow dots for orange.
- Overlap dots slightly to achieve smoother transitions between hues.

5. Refine Texture and Light - Adjust dot size and density to create texture:
- Small, denser dots produce smooth areas; large dots spaced apart create rough textures.
- Add lighter dots for highlights and darker ones for shadows for depth and light effects.

6. Complete Your Artwork - Step back frequently to assess your progress from afar. The image will look more cohesive at a distance. Add final details with white or light-coloured dots until you're satisfied with the result.

Pointillism isn't limited to traditional mediums; digital tools offer exciting possibilities:

Digital Techniques

Software like Photoshop, GIMP or Procreate allows artists to replicate pointillism effects:
- Adjust brush settings for dot size and opacity.
- Layer colours digitally to mimic optical blending.
- Experiment with undo functions for easy corrections.

Advantages of Digital Pointillism
- Accessible for beginners without costly materials.
- Timesaving compared to manual methods.
- Encourages experimentation with colours and patterns.

Whether traditional or digital, pointillism invites creativity while fostering mindfulness, a perfect blend of art and wellbeing! It is more than just an art technique; it's a meditative practice that combines creativity with therapeutic benefits. By focusing on individual dots to form intricate images, you can experience relaxation, improve concentration, and express emotions in unique ways. Whether you're painting on canvas or exploring digital platforms, pointillism offers endless possibilities for artistic growth and personal fulfilment! Start small today and discover the joy hidden in every dot!

Activity 122. Make a solar oven

A solar oven is a delightful DIY gadget that turns sunshine into a source of delicious food. Building and using one is a mindful, creative, and eco-friendly project, perfect for anyone in recovery or simply looking to boost wellbeing, learn new skills, and have some fun outdoors.

Why Try It?

- **Mental and Emotional Wellbeing:**
  Brings focus and calm, provides a sense of accomplishment, and serves as a mindful, constructive distraction from cravings or stress.
- **Physical Health:**
  Safe (no flames), promotes healthier eating, gets you moving, and gives a welcome dose of vitamin D!
- **Eco-Friendly:**
  Uses only solar energy, teaching sustainable habits with a tangible, tasty reward.
- **Community:**
  Perfectly shareable—invite friends or family to join the experiment and enjoy your sun-powered creations together.

What You'll Need

- Large cardboard (pizza) box
- Aluminium foil
- Black construction paper/card
- Clear plastic wrap/cling film
- Tape (clear or duct)
- Scissors/box cutter
- Ruler
- Stick/skewer (to prop open flap)

How To Build It

1. **Cut the Flap:** Draw a square on the top of the box lid, 2.5 cm/1 inch from three sides. Cut along these lines, leaving one edge attached for a flap.

2. **Line With Foil:** Cover the inside of the flap and the base of the box with foil (shiny side up), taping it smooth.

3. **Plastic Window:** Tape plastic wrap tightly over the opening in the lid (double layer if possible) for an airtight seal.

4. **Add Absorber:** Place black paper/card flat on the bottom inside the box.

5. **Set Up:** Close the lid, keep the plastic window taut, and prop the flap open with your stick so it faces the sun. Sit the oven in strong sunlight and preheat for 30 minutes.

How To Use

- Use lightweight, dark baking trays or foil pans.
- Cooking takes 30 minutes to 2 hours—be patient, and peek as little as possible to retain heat.
- Caution with hot steam, but boxes don't usually get burn-hot.

Solar Recipes

S'mores: Layer graham crackers or digestives, a marshmallow, and a piece of chocolate in a foil pan. Place in oven; wait 30–60 mins till gooey.

English Muffin Pizza: Split muffins, top with sauce, cheese, extras. Bake in pan for 40–50 mins till melty and crisp.

Breakfast Frittata: Whisk eggs, splash of milk, chopped veg, and cheese—season to taste. Pour into oiled dish or foil pan, bake 35–60 mins until set.

Solar Lasagna: Layer sauce, noodles, ricotta, and cheese in a baking dish. Repeat if space allows. Bake 90+ mins until hot and bubbling.

Roasted Cauliflower & Chickpeas: Mix cauliflower florets, rinsed chickpeas, olives, garlic, olive oil, and seasoning. Spread in dish, roast about 1 hour, shake midway.

Nachos: Spread chips in pan, cover with cheese and toppings, bake 20–30 mins until cheese is gooey.

Tips & Extras
- Don't open the oven too often—heat escapes!
- Decorate your solar oven and make it yours.
- Try the activity with others and compare results.
- Enjoy the process: sunbathing, reading, or chatting while your meal cooks.

A solar oven is more than a kitchen project—it's about connection, creativity, and harnessing nature's power in a positive, mindful way. Enjoy experimenting, savour every sun-cooked treat, and celebrate each small success in your journey.

Activity 123. Research local attractions

Researching local attractions involves exploring the landmarks, activities, and cultural experiences available in your area. Whether you're a resident or a visitor, this process helps you uncover popular destinations, hidden gems, and unique events that define the character of your community. From historical sites and museums to parks and festivals, local attractions provide opportunities for entertainment, education, and connection with your surroundings.

I felt really down a few weeks ago, I had been sat at my laptop for far too many hours and my husband said, 'Pick somewhere, anywhere and we will go out for the day, anywhere you want!' I thought about it and had a little Google and said 'The Big Pit Coal Mine' (It's a museum, a former working coal mine located in Blaenavon in South Wales). He looked at me daft, 'I've offered to take you anywhere and you want to go down a coal mine' and I said 'Yeap!' It was only 15 miles down the road and what a brilliant day we had. I also brought a book on the women and children who worked down the coal mines and whoa, I can not find the words for their fight for food and family survival!

- **Mental Wellbeing**: Exploring the mine and learning about the lives of miners (and the horses!) fosters appreciation for history and human resilience. The immersive tours encourage mindfulness as visitors focus on their surroundings and the stories shared by guides.
- **Physical Wellbeing**: The underground tour involves walking through tunnels, engaging visitors in light physical activity. Experiencing the environment where miners worked promotes gratitude and reflection, enhancing emotional health. Additionally, the surrounding Blaenavon landscape offers opportunities for outdoor exploration which is just beautiful, which can boost mood and energy levels.

We can all do this and do not have to go far, the coal museum was free. In general, exploring local attractions offers numerous benefits:

- **Mental Wellbeing**: Discovering new places stimulates curiosity and creativity. It encourages mindfulness as you engage with your environment, helping you focus on the present moment. Visiting cultural or natural sites can also reduce stress by providing a sense of escape and relaxation.
- **Physical Wellbeing**: Many local attractions involve physical activity, such as walking tours, hiking trails, or outdoor festivals. These activities promote cardiovascular health, improve stamina, and boost energy levels. Additionally, spending time outdoors enhances mood by increasing exposure to sunlight and fresh air.

Researching attractions also fosters social connections by encouraging participation in community events or interactions with locals. This sense of belonging can significantly improve emotional resilience and overall happiness.

Online Resources

The internet is a powerful tool for discovering attractions:

1. TripAdvisor: Browse top-rated destinations and read user reviews for honest insights into local experiences.
2. Tourism Board Websites: Visit your city's official tourism site for comprehensive lists of attractions, events, and seasonal activities.
3. Social Media Platforms: Use Instagram location tags or Pinterest boards to find visually appealing spots and hidden gems. Facebook events near you is also a great resource.
4. Travel Blogs: Search for bloggers who have visited your area. They often share personal experiences and insider tips that go beyond mainstream recommendations.

Local Connections

Engaging with the community can reveal authentic experiences:

1. Community Events: Attend festivals, farmers' markets, or cultural gatherings to discover attractions while immersing yourself in local traditions.
2. Talk to Residents: Strike up conversations with locals at cafes or shops—they often know the best spots that aren't listed online!
3. Local Businesses: Staff at restaurants or boutiques can offer valuable recommendations tailored to your interests.

Specialised Platforms

Explore unique experiences through niche platforms:

1. AirBnB Experiences: Discover tours and workshops hosted by individuals passionate about their city.
2. Withlocals: Connect with local hosts offering personalized activities like cooking classes or guided walks.

Off-the-Beaten-Path Exploration

Sometimes the best discoveries happen spontaneously:
1. Venture into neighbourhoods outside tourist districts to uncover hidden treasures like street art or independent galleries.
2. Follow curiosity and wander through parks or alleys that catch your eye (be careful, not that should have to even say this, but please use your discretion).

3. Research niche interests like historical landmarks or specialty museums tailored to your hobbies.

Utilise Podcasts for Local Insights

Podcasts are an excellent way to learn about attractions before visiting:
1. Search podcast platforms like Spotify or Apple Podcasts using keywords like "travel" + your destination name.
2. Explore podcasts produced by tourism boards or local media—they often provide insider knowledge.
3. Check travel blogs—many bloggers create podcasts sharing their experiences in specific locations.

Apps for Location-Based Exploration

- TrailTale: is a free app focused entirely on Great Britain. It offers self-guided walking tours and trails across cities, towns, and villages throughout the UK. It includes historical insights, fun facts, and even trivia about famous filming locations like those from Harry Potter.
- Places and Trails: This app specialises in GPS-triggered self-guided tours across England and Wales. It features walking, cycling, and driving trails with insights from local experts.
- Tourist Walks: provides GPS-guided audio tours for various UK cities. The app includes offline maps and audio commentary tailored to famous landmarks and hidden gems.

These apps are excellent for exploring attractions in the UK!

Tips for Success

- Keep an open mind, as lesser-known attractions often provide the most memorable experiences.
- Plan visits during off-peak hours to avoid crowds and enjoy a more relaxed atmosphere.
- Combine multiple resources (online tools, local advice, specialised platforms) for a well-rounded exploration.

Researching local attractions is more than just planning outings, it's an opportunity to connect with your surroundings while enhancing mental clarity and physical vitality. By combining online tools, community engagement, and spontaneous exploration, you can uncover a wealth of experiences that enrich your life and deepen your appreciation for the world around you. So start today, whether it's discovering a new park, attending a local festival or heading down a coal mine and embrace the joy of exploration!

Activity 124. Create a travel emergency kit or one for your home, you never know when you might need it!

Create a emergency travel kit, ready for your travels or for your household as you never know when you might need it. It is a compact collection of all essential supplies designed to address minor injuries, illnesses, and unexpected situations. It serves as a portable first aid resource, ensuring you're equipped to handle emergencies while traveling. Whether you're on a road trip, on a couch, flying abroad, or exploring remote destinations, having a well-stocked kit can make all the difference in staying safe and comfortable.

Creating and carrying a travel emergency kit offers numerous benefits for both mental and physical health:

- **Mental Wellbeing:** Knowing you're prepared for emergencies provides peace of mind and reduces anxiety, especially in unfamiliar environments. It fosters confidence, allowing you to focus on enjoying your trip rather than worrying about potential issues.
- **Physical Wellbeing:** A travel emergency kit ensures immediate access to supplies for treating minor injuries, illnesses, or discomforts. Quick responses to ailments like cuts, burns, or allergic reactions can prevent complications and promote faster healing. Additionally, items like sunscreen and insect repellent protect against environmental risks, contributing to overall health during travel.

How to Create a Travel Emergency Kit

Step 1: Choose the Right Container - Select a durable, water-resistant container that's easy to carry. A small zip-up bags or hard-shell box work well and label it clearly as "Emergency Kit" for quick identification.

Step 2: Pack Essential First Aid Items - Include basic supplies for treating minor injuries:
- Bandages (assorted sizes)
- Gauze pads and rolls
- Adhesive tape
- Scissors (check airline regulations)
- Antiseptic wipes
- Antibiotic ointment
- Tweezers
- Disposable gloves

Step 3: Add Medications - Pack medications for common travel ailments:
- Pain relievers (e.g., acetaminophen or ibuprofen)
- Antihistamines for allergies
- Antacids for indigestion
- Anti-diarrheal medicine

- Motion sickness medication
- Any prescription medications specific to your needs

Step 4: Include Travel-Specific Items - Prepare for environmental factors:
- Hand sanitizer
- Insect repellent
- Sunscreen (SPF 30 or higher)
- Aloe gel for sunburn relief
- Rehydration salts for dehydration

Step 5: Tailor to Your Destination - Consider location-specific needs:
- Malaria prevention medication for tropical regions.
- Cold-weather gear like heat packs if traveling to snowy areas.

Step 6: Include important information in your kit such as a list of current medications and allergies, emergency contact details and copies of your health insurance card or travel insurance policy.

Conduct a thorough inspection/annual review once a year:
1. Check expiration dates on medications and supplies.
2. Replace expired or damaged items promptly.
3. Clean the container to remove dust or debris.
4. Document the review date for future reference.

Pre-Trip check before every trip to verify that all items are in good condition and haven't expired since your last check, plus add destination-specific supplies based on weather, activities, or health risks. Post-Emergency restock after using any item from your kit during an emergency, replace it immediately so the kit remains fully stocked.

Some items require more frequent updates than others:
1. Bandages and adhesives: Replace every 3–5 years or sooner if they lose adhesiveness.
2. Medications: Check expiration dates regularly; replace as needed.
3. Sterile items: Replace immediately if packaging is damaged, even if not expired.

Benefits of having an emergency kit include having peace of mind, saving money and the ability to react quickly to emergencies. It is an essential step toward ensuring safety and wellbeing during travel, whether you're exploring bustling cities or remote landscapes, this small investment in preparedness can make all the difference in enjoying your travels with confidence and peace of mind!

Activity 125. Practice cloud watching and imagination

Cloud watching is the simple art of lying back, observing clouds drifting by, and using imagination to find shapes or invent stories inspired by what you see. This creative, mindful activity needs nothing but a good view of the sky and a playful spirit—it's accessible, low-cost, and brings you closer to nature, with no tools required!

Benefits

- **Reduces Stress:** The slow movement of clouds soothes the mind, much like meditation.
- **Lifts Mood:** The beauty and wonder of cloud shapes create joy and contentment.
- **Boosts Creativity:** Finding animals or crafting stories from cloud shapes sparks creative thinking.
- **Enhances Mindfulness:** Cloud watching helps you stay present and aware of your surroundings.
- **Builds Resilience:** Playful imagination fosters a positive mindset.
- **Mental Agility:** Interpreting what you see exercises flexible thinking and memory.

How To Cloud Watch

1. **Find Your Spot:** Choose a spot with a clear sky view—park, garden, or beach—and get comfortable.
2. **Observe:** Focus on the clouds' shapes, colours, and how they move. Let your thoughts drift, noticing patterns or stories.
3. **Use Imagination:** Spot animals or objects in the clouds, or invent stories about cloud adventures.
4. **Repeat Regularly:** Make it a regular mindful habit, even for a few minutes a day.
5. **Try Closing Your Eyes:** Afterwards, imagine scenes based on the clouds you saw to boost visualization skills.
6. **Combine with Meditation:** Pair with deep breathing for extra relaxation and mental clarity.

Cloud Types to Spot

- **Cirrus:** High, wispy streaks; fair weather, change coming.
- **Cumulus:** Puffy, cotton-like; usually fair weather, can bring storms if they grow tall.
- **Stratus:** Low, flat layers; often grey and bring drizzle (very UK!).

Unique & Striking Formations

- **Nacreous:** Iridescent "mother-of-pearl" clouds at dawn/dusk.
- **Mammatus:** Bulging, pouch-like under storm clouds.
- **Lenticular:** Smooth, lens-shaped, often near hills.

- **Noctilucent:** Night-visible, glowing high clouds.
- **Kelvin-Helmholtz, Undulatus Asperatus, Roll, Fallstreak Hole:** Rare, striking cloud forms for the keen observer.
- **Iridescence, Pileus, Actinoform:** Rainbow effects, "cap" clouds, or large patterns.

Make It More Fun
- Take photos or create art and stories inspired by the clouds.
- Play guessing games—who finds the funniest shape?
- Try it at different times of day for dramatic light effects.
- Go barefoot outside for a deeper sensory experience.

Practicing cloud watching and imagination is an enriching way to connect with nature while nurturing creativity and calmness within yourself. This simple yet profound activity invites you to slow down, appreciate life's beauty, and let your imagination soar all while reaping mental health benefits like reduced stress and enhanced mindfulness. So next time you see fluffy white clouds floating overhead, take a moment to pause, look up, and let your mind wander, you might just discover something magical!

Go on have a look out the window or for the ultimate go outside, take your shoes off, feel the ground below your feet and find those beauties in the sky!

Activity 126. Solve a riddle

Solving riddles is a fun and brain-boosting activity, well for some. A riddle is a type of puzzle or question that requires creative thinking and problem-solving to uncover the answer. Often presented as clever wordplay, riddles challenge the mind by combining logic, imagination, and linguistic skills. They can range from simple and humorous to complex and thought-provoking, making them a versatile and enjoyable mental exercise for people of all ages.

Engaging with riddles offers numerous benefits for both mental and emotional health:

Mental Benefits
- Enhances Critical Thinking: Riddles require analysing clues, thinking logically, and finding creative solutions, which strengthens critical thinking skills.
- Improves Problem-Solving: By identifying problems and exploring different approaches, riddles enhance your ability to solve challenges in everyday life.
- Boosts Creativity: Riddles encourage out-of-the-box thinking, fostering imagination and expanding your ability to approach problems unconventionally.
- Strengthens Memory and Concentration: Solving riddles requires focus and attention to detail, improving memory retention and concentration over time.
- Develops Flexible Thinking: Many riddles involve wordplay or twists that challenge you to consider alternative perspectives, promoting adaptability in thought processes.
- Stimulates Brain Activity: Riddles engage both the logical (left) and creative (right) sides of the brain, increasing cognitive function and mental sharpness.

Emotional Benefits
- Boosts Confidence: Successfully solving a riddle provides a sense of accomplishment that builds self-esteem and confidence in your problem-solving abilities.
- Provides Enjoyment: The playful nature of riddles makes them a fun activity that can lift your mood and reduce stress levels.

How to Solve Riddles Effectively

Step 1: Read Carefully - Pay close attention to the wording of the riddle, as it often contains subtle clues or wordplay that guide you toward the answer.

Step 2: Break It Down - Divide the riddle into smaller parts to analyse each segment individually. This helps you identify patterns or hidden meanings more easily.

Step 3: Think Creatively - Riddles often require unconventional thinking, so consider metaphors, puns, or double meanings to uncover the solution.

Step 4: Visualise Scenarios - For riddles involving objects or situations, try visualising the scene in your mind to better understand the context or relationships between elements.

Step 5: Take Your Time - Don't rush, solving riddles is about enjoying the process as much as finding the answer. If you're stuck, step away for a moment and revisit it later with fresh eyes.

Step 6: Practice Regularly - The more riddles you solve, the better you'll become at recognizing patterns, interpreting clues, and thinking creatively. Here are some fun examples:

1. What has to be broken before you can use it?
2. I'm tall when I'm young, and I'm short when I'm old. What am I?
3. What is full of holes but still holds water?
4. What has hands but can't clap?
5. What has a head and a tail but no body?
6. I have cities but no houses, mountains but no trees, water but no fish. What am I?
7. What comes once in a minute, twice in a moment, but never in a thousand years?
8. I'm not a blanket yet I cover the ground; a crystal from heaven that doesn't make a sound. What am I?
9. What gets bigger the more you take away?
10. What has many teeth but can't bite?

Take your time, they are designed to challenge your brain while providing entertainment!

Tips for Incorporating Riddles Into Your Routine:
- Daily Challenge: Solve one riddle every day as part of your morning routine to kickstart your brain activity.
- Family Fun: Share riddles with family members or friends during meals or gatherings for interactive entertainment.
- Creative Writing: Use riddles as inspiration for crafting stories or poems that incorporate clever wordplay.
- Educational Games: Incorporate riddles into classroom activities or learning sessions to make problem-solving fun for kids.

Solving riddles is more than just an enjoyable pastime, it's a powerful way to sharpen your mind, boost creativity, and improve problem-solving skills while having fun! Whether you're tackling classic brainteasers or crafting your own clever puzzles, this activity encourages mental agility while providing moments of joy and accomplishment. So, grab a riddle today, challenge yourself, and let your imagination take centre stage!

Activity 127. Take macro photos of nature

Macro photography is a technique that involves taking close-up images of small subjects, revealing intricate details that are often invisible to the naked eye. In nature, this style of photography focuses on subjects like flowers, insects, water droplets, and plant textures, showcasing their beauty at a miniature scale. By magnifying these elements, macro photography transforms everyday objects into extraordinary works of art, allowing viewers to appreciate the hidden intricacies of the natural world.

Common Subjects in Macro Nature Photography include: delicate petal textures and intricate centres like stamens and pistils. Capturing the eyes of insects, wing patterns, fine hairs, and iridescent exoskeletons. Showcasing surface tension and reflections on grass blades or leaves and revealing leaf veins, spiralling fern fronds and bark textures.

Macro photography offers several benefits for mental and emotional health:

- Encourages Mindfulness: Observing minute details in nature fosters a sense of presence and appreciation for the world around you.
- Boosts Creativity: Experimenting with angles, lighting, and compositions stimulates creative thinking and artistic expression.
- Reduces Stress: Immersing yourself in nature while focusing on photography can be calming and meditative, helping to lower anxiety levels.
- Promotes Curiosity: Exploring the hidden beauty of plants or insects sparks curiosity and wonder about the natural world.
- Encourages Outdoor Activity: Macro photography often involves walking in parks or gardens to find subjects, promoting physical movement and fresh air exposure.
- Improves Focus and Patience: The careful process of capturing detailed shots helps develop concentration and patience over time.

What You'll Need

- A smartphone (or camera)
- A simple clip-on macro lens for your phone (optional, but makes details clearer)

How to Get Started

1. **Pick Your Subject:**
   Look for small things outside—petals on flowers, bugs on leaves, raindrops on grass, or interesting plant patterns.
2. **Get Close, But Not Too Close:**
   Move your phone or lens about 2–7 cm from the subject. Slow, gentle movement helps you find sharp focus.

3. **Use Good Light:**
   Natural light is best. Early morning or late afternoon works well; avoid harsh midday sun.
4. **Steady Your Shot:**
   Rest your phone (or hands) on something solid—a wall, your knee, or use a tripod. Press the shutter with a timer or headphones to avoid blurriness.
5. **Try Different Angles:**
   Take photos from above, below, or the side to find new perspectives.
6. **Focus on the Details:**
   Tap your phone screen on the main part of your subject to improve focus. Don't use digital zoom—just move closer instead.
7. **Play With Composition:**
   Put interesting shapes or patterns in the centre or off to the side of your shot. Let some parts blur for an artistic effect.

Why Try Macro Photography?

- Encourages *mindfulness*—you notice and appreciate the world around you.
- *Boosts creativity* and curiosity about plants and creatures.
- The slow, careful process is calming and relaxing.
- Exploring outdoors helps you move and get fresh air.

Helpful Tips

- Practice lots—you'll get better at spotting cool details.
- Parks, gardens, or even your own backyard offer endless subjects.
- Learning what you photograph (like flower parts or bug types) makes the experience richer.

By looking closer at nature through macro photography, anyone can discover surprising beauty and enjoy a relaxing, creative hobby—even with just a phone and a little patience.

Macro photography is more than just capturing close-up images, it's an invitation to explore the intricate beauty hidden in nature's smallest details. By engaging in this art form, you can cultivate mindfulness, boost creativity, and deepen your connection with the natural world while enjoying its therapeutic benefits for mental wellbeing. So, grab your smartphone or camera today and start discovering the extraordinary within the ordinary!

Activity 128. Update your CV

Updating your CV shouldn't feel intimidating, but for many, it brings up stress—especially if you haven't checked it in a while. As a former Virtual Assistant, I've helped countless friends and clients in a last-minute panic after a job interview, desperately trying to recall job dates and achievements. The best way to avoid that scramble? Make your CV a living document: something you update regularly so you're always ready for new opportunities, less anxious, and proud to put your best foot forward.

Why Keeping Your CV Fresh Matters
- **Ready for Opportunities:** Employers, recruiters, or even chance encounters can happen anytime. An up-to-date CV means you're ready to go.
- **Boosts Confidence:** Reflecting on your skills, growth, and successes reminds you how far you've come—and reminds you that you *do* have a lot to offer.
- **Reduces Last-Minute Panic:** No more digging through old emails or guessing employment dates—everything is there, accurate and ready.
- **Supports Reflection and Goal Setting:** Noticing your progress can help clarify what's next for your career, and highlight what you've done well

Step-by-Step: Writing and Updating Your CV
1. Start With the Basics
- Use your full name and add a LinkedIn profile or portfolio link if you have one.
- Triple-check your phone number and email for typos.
- Make sure your voicemail and email address sound professional.

2. Write a Personal Statement
- Think of this as your elevator pitch, a short paragraph (3–5 lines) at the top.
- Clearly state who you are, what you do, and your career goals or specialism.
- Example: "Detail-oriented admin professional with 6+ years' experience supporting busy teams. Skilled in schedule management, project delivery, and customer relations. Now seeking a new challenge in creative industries."

3. Work Experience—Show Off
- List jobs (with job title, employer, and years).
- Start with the most recent and work backwards.
- For each job, add a few bullet points about your achievements—don't just list duties.
    - Begin each point with a strong verb: managed, created, improved, delivered, supported, implemented.
    - Where possible, add numbers and results: "Increased sales by 18%," "Coordinated schedules for a team of 20+ staff."
- Focus on achievements, not just tasks.

4. **Skills Section—Highlight Your Value**
   - Include both technical (e.g., Excel, social media management, bookkeeping) and personal skills (e.g., teamwork, problem-solving, organisation).
   - Tailor this section for the role you want. If you're applying for customer service, spotlight communication and empathy.

5. **Education and Qualifications**
   - Most recent/relevant courses or degrees first.
   - Include the institution, qualification title, and year.
   - Add in new certifications or trainings—even those completed online.

6. **Add Extras (if relevant)**
   - Volunteering: Showcase community work, especially if it backs up your skills.
   - Projects: Briefly describe recent projects that prove initiative or creativity.
   - Awards/Publications: Mention recognitions, articles, or blogs.
   - Languages: Even conversational skills can be a plus.

7. **Tidy Up Your Formatting**
   - Stick to clean fonts (Arial, Calibri, Verdana).
   - Use logical section headers and bullet points.
   - Keep sentences clear and direct—don't overdo jargon.
   - Aim for 1–2 pages (not an essay!).
   - Save as PDF for emailing, so the layout doesn't shift.

Making Your CV Stand Out

- **Tailor for Each Application:** Tweak your CV for every job. Match keywords and phrases from the job description. Your CV should "echo" the language employers use.
- **Action Words:** Always start your achievements with action verbs (not "responsible for"—say "kickstarted," "streamlined," "executed," etc.).
- **Quantify Achievements:** Numbers grab attention—how many, how much, what percentage?
- **Show Your Personality:** Let passion for your field shine through, especially in your personal statement.

Even More Practical Tips

- Review/update your CV every 6–12 months, and each time you finish a big project or role.
- Keep a "brag file" on your phone or computer. Log wins, praise, certifications, anything you might forget later.
- Use the STAR technique for achievements: Situation, Task, Action, Result.
- Get feedback—from a friend, mentor, or career coach.
  - Don't worry if your job history isn't perfect—use volunteer work, parenting, or freelance gigs to showcase skills too.

Activity 129. Improve your work area ergonomics

Work area ergonomics refers to designing and arranging your workspace to promote comfort, efficiency, and safety. It involves adjusting furniture, tools, and equipment to fit your body's needs and reduce strain during daily activities. Whether you work from home, in an office, or spend time at a desk for hobbies or personal projects, an ergonomic setup can make a significant difference in your physical health and mental wellbeing.

Mental & Physical Wellbeing Benefits

1. Prevents Musculoskeletal Disorders (MSDs): Poor posture and repetitive movements can lead to back pain, neck strain, and other injuries. An ergonomic workspace reduces these risks by supporting proper alignment and minimising strain.
2. Enhances Comfort: Sitting or working in a well-designed space reduces physical discomfort, allowing you to focus on tasks without distractions caused by aches or fatigue.
3. Promotes Movement: Incorporating ergonomic principles encourages regular movement, improving circulation and reducing the risk of stiffness or long-term health issues associated with prolonged sitting.
4. Reduces Stress: A comfortable workspace minimises physical discomfort, which can lower stress levels and improve focus.
5. Boosts Productivity: When your environment supports your body's needs, you can work more efficiently and feel more accomplished at the end of the day.
6. Improves Mood: Feeling comfortable and supported while working fosters positivity and enhances overall job satisfaction—even if you're not working professionally but using the space for personal projects or hobbies.

Step 1: Choose the Right Chair - Invest in a chair with lumbar support to maintain the natural curve of your spine. Ensure your chair height allows your feet to rest flat on the floor with knees at a 90-degree angle.

Step 2: Desk Height and Setup - Adjust your desk height so your elbows remain at a 90-degree angle while typing. Use books or risers if needed to achieve the correct height. Ensure there's ample space under your desk for leg movement.

Step 3: Monitor Positioning - Position your monitor so the top of the screen is at or slightly below eye level to prevent neck strain. Keep the monitor about an arm's length away to reduce eye strain.

Step 4: Keyboard and Mouse Placement - Place your keyboard and mouse close enough so your arms remain relaxed at a 90-degree angle while typing or clicking. Use wrist supports or ergonomic keyboards/mice to maintain neutral wrist positioning.

Step 5: Lighting Considerations - Use natural light whenever possible but avoid glare on screens by positioning monitors perpendicular to windows. Add task lighting with adjustable lamps for focused illumination without causing eye strain.

Step 6: Organise Your Workspace - Keep frequently used items within easy reach to minimise stretching or straining. Declutter your workspace regularly to reduce distractions and promote focus.

Step 7: Incorporate Movement - Take breaks every hour to stand up, stretch, or walk around, this reduces tension and improves circulation. Alternate between sitting and standing using a sit-stand desk or DIY solutions like stacking books for height adjustments.

Creating an ergonomic home workspace doesn't have to break the bank. Small, inexpensive changes can significantly improve your comfort, productivity, and overall wellbeing. Whether you work from home full-time, occasionally, or simply spend time at a desk for personal projects, these budget-friendly adjustments can make a big difference.

If you're on a tight budget, get creative with items you already have at home:

1. Monitor Riser: Stack books Stack sturdy shoeboxes, plastic containers, or unused storage bins to elevate your monitor or laptop screen to eye level.
2. Lumbar Support: Roll up a towel, blanket, use a cushion or rolled-up yoga mat as back support in your chair. Use an inflatable travel pillow as an adjustable lumbar support option.
3. Footrest Alternative: Repurpose an old shoebox, stack magazines, a small wooden crate or box under your feet for elevation.
4. Document Holder: Use a clipboard propped against books as an affordable way to hold papers upright or create a DIY document holder by folding cardboard into an upright stand.
5. Keyboard and Mouse Placement: Use a flat tray or cutting board as a temporary keyboard tray to adjust its height relative to your desk. Add wrist support by rolling up soft towels and placing them under your wrists while typing or using the mouse.

If your chair is too low or high: Add cushions or folded blankets to increase seat height. Place sturdy books under the chair legs to adjust its height (if safe).

If your desk is too low: Raise it using furniture risers or blocks.
If it's too high: Adjust the height of your chair and add a footrest to maintain proper posture.

Lighting Adjustments: Redirect existing lamps from other parts of your home toward your workspace for better task lighting. Use mirrors strategically to reflect natural light onto your desk area.

Movement is essential for maintaining physical health during long periods of sitting:

1. Stretch Breaks: Set timers every hour to remind yourself to stand up, stretch, and move around for 2–5 minutes. Apps like "Stand Up!" can help with reminders.
2. DIY Standing Desk: Alternate between sitting and standing by stacking boxes or books on your desk temporarily.
3. Active Sitting: Use an exercise ball as a chair alternative for short periods, it encourages core engagement and improves posture.

Tips for Maintaining an Ergonomic Workspace

1. Conduct regular self-assessments using ergonomic checklists—adjust as needed based on comfort levels.
2. Experiment with different setups until you find what works best for your body.
3. Use timers or apps to remind yourself to take breaks throughout the day.
4. Reassess your setup periodically as your needs change over time.

Improving work area ergonomics is essential not just for professionals but for anyone who spends time working at a desk, whether it's crafting, studying, gaming, or managing personal tasks from home. A comfortable workspace enhances physical health by reducing strain while boosting mental clarity and productivity through better focus and reduced stress levels. With affordable accessories and DIY solutions readily available, creating an ergonomic setup is achievable for everyone—even on a budget! Take the time today to evaluate your workspace—you'll be amazed at how small changes can make a big difference in how you feel and perform every day!

Activity 130. Practice Visualisation techniques

Visualisation is a mental technique that involves creating vivid mental images or scenarios to influence emotions, behaviours, and physiological responses. By imagining desired outcomes or calming scenes, you can train your mind to focus on positivity, success, and relaxation. This practice is widely used in sports, personal development, and therapy to enhance performance, reduce stress, and foster emotional resilience. Why Is Visualisation Good for Mental and Physical Wellbeing?

Mental Wellbeing
1. Reduces Stress: Imagining peaceful environments or successful outcomes activates the body's relaxation response, lowering cortisol levels and promoting calmness.
2. Boosts Confidence: Mentally rehearsing success builds self-efficacy, the belief in your ability to succeed and reduces self-doubt.
3. Improves Emotional Regulation: Visualisation helps steer thoughts away from negativity, fostering feelings of joy, calmness, and optimism.
4. Enhances Focus and Motivation: By vividly imagining your goals, you create a mental roadmap that keeps you motivated and committed to achieving them.

Physical Wellbeing
1. Improves Performance: Athletes use visualisation to mentally rehearse movements, enhancing muscle coordination and strength through neural activation. This technique can also be applied to work tasks, public speaking, or interviews.
2. Promotes Relaxation: Techniques like guided imagery reduce physical tension by calming the nervous system, which can alleviate headaches or muscle pain caused by stress.
3. Supports Better Sleep: Visualising serene scenes before bed can help quiet the mind and improve sleep quality.

Here are several effective methods to integrate visualisation into your daily routine:

1. Guided Visualisation: Use audio recordings or apps that lead you through calming scenarios or goal-focused exercises. Engage all your senses - imagine what you see, hear, smell, taste, and feel in the scene being described.

2. Vision Boards: Create a physical or digital board filled with images, quotes, and symbols representing your goals and aspirations. Place it somewhere visible to remind yourself daily of what you're working toward.

3. Candle Visualisation: Light a candle and focus on its flame for a few minutes; observe its colours and movements. Close your eyes and visualise the flame vividly in your mind to improve concentration.

4. Outcome Visualisation: Picture what your life will look like once you've achieved your goals. Imagine the environment, people round you, how you feel emotionally and physically.

5. Process Visualisation: Visualise steps required to reach your goals in detail, from preparation to execution, helping to clarify the path forward, reducing anxiety about the process.

6. Daily Affirmations with Visualisation: Combine positive affirmations with mental imagery (e.g., "I am confident" while visualising yourself succeeding in a specific task).

7. Safe Place Visualisation: Create a mental sanctuary where you can retreat during stressful times, imagine this space in detail using all your senses.

Tips for Effective Practice

1. Consistency Matters: Practice visualisation daily, even just 5–10 minutes can make a difference over time.
2. Engage All Senses: The more detailed and sensory-rich your visualisations are, the more impactful they'll be.
3. Stay Relaxed: Find a quiet space where you won't be disturbed and relax fully.
4. Start Small: Begin with manageable goals before visualising larger aspirations.
5. Be Patient: Like any skill, visualisation takes time to develop, give yourself grace as you practice.

Common Mistakes to Avoid

1. Negative Imagery: Avoid focusing on failures or negative outcomes; always visualise success and positivity.
2. Rushed Sessions: Don't rush through visualisation—take time to create vivid mental images that fully engage your senses.
3. Unrealistic Goals: Start with achievable goals before moving on to larger ones; this builds confidence without overwhelming yourself.
4. Lack of Detail: Vague images are less effective—ensure your visualisations are clear and precise.

Signs That Visualisation Is Working

1. As you practice regularly, watch for these signs that indicate progress:
2. Increased motivation to take actionable steps toward your goals.
3. Enhanced clarity of objectives - your vision becomes more defined over time.
4. Improved confidence in handling challenges or pursuing aspirations.
5. Reduction in anxiety when preparing for stressful situations like interviews or public speaking.
6. Positive emotional responses during or after sessions (e.g., joy or calmness).
7. Tangible results—achieving milestones or noticing opportunities aligned with your goals.

Advanced Techniques for Beginners

1. Once comfortable with basic visualisation techniques, try these advanced methods:
2. Creative Visualisation: Use tools like vision boards or journals to outline goals while engaging all five senses in imagining success.
3. Sensory Anchoring: Associate specific scents or sounds with your visualizations (e.g., lavender for relaxation) to deepen their impact.
4. Meditative Visualisation: Combine mindfulness meditation with goal-focused imagery for enhanced relaxation and focus.

Visualisation is more than just imagining, it's a powerful tool for shaping your mindset, boosting confidence, reducing stress, and achieving personal growth through focused mental imagery. By practicing regularly using techniques like guided visualisation or vision boards and avoiding common mistakes, you can harness this skill to improve both mental clarity and physical performance while staying motivated toward achieving your dreams!

Activity 131. Do a quick yoga flow

A quick yoga flow is a short sequence of yoga poses designed to stretch, strengthen, and relax your body in just a few minutes. It's a simple and effective way to refresh your mind and body, whether you're starting your day, taking a break, or winding down in the evening. This practice is accessible to all levels, including beginners, and can be done at home or anywhere you have a little space.

Mental Wellbeing
1. Reduces Stress: Yoga encourages deep breathing and mindfulness, helping to lower stress levels and calm the mind.
2. Boosts Mood: The gentle movement and focus on breathing release endorphins, improving your overall mood.
3. Enhances Focus: Practicing yoga helps clear mental clutter, allowing you to feel more present and focused.

Physical Wellbeing
1. Improves Flexibility: A quick flow stretches tight muscles, enhancing flexibility over time.
2. Relieves Tension: Targeted poses release tension in common problem areas like the neck, shoulders, and lower back.
3. Boosts Circulation: Flowing through poses increases blood flow, energizing the body and reducing fatigue.
4. Strengthens Muscles: Even a short sequence can engage core muscles and improve overall strength.

This 5-minute yoga flow is perfect for beginners or for a quick reset during the day:

1. **Child's Pose (Balasana):** Begin kneeling on the floor. Sit back on your heels and stretch your arms forward on the mat, letting your forehead rest on the ground. Hold for 8 deep breaths. Benefits: Gently stretches the hips, thighs, and back while calming the mind.
2. **Cat-Cow Stretch (Marjaryasana-Bitilasana):** Move onto all fours with wrists under shoulders and knees under hips. Inhale as you arch your back (Cow), lifting your head and tailbone; exhale as you round your spine (Cat), tucking your chin to your chest. Repeat for 8 breaths. Benefits: Improves spinal flexibility and relieves tension in the back.
3. **Low Lunge (Anjaneyasana):** From all fours, step your right foot forward between your hands into lunge position, lower your back knee to the floor and lift your arms overhead, keeping them close to your ears. Switch sides after holding the pose on one side. Hold for 8 breaths per side. Benefits: Opens up tight hips and stretches the thighs while building leg strength.
4. **Rag Doll Pose (Uttanasana):** From standing or Downward Dog, fold forward at the hips with knees slightly bent. Let your upper body hang heavy and grab

opposite elbows to sway gently side to side. Hold for 8 breaths. Benefits: Releases tension in the hamstrings, lower back, and shoulders.
5. **Garland Pose (Malasana)** - Instructions: Stand with feet slightly wider than hip-width apart and squat down deeply with hands at heart centre in prayer position. Hold for 8 breaths. Benefits: Opens up tight hips and strengthens the lower body.
6. **Boat Pose (Navasana):** Sit on the floor with knees bent. Lean back slightly while lifting your feet off the ground, balancing on your sit bones. Extend arms forward or overhead for an extra challenge. Hold for 8 breaths. Benefits: Strengthens core muscles and improves balance.
7. **Savasana (Corpse Pose):** Lie flat on your back with legs extended and arms resting at your sides, palms facing up. Close your eyes and relax completely. Stay here for at least 1–2 minutes if time allows. Benefits: Promotes deep relaxation and integrates the benefits of the practice.

Tips for Success

- **Breathe Deeply:** Focus on slow, deep breaths throughout each pose to enhance relaxation and oxygenate your body more effectively.
- **Modify as Needed:** Use props like blocks or cushions to support yourself if any pose feels uncomfortable.
- **Listen to Your Body:** Avoid pushing into pain—yoga should feel good! Adjust poses to suit your flexibility level.
- **Create a Calm Space:** Practice in a quiet area where you won't be disturbed to fully immerse yourself in the flow.

Variations for Different Times of Day

- Morning Flow: Energise Your Day - Incorporate poses like Mountain Pose (Tadasana) or Warrior I (Virabhadrasana I) into this sequence to wake up your body and mind.
- Midday Reset: Combat Fatigue - Focus on stretches like Downward Dog (Adho Mukha Svanasana) or Triangle Pose (Trikonasana) to release tension from sitting.
- Evening Wind Down: Relax Before Bed - Add gentle twists or seated forward folds to calm the nervous system before sleep.

A quick yoga flow is more than just physical exercise, it's an opportunity to reconnect with yourself amidst life's busyness. Whether you're looking to reduce stress, relieve tension, or simply take a mindful pause during your day, this short practice offers immense benefits for both mental clarity and physical vitality. Remember that yoga is about progress, not perfection, so roll out your mat, take a few deep breaths, and enjoy the journey!

Activity 132. Try fruit and vegetable carving

Please if you still have the shakes or have a history of self-harm, think before embarking on this activity.

Fruit and vegetable carving is a fun and rewarding hobby that offers numerous benefits beyond creating visually stunning edible art. I know, bear with me with this one! Here's are just some of the reasons why:

Creative Expression - Carving fruits and vegetables allows you to unleash your creativity and Creative Expression transform ordinary produce into extraordinary masterpieces (with a little practice). You can create intricate designs, from floral arrangements to animal sculptures, letting your imagination run wild.

Stress Relief - The process of carving can be therapeutic, helping to reduce stress, anxiety, and depression. It provides an opportunity to slow down and focus on the present moment, offering a meditative experience.

Skill Development - As you practice carving, you'll develop precision, patience, and fine motor skills (Fine motor skills are the precise movements and coordination of small muscles, primarily in the hands, fingers, and wrists, often in conjunction with the eyes. These skills involve complex coordination between the nervous system and muscles, allowing for intricate tasks). The satisfaction of seeing your skills improve over time can be incredibly rewarding.

Enhancing Culinary Experiences - Your carved creations can elevate the presentation of meals, making them more visually appealing and appetising (also see Activity 81). This can be especially fun when entertaining guests or preparing special occasions.

Nutritional Benefits - Carving can make fruits and vegetables more appealing, especially to children and picky eaters, potentially encouraging healthier eating habits.

By engaging in fruit and vegetable carving, you're not just creating art – you're embarking on a journey of self-expression, relaxation, and culinary exploration that can bring joy to both you and those around you.

Materials Needed
- Sharp paring knife
- Cutting board
- Firm fruits or vegetables (e.g., watermelon, pumpkin, cucumber, carrot)
- Melon baller or small scoop (optional)
- Toothpicks (optional)

1. Choose Your Produce - Select firm, ripe fruits or vegetables with smooth surfaces, clean thoroughly and pat dry. For large items like watermelons, cut a flat base for stability.

2. Start with Simple Shapes - Begin by carving basic shapes like triangles or crescents, practicing on easier produce like a cucumber.

3. Try Basic Techniques:
    - V-cut: Make two angled cuts to remove a V-shaped wedge.
    - Peel carving: Remove skin in patterns to create contrast.
    - Slice and lift: Cut thin slices and lift edges for 3D effects.

4. Experiment with Designs:
    - Start with simple flowers or leaves.
    - Use a melon baller to create spheres or scoop out areas.

5. Add Details:
    - Use the tip of your knife to add fine lines or textures.
    - Create depth by varying the depth of your cuts.

6. Assemble and Display:
    - For complex designs, use toothpicks to attach separate pieces.
    - Arrange your carved produce on a platter for presentation.

Remember, fruit and vegetable carving takes practice. Start with simple designs and gradually work your way up to more complex creations. Always prioritise safety when handling sharp knives, so definitely not ideal if you have the DT's and shakes! Here are some fruit and vegetable carving shapes that are easy to make:

Cucumber Flowers
- **How to Make:** Slice a cucumber into thick coins. Use a small knife to cut shallow V-shapes around the edge, creating petals. Gently press the centre to slightly pop it up for a raised flower look.
- **Tips:** Try with carrots or radishes for colourful mini flowers.Edited-May-2025-Evolve-draft-formatting-7x10.docx
- **Melon or Apple Wedges "Leaves"**
- **How to Make:** Cut melon or apple slices into thin wedges. Use a knife to cut small diagonal notches along one side to form a simple leaf pattern.
- **Tips:** Arrange around a fruit platter for a decorative, leafy accent.Edited-May-2025-Evolve-draft-formatting-7x10.docx
- These shapes are quick, require only a basic kitchen knife, and add a touch of creativity to snacks or party trays!

Activity 133. Practice nonverbal communication skills

Nonverbal communication skills involve using body language, facial expressions, posture, gestures, tone of voice, and personal space to convey emotions and messages. These cues often complement or even replace spoken words, making them a crucial part of effective communication. Mastering nonverbal communication allows you to express yourself clearly, build rapport with others, and interpret their emotions more accurately.

1. Enhances Emotional Intelligence: Understanding nonverbal cues helps you empathise with others and navigate social situations more effectively.
2. Builds Confidence: Practicing open body language and positive facial expressions boosts self-assurance during interactions.
3. Reduces Miscommunication: Improved nonverbal skills minimize misunderstandings and foster clarity in conversations, reducing stress in social or professional settings.
4. Strengthens Relationships: Effective nonverbal communication fosters trust and connection, leading to healthier personal and professional relationships.
5. Promotes Relaxation: Practicing relaxed posture and facial expressions reduces physical tension caused by stress or anxiety.
6. Improves Posture: Exercises to refine body language encourage proper alignment, reducing strain on muscles and joints.
7. Supports Active Listening: Leaning slightly forward or maintaining eye contact during conversations improves engagement and focus, benefiting cognitive health.

Step 1: Observe and Learn - Watch others in various settings, in meetings, social gatherings, or public speaking events and note their body language, facial expressions, and gestures. Identify effective communicators and analyse what makes their nonverbal cues impactful (e.g., confident posture or warm smiles).

Step 2: Develop Self-Awareness - Stand in front of a mirror and practice different facial expressions (e.g., happiness, curiosity, concern) to see how you naturally convey emotions. Pay attention to your posture - are you slouching or crossing your arms? Adjust to appear open and confident.

Step 3: Practice Eye Contact - During conversations, maintain appropriate eye contact to show engagement without staring or intimidating the other person. Practice looking at the person's face while they speak and when you reply, this conveys attentiveness.

Step 4: Refine Body Language - Stand or sit up straight with shoulders back and chest slightly forward to project confidence. Avoid crossing your arms or legs, as this can appear defensive or disengaged. Lean slightly toward the speaker during conversations to demonstrate interest.

Step 5: Control Facial Expressions - Relax your facial muscles by practicing in front of a mirror, this helps avoid appearing tense or disengaged during interactions. Work on conveying an open, attentive expression that matches the tone of the conversation.

Step 6: Improve Gestures - Use hand gestures naturally to emphasise points but avoid overdoing them as they should complement your words rather than distract from them. Practice subtle gestures like nodding to show understanding or agreement.

Step 7: Modulate Your Voice - Record yourself speaking and listen for tone, pitch, pace, and inflection - are you monotone or overly fast? Adjust accordingly for clarity and emotional impact. Practice varying your vocal inflections to convey enthusiasm, empathy, or authority depending on the context.

Step 8: Respect Personal Space - Be mindful of maintaining appropriate distances during conversations, typically about 4 feet away in professional settings unless otherwise indicated. Observe others' reactions to gauge if you're too close or too far.

Step 9: Practice Active Listening - Focus entirely on the speaker without planning your response while they talk, this improves connection and understanding. Use nonverbal cues like nodding or maintaining eye contact to demonstrate engagement.

Nonverbal communication shapes how people perceive you. It can make you appear approachable, confident, empathetic, or disengaged depending on how well you use it. Regular practice ensures that these cues align with your intentions while helping you adapt to different situations more effectively.

Nonverbal communication is a powerful tool that shapes how we connect with others without saying a word. By practicing techniques like observing body language, refining gestures, maintaining eye contact, and being mindful of cultural differences, you can enhance both personal relationships and professional interactions significantly. With consistent effort, these silent skills will become second nature, helping you express yourself confidently while building meaningful connections wherever you go!

Activity 134. Give yourself a foot rub

Taking time to care for your feet through a self-administered foot massage is more than just a simple act of self-care, it's a practice that can significantly enhance both your physical and mental well-being. Often overlooked, the feet bear the weight of our daily lives and giving them attention can lead to profound relaxation and rejuvenation. A foot massage offers numerous benefits that extend beyond the physical realm.

Here's why it's worth incorporating into your routine:

- **Physical Benefits**: Massaging your feet stimulates circulation, which helps flush out toxins and deliver oxygen and nutrients throughout your body. Improved blood flow can alleviate muscle tension, reduce pain, and enhance overall foot health. Regular massages may even help prevent common foot issues like plantar fasciitis or soreness from prolonged standing.
- **Mental Benefits**: The gentle pressure applied during a foot rub encourages the release of endorphins—natural mood elevators and painkillers. This can lower stress levels, alleviate anxiety, and improve sleep quality. Additionally, focusing on specific pressure points may relieve headaches, boost cognitive function, and promote a sense of calm.
- **Holistic Well-Being**: A foot massage is an act of mindfulness. By dedicating time to this soothing ritual, you connect with your body, fostering self-awareness and grounding yourself in the present moment.

If you're not fond of touching your feet, consider massaging your ankles and lower legs instead for similar benefits and follow this step-by-step guide to create a relaxing massage:

1. **Preparation**
    - Wash your feet thoroughly and dry them.
    - Sit in a comfortable position.
    - Apply a small amount of lotion or oil to your hands (refer to oil blends below).

2. **Warm-Up**
    - Hold your foot with both hands and gently rotate your ankle in both directions.
    - Flex and point your toes to loosen up stiff joints.

3. **Massage Techniques**
    - Sole Massage: Use your thumbs to make circular motions across the sole, starting at the heel and working toward the toes. Apply firm yet even pressure.

- Arch Massage: Press your thumbs into the arch of your foot, making small circular motions from the heel to the ball of the foot.
- Heel Massage: Cup your heel with one hand while using your thumb to apply circular pressure.
- Ball of Foot: Massage the padded area below your toes with firm circular motions using your thumbs.
- Toe Massage: Gently pull each toe and massage its base using your thumb and index finger.
- Top of Foot: Use your knuckles to gently massage from the ankle toward the toes.

4. Finish Up
- Squeezing your foot gently with both hands before repeating on the other foot.
- Adjust pressure based on comfort level, focusing on areas that feel particularly tense or sore.
- Be mindful of unabsorbed oils that could make walking slippery afterward.

Incorporating regular foot massages into your self-care routine can help you unwind after long days, improve circulation, and keep your feet healthy. It's also an excellent way to nurture yourself without requiring expensive tools or treatments. By taking time for this simple practice, you're investing in both physical relief and emotional restoration.

Enhance your foot rub by using essential oils blended with carrier oils for added therapeutic effects. Here's how:

Dilution Guidelines
- For adults: Use a 2% dilution ratio (12 drops of essential oil per 30ml carrier oil).
- For sensitive skin or elderly individuals: Use 1% dilution (6 drops per 30ml carrier oil).
- Never exceed 5% dilution for topical applications.

Perform a patch test before applying any oil blend to ensure compatibility with your skin.

Carrier Oils
- Coconut oil: Deeply hydrating; absorbs quickly.
- Jojoba oil: Lightweight; suitable for all skin types.
- Almond oil: Softens and moisturises skin.

Essential Oils
- Lavender: Relaxes muscles; promotes calmness.
- Peppermint: Cooling effect; relieves pain and swelling.

- Eucalyptus: Improves circulation; antibacterial properties.
- Rosemary: Eases muscle aches; supports circulation.
- Tea tree: Antifungal properties; ideal for athlete's foot.
- Lemongrass: Refreshing scent; may help with muscle pain.

Experiment with combinations like lavender for relaxation or peppermint for cooling relief after a long day on your feet.

By dedicating just ten minutes to this practice each day or as needed, you'll find yourself reaping its many benefits, both physically and mentally, while fostering a deeper connection with yourself.

Activity 135. Read inspirational quotes

Incorporating inspirational quotes into your daily routine is a simple yet impactful way to nurture your mental and emotional well-being. These concise pieces of wisdom have the ability to uplift, motivate, and transform your outlook on life, offering comfort during difficult times and encouraging personal growth.

Inspirational quotes provide a wide range of benefits for both mental and emotional health:
- **Motivation and Encouragement**: Quotes act as a form of personal coaching, offering encouragement to persevere through challenges. They can spark new ideas, inspire action, and foster personal growth by reminding you of your inner strength and potential.
- **Emotional Support**: During periods of stress or uncertainty, reading quotes can boost your mood, reduce feelings of isolation, and provide comfort. They validate your experiences and offer empathy, reminding you that others have faced similar struggles and triumphed.
- **Perspective Shifts**: Inspirational quotes can help reframe negative thoughts into positive ones. They encourage you to focus on possibilities for growth rather than limitations, helping you see challenges in a new light.
- **Improved Self-Reflection**: By engaging with meaningful quotes, you can deepen self-awareness and better understand your emotions. They often prompt introspection, helping you identify areas for growth or healing.

Here's how you can make reading inspirational quotes a regular part of your routine:

1. **Morning Motivation** - Start your day with a quote that resonates with you. Write it down or place it somewhere visible like on your mirror or desk to set a positive tone for the day.
2. **Daily Reflection** - Choose a quote that aligns with your current challenges or goals. Reflect on its meaning and how it applies to your life during quiet moments or journaling sessions.
3. **Create a Quote Collection** - Compile quotes that inspire you in a notebook, digital folder, or even on sticky notes. Refer to them when you need encouragement or clarity.
4. **Use Quotes as Affirmations** - Recite empowering quotes aloud as affirmations to reinforce positivity and self-belief.
5. **Share Inspiration** - Share quotes with friends or loved ones who may benefit from their wisdom. This not only spreads positivity but also strengthens connections.

Why Make This Part of Your Routine? Reading inspirational quotes regularly can help cultivate a positive mindset, especially during tough times. They serve as reminders of resilience, perseverance, and the human capacity for growth despite adversity. Quotes are quick to read yet impactful, offering "a shot of espresso for your psyche" whenever you need it most.

By engaging with these nuggets of wisdom, you learn to reframe challenges as opportunities for growth and develop healthier coping mechanisms for stress or uncertainty.

Here are some timeless inspirational quotes to motivate and uplift you:

- *"Life doesn't get easier or more forgiving; we get stronger and more resilient."* — Steve Maraboli
- *"Do not judge me by my success; judge me by how many times I fell down and got back up again."* — Nelson Mandela
- *"I can be changed by what happens to me. But I refuse to be reduced by it."* — Maya Angelou
- *"Rock bottom became the solid foundation on which I rebuilt my life."* — J.K. Rowling
- *"Our greatest glory is not in never falling, but in rising every time we fall."* — Confucius

And one of my favourites that I have on my wall so I can see it every day – *"When you're backed against the wall, break the goddamn thing down"* — Harvey Specter, TV series *Suits*.

These words remind us that setbacks are not the end—they are stepping stones toward strength and resilience.

Practical Applications. Inspirational quotes are versatile tools for personal development:

- Quick Boosts: When time is limited, reading a single quote can provide instant motivation.
- Coping Mechanisms: In moments of difficulty, quotes offer hope and positivity.
- Mindfulness Practice: Reflecting on meaningful phrases encourages mindfulness and presence.

By making inspirational quotes part of your daily life, whether through reading them in the morning, reflecting during quiet moments, or sharing them with others, you'll find yourself equipped with renewed energy and perspective to face life's challenges head-on. Get on Google and find some inspirational, then put it somewhere you can see every day.

Top Tip: Make it into your phone screen saver!

Activity 136. Organise your desktop icons

Organising your desktop icons is a simple yet effective way to improve your mental and physical well-being. A cluttered digital workspace can create unnecessary stress, reduce productivity, and even impact your overall mood. By taking the time to declutter and organise your desktop, you can foster a sense of control, clarity, and efficiency in your daily life.

Why Is Organising Your Desktop Good for You? Honestly, there is a good reason, well many good reasons why this is in the book! Here are the key benefits of organising your desktop icons:

- **Reduced Stress and Anxiety**: A messy desktop can feel overwhelming, increasing cognitive load and creating a sense of chaos. Organising your icons creates a serene digital environment, reducing stress and anxiety associated with clutter.
- **Improved Focus and Productivity**: An organised desktop allows you to quickly access important files and applications, saving time and energy. This efficiency boosts focus and productivity, giving you a sense of accomplishment.
- **Enhanced Sense of Control**: Taking charge of your digital space fosters a feeling of mastery over your environment. This sense of control can translate into improved confidence and reduced stress in other areas of life.
- **Clearer Mental Space**: Digital clutter has a similar effect on the mind as physical clutter, it can cloud your thoughts. Organising your desktop helps clear mental space, allowing for better cognitive processing and decision-making.
- **Improved Work Satisfaction**: A tidy desktop contributes to a more professional and efficient work environment. This can lead to greater job satisfaction and a more positive outlook on your tasks.

Follow these steps to create an organised and visually appealing desktop:

1. **Create an Archive Folder**: Move old or rarely used files into an "Archive" folder to declutter your workspace while keeping them accessible if needed.

2. **Group Related Icons into Folders**: Organise similar files into folders (e.g., "Work Documents," "Personal Photos," "Software"). This reduces visual clutter and makes navigation easier.

3. **Use Naming Conventions**: Name files and folders clearly for quick identification (e.g., "Project_Report_March2025" instead of "Document1").

4. **Limit the Number of Icons**: Keep only essential files on your desktop to maintain a clean look. Move non-essential items to folders or other storage locations.

5. **Consider Desktop Organisation Tools**: Use software like Fences or Rainmeter for advanced sorting and customisation to create a visually appealing layout.

6. **Backup Files Simultaneously**: While organising your icons, take the opportunity to back up important files. This ensures that your data is safe in case of hardware failure or accidental deletion.

Organising your desktop is not just about aesthetics—it's about creating a functional space that supports your mental health and productivity. By keeping your digital workspace tidy, you reduce stress, improve focus, and foster a sense of control over your environment. Regularly decluttering ensures that you're always working in an efficient and calming space.

Don't forget to tidy up your phone while organising your digital life! Unused apps take up storage and slow down your device, so clearing them out can make a big difference. My husband keeps only the apps he uses, while I tend to hoard hundreds—it's worth trimming them down!

If you have loads of loyalty card apps for places like Boots, Superdrug, Tesco, or Holland & Barrett, you can save space by using one app to store them all. Check out these handy UK apps:

- Stocard: Scan your loyalty cards and keep them all in one place. It's easy to use and even shows offers from stores like Tesco and Boots.
- SuperCards: Another great option for storing all your loyalty cards digitally—no more juggling multiple apps!

1. Delete apps you don't use anymore.
2. Group similar apps into folders (e.g., "Shopping" or "Social Media").
3. Back up important files like photos and videos to cloud storage (Google Drive or iCloud).
4. Use apps like Stocard to free up space from loyalty card clutter.

A tidy phone means less stress, more storage, and quicker access to what you need—plus it just feels good! Take a few minutes today to declutter and enjoy a smoother digital experience. While organising your desktop icons, it's essential to back up important files at the same time.

By organising your desktop icons regularly and backing up files simultaneously, you create a digital workspace that supports productivity, reduces stress, and safeguards valuable data. This small habit can have far-reaching benefits for both your mental health and efficiency!

Activity 137. Make a terrarium

I absolutely love this activity. Imagine having your very own tiny garden, a living masterpiece that brings a slice of nature indoors. A terrarium is more than just a DIY project, it's a chance to create a miniature world filled with plants and personalised touches that reflect your passions and creativity. Whether it's a lush rainforest in a jar or a desert oasis in a vase, terrariums are the perfect blend of art, nature, and fun.

Building and caring for a terrarium isn't just enjoyable, it's great for your mental and physical well-being too! Here's why:

- **Stress Relief**: Working with plants and soil is calming and therapeutic. It's like meditation, but with dirt!
- **Boosts Creativity**: Designing your terrarium allows your imagination to run wild. You can create anything from a fairy garden to a mini library.
- **Improves Air Quality**: Plants help purify the air, making your indoor space fresher and healthier.
- **Sense of Accomplishment**: Watching your tiny garden thrive gives you a sense of pride and achievement.
- **Connection with Nature**: A terrarium brings the outdoors inside, helping you feel grounded and connected to the natural world.

Ready to get started? Follow these steps to craft your own little green paradise:

1. **Choose Your Container**
   Head to your local charity shop or rummage through your cupboards for the perfect glass container. It could be an old fishbowl, mason jar, geometric terrarium, or even that oddly shaped vase you never use. Open containers are great for succulents and cacti, while closed ones are ideal for tropical plants that love humidity.

2. **Gather Your Materials - Here's what you'll need:**
   - Drainage Material: Gravel, pebbles, or colourful fish tank stones (check charity shops or collect some from outside).
   - Activated Charcoal: Keeps bacteria at bay—essential for closed terrariums.
   - Moss: Adds texture and helps separate layers.
   - Potting Soil: Use regular soil or a mix designed for terrariums.
   - Plants: Small ones like ferns, mosses, succulents, or air plants work best.
   - Decorative Elements: This is where the fun begins! Think tiny figurines, shells, pebbles, or even mini furniture.

3. **Layer Your Terrarium**
   Start building your magical world layer by layer:
   a) Add 1–2 inches of gravel or pebbles at the bottom for drainage.

    b) Sprinkle a thin layer of activated charcoal over the gravel to keep things fresh.
    c) Add moss to separate the charcoal from the soil—it also looks lovely!
    d) Pour in 1–2 inches of soil as the base for your plants.

4. **Plant Your Garden**
Now it's time to bring your terrarium to life:
    a) Remove plants from their pots and gently loosen their roots.
    b) Create small holes in the soil and carefully place each plant inside, starting with the largest ones first. Use chopsticks or tweezers for tricky spots!
    c) Add moss around the plants for extra charm.

5. **Decorate Your World**
    Here's where you can let your imagination run wild! Love knitting? Add a mini chair with tiny knitting needles made from toothpicks. A bookworm? Craft a mini bookshelf out of lollypop sticks and fill it with tiny books made from folded paper scraps. Create pebble paths, add shells for ponds, or even sprinkle glitter for some magical sparkle.

6. **Finish Up**
Top it all off with small pebbles or sand for polish, then lightly mist with water using a spray bottle.

Creating and maintaining a terrarium is more than just crafting, it's about nurturing something beautiful that brings joy into your daily life. Every time you glance at it; you'll be reminded of the creativity and care you poured into it.

- Maintenance Made Easy: Closed terrariums need very little watering—just seal them up and let nature do its thing! Open ones require occasional watering based on the plants you've used (succulents need less water than ferns). Place them in bright but indirect light to keep them happy.
- Reuse & Recycle: Get creative with materials, charity shops are treasure troves for containers and decorative items.
- Personalise It: Make it uniquely yours by incorporating elements that reflect your hobbies or interests.

Your terrarium can be anything you want it to be—a peaceful forest retreat, an enchanted fairyland, or even a quirky scene inspired by your favourite hobby. The possibilities are endless! So, grab some soil, let your creativity flow, and build yourself a little world where imagination meets nature.

Remember: There's no right or wrong way to create a terrarium—it's all about having fun and making something that brings you joy!

Activity 138. Learn how to deal with Chronic pain

Chronic pain is a persistent discomfort that lasts beyond the typical recovery period or occurs without an obvious injury. Unlike acute pain, which signals immediate harm, chronic pain can be influenced by emotional, psychological, and physical factors. It can affect every aspect of life, but with the right strategies, it's possible to manage pain effectively and improve your overall quality of life. How is managing chronic pain good for mental and physical wellbeing?

Mental Wellbeing
1. Reduces Stress and Anxiety: Chronic pain often triggers emotional distress. Learning how to manage it can help lower stress levels and improve mental clarity.
2. Improves Emotional Resilience: Coping techniques like mindfulness meditation or support groups foster a positive mindset, helping you navigate challenges more effectively.
3. Promotes Relaxation: Techniques such as progressive muscle relaxation (PMR) and guided imagery encourage calmness and reduce the perception of pain.

Physical Wellbeing
1. Enhances Mobility: Gentle exercises like yoga or walking improve flexibility and reduce stiffness caused by inactivity or prolonged discomfort.
2. Relieves Muscle Tension: Therapies such as massage or hot/cold treatments target areas of tension, providing relief from physical strain.
3. Supports Better Sleep: Managing pain through relaxation techniques improves sleep quality, which is vital for overall health and healing.

How to Manage Chronic Pain Effectively

Step 1: Physical Therapies
1. Exercise: Engage in low-impact activities like swimming, walking, or yoga to strengthen muscles and improve mobility. Even light stretching can make a difference when done regularly.
2. Hot and Cold Therapy: Apply heat packs to relax tight muscles or cold packs to reduce inflammation and numb sharp pain. Alternate between the two for maximum relief.
3. Massage Therapy: Use therapeutic massage to alleviate muscle tension and promote relaxation, even if temporary relief is all that's achieved.

Step 2: Psychological Approaches
1. Cognitive Behavioural Therapy (CBT): Work with a therapist to reframe negative thoughts about pain and develop coping mechanisms for emotional distress.
2. Mindfulness Meditation: Focus on the present moment without judgment, this practice reduces stress and helps you respond to pain more calmly.

3. Support Groups: Join local or online groups where you can share experiences and learn practical tips from others dealing with chronic pain.

Step 3: Lifestyle Modifications
1. Healthy Diet: Incorporate anti-inflammatory foods like fruits, vegetables, whole grains, and lean proteins into your meals to support overall health and potentially reduce pain sensitivity.
2. Sleep Hygiene: Prioritise consistent sleep schedules and create a restful environment by limiting screen time before bed or using blackout curtains.
3. Maintain Routine: Keeping a regular schedule for daily activities provides structure that can help manage pain levels.

Non-Medication Strategies for Pain Relief. If you prefer managing chronic pain without medication, here are effective alternatives:

Mind-Body Techniques
1. Yoga and Tai Chi: These practices combine gentle movements with breath control and meditation, helping to relieve tension while improving flexibility.
2. Biofeedback: Learn how to control physiological functions like heart rate or muscle tension using real-time feedback, this technique helps identify stress responses that exacerbate pain.
3. Guided Imagery: Visualise peaceful scenes or experiences to distract from discomfort.

Alternative Therapies
- **Acupuncture**: Thin needles inserted at specific points stimulate energy flow, which many studies suggest can alleviate chronic pain.
- **Transcutaneous Electrical Nerve Stimulation (TENS)**: Low-voltage electrical currents interrupt pain signals sent to the brain, often used for back pain or arthritis.

Relaxation Techniques for Chronic Pain Management

Deep Breathing Exercises
- Find a quiet space to sit or lie down comfortably.
- Inhale deeply through your nose, hold for a few seconds, then exhale slowly through your mouth.
- Repeat for several minutes while focusing on the sensation of your breath.

Progressive Muscle Relaxation (PMR)
- Tense each muscle group in your body for 5–10 seconds before relaxing completely.
- Start with your feet and gradually move upward through your calves, thighs, abdomen, arms, shoulders, neck, and face.

Mindfulness Meditation
- Sit comfortably with eyes closed.
- Focus on your breath or bodily sensations without judgment.
- If your mind wanders, gently bring it back to the present moment.

Resources for Chronic Pain Management

Online Resources
1. NHS Guidance: Offers comprehensive advice on staying active and managing chronic pain through self-care strategies.
2. Flippin' Pain: Provides educational materials designed by individuals living with chronic pain for those experiencing it.

Books
1. 'Explain Pain' by David Butler & Lorimer Moseley: Explains how pain works in the body with practical strategies for relief.
2. 'The Body Keeps the Score' by Bessel van der Kolk: Explores how trauma affects physical health, useful insights for managing chronic pain, I really like this book.

Join communities like the Chronic Pain Support Group (local or online) to connect with others who understand your experience.

Managing chronic pain requires a multifaceted approach tailored to individual needs—from physical therapies like exercise or massage to psychological strategies such as CBT or mindfulness meditation. Lifestyle changes like maintaining a healthy diet and prioritising sleep also play a crucial role in reducing discomfort while enhancing overall wellbeing. By combining these techniques with support from healthcare professionals and resources like books or online groups, you can take meaningful steps toward reclaiming control over your life despite chronic pain challenges.

Activity 139. Create a mini scrapbook page

A mini scrapbook page is a creative, therapeutic, and meaningful way to capture memories in a compact format. Whether you're celebrating milestones, documenting recovery progress, or simply expressing yourself artistically, this activity provides a space-saving and portable option for storytelling. I have so many for different occasions. Scrapbooking is not only enjoyable but also beneficial for mental and physical well-being, especially for those navigating life changes like addiction recovery.

Scrapbooking offers more than just a creative outlet; it has profound benefits for your mental health and emotional resilience:

- **Stress Relief**: Engaging in creative activities like scrapbooking reduces stress and anxiety by encouraging mindfulness and focus. The act of arranging photos and embellishments can be soothing and meditative.
- **Therapeutic Benefits**: Scrapbooking fosters self-expression, helping you process emotions and reflect on personal growth. For individuals in recovery, it provides a healthy alternative to negative coping mechanisms.
- **Sense of Accomplishment**: Completing a scrapbook page gives you a tangible sense of achievement. It's a reminder of how far you've come and the memories you've created along the way.
- **Connection to Positive Moments**: By focusing on uplifting memories, scrapbooking reinforces positive reinforcement and gratitude, which are vital for maintaining emotional well-being.
- **Compact Creativity**: Mini scrapbook pages are less overwhelming than full-sized projects, making them ideal for beginners or those with limited time or space.

Materials Needed

- Cardstock or scrapbook paper (4x6 or 6x6 inches—perfect for compact pages).
- Photos (print smaller sizes for easy arrangement).
- Embellishments (stickers, washi tape, stamps, etc.).
- Adhesive (glue stick or double-sided tape).
- Scissors or paper trimmer.
- Journaling pen for captions or notes.

Step-by-Step Guide

1. Choose Your Theme: Decide on the memory or event you want to highlight—this could be a celebration, milestone, or even an everyday moment that brings joy.

2. Select Background Paper: Pick scrapbook paper that complements your theme. For example, pastel tones for calming memories or bold patterns for exciting events.
3. Trim Your Photos: Cut your photos into smaller sizes (2–3 images work best) to fit the mini page format without overcrowding it.
4. Arrange Before Adhering: Lay out your photos and embellishments before sticking them down to ensure everything fits well visually.
5. Add Embellishments: Use stickers, washi tape, or small decorative elements sparingly to enhance the design without overwhelming the page.
6. Include Journalling: Write a brief caption or note about the memory—this could be a date, feeling, or reflection tied to the event.
7. Add a Title: Use letter stickers or hand lettering to create an eye-catching title that ties the theme together (e.g., "New Beginnings" or "Family Fun").
8. Secure Everything: Use adhesive to stick down all elements firmly.

Creating mini scrapbook pages regularly is an excellent way to practice mindfulness while preserving memories in manageable chunks. It's perfect for busy schedules since it doesn't require much time or space—and the results are deeply rewarding.

Here are some ideas for themed mini scrapbook pages:

- Recovery Scrapbook - Perfect for those in addiction recovery, this type of scrapbook can document progress while serving as a positive coping mechanism.
- Travel Scrapbook
- Family & Friends Scrapbook
- Seasonal Scrapbook

Hobby Scrapbook

Scrapbooking is particularly beneficial for individuals in recovery because it allows them to focus on positive moments without pressure:

- **Nonlinear Progress Tracking**: Unlike traditional methods like counting days sober, scrapbooking highlights achievements without rigid timelines, perfect for those who prefer flexibility in their journey.
- **Creative Expression**: Recovery involves rebuilding identity; scrapbooking offers an outlet for self-discovery through art.
- **Portable & Accessible**: Mini pages are easy to create anywhere, whether at home, in therapy sessions, or during quiet moments.
- **Affordable Hobby**: You don't need expensive materials, recycled paper scraps, old photos, and basic stationery work beautifully.

By creating mini scrapbook pages tailored to your life experiences, you're not just preserving memories, you're actively nurturing your mental health and celebrating your journey one page at a time!

Activity 140. Practice progressive muscle relaxation

Progressive Muscle Relaxation (PMR) is a relaxation technique that involves systematically tensing and relaxing different muscle groups in the body. By focusing on the contrast between tension and relaxation, PMR helps you become more aware of physical stress and teaches you how to release it effectively. This method is simple, accessible, and can be practiced almost anywhere, making it an excellent tool for managing stress and promoting overall wellbeing, even if you don't work from home or have a sedentary lifestyle.

Why Is PMR Good for Mental and Physical Wellbeing?

- **Reduces Stress and Anxiety**: PMR helps calm the mind by releasing physical tension associated with emotional stress. Studies show that regular practice can significantly lower anxiety levels.
- **Improves Sleep Quality**: Practicing PMR before bedtime relaxes both the mind and body, making it easier to fall asleep and stay asleep.
- **Enhances Focus and Mindfulness**: The practice encourages mindfulness by promoting awareness of bodily sensations, helping you stay present in the moment.
- **Supports Emotional Regulation**: PMR provides tools to manage stress responses effectively, fostering resilience in challenging situations.
- **Relieves Muscle Tension**: PMR reduces tightness in muscles caused by prolonged sitting, repetitive movements, or physical strain, making it ideal for people with active or sedentary lifestyles.
- **Alleviates Chronic Pain**: Regular practice can help manage discomfort associated with conditions like back pain, arthritis, or headaches by reducing muscle tension and altering pain perception.
- **Promotes Relaxation Response**: PMR activates the parasympathetic nervous system (rest-and-digest mode), leading to lower heart rate, reduced blood pressure, and decreased overall tension.

Step 1: Find a Quiet Space - Choose a calm environment where you won't be disturbed. You can sit in a chair or lie down on your back for maximum comfort.

Step 2: Get Comfortable - Wear loose clothing and remove distractions like phones or loud noises.

Step 3: Start with Your Feet - Tense: Curl your toes tightly and tense the muscles in your feet for about 5–10 seconds. Then Relax: Release the tension suddenly and notice how your feet feel as they relax completely.

Step 4: Move Up Your Body - Continue this process systematically through each muscle group:
- Calves: Tense the calf muscles, hold for 5–10 seconds, then relax.

- Thighs: Squeeze the thigh muscles together, hold, then relax.
- Buttocks: Tighten the buttocks, hold, then release.
- Abdomen: Suck in your stomach muscles tightly, hold, then relax.
- Hands: Make fists with your hands, hold the tension, then release.
- Arms: Squeeze your arm muscles tightly, hold, then relax.
- Shoulders: Shrug your shoulders up toward your ears, hold the tension, then release.
- Neck: Push your head back slightly to tense neck muscles, hold briefly, then relax.
- Face: Scrunch up your facial muscles (eyes and mouth), hold the tension, then release.

Step 5: Full Body Tension: After working through each muscle group individually, tense all the muscles in your body at once—hold for a few seconds—then release completely.

Step 6: Focus on Relaxation: Take a moment to notice how relaxed you feel after releasing tension from each muscle group.

Step 7: Breathe Deeply - Inhale deeply through your nose and exhale slowly through your mouth throughout the exercise to enhance relaxation.

Step 8: Finish Slowly - When you've completed the exercise, take a few moments to enjoy the feeling of relaxation before slowly getting up or opening your eyes.

Practicing PMR regularly—ideally daily or several times a week—can lead to lasting improvements in how you respond to stressors in life.

Tips for Success
1. Practice PMR at the same time each day to build a habit, morning or bedtime works well.
2. Use guided audio if you're new to PMR, they provide step-by-step instructions.
3. Combine PMR with other relaxation techniques like deep breathing or visualisation for enhanced effects.
4. Be patient, it may take time to fully recognise tension patterns in your body and learn how to release them effectively.

Progressive Muscle Relaxation is an accessible and impactful technique that benefits both mental clarity and physical health. Whether you're managing stress at work or seeking relief from chronic pain at home, PMR provides a simple yet powerful way to reconnect with your body and promote relaxation. By incorporating this practice into your routine regularly, you'll not only reduce tension but also cultivate mindfulness and resilience that positively impact every aspect of your life!

Activity 141. Write a list of goals

Creating a list of goals or a bucket list is a powerful exercise in self-discovery, planning, and motivation. It's more than just jotting down dreams—it's a structured way to bring clarity to your aspirations and take actionable steps toward achieving them. Whether it's short-term goals or lifelong ambitions, this practice can have profound effects on your mental and emotional well-being.

Writing down your goals benefits both your mental and emotional health in several ways:

Reduced Stress and Anxiety: Putting your goals on paper externalizes them, reducing the mental burden of trying to remember everything. Breaking larger goals into smaller steps makes them feel less overwhelming, helping you approach them with confidence.

Improved Focus and Clarity: Writing goals allows you to clarify what you truly want to achieve. This process provides direction and purpose, helping you prioritize what matters most while eliminating mental clutter.

Sense of Control and Accomplishment: A written list gives you a sense of control over your future. Checking off completed goals is deeply satisfying, boosting self-esteem and reinforcing your ability to achieve what you set out to do.

Enhanced Motivation: Goals written down act as constant reminders of what you're working toward. They provide motivation during challenging times by keeping your focus on the bigger picture.

To maximise the benefits of goal-setting, follow these steps:

1. **Use the SMART Framework** (See Activity 35) - Ensure your goals are:
   - Specific: Clearly define what you want to achieve.
   - Measurable: Include criteria to track progress.
   - Achievable: Set realistic and attainable goals.
   - Relevant: Align them with your broader life objectives.
   - Time-bound: Assign deadlines to create urgency and focus.

2. **Break Down Larger Goals**: Divide big ambitions into smaller, manageable tasks. For example, if your goal is to write a book, start with outlining chapters or writing 500 words a day. Assign timelines for each task to maintain steady progress.

3. **Write Positively and Actionably**: Frame your goals in positive terms and actionable language. Start each statement with "I will" instead of "I want" or "I might." For example, write "I will save £5,000 for travel by December" rather than "I want to save money."

4. Review and Adjust Regularly: Periodically revisit your list to ensure it remains relevant as your circumstances or priorities change. Flexibility is key, adjust deadlines or modify goals as needed without feeling discouraged.

Writing a list of goals is not just about achieving things, it's about creating a roadmap for personal growth and fulfilment. Here's why it's worth doing:

- It helps you stay organised and reduces the chaos of juggling multiple aspirations in your mind.
- It fosters mindfulness by encouraging you to focus on what truly matters.
- It builds resilience by teaching you how to break down challenges into manageable steps.
- It provides a sense of purpose, which is essential for long-term happiness and mental well-being.

Additionally, having a bucket list can inspire excitement about the future. Whether it's traveling to dream destinations, learning new skills, or achieving career milestones, these ambitions give life meaning and direction.

Here are some extra ideas to enhance your goal-setting process:

- Categorise Your Goals: Divide them into areas like personal growth, career, health, relationships, finances, or leisure activities (e.g., travel or hobbies). This ensures balance across different aspects of life.
- Visualise Success: Imagine how accomplishing each goal will feel. Visualisation can boost motivation and help you stay committed.
- Celebrate Small Wins: Acknowledge progress along the way by celebrating milestones. This reinforces positive habits and keeps you motivated.

Need inspiration?

Small Bucket List Ideas: These are simple, low-cost, or easily achievable goals that can bring joy and fulfilment to your daily life:

- Write a handwritten letter to a loved one.
- Watch the sunrise or sunset from a scenic spot.
- Bake a cake from scratch.
- Start a gratitude journal and write in it daily.
- Learn to meditate or practice mindfulness for 10 minutes a day.
- Plant and care for a small herb garden at home.
- Attend a free local event, such as a farmers' market or art exhibit.
- Try a new recipe from a different cuisine.
- Go on a picnic in the park with homemade food.
- Take an evening walk without any technology, just enjoying nature.

Medium Bucket List Ideas: These goals require more planning or resources but are still achievable with some effort:

- Take a weekend road trip to explore nearby towns or attractions.
- Learn a new skill, such as playing an instrument, painting, or photography.
- Host a themed dinner party for friends or family.
- Volunteer for a cause you care about, like helping at an animal shelter or food bank.
- Complete a fitness challenge, such as running a 5K or doing yoga for 30 days.
- Take up an outdoor activity like kayaking, paddleboarding, or hiking.
- Join a class to learn something new - cooking, pottery, or calligraphy.
- Start a passion project, like writing a blog or creating art to sell online.
- Visit a national park you've never been to before.
- Organise your own scavenger hunt with friends in your city.

Large Bucket List Ideas: These are ambitious goals that may take significant time, effort, or resources but can be life-changing:

- Travel to all seven continents or visit all 50 U.S. states.
- Climb a major mountain like Kilimanjaro or hike the Appalachian Trail.
- Write and publish a book, whether fiction or nonfiction.
- Start your own business or side hustle based on your passion.
- Learn to speak another language fluently and use it while traveling abroad.
- Go scuba diving in the Great Barrier Reef or see the Northern Lights in Iceland.
- Take part in an iconic event like the Holi Festival in India or Oktoberfest in Germany.
- Build your dream home or renovate your current space to reflect your style.
- Complete an advanced degree or certification in your field of interest.
- Experience zero gravity or take part in space tourism.

By writing down everything you wish to achieve, whether it's small daily tasks or lifelong dreams, you create a tangible guide that keeps you focused on living intentionally. Goal setting isn't just about achieving; it's about becoming the best version of yourself while enjoying the journey along the way!

Activity 142. Update your online profiles

Your online profiles are a reflection of who you are, both personally and professionally. Whether it's LinkedIn, Instagram, or even niche platforms like GitHub or Behance, keeping your profiles up-to-date ensures they accurately represent your current skills, achievements, and goals. In today's digital world, these profiles often serve as the first impression others have of you—so it's worth investing time to make them shine. Regularly refreshing your online profiles isn't just about looking good online, it can also positively impact your mental and professional well-being:

- **Improved Visibility and Opportunities**: Updated profiles are more likely to appear in searches, boosting your visibility to potential employers, collaborators, or clients. This can lead to new career opportunities, partnerships, or personal connections.
- **Enhanced Confidence**: Knowing your profiles are polished and current gives you a sense of control over how you're perceived online. This can reduce stress about outdated information and boost your confidence in presenting yourself to the world.
- **Professional Growth**: By showcasing your latest skills, projects, and accomplishments, you establish credibility and thought leadership in your field. This helps build trust with others and supports long-term career development.
- **Reduced Digital Clutter**: Just like decluttering a physical space can bring peace of mind, tidying up old or irrelevant information on your profiles creates a cleaner digital presence. It feels satisfying and helps you stay organised.
- **Stronger Personal Branding**: Consistently updating your profiles ensures that they align with your evolving personal or professional brand. This keeps you relevant in fast-changing industries or social circles.

Refreshing your online presence doesn't have to be overwhelming:

1. Review Regularly: Aim to review all your profiles every three to six months. This ensures that any new roles, skills, or achievements are reflected promptly.
2. Ensure Consistency: Use the same tone, style, and up-to-date information across all platforms to present a cohesive image.
3. Optimise for Search Engines: Incorporate relevant keywords into bios and descriptions to improve visibility on platforms like LinkedIn or Google searches.

LinkedIn: Add recent roles, certifications, skills, or accomplishments under the "Experience" section. Update your headline and summary ("About" section) to reflect current goals or aspirations. Request recommendations from colleagues or clients and endorse others' skills to keep your profile dynamic. Share recent projects or articles that demonstrate expertise in your field.

Facebook/Instagram: Refresh profile pictures and bios with updated information about work, education, or interests. Use Instagram's "Highlights" feature to showcase key moments or projects in an organised way.

Twitter/X: Update your bio with relevant hashtags or keywords related to your industry or interests. Pin an important tweet (e.g., an announcement or portfolio link) at the top of your profile for easy visibility.

TikTok/YouTube: Revise channel descriptions and links to align with your latest content strategy. Update playlists (on YouTube) or pinned videos (on TikTok) to reflect current priorities.

If you use specialised platforms for work or hobbies, don't forget those also. Updating your online profiles is an ongoing process that ensures you're always putting your best foot forward in the digital space. Here's why it should become part of your routine:

1. Stay Relevant: Industries evolve quickly; keeping profiles updated ensures you stay competitive and visible in searches.
2. Showcase Growth: Regular updates highlight how you're growing professionally or personally over time.
3. Build Connections: Updated profiles attract the right people, whether they're potential employers, collaborators, or friends.

To make the most of updating your profiles:
1. Use High-Quality Photos: A professional-looking profile picture makes a strong first impression.
2. Highlight Achievements: Don't shy away from showcasing awards, certifications, or major milestones.
3. Pin Key Content: Pin important posts so they're always visible at the top of your profile.
4. Backup Old Content: Save older portfolio items elsewhere if you no longer want them on display but might need them later.
5. Custom URLs: Personalise URLs (e.g., LinkedIn.com/in/YourName) for a more professional look that's easy to share.

If managing multiple profiles feels overwhelming, just focus on platforms most relevant to your goals (e.g., LinkedIn for professional networking; Instagram for creative pursuits) and set reminders every few months to review all profiles, it's easier when done regularly rather than letting it pile up. By keeping your online profiles fresh and relevant, you maintain a dynamic digital presence that reflects who you are today while opening doors for future opportunities. Whether it's landing a new job, connecting with like-minded individuals, or simply feeling confident about how you're represented online, updating your profiles is an investment in yourself!

Activity 143. Plant microgreens

Microgreens are tiny, nutrient-packed greens harvested when they're just a few inches tall. Perfect for growing indoors, they're quick, easy, and incredibly rewarding. Whether it's spicy radish, earthy beetroot, or peppery rocket, British microgreens are a fantastic way to bring fresh flavour and greenery into your home—all from the comfort of your windowsill.

Planting microgreens offers more than just fresh greens; it's an activity that nurtures your mental and physical health:

- **Stress Relief**: Watching seeds sprout and grow is calming and therapeutic. Gardening even on a small scale can lower anxiety and promote mindfulness.
- **Sense of Achievement**: Microgreens grow fast, most varieties are ready to harvest in just 7–14 days. Seeing progress every day provides a sense of accomplishment and boosts self-esteem.
- **Connection to Nature**: Growing microgreens indoors creates a little green haven in your home, helping you feel grounded and connected to nature even in urban settings.
- **Nutritional Benefits**: These tiny greens are packed with vitamins, minerals, and antioxidants that support brain health, reduce stress hormones, and boost energy levels.
- **Convenience of Indoor Gardening**: Microgreens require minimal space, making them ideal for apartments or homes without outdoor gardens. You can grow them year-round regardless of the weather.

Here are some popular microgreens that thrive indoors and add a burst of flavour to your dishes:

1. Radish Microgreens: Radish varieties like Rambo Radish (with vibrant purple stems) or Daikon Radish (with mild peppery leaves) are quick to grow—ready in as little as 7 days! They add a spicy crunch to salads, sandwiches, and soups.
2. Rocket (Arugula): Known for its sharp peppery flavour, rocket microgreens grow in just 7 days and are perfect for adding zest to salads or stir-fries.
3. Beetroot Microgreens: With striking red stems and earthy flavour, beetroot microgreens brighten up dishes while providing essential nutrients. They're ready to harvest in about 10 days.
4. Mustard Greens: Fiery mustard microgreens with frilly leaves add bold flavour to stir-fries or Asian dishes. They're ready in 7–10 days.
5. Broccoli Microgreens: These nutrient-dense microgreens have a mild spicy flavour and are ready in just 7 days—perfect for salads or omelettes.
6. Spinach Microgreens: Mild yet packed with nutrients, spinach microgreens take about 10 days to grow and work well in risottos or smoothies.

Growing microgreens is simple and requires minimal equipment:
1. Choose Your Seeds: Select British favourites like radish, rocket, or beetroot for quick-growing greens.
2. Prepare Your Container: Use a shallow tray with drainage holes—or repurpose items like takeout containers.
3. Add Growing Medium: Fill the tray with organic compost or soilless mix like coconut coir.
4. Sow Seeds Evenly: Sprinkle seeds across the soil surface without overcrowding.
5. Mist & Cover: Lightly mist the soil with water and cover the tray with a clear lid or plastic wrap.
6. Provide Light: Once seeds germinate (in 3–7 days), remove the cover and place the tray on a sunny windowsill or under grow lights.
7. Water Regularly: Keep the soil moist but avoid overwatering—use a spray bottle for gentle misting.
8. Harvest Your Greens: When the first true leaves appear (usually within 7–14 days), use scissors to snip the greens just above the soil line.

Growing microgreens is an easy way to incorporate gardening into your daily life without needing outdoor space or fancy equipment. It's perfect for busy schedules, just sow seeds once every couple of weeks for a continuous supply of fresh greens.

- Prevent Mould: Ensure good air circulation by spacing out seeds and avoiding overwatering.
- Experiment with Flavors: Mix different seeds like spicy radish with mild spinach for unique taste combinations.
- Reuse Containers: Repurpose jars, trays, or even old baking tins as eco-friendly growing containers.
- Rotate Crops: Start new trays every week so you always have fresh greens ready.

Microgreens aren't just nutritious—they're versatile! Add them to your meals in creative ways such as rocket in soup or radish microgreens on egg sandwiches for extra spice.

Growing microgreens indoors is not only convenient but also incredibly rewarding. With British favourites like radish and rocket ready in just days, you can enjoy fresh greens year-round while boosting your mood and health—all from the comfort of your kitchen!

Activity 144. Do a Mindful Eating Exercise

In today's fast-paced world, many of us are guilty of rushing through meals. Whether it's grabbing a quick snack between meetings or eating while scrolling through our phones, we often treat food as an afterthought. However, food is more than just fuel for our bodies—it's an experience that deserves our attention. How we eat is just as important as what we eat. When I first met my husband, I noticed he barely chewed his food. Growing up as one of six kids, he had learned to eat quickly to avoid his siblings snatching his meal. Over time, he slowed down and began chewing properly, and he was amazed at how much more he could taste and enjoy his food.

Eating too quickly places unnecessary stress on the digestive system, which can leave us feeling tired and sluggish. Mindful eating offers a way to counteract this habit by encouraging us to slow down and fully engage with the act of eating.

The Science and Benefits of Mindful Eating

Mindful eating is a practice rooted in mindfulness that encourages you to focus on the present moment during meals. It involves paying attention to your food—its taste, texture, aroma, and how it makes you feel—without distractions or judgment. This approach has been shown to have profound benefits for both physical and mental health.

Research indicates that mindful eating can help reduce emotional eating by making individuals more aware of their triggers and patterns. For example, instead of reaching for comfort food out of stress or boredom, mindful eaters learn to distinguish between emotional cravings and genuine physical hunger. Studies have also shown that practicing mindful eating can improve digestion, reduce overeating, and even alleviate symptoms of stress-related digestive issues like irritable bowel syndrome (IBS).

One study found that mindfulness meditation training altered brain connectivity between regions responsible for stress regulation and reward processing—highlighting how mindful eating can help regulate cravings. Another review of 68 studies concluded that mindfulness interventions were effective in reducing binge eating and emotional eating over time.

While mindful eating may not always lead to immediate weight loss, its ability to foster healthier relationships with food makes it a valuable tool for long-term well-being. By promoting self-awareness and self-compassion, it helps individuals move away from cycles of guilt or restriction toward understanding and kindness.

A Simple Mindful Eating Exercise

Practicing mindful eating doesn't require any special equipment or preparation—just your willingness to slow down and focus. Here's a step-by-step guide to try:

- Choose a small piece of food, such as a raisin, nut, or piece of chocolate.
- Find a quiet place where you can sit comfortably without distractions.
- Take a few deep breaths to centre yourself.

1. **Observe the Food**: Look closely at the food item in your hand. Notice its shape, colour, and texture as if you're seeing it for the first time.
2. **Feel the Texture**: Close your eyes and explore the food with your fingers. Is it smooth, rough, sticky?
3. **Smell the Aroma**: Bring the food close to your nose and take a deep breath. What scents do you notice?
4. **First Bite**: Place the food in your mouth but don't chew yet. Pay attention to how it feels on your tongue.
5. **Chew Slowly**: Begin chewing very slowly, noticing how the texture changes with each bite. Focus on the flavours as they unfold.
6. **Swallow Mindfully**: Observe the urge to swallow and notice the sensation as the food moves down your throat.
7. **Reflect**: After swallowing, take a moment to notice any lingering tastes or sensations in your mouth.

Tips for Success
- Take at least 20 seconds per bite.
- If your mind wanders (which is natural), gently bring your focus back to the experience.
- Avoid judging yourself or the exercise; simply observe what you notice.

By practicing this exercise regularly—even with just one meal or snack per day—you can develop a deeper connection with your body's hunger cues and improve your overall relationship with food.

Mindful eating transforms mealtime into an opportunity for self-care rather than another task on your to-do list. It helps you savour each bite while fostering gratitude for the nourishment food provides. Over time, this practice can lead to better control over impulsive eating behaviours, reduced stress around meals, and greater enjoyment of food.

So next time you sit down for a meal or snack, pause for a moment. Engage all your senses in the process of eating—and see how this simple act can bring more balance and joy into your life.

Activity 145. Practice Balance Exercises

Balance exercises are an excellent way to improve both physical and mental well-being. They are particularly beneficial for individuals in alcohol recovery, offering unique advantages that support the healing process. By focusing on balance, you can enhance coordination, mindfulness, and self-confidence, all essential components of a holistic recovery journey.

Balance exercises go beyond simply improving physical stability; they offer a range of benefits that can positively impact your recovery experience:

1. **Improved Physical Coordination**: Alcohol abuse often affects coordination and balance. Regular practice can help restore these abilities, allowing you to feel more stable and confident in your movements.
2. **Increased Body Awareness**: These exercises require focus on body positioning and movement, promoting mindfulness and a stronger mind-body connection. This heightened awareness can help you stay present and attuned to your physical and emotional states.
3. **Stress Reduction**: The focus required for balance exercises acts as a form of moving meditation, helping to reduce stress and anxiety—common challenges during recovery.
4. **Enhanced Self-Confidence**: As you improve your balance skills, you'll likely experience a boost in self-esteem and confidence, which is crucial for rebuilding self-worth in recovery.
5. **Neuroplasticity Support**: Balance exercises engage multiple areas of the brain, supporting neuroplasticity—the brain's ability to form new neural pathways. This is particularly important as the brain heals from the effects of alcohol use.
6. **Fall Prevention**: Improved balance reduces the risk of falls, enhancing safety and overall health—especially if physical coordination has been affected by alcohol use.
7. **Complementary to Other Exercises**: Balance exercises can be easily incorporated into broader fitness routines, amplifying the benefits of physical activity such as better mood, improved sleep, and reduced cravings.

By incorporating balance exercises into your daily routine, you can support both your physical and mental well-being while fostering a sense of control and stability in your recovery journey. Here are some easy balance exercises you can practice at home. They require minimal equipment and are suitable for beginners:

Standing Balance Exercises
1. One-Leg Stand
- Stand on one leg for up to 30 seconds.
- Switch legs and repeat.
- For an added challenge, try closing your eyes or holding onto a stable surface lightly for support.

2. Heel-to-Toe Walk
- Walk in a straight line, placing the heel of one foot directly in front of the toes of the other foot with each step.
- Take 10–20 steps forward, then walk backward using the same technique.

3. Flamingo Stand
- Stand on one leg while extending the other leg forward or behind you.
- Hold this position for up to 15 seconds before switching legs.

Dynamic Balance Exercises
1. Sideways Walking
- Take 10 steps sideways in one direction without crossing your feet over each other.
- Return with 10 steps in the opposite direction.

2. Rock the Boat
- Stand with feet hip-width apart.
- Shift your weight onto one foot while lifting the other slightly off the ground.
- Hold for up to 30 seconds before switching sides.

3. Sit-to-Stand Exercise
- Rise from a seated position without using your hands for support.
- Slowly lower yourself back down into the chair or surface you were sitting on.
- Repeat this movement 5–10 times.

Advanced Balance Exercises - If you're ready for a challenge, try these more advanced moves:

Single-Leg Exercises
1. Single-Leg Reach
- Balance on one leg while extending the other leg behind you as you lower your chest forward slightly.
- Raise your arms overhead simultaneously to create a straight line from fingers to toes.

2. Single-Leg Stand with Eyes Closed
- Stand on one leg for up to 30 seconds but close your eyes for added difficulty.

Dynamic Balance Moves
1. Lateral Lunge
- Take a large step sideways into a lunge position, keeping your torso upright and knee tracking over your toes.
- Push back to the starting position and repeat on the other side.

2. Box Step-Up with Knee Drive
- Step onto a sturdy box or bench with one foot while driving the opposite knee up toward your chest.
- Lower back down and alternate legs.

Core-Focused Balance
1. Plank with Shoulder Tap
- Begin in a plank position (push-up stance).
- Tap your left shoulder with your right hand while keeping hips level, then switch sides.

2. Standing Elbow-to-Knee Exercise
- While standing upright, bring your right knee toward your left elbow by twisting slightly at the torso.
- Return to starting position and alternate sides.

Tips for Safe Practice

- Perform these exercises near a stable surface (like a wall or chair) for support if needed.
- Start with easier variations before progressing to advanced moves.
- Focus on proper form rather than speed—quality is more important than quantity.
- Gradually increase repetitions or duration as you build confidence and strength.

Balance exercises aren't just about physical stability—they're about cultivating mindfulness through movement, improving brain function, and boosting emotional resilience during recovery. By practicing these exercises regularly (even just six minutes at a time), you'll develop greater control over both body and mind while enhancing overall well-being.

So, take a moment today—stand tall, focus deeply, and embrace balance as part of your journey toward lasting health and recovery!

Activity 146. Observe and Record Weather Patterns

Engaging with the weather can be a fascinating way to distract yourself from cravings while building mindfulness and a deeper connection to nature. Observing and recording weather patterns is not only meditative but also educational, offering insights into local climate conditions. This activity encourages you to pause, look up, and appreciate the beauty of the world around you—an antidote to the busyness of modern life.

Taking time to observe and record weather patterns provides several benefits:

1. **Mindfulness**: Observing the sky and weather helps you stay present in the moment, creating a calming, meditative experience.
2. **Connection with Nature**: Understanding weather patterns fosters a deeper appreciation for the environment.
3. **Practical Insights**: By tracking daily weather, you can make more accurate predictions for outdoor activities or gardening.
4. **Climate Awareness**: Recording changes in weather can increase your understanding of local environmental conditions and climate change.

This activity is simple yet rewarding, requiring only a few tools and consistent practice.
To begin observing and recording weather patterns, follow these steps:

1. Find a Quiet Space - Choose an open area where you can observe the sky without obstructions like buildings or trees.

2. Gather Equipment - You don't need expensive tool, many weather instruments can be made at home or purchased inexpensively:
- Thermometer: Measures temperature (place in a shaded area for accuracy).
- Barometer: Tracks air pressure changes to predict upcoming weather shifts.
- Rain Gauge: Measures precipitation levels (easily made from a plastic bottle).
- Anemometer: Estimates wind speed (can be crafted using cups and straws).
- Wind Vane: Determines wind direction (create one with cardboard and a pencil).

3. Create a Weather Log - Record your observations daily in a notebook or digital spreadsheet. Include details like temperature, humidity, cloud types, visibility, wind speed, and precipitation levels.

4. Consistent Timing - Take measurements at the same time each day for consistency in your data collection.

If you're feeling creative, try making your own weather station with household items:

Rain Gauge - Materials: Clear plastic bottle, ruler, scissors, pebbles for weight

1. Cut the top off the bottle and invert it to create a funnel shape inside the base.
2. Add pebbles to stabilise the gauge outdoors.
3. Mark measurements on the side of the bottle using a ruler for tracking rainfall amounts.

Barometer - Materials: Glass jar, balloon, rubber band, straw, tape
1. Stretch a balloon tightly over the jar's opening and secure it with a rubber band.
2. Tape a straw horizontally across the balloon as an indicator of pressure changes.
3. Observe how the straw moves up or down as atmospheric pressure fluctuates.

Anemometer (Wind Speed) - Materials: 4 plastic cups, 2 straws, pencil with eraser, pushpin
1. Attach cups to both ends of two intersecting straws using tape.
2. Secure the straws to the pencil eraser with a pushpin so they can rotate freely.
3. Count rotations over time to estimate wind speed.

Wind Vane (Wind Direction) - Materials: Plastic bottle, straw, cardboard cutout (arrow shape), pencil with eraser
1. Attach an arrow-shaped cardboard piece to one end of a straw.
2. Secure the straw vertically on top of a pencil using a pushpin.
3. Place it in an open area and observe how it aligns with wind direction.

Once you've mastered basic tools, expand your weather tracking with these activities: Sense-Based Observations - Pay attention to visual details like cloud formations or colours during sunrise and sunset. Note sounds like rustling leaves or distant thunder.

Seasonal Changes - Track how temperature and precipitation vary across weeks or months to identify seasonal patterns and Compare Predictions - Compare your observations with official weather forecasts to test accuracy.

Observing weather isn't just about science—it's also about mindfulness and slowing down to appreciate nature's beauty. Reflect on moments like watching clouds drift across the sky or feeling raindrops on your skin; these experiences can ground you in the present moment and provide relief from cravings or stress.

This activity engages both your mind and body by combining observation skills with creativity through DIY projects. It's an excellent way to shift focus from cravings while fostering curiosity about the world around you.

So next time you feel overwhelmed or tempted by cravings, step outside - look up at the sky - and start recording what you see! Over time, this practice may become not only an enjoyable distraction but also a meaningful ritual that connects you more deeply with nature.

Activity 147. Research Traditional Foods

Exploring traditional foods is an engaging activity that not only distracts from cravings but also enriches your understanding of global cultures and culinary heritage. Whether you're delving into the origins of Italian pasta, the art of Japanese sushi, or the spices of Indian curries, researching traditional foods is a journey filled with discovery, creativity, and connection.

Learning about traditional foods offers a wide range of benefits:
1. **Cultural Connection**: Traditional foods are deeply tied to cultural heritage and history, offering insights into the values, traditions, and lifestyles of different societies.
2. **Nutritional Benefits**: Many traditional diets, like the Mediterranean diet, are nutrient-dense and associated with lower risks of chronic diseases such as heart disease and diabetes.
3. **Culinary Inspiration**: Researching traditional recipes introduces you to new ingredients, flavours, and cooking techniques that can transform your meals.
4. **Mindful Distraction**: Cooking and learning about food can serve as a therapeutic activity, keeping your hands and mind busy while fostering mindfulness.
5. **Social Bonding**: Sharing traditional dishes with friends and family creates opportunities for connection and celebration.
6. **Sustainability**: Many traditional food systems emphasize biodiversity and sustainable agriculture, offering solutions to modern environmental challenges.

By immersing yourself in the world of traditional foods, you can discover new ways to nourish both your body and soul while gaining a deeper appreciation for global diversity.

One day, I ordered a dessert through HelloFresh that I couldn't stop thinking about—it was a delightful mixture of dough, walnuts, cinnamon, sugar, and honey. Inspired by its flavours, I recreated it at home by mixing walnuts with cinnamon powder, sugar, and honey. I placed spoonful's of this mixture onto small circles of rolled-out pizza dough, folded them into little parcels, and baked them for 12 minutes. To top it off, I dipped them in melted chocolate! The result was a delicious treat that felt both indulgent and unique; a perfect example of how exploring traditional recipes can spark creativity in the kitchen.

Need more reasons to dive into this culinary adventure? Here's why exploring traditional foods is worth your time:
- Rich in Nutrients: Traditional dishes often use whole foods packed with essential vitamins, minerals, and antioxidants.
- Balanced Diets: Many traditional cuisines emphasize balance through diverse ingredients—think Mediterranean olive oil or Japanese fermented foods like miso.

- Health Benefits: Traditional diets are often linked to lower risks of obesity and other modern health issues due to their reliance on fresh, unprocessed ingredients.
- Preserving Heritage: Learning about these foods helps preserve cultural identity and culinary traditions for future generations.
- Community Support: Supporting local food producers who specialize in traditional ingredients helps sustain local economies.
- Solutions to Modern Challenges: Traditional food systems often align with sustainable practices that address current nutritional and environmental issues.

1. Choose a Region or Culture - Pick a cuisine that interests you—Italian, Japanese, Indian, Mexican—and dive into its history and signature dishes.
2. Understand the Ingredients - Learn about the key ingredients used in that cuisine—like olive oil in Mediterranean cooking or tamarind in Indian curries—and their health benefits.
3. Explore Cooking Techniques - Research how these dishes are traditionally prepared—whether it's hand-rolling pasta or fermenting vegetables—and try replicating them at home.
4. Look for Authentic Recipes - Find reliable sources for recipes that stay true to their cultural roots (see the list below). Authentic recipes often include stories or tips that deepen your understanding of the dish.

To get started with cooking traditional dishes at home, check out some of these trusted websites: Hot Thai Kitchen (Thai cuisine), Maangchi & Korean Bapsang (Korean cuisine), Omnivore's Cookbook & The Woks of Life (Chinese cuisine), Just One Cookbook (Japanese cuisine), The Storied Recipe (Global cuisines with cultural insights), Foolproof Living (Turkish, Mexican, Asian recipes) and BBC Good Food & Taste of Home (International recipes). Alternatively, visit charity shops for second-hand cookbooks dedicated to specific cuisines—you might stumble upon hidden gems!

Cooking traditional dishes isn't just about food—it's about storytelling through flavour and technique. Each dish carries with it centuries of history and cultural significance that you can bring to life in your own kitchen. Whether you're preparing a hearty Italian lasagna or crafting delicate Japanese sushi rolls, these meals offer an opportunity to connect with people across time and space.

Researching traditional foods engages your curiosity while keeping your hands busy if you decide to cook them yourself! It's an immersive activity that shifts your focus away from cravings toward something creative and fulfilling.

So next time you feel tempted by cravings or simply want to try something new dive into the world of traditional foods! You'll not only satisfy your taste buds but also gain a greater appreciation for global cultures along the way.

Activity 148. Do a Quick Personality Assessment

A personality assessment is a simple yet impactful activity that can provide valuable insights into your unique traits, behaviours, and tendencies. By taking just a few minutes to explore your personality, you can enhance self-awareness, improve relationships, and even gain clarity on personal or professional goals. Whether you're curious about how you interact with others or seeking ways to grow, a quick personality assessment is an engaging and meaningful way to distract yourself from cravings while fostering personal development.

Personality assessments are more than just fun quizzes—they can positively impact your mental and emotional health in several ways:

1. **Enhanced Self-Awareness**: Understanding your personality helps you identify strengths, areas for growth, and behavioural patterns. This self-awareness can improve decision-making and emotional regulation.
2. **Stress Management**: By recognising how you respond to stress, you can develop healthier coping mechanisms tailored to your personality type.
3. **Improved Relationships**: Learning about different personality types fosters empathy and communication, reducing misunderstandings in personal and professional interactions.
4. **Boosted Confidence**: Identifying your natural talents and strengths can increase self-esteem and motivation to pursue goals.
5. **Mindful Distraction**: Focusing on self-reflection through a personality assessment offers a constructive way to redirect attention from cravings or stressors.

You don't need hours or professional guidance to complete a personality assessment—many quick and accessible options are available online or through simple exercises. Here are three easy methods to try:

1. Take an Online Test
Several free online tests provide fast insights into your personality:

- 16 Personalities Test: Based on the Myers-Briggs framework, this test takes 10–15 minutes and offers a detailed profile of your traits, including how you interact with others and make decisions.
- Big Five Personality Test: Measures five core dimensions of personality (openness, conscientiousness, extraversion, agreeableness, neuroticism) in about 10 minutes.
- TestColour: A unique 5-minute test that uses colour preferences to reveal personality traits in an intuitive way.

2. Try a Self-Reflection Exercise
For a quicker, introspective approach:

- Think about how you behave in different situations—at work, in social settings, or under stress.
- Reflect on your preferences for socialising (introverted vs extroverted), decision-making (logical vs emotional), and handling new experiences (structured vs spontaneous).
- Consider how others describe you—do they see you as empathetic, assertive, analytical?

3. Use Rapid Assessment Tools
If you prefer something structured but quick:
- True Colours Test: Categorises personalities into four colour types (blue, green, gold, orange) based on behavioural tendencies—takes only a few minutes.
- DISC Personality Assessment: Measures four behavioural traits (dominance, influence, steadiness, conscientiousness) in a condensed format.

Taking time for a quick personality assessment isn't just entertaining—it serves practical purposes that can enrich various aspects of your life:

1. Self-Growth: Gain clarity on who you are and where you want to grow personally or professionally.
2. Improved Communication: Learn how to adapt your communication style to connect better with others.
3. Career Insights: Many assessments highlight strengths that align with specific roles or industries, helping guide career decisions.
4. Team Dynamics: If done with colleagues or friends, these assessments can foster understanding and collaboration by revealing complementary traits within the group.

Keep in Mind that personality assessments provide insights but should not be treated as absolute truths about who you are. Use them as a tool growth and focus on what the results reveal about your strengths and areas for improvement. Personalities evolve over time, retake assessments occasionally to reflect changes in your life.

Many tests are free online; simply search for the ones mentioned above (e.g., "16 Personalities" or "Big Five Personality Test"). Alternatively, explore books or apps dedicated to self-discovery for more in-depth options.

A quick personality assessment is more than just an entertaining distraction, it's an opportunity for meaningful self-reflection that benefits both mental and physical wellbeing. By understanding yourself better through these tools, you'll not only gain clarity but also build stronger relationships and make more informed choices in life. So next time you feel the pull of cravings or stress creeping in, take six minutes to dive into a personality test—you might just discover something new about yourself!

Activity 149. Clean Window Tracks

Cleaning window tracks is a simple yet impactful activity that can refresh your living space while offering mental and physical benefits. Window tracks often collect dust, dirt, and debris over time, making them a hidden culprit of indoor grime, which is often overlooked (excuse the pun) and forgotten. Taking just a few minutes to clean them not only improves the appearance and functionality of your windows but also provides a satisfying sense of accomplishment.

Cleaning window tracks might seem like a mundane task, but it can positively impact your wellbeing in several ways:

1. **Promotes Mindfulness**: Focusing on small, detailed tasks like cleaning tracks encourages you to stay present, helping to reduce stress and anxiety.
2. **Boosts Productivity**: Completing this task provides a quick win, motivating you to tackle other household chores or personal goals.
3. **Improves Air Quality**: Removing built-up dirt and debris prevents dust from circulating indoors, which can benefit your respiratory health.
4. **Physical Activity**: Cleaning requires movement, stretching, and bending, offering light physical exercise that contributes to overall wellness.
5. **Sense of Accomplishment**: A clean home environment fosters positivity and satisfaction, enhancing your mood and mental clarity.

Follow these simple steps to clean your window tracks effectively:

1. Remove Loose Debris - Use a vacuum cleaner with a narrow nozzle or brush attachment to remove dust and loose dirt from the tracks. If you don't have a vacuum handy, use a small paintbrush or dry toothbrush to sweep debris out of the grooves.

2. Apply Cleaning Solution - Mix warm water with mild dish soap or equal parts water and white vinegar for an eco-friendly option. For stubborn dirt, sprinkle baking soda along the tracks and add vinegar to create a natural cleaning paste.

3. Scrub Thoroughly - Use an old toothbrush or small scrub brush to clean the tracks, paying attention to corners and grooves where dirt accumulates most. For hard-to-reach areas, wrap a damp cloth around a butter knife or putty knife to scrape out grime.

4. Wipe Clean - Use a microfiber cloth or paper towels to wipe away loosened dirt and cleaning solution. Repeat until the tracks are visibly clean.

5. Dry Completely - Allow the tracks to air dry or use a clean, dry cloth to speed up the process.

6. Lubricate (Optional) - For sliding windows, apply a silicone-based lubricant along the tracks to ensure smooth operation.

Cleaning window tracks isn't just about aesthetics—it's about creating an environment that feels fresh and functional while giving yourself a productive outlet for distraction from cravings or stress. Here's why this task is worth doing:

1. Improved Functionality: Dirt buildup can hinder the smooth operation of sliding windows; cleaning ensures they glide effortlessly.
2. Seasonal Preparation: Clean tracks prevent debris from blowing indoors during spring or summer when windows are frequently opened.
3. Home Maintenance: Regular cleaning prevents long-term damage caused by mould or corrosion in metal tracks, saving you money on repairs or replacements.
4. Mental Reset: Tackling small tasks like cleaning window tracks can help reset your mind during moments of stress or indecision.

If your window tracks haven't been cleaned in years or are especially grimy, try these:

1. Handheld Steamer: Use steam to loosen stubborn grime for easier scrubbing.
2. Custom Sponge Tool: Cut grooves into a sponge that match the shape of your window track for effortless cleaning.
3. Mould Removal: For mouldy areas, use diluted bleach or hydrogen peroxide—but ensure proper ventilation and avoid mixing chemicals.

In the UK, where damp weather can contribute to mould growth in window tracks, regular cleaning is especially important for maintaining indoor air quality and preventing damage caused by moisture buildup.

Cleaning window tracks may seem like a minor task, but its benefits go far beyond aesthetics—it enhances air quality, improves functionality, and offers an opportunity for mindfulness and physical activity in just six minutes! By incorporating this simple chore into your routine, you'll not only refresh your home but also boost your mood and mental clarity.

So grab an old toothbrush today—clean those neglected window tracks—and enjoy the satisfaction of a fresher living space!

Activity 150. Organise a Spice Rack Plus Other Ideas

Organising a spice rack is a simple yet transformative activity that can enhance your cooking experience while offering mental and physical benefits. A tidy spice rack not only saves time but also inspires creativity in the kitchen, making meal preparation more enjoyable. Whether you're a seasoned chef or a casual cook, this activity can bring order to your kitchen and spark joy through organisation.

Organising your spice rack may seem like a small task, but it has surprising benefits for your overall wellbeing:

1. **Promotes Mindfulness**: Sorting spices requires focus and attention to detail, helping you stay present and calm during the process.
2. **Reduces Stress**: A clutter-free and organised space can reduce feelings of overwhelm, creating a sense of control and order.
3. **Boosts Creativity**: An accessible spice rack encourages experimentation with flavours, making cooking more fun and fulfilling.
4. **Supports Healthy Eating**: Having spices readily available makes it easier to prepare nutritious meals at home, reducing reliance on processed foods.
5. **Physical Activity**: The task involves movement—reaching, sorting, and arranging—which contributes to light physical exercise.

Follow these steps to organise your spice rack effectively:

1. Declutter and Sort
- Remove all spices from your rack or drawer.
- Check expiration dates and discard any old or stale spices.

2. Choose an Organisation Method
Select a system that works best for you:
- Alphabetical Order: Arrange spices from A to Z for quick access.
- By Cuisine: Group spices by the cuisine they're commonly used in (e.g., Italian herbs together, Indian spices together).
- Frequency of Use: Place frequently used spices at eye level or in easy-to-reach spots; store less-used ones higher or lower.
- Type of Spice: Group herbs, seeds, powders, and blends separately for easier recipe-following.

3. Transfer to Uniform Containers
- Use matching jars or containers for a cohesive look—clear containers are ideal for visibility.
- Label each container with the spice name and expiration date.

4. Maximise Space with Creative Solutions
Consider these storage ideas:
- Tiered Shelving: Use risers or stepped organisers to make all spices visible at once.
- Magnetic System: Attach metal containers to a magnetic board or fridge for modern storage that saves counter space.
- Drawer Inserts: Use custom drawer organisers to keep spices tidy and hidden yet easily accessible.
- Lazy Susan: Place spices on a rotating tray for effortless access in cabinets or on countertops.

5. Maintain Regularly
Check your spice rack every few months to ensure freshness and organisation.

Organising your spice rack isn't just about tidiness—it's about creating an environment that supports creativity, efficiency, and health in the kitchen. Here's why it's worth doing:
1. Improved Cooking Experience: A well-organised spice rack saves time during meal prep and makes cooking more enjoyable by eliminating frustration from searching for ingredients.
2. Encourages Experimentation: Having all your spices visible inspires you to try new recipes and flavour combinations, adding variety to your meals.
3. Supports Healthy Habits: Easy access to spices encourages home cooking over ordering takeaway, promoting healthier eating patterns.
4. Aesthetic Appeal: A neatly arranged spice rack adds style to your kitchen, making it a more inviting space.

Damp weather can affect the longevity of certain spices like dried herbs or powders stored improperly—ensure airtight containers are used to preserve freshness longer.

Organising a spice rack is more than just tidying—it's an opportunity to create a functional and inspiring space that enhances your cooking experience while promoting mindfulness and creativity. By dedicating just six minutes to this task, you'll not only transform your kitchen but also gain a sense of accomplishment that boosts mental clarity. So, grab those jars today—sort them out—and enjoy the satisfaction of an organised spice rack that makes every meal preparation feel effortless!

Here are some ideas for items around the house that can be arranged or ordered to improve functionality and aesthetics. Organising these items not only declutters your space but also makes daily tasks more efficient.

Kitchen
- Spices: Organise by type, cuisine, or frequency of use.
- Pantry: Group items by category (e.g., canned goods, grains, snacks).
- Utensils: Arrange by size or purpose in drawers or holders.
- Fridge: Categorise shelves for dairy, vegetables, condiments, etc.

Living Room
- Books: Sort by genre, author, or colour for a decorative touch.
- Magazines: Stack neatly or store in magazine holders.
- Decor Items: Arrange vases, candles, and frames for a cohesive look.
- Remote Controls: Place in a designated tray or organiser.

Bedroom
- Clothing: Organise by type (e.g., shirts, trousers) or season.
- Jewellery: Use trays or boxes to separate pieces by type.
- Shoes: Arrange by style or frequency of wear in racks or shelves.
- Bedside Table: Keep essentials like books, chargers, and lamps tidy.

Bathroom
- Toiletries: Group items like skincare products, shampoos, and dental care supplies.
- Towels: Fold neatly and arrange by size or colour.
- Makeup: Use organisers to separate brushes, palettes, and lipsticks.
- Cleaning Supplies: Store under the sink in bins or caddies.

Home Office
- Files: Categorise documents into folders for easy access.
- Stationery: Arrange pens, paperclips, and sticky notes in desk organisers.
- Books and Manuals: Sort by topic or frequency of use on shelves.
- Cables and Chargers: Use cable ties or organisers to prevent tangling.

Miscellaneous
- Tools: Arrange screwdrivers, hammers, and other tools in a toolbox.
- Craft Supplies: Store items like paints, brushes, and fabrics in bins or drawers.
- Toys: Use labelled bins to separate toys by type (e.g., puzzles, action figures).
- Shoes at Entryway: Use racks or baskets to keep them tidy.

Activity 151. Create Care Packages

Creating care packages is a thoughtful and meaningful way to show kindness—whether for yourself or others. These packages can be tailored to meet specific needs, interests, or occasions, making them a versatile and personal gift. Whether you're assembling one for a loved one or crafting a self-care kit for yourself, this activity promotes connection, comfort, and mindfulness. Care packages offer several benefits for both the giver and recipient:

For Recipients:
1. **Boosts Emotional Wellbeing**: Receiving a personalised care package reminds someone that they are loved and valued, helping to reduce feelings of loneliness or stress.
2. **Encourages Relaxation**: Including items like scented candles or bath bombs promotes relaxation and self-care, aiding mental health.
3. **Provides Practical Support**: Thoughtfully chosen items can address specific needs, such as skincare products or comforting snacks, enhancing physical wellbeing.

For Givers:
1. **Promotes Mindfulness**: Selecting items with care requires focus and thoughtfulness, encouraging you to be present in the moment.
2. **Fosters Connection**: Creating a care package strengthens bonds with others by showing empathy and understanding of their needs.
3. **Boosts Mood**: The act of giving brings joy and fulfilment, contributing to your own emotional wellbeing.

Follow these steps to create a meaningful care package:
1. **Choose a Theme** - based on the recipient's interests or needs. Some ideas include:
    - Relaxation and Self-Care: Items that promote calmness and pampering (e.g., bath products, aromatherapy oils).
    - Comfort Food and Snacks: A selection of favourite treats like biscuits, teas, or chocolates.
    - Entertainment: Books, puzzles, or games to keep them engaged and entertained.
    - Hobby-Focused: Supplies for their favourite activities (e.g., knitting/art supplies).
2. **Select Appropriate Items** - choose items that fit your theme while keeping the recipient's preferences in mind:
    - Comfort Items: Fuzzy socks, cozy blankets, or soft robes for warmth and relaxation.
    - Self-Care Products: Face masks, bath bombs, scented candles, or pillow sprays.
    - Snacks and Treats: Gourmet popcorn, herbal teas, or their favourite sweets.
    - Entertainment: Crossword puzzles, colouring books, magazines, or small games.

- Personal Touches: Handwritten notes, printed photos, or handmade crafts.
3. **Packaging Your Care Package**
    - Select a container that suits your theme—such as a decorative tin, basket, or box.
    - Add cushioning like tissue paper or shredded paper to protect items during delivery.
    - Arrange the items attractively within the container for visual appeal.
4. **Add Personal Touches**
    - Write a heartfelt note explaining why you chose each item—it adds meaning to the gift.
    - Include small decorations like stickers or ribbons for extra charm.
    - Consider handmade items (e.g., a knitted scarf or painted card) for an extra-special touch.

Here are some examples of themed care packages you can create:
- Relaxation - Bath bombs, lavender pillow spray, fuzzy socks
- Comfort Food - Hot chocolate mix, biscuits, gourmet popcorn
- Entertainment - Crossword puzzles, novels by UK authors, playing cards
- Hobby-Focused - Art supplies (sketchbook/pencils), gardening tools (seeds/gloves)
- Self-Care - Jade roller for facial massage, scented candles

Care packages aren't just about giving physical items—they're about showing thoughtfulness and creating moments of joy for yourself or someone else. Here's why it's worth doing:
1. **Strengthen Relationships**: Thoughtfully curated packages show recipients you understand their needs and care about their wellbeing.
2. **Encourage Self-Care**: Creating one for yourself is an act of kindness toward your own mental health—reminding you to slow down and prioritise relaxation.
3. **Spread Positivity**: Whether it's for friends, family members, or strangers in need (e.g., nursing home residents), care packages bring happiness and connection.

Consider sending care packages to those who may need extra support in the UK:
1. NHS Staff: Create thank-you packages with snacks and self-care items for local healthcare workers.
2. Charities Supporting Vulnerable Groups: Organisations like Shelter accept donations that can include comfort-focused care packages.
3. Military Personnel Abroad: Send morale-boosting packages through initiatives like *Support Our Soldiers*.

Creating care packages is more than just assembling items—it's about spreading kindness and connection through thoughtful gestures that brighten someone's day while promoting your own sense of fulfilment. Take six minutes today—choose a theme—and start crafting your perfect care package! Whether it's for yourself or someone else in need of support, this simple act can make a world of difference!

Activity 152. Research Money-Saving Tips

Researching money-saving tips is a practical and empowering activity that can help you take control of your finances while fostering mental clarity and reducing stress. Whether you're looking to cut down on household expenses or save for a specific goal, exploring ways to manage your money effectively can improve your overall wellbeing and provide a sense of accomplishment.

Understanding and implementing money-saving strategies offers several benefits for both mental and physical health:
1. **Reduces Financial Stress**: Learning how to save money and manage expenses alleviates anxiety about financial uncertainties, promoting peace of mind.
2. **Boosts Confidence**: Gaining knowledge about budgeting and saving empowers you to make informed decisions, enhancing self-esteem.
3. **Encourages Mindfulness**: Tracking expenses and researching savings techniques encourages thoughtful spending, helping you stay present and intentional with your money.
4. **Improves Physical Health**: Financial stability allows you to invest in healthier food options, maintain essential utilities, and afford preventative healthcare measures.
5. **Supports Long-Term Goals**: Saving money consistently helps you achieve milestones like buying a home, planning a holiday, or securing retirement funds, which can improve overall life satisfaction.

Follow these steps to start researching money-saving tips effectively:

1. **Utilise Online Resources**
   - Explore reputable personal finance websites like MoneySavingExpert.com or Which? for UK-specific advice.
   - Read reviews of budgeting apps such as Yolt or Emma to find tools that suit your needs.
   - Search for articles on frugal living or energy-saving tips tailored to your lifestyle.

2. **Leverage Your Local Library**
   - Borrow books on personal finance, such as *The Money Diet* by Martin Lewis or *Your Money or Your Life* by Vicki Robin.
   - Use free internet access at the library to research online if needed.
   - Check if your library offers financial literacy workshops or classes.

3. **Explore Social Media**
   - Follow financial experts like Martin Lewis on Twitter or Instagram for daily advice.
   - Join Facebook groups dedicated to frugal living or budgeting tips (e.g., UK Money Saving & Budgeting).
   - Use Pinterest to find infographics on meal planning, DIY household hacks, and energy-saving ideas.

4. Consult Financial Professionals
- Schedule a meeting with a financial advisor at your bank for personalised recommendations.
- Attend free seminars offered by local credit unions or community centres focused on budgeting and saving strategies.

5. Track Your Expenses
- Use budgeting apps like Monzo or spreadsheets to monitor spending habits over a month.
- Analyse where your money goes—identify areas where you can cut back (e.g., unused subscriptions).
- Set realistic savings goals based on your findings.

6. Network with Friends and Family
- Share tips with trusted friends or relatives who have successfully saved money.
- Form an accountability group where members motivate each other to stick to savings plans.

Here are some actionable strategies to help reduce household expenses:

Energy Efficiency
- Switch off appliances when not in use and unplug chargers overnight.
- Install energy-efficient light bulbs like LEDs.
- Use smart thermostats (e.g., Hive or Nest) to optimise heating schedules in the UK's colder months.

Grocery Shopping and Meal Planning
- Plan meals weekly to avoid impulse purchases at the supermarket.
- Buy generic brands instead of premium ones—they often taste just as good!
- Use loyalty cards like Tesco Clubcard or Nectar points for discounts and rewards.

Household Supplies
- Make homemade cleaning products using vinegar, baking soda, and essential oils.
- Opt for reusable alternatives like cloth napkins instead of paper towels.
- Shop at discount stores like Poundland for everyday essentials.

Transportation
- Compare fuel prices using apps like PetrolPrices.com before refuelling your car.
- Consider carpooling with colleagues or using public transport when possible—many cities offer discounted travel cards (e.g., Oyster Card in London).

Entertainment and Subscriptions
- Cancel subscriptions you don't use (e.g., streaming services) or share accounts with family members where possible.

- Take advantage of free community events such as festivals, museum days, or library programs.
- Borrow DVDs from libraries instead of paying for rentals.

Home Maintenance
- Perform regular upkeep tasks like clearing gutters or sealing windows to prevent costly repairs later.
- Learn basic DIY skills through YouTube tutorials for small fixes around the house.
- Compare quotes from service providers before committing to repairs.

Researching money-saving tips isn't just about cutting costs—it's about creating financial stability that supports your lifestyle and goals while reducing stress associated with money management challenges. Here's why it's worth doing:

1. Empowerment: Understanding how to save money equips you with tools to make smarter financial decisions, giving you greater control over your life.
2. Preparedness: Saving consistently builds an emergency fund that can protect you during unexpected situations like job loss or medical expenses.
3. Freedom: Financial stability allows you to focus on experiences that matter—whether it's travelling, pursuing hobbies, or spending quality time with loved ones.

Here are some helpful resources tailored for UK residents:
1. MoneySavingExpert.com: Offers expert advice on everything from energy bills to supermarket shopping hacks.
2. Which? Magazine: Provides reviews on products and services alongside consumer rights information.
3. Citizens Advice Bureau: Offers free guidance on managing debt and budgeting effectively.
4. Local Council Websites: Many councils provide information on grants, discounts, or schemes available in your area (e.g., council tax reductions).

Researching money-saving tips is more than just an exercise in frugality—it's an opportunity to build confidence, reduce stress, and create a foundation for achieving long-term goals. By dedicating just six minutes today to exploring ways to save money, you'll gain valuable insights that can transform how you manage your finances while improving overall wellbeing.

So grab a notebook—start researching—and take the first step toward smarter spending and greater financial freedom!

Activity 153. Do Some Gardening or Weeding

Gardening and weeding are therapeutic activities that allow you to connect with nature, improve your surroundings, and enjoy a sense of accomplishment. Whether you have a sprawling garden or just a windowsill, engaging with plants can boost your mental and physical wellbeing. For those in addiction recovery, gardening offers a calming and purposeful activity that promotes mindfulness and resilience. Gardening provides numerous benefits for both mental and physical health:

Mental Health Benefits

1. **Reduces Stress**: Outdoors working with plants lowers cortisol, promoting relaxation.
2. **Boosts Mood**: Gardening releases endorphins, improving overall happiness and reducing symptoms of depression.
3. **Encourages Mindfulness**: Focusing on tasks like weeding or planting helps you stay present, fostering clarity and calmness.
4. **Promotes Connection**: Gardening connects you to nature, creating a sense of harmony and grounding.

Physical Health Benefits

1. **Improves Strength**: Digging, weeding, and lifting improve muscle tone and flexibility.
2. **Encourages Movement**: Gardening is a light form of exercise that increases circulation and burns calories.
3. **Supports Immune Health**: Exposure to soil microbes can strengthen your immune system.

For individuals in addiction recovery, gardening provides a structured activity that builds focus, patience, and self-esteem—key qualities for maintaining sobriety. Follow these steps to start gardening or weeding, whether you have an outdoor garden or not:

If You Have a Garden:
1. **Assess Your Space** - Observe your garden at different times of day to note sunny and shady areas. Identify existing plants, weeds, and areas that need attention.
2. **Gather Essential Tools** - Start with basics like a hoe, hand fork, spade, gloves, and weeding knife. Ensure access to water, ideally with a hose or watering can.
3. **Learn About Weeds** - Research common weeds in your area or ask an experienced gardener for advice. Use photos or guides to help identify weeds versus beneficial plants.
4. **Begin Weeding** - Use a hoe for small weeds on warm, dry days to disturb their roots. Pull out annual weeds by hand; dig out deeper-rooted perennial weeds with tools like a hand fork or spade.

5. **Prevent Weed Growth** - Cover empty beds with cardboard during winter to suppress weeds naturally. Apply organic mulch (10–20cm) around plants to smother weeds while enriching the soil.
6. **Start Small** - Focus on one area at a time to avoid feeling overwhelmed progress is key!
7. **Choose Low-Maintenance Plants** - If time is limited, opt for hardy trees, shrubs, or perennials that require minimal upkeep.

If You Don't Have a Garden: You can still enjoy gardening through these creative alternatives:

1. **Indoor Gardening** - Grow herbs like basil or mint on a windowsill for fresh flavours in cooking, microgreens in trays, as they grow quickly and are nutritious! Even create terrariums with succulents or moss for decorative indoor greenery.
2. **Container Gardening** - Use pots or planters on balconies or patios to grow vegetables like tomatoes or chilies, or window boxes with colourful flowers or aromatic herbs for visual appeal.
3. **Community Gardening** - Join local community garden projects, many cities have shared spaces where you can tend plants alongside others or volunteer at gardening initiatives hosted by community centres or charities.
4. **Do Creative Gardening Projects** - Make kokedama (Japanese moss ball planting) for unique indoor displays. Grow beansprouts in jars, it's a fun way to cultivate food indoors! Or set up small hydroponic systems for growing leafy greens without soil.

Gardening isn't just about tending plants—it's about nurturing yourself through the process of growth and care. Here's why it's worth doing:

1. **Reconnect with Nature**: Spending time outdoors helps you feel grounded and connected.
2. **Build Confidence**: Watching plants thrive under your care reinforces self-esteem and accomplishment.
3. **Encourage Healthy Habits**: Growing your own food promotes healthier eating while reducing reliance on processed options.
4. **Support Recovery Goals**: Gardening provides structure and mindfulness, two essential elements for staying focused in addiction recovery.

Take six minutes today, grab some gloves and start tending to your space! You'll not only create beauty but also discover new strengths within yourself along the way!

Activity 154. Plan a Day Trip

Planning a day trip is a fun and imaginative way to explore new places, break free from routine, and create lasting memories. Whether you're seeking adventure, relaxation, or cultural experiences, the UK offers countless hidden gems that cater to every mood and interest. For those in addiction recovery, day trips provide a positive focus, promote mindfulness, and encourage healthy exploration.

Day trips offer numerous benefits for your mental and physical health:

Mental Health Benefits
1. Reduces Stress: Escaping to new surroundings helps clear your mind and alleviate daily worries.
2. Boosts Mood: Exploring beautiful landscapes or engaging in fun activities releases endorphins, lifting your spirits.
3. Encourages Mindfulness: Immersing yourself in nature or culture keeps you present in the moment.
4. Fosters Connection: Sharing the experience with friends or family strengthens relationships and creates positive memories.

Physical Health Benefits
1. Promotes Movement: Activities like hiking, walking tours, or exploring attractions encourage physical exercise.
2. Improves Energy Levels: Fresh air and natural surroundings rejuvenate your body and mind.

For individuals in addiction recovery, day trips can provide structure, motivation, and opportunities to rediscover joy in simple pleasures.

Follow these steps to plan an affordable and enjoyable day trip:

1. Choose Your Destination
- Think outside the box—explore lesser-known attractions like waterfalls, caves, or quirky museums (e.g., Swallow Falls in Wales or Cathedral Cave in the Lake District).

2. Set Your Budget
- Estimate costs for transportation, food, entrance fees, and any extras (e.g., souvenirs).
- Look for free or low-cost attractions like nature reserves or public parks (e.g., Kyoto Gardens in London).

3. Plan Your Activities
- Include a mix of relaxation and exploration—such as hiking trails followed by a picnic or visiting a museum before strolling through nearby gardens.

- Research hidden gems using platforms like Atlas Obscura or local blogs for unique ideas.

4. Pack Smart
- Bring essentials like water bottles, snacks, sunscreen, comfortable shoes, and weather-appropriate clothing.
- If visiting nature spots like beaches or caves, pack items like towels or flashlights.

5. Use Public Transport
- Save money by using trains or buses—check for discounts through National Railcards or group travel offers.

6. Be Flexible
- Allow time for spontaneity—some of the best experiences come from unexpected discoveries during your trip.

Planning a day trip isn't just about exploring—it's about creating moments of joy and connection that positively impact your mindset. Here's why it's worth doing:

- **Escape Routine**: A change of scenery refreshes your perspective and boosts creativity.
- **Celebrate Sobriety Milestones**: For those in recovery, day trips can mark progress by celebrating achievements with meaningful experiences.
- **Build Confidence**: Navigating new places fosters independence and problem-solving skills.
- **Reconnect with Nature**: Spending time outdoors promotes grounding and mindfulness.

Here are some imaginative ideas tailored to different moods:

Adventure Seekers - Explore Hawkstone Park Follies in Shropshire with sandstone cliffs and hidden paths
Nature Lovers - Grey Mare's Tail Nature Reserve in Scotland for waterfalls and rare wildlife
History Buffs - Tour Amberley Museum in West Sussex for industrial heritage exhibits
Relaxation Seekers - Stroll through Kyoto Gardens in London for peaceful reflection
Unique Experiences - Discover Alnwick Poison Garden featuring toxic plants
Family Fun - Spend the day at Crealy Resort in Devon with rides and farm animals

How to Deal with Anxiety Around New Places
If you feel nervous about visiting unfamiliar locations, try these tips to ease anxiety:

1. **Plan Ahead**: Research maps, transportation options, and attractions thoroughly so you know what to expect.

3. **Start Small**: Begin with destinations close to home before venturing further afield.
4. **Bring Support**: Invite a trusted friend or family member to join you—they can provide encouragement and companionship.
5. **Practice Mindfulness**: Focus on your surroundings—notice the colours, sounds, and smells of the place to stay grounded.
6. **Take Breaks**: Allow yourself time to rest if exploring feels overwhelming.

Day trips can play a vital role in recovery by offering positive distractions and opportunities for growth:

1. Focus on Positivity: Exploring new places shifts attention away from cravings toward uplifting experiences.
2. Celebrate Progress: Use day trips as rewards for reaching sobriety milestones—each outing becomes a celebration of your journey.
3. Build Resilience: Navigating challenges during travel (e.g., finding routes or managing schedules) teaches adaptability and problem-solving skills.
4. Reconnect with Joy: Rediscovering simple pleasures like walking through nature or enjoying local food fosters gratitude.

Planning a day trip is more than just an activity—it's an opportunity to escape routine, embrace adventure, and create meaningful memories that enrich your life. Whether you're hiking to Swallow Falls or exploring quirky sites like The Smallest House in Great Britain, this experience allows you to reconnect with yourself while discovering new places.

Take six minutes today—choose a destination that excites you—and start planning! You'll not only enjoy the journey but also uncover new strengths along the way!

Activity 155. Start a Fundraiser

Starting a fundraiser is a meaningful way to support a cause you care about while fostering personal growth and community engagement. Whether it's organising an event, taking on a challenge, or launching an online campaign, fundraising can make a significant difference in people's lives. For those in addiction recovery, this activity can provide purpose, structure, and opportunities to connect with others.

Fundraising benefits your mental and physical health in several ways:

Mental Health Benefits
1. Boosts Self-Esteem: Successfully raising funds for a cause reinforces your sense of purpose and accomplishment.
2. Reduces Stress: Focusing on helping others shifts attention away from personal challenges, promoting positivity.
3. Builds Community: Collaborating with others fosters a sense of belonging and combats feelings of isolation.
4. Encourages Gratitude: Supporting a cause helps you appreciate what you have while giving back to others.

Physical Health Benefits
1. Promotes Activity: Challenges like charity runs or walks encourage physical exercise.
2. Improves Heart Health: Acts of kindness, such as fundraising, release oxytocin, which reduces blood pressure and promotes cardiovascular health.

For individuals in recovery, fundraising can also reinforce sobriety by providing structure, purpose, and opportunities to connect with others in meaningful ways. Follow these steps to start your own fundraiser:

1. **Choose a Cause** - Select a charity or cause that resonates with you personally or aligns with your recovery journey (e.g., addiction support programs or mental health charities).

2. **Set Clear Goals** - Decide how much money you want to raise and set a deadline for achieving it. Clear goals inspire donors to contribute and keep you motivated.

3. **Select a Fundraising Method** -
   - Challenges: Take on something daring like a skydive, marathon, or sponsored hike.
   - Events: Organise bake sales, quiz nights, or fun runs.
   - Creative Campaigns: Try unique ideas like a "no social media" challenge—encouraging participants to disconnect while raising funds for addiction recovery or mental health awareness.

4. **Create a Budget** - Outline expected costs (e.g., venue hire, materials) and potential income sources (e.g., ticket sales, donations). Ensure the majority of funds go directly to the cause.

5. **Promote Your Fundraiser** - Use social media platforms like Instagram or Facebook to share your story and invite people to donate. Create posters for local community boards or reach out to local newspapers for coverage.

6. **Follow Legal Requirements** - Ensure compliance with UK fundraising regulations by checking guidelines on the Fundraising Regulator website and obtaining necessary permissions if required.

Starting a fundraiser isn't just about raising money—it's about making an impact while growing personally and connecting with others. Here's why it's worth doing:

1. Make a Difference: The funds you raise can directly support people in need or advance causes close to your heart.
2. Build Resilience: Planning and executing a fundraiser teaches perseverance and problem-solving skills.
3. Raise Awareness: Fundraising events educate others about important issues like addiction recovery or mental health.
4. Celebrate Sobriety: For those in recovery, fundraising can be a way to give back while celebrating personal milestones.

Here are some creative ideas to inspire your fundraiser:

- Personal Challenges - Sponsored hikes, skydives, marathons
- Community Events - Quiz nights, BBQs, talent shows
- Awareness Campaigns - Recovery storytelling nights, wellness challenges
- Digital Campaigns - Sponsored "no social media" challenges, this encourages participants to disconnect for mental clarity while raising funds for addiction recovery programs.

If you're based in the UK, these resources can help you get started:

1. JustGiving & Virgin Money Giving: Popular platforms for creating online fundraising pages tailored to UK audiences.
3. Fundraising Regulator Guidelines: Ensure your fundraiser complies with legal requirements.
4. Local Charities & Organisations: Partner with charities like Alcohol Change UK or Mind for support and promotion.

Take six minutes today, choose a cause that inspires you and start planning your fundraiser! You'll not only make an impact but also discover new strengths within yourself along the way!

Activity 156. Practice remembering phone numbers

Practicing the skill of remembering phone numbers is an excellent way to strengthen memory, enhance cognitive abilities, and prepare for emergencies where technology may not be available. In today's world, phone numbers are often stored in devices, leaving many of us unable to recall even the most important ones without assistance. By learning to memorise phone numbers, you can improve your mental resilience and develop a valuable life skill. Memorising phone numbers involves using techniques to encode numerical sequences into your memory for easy recall. This practice is more than just a mental exercise; it has tangible benefits for both mental and physical well-being.

- **Improved Memory**: Practicing recall strengthens neural pathways, boosting overall memory retention and cognitive function.
- **Reduced Anxiety**: Knowing you can recall important numbers without relying on technology provides peace of mind in high-pressure situations.
- **Brain Stimulation**: Memorisation exercises promote neuroplasticity, helping the brain adapt and grow, which is particularly beneficial as we age.
- **Stress Management**: The focus required for memorisation can serve as a mindfulness exercise, reducing stress levels.
- **Emergency Preparedness**: In situations where phones or internet access are unavailable, knowing key numbers can be lifesaving.

Step 1: Choose Key Numbers: Start by selecting three essential phone numbers you want to memorise such as family members, emergency services, or close friends.

Step 2: Break Down the Number (Chunking): Divide the number into smaller groups of digits (e.g., 555-123-4567). Chunking makes long sequences easier to remember.

Step 3: Use Mnemonics: Create associations for each chunk:
- Link digits to familiar concepts (e.g., 555 could remind you of "triple luck").
- Turn numbers into words using keypad letters (e.g., 2 = A, B, C).

Step 4: Create Stories or Visual Images - Turn the number into a memorable narrative or picture. For 1234, imagine "12 swans swimming in a pond with 34 flowers." Or use surreal imagery to make it stick, like balloons floating over a snowman (for digits 8 and 9).

Step 5: Apply Repetition - Practice recalling the number daily using spaced repetition techniques such as repeat it immediately after learning, then test yourself after an hour, after a day, and so on.

Step 6: Use Rhymes or Songs - Set the number to a tune or rhyme. For example:
Sing your phone number to the melody of "Jingle Bells" or "Twinkle Twinkle Little Star."

Memorising phone numbers offers practical benefits:
1. Emergency Readiness: If your phone is lost or dead, remembering ensures you get help.
2. Mental Exercise: Strengthening memory improves problem-solving skills and focus.
3. Self-Reliance: Relying less on technology fosters independence and confidence.

For individuals in addiction recovery or managing mental health challenges, this practice can be particularly empowering:
- It helps build focus and discipline, skills that are crucial during recovery journeys.
- Memorisation exercises provide a calming activity that reduces stress and anxiety.
- The sense of accomplishment from recalling numbers boosts self-esteem.

Examples of Memorisation Techniques

1. **Memory Palace** - Picture your home and assign chunks of the number to different rooms:
   - Place "555" in the living room.
   - Visualise "123" on the kitchen table.
   - Imagine "4567" written on the bedroom wall.
2. **Visualisation** - Use shapes or objects that resemble digits (e.g., "8" as a snowman or "7" as a cliff) and create vivid mental images linking these shapes in sequence.
3. **Association**: Link digits to meaningful events (e.g., "1986" could remind you of a personal milestone).

Suggestions for Practice
1. Write down the number repeatedly until you can recall it without looking.
2. Test yourself by reciting the number backward or skipping chunks.
3. Use apps designed for memory training to gamify the process.

Tips for Success
1. Start small with shorter numbers before progressing to longer ones.
2. Make it fun, use creative stories or songs that resonate with you.
3. Stay consistent; regular practice strengthens long-term recall.

In summary, practicing remembering phone numbers is more than just a mental exercise, it's an empowering tool that enhances memory, builds self-reliance, and prepares you for critical situations where technology may fail. Whether through chunking, mnemonics, visualisation, or repetition, this skill offers lasting benefits for cognitive health and emotional resilience. For those navigating addiction recovery or mental health challenges, it serves as both a grounding activity and a confidence booster, helping individuals take charge of their minds while fostering personal growth.

Activity 157. Create nature rubbings with paper and crayons

Creating nature rubbings with paper and crayons is a simple yet creative activity that combines art with mindfulness and exploration. By capturing the textures of natural objects like leaves, bark, or stones, this practice fosters a deeper connection to the environment while promoting mental and physical well-being. It's an accessible activity for people of all ages, including those in addiction recovery or managing mental health challenges. Nature rubbings involve placing paper over textured natural items and rubbing crayons or other drawing tools across the surface to reveal intricate patterns. This activity is not only fun but also offers significant benefits for mental and physical health.

Mental Well-Being Benefits
- Stress Reduction: The repetitive motion of rubbing and the focus on textures create a meditative effect, lowering stress and anxiety levels.
- Mindfulness: Engaging with nature through rubbings encourages present-moment awareness, helping individuals stay grounded.
- Creativity Boost: Exploring textures and experimenting with colours stimulates creative thinking and problem-solving.
- Emotional Expression: Creating art provides an outlet for emotions that may be difficult to verbalise.

Physical Well-Being Benefits
- Improved Focus: The attention required for creating rubbings enhances concentration.
- Relaxation Response: The calming nature of this activity can lower heart rate and blood pressure.
- Motor Skill Development: Handling crayons and positioning paper improves fine motor coordination.

Step 1: Gather Materials
You'll need:
- Paper (preferably thicker sheets to prevent tearing).
- Crayons (wax crayons work best; remove the wrappers for easier handling).
- Optional tools like coloured pencils, charcoal, or chalk for varied effects.

Step 2: Collect Natural Items - Walk in your yard, park, or neighbourhood to collect textured items such as leaves (fresh or fallen), tree bark, stones or pebbles, flowers and grass blades.

Step 3: Position the Item - Place your chosen item under the paper with its textured side facing up. Secure it with tape if necessary to prevent movement.

Step 4: Rub with Crayon - Hold the crayon sideways and gently rub over the paper where the item is placed. Experiment with different colours, pressures, and angles to enhance the texture.

Step 5: Layer Colours - For added depth, layer multiple colours over the same rubbing or combine rubbings from different items into one artwork.

Step 6: Add Details - After completing your rubbings, you can embellish them by colouring around them or incorporating them into larger art projects like collages or greeting cards.

Nature rubbings offer both immediate relaxation and long-term creative benefits:
1. Connection to Nature: This activity fosters appreciation for the environment by highlighting its intricate textures.
2. Mindful Creativity: The focus required helps quiet racing thoughts and promotes mindfulness.
3. Accessible Art: It's easy to do anywhere, requiring minimal supplies and no prior artistic skills.

For individuals in addiction recovery or managing mental health challenges, nature rubbings provide additional advantages as it offers a calming distraction during moments of distress, encourages exploration of surroundings, which can reduce feelings of isolation and supports emotional regulation by focusing on sensory experiences rather than triggers.

Suggestions for Enhancing Creativity
1. Experiment with different materials like oil pastels or chalk for varied textures.
2. Try rubbing on unconventional surfaces like fabric or aluminium foil for new effects.
3. Incorporate digital manipulation by scanning your rubbings into software to create collages or abstract designs.

Tips for Success
1. Focus on items with pronounced textures; smooth surfaces won't produce clear impressions.
2. Use thicker paper to prevent tearing during vigorous rubbing.
3. Embrace imperfections- each rubbing is unique and reflects the beauty of nature's diversity.

Creating nature rubbings is more than just an art project, it's a therapeutic practice that nurtures mindfulness, creativity, and connection to the natural world. Whether capturing the delicate veins of a leaf or the rugged texture of tree bark, this activity offers an accessible way to explore art while fostering mental clarity and emotional resilience. For those navigating addiction recovery or mental health challenges, it provides a grounding tool that combines creativity with healing through nature's restorative power.

Activity 158. Write Thank-You Notes

Writing thank-you notes is a simple yet impactful way to express gratitude and strengthen relationships. Whether you're thanking family, friends, professionals, or community members, this thoughtful gesture fosters connection and positivity. The act of writing a heartfelt note benefit both the sender and recipient, creating moments of appreciation that can have lasting effects on emotional wellbeing.

Thank-you notes go beyond polite gestures—they offer tangible benefits for mental and emotional health:

For Recipients:
1. Boosts Emotional Wellbeing: Receiving a thank-you note makes people feel valued and appreciated, lifting their mood and fostering a sense of belonging.
2. Strengthens Relationships: Acknowledging someone's kindness or support deepens bonds and creates a positive cycle of goodwill.
3. Encourages Reflection: Recipients often reflect on their contributions, reinforcing their sense of purpose and self-worth.

For Writers:
1. Promotes Gratitude: Writing thank-you notes cultivates a positive mindset by focusing on the good in your life.
2. Reduces Stress: The act of expressing appreciation can lower stress levels and improve overall mood.
3. Fosters Mindfulness: Crafting a thoughtful message requires focus and reflection, helping you stay present in the moment.
4. Builds Empathy: Thanking others encourages you to consider their efforts and contributions, enhancing emotional intelligence.

Follow these steps to write meaningful thank-you notes:

1. Choose Your Recipient
Think about someone whose kindness or support has made an impact on you—this could be a family member, friend, colleague, or even a service provider.

2. Craft Your Message
- Start with a warm greeting like *"Dear [Name]"*.
- Express your gratitude clearly: *"Thank you so much for [specific action or gift]."*
- Add personal details to make your note unique: *"Your thoughtful gift card will help me buy that cookbook I've been eyeing—I can't wait to try new recipes!"*
- Close with kind wishes: *"Wishing you all the best—you've truly made my day brighter!"*

3. Make It Personal
Include specific details that highlight why you're thankful—this makes the message more heartfelt and memorable.

4. Add Creative Touches
- Incorporate drawings, stickers, or decorative elements for visual appeal.
- Use colourful pens or stationery to make the note stand out.

5. Deliver Thoughtfully
- Hand-deliver your note for a personal touch or send it via post for added surprise.
- If appropriate, attach the note to a small gift (e.g., flowers or chocolates).

Here are some examples to inspire your writing:

Family Member- "Dear Mum, thank you for always being there for me, I couldn't have done it without your love and support."
Friend - "Dear Sarah, thank you for helping me move last weekend, you made what could have been stressful so much easier!"
Colleague - "Dear John, I appreciate your guidance on the project, it truly helped me grow professionally."
Healthcare Provider - "Dear Dr Smith, thank you for your care during my recovery, you've made such a difference in my life."

Writing thank-you notes isn't just about showing appreciation; it's about creating moments of connection that enrich relationships and foster positivity in your life.

Here's why it's worth doing:

- **Strengthen Bonds**: A heartfelt note deepens relationships by acknowledging someone's efforts or kindness.
- **Spread Positivity**: Expressing gratitude creates a ripple effect of goodwill that can brighten someone's day.
- **Cultivate Gratitude**: Reflecting on what you're thankful for helps shift focus toward the positive aspects of life.

Here are some ideas for recipients who would appreciate your gratitude:

1. Consider writing thank-you notes to individuals who contribute to your daily life or community:
2. NHS Staff: Thank healthcare workers for their dedication during challenging times.
3. Delivery Drivers: Show appreciation for their hard work in ensuring timely deliveries.
4. Local Shop Owners: Acknowledge their service in supporting your neighbourhood.

5. Sponsors or Mentors: Thank them for their guidance, accountability, and encouragement in your recovery.
6. Therapists or Counsellors: Appreciate their compassionate support and tools for navigating challenges.
7. Family Members: Acknowledge their love, patience, and unwavering support during tough times.
8. Friends: Thank them for their loyalty, positivity, and belief in your journey.
9. Healthcare Providers: Recognise their care and expertise in managing your treatment.
10. Employers or Colleagues: Thank them for their understanding and creating a supportive work environment.
11. Addiction Treatment Centre Staff: Acknowledge their dedication to your care and recovery structure.
12. Sober Living House Managers or Roommates: Appreciate the safe, supportive living environment they provided.
13. Religious or Spiritual Leaders: Thank them for offering hope, guidance, and spiritual support.
14. Social Workers or Case Managers: Recognise their help in coordinating resources that supported your recovery.
15. Probation Officers or Legal Professionals: Appreciate their fairness and encouragement during rehabilitation.
16. Teachers or Educators: Thank them for accommodating your needs and encouraging personal growth.
17. Neighbours: Acknowledge their kindness and practical support during your journey.
18. Community Outreach Workers: Thank them for connecting you with essential resources during recovery.

Writing thank-you notes is more than just etiquette—it's an opportunity to connect with others while cultivating gratitude and positivity in your own life. By taking six minutes today to craft a thoughtful message, you can brighten someone's day while boosting your own emotional wellbeing.

Grab some paper—choose your recipient—and start writing! Your small gesture could make a big difference!

Activity 159. Practice Mindful Listening

Listening is a skill we often take for granted. Many people hear, but they don't truly listen. Have you ever had this scenario? You ask your partner or family member, "Can you empty the recycling and put the bin out, please?" ... No response. You follow up with, "Did you hear me?" and they reply, "Yes, the bins." But you know they didn't really listen—chances are, if they do put the bin out, they'll forget about the recycling!

I can always tell when my husband is listening versus when he's simply hearing my voice. The difference is profound, especially when I'm feeling emotional and need to be heard. Mindful listening is not just about hearing words—it's about creating a space where someone feels understood and valued. This skill is essential in every type of relationship: with partners, parents, children, friends, or colleagues. Mindful listening goes beyond basic communication; it fosters deeper connections and builds trust. When practiced regularly, it can transform relationships by making conversations more meaningful and productive. Here are some key benefits of mindful listening:

- **Improves Communication**: Strengthens relationships by reducing misunderstandings.
- **Enhances Empathy**: Helps you understand others' emotions and perspectives.
- **Reduces Conflicts**: Creates clarity and prevents unnecessary arguments.
- **Regulates Emotions**: Helps you stay calm and present during difficult conversations.
- **Encourages Growth**: Allows you to learn from others' experiences and viewpoints.
- **Promotes Presence**: Keeps you focused on the moment instead of distractions.
- **Makes Others Feel Valued**: Shows people that their words matter to you.

Mindful listening creates a safe space for authentic expression, which can lead to more satisfying personal and professional relationships. Mindful listening requires intention and focus. It's not about preparing your response while someone speaks, it's about fully immersing yourself in what they're saying without judgment or distraction. Here's how to get started:

1. Set an Intention: Before a conversation begins, decide to listen mindfully.
2. Give Full Attention: Eliminate distractions like phones or background noise.
3. Focus on Details: Pay attention to the speaker's words, tone, and body language.
4. Redirect Wandering Thoughts: If your mind drifts, gently bring it back to the conversation.
5. Ask Open-Ended Questions: Show engagement by asking questions that invite deeper sharing.
6. Reflect Back: Summarize what you've heard to confirm understanding.
7. Be Patient: Avoid interrupting or reacting immediately; let the speaker finish their thoughts.

To develop this skill further, try these practical exercises:

1. **Three-Minute Breathing Space**
   - Find a quiet place and set a timer for three minutes.
   - Close your eyes and focus on your breath as it flows in and out.
   - If your mind wanders, gently bring your attention back to breathing.
   - When the timer ends, open your eyes and notice how calm and cantered you feel.

2. **Mindful Conversation Practice**
   - Choose a topic with a partner and set a time limit (e.g., five minutes each).
   - One person speaks while the other listens attentively without interrupting.
   - The listener can only ask open-ended questions for clarification (no commentary)!
   - Switch roles and repeat.

3. **Active Listening to Media**
   - Select a podcast, video, or speech (keep it short—five to ten minutes).
   - Listen with full attention—no multitasking or note-taking allowed!
   - Afterward, summarize the main points, details, and even the speaker's tone or purpose.

4. **Silent Listening Exercise**
   - Ask someone to share something important with you, a story or concern they care about.
   - Listen silently without interrupting or commenting; use only body language (eye contact, nodding) to show engagement.
   - Afterward, thank them for sharing and reflect together on how the experience felt.

5. **Mindful Sound Awareness**
   - Sit quietly in a room or outdoors and close your eyes.
   - Focus on identifying as many sounds as possible—birds chirping, cars passing by, distant voices—without judgment.
   - Practice this regularly to sharpen your overall listening awareness.

Mindful listening isn't just about hearing words, it's about giving someone your undivided attention in a way that makes them feel truly seen and heard. It strengthens bonds by fostering mutual respect and understanding while helping you stay grounded in the present moment. The beauty of mindful listening lies in its simplicity—you don't need fancy tools or hours of practice to start seeing results! Just commit to being fully present during conversations with loved ones or colleagues. Over time, this skill will enhance not only your relationships but also your ability to connect deeply with others. So next time someone speaks to you, whether it's a casual chat or an emotional discussion, pause for a moment before responding. Focus on their words with curiosity and compassion and watch how this small shift transforms your interactions.

Activity 160. Practice Decision-Making Skills

Decision-making is an essential life skill that influences every aspect of our personal and professional lives. By practicing and refining these skills, you can enhance your ability to navigate challenges, reduce stress, and build confidence in your choices. Whether you're recovering from addiction, striving for career growth, or simply seeking to improve your daily decision-making, this activity can empower you to take control of your life with clarity and purpose. Practicing decision-making skills offers significant benefits for both mental and physical health:

- **Improved Problem-Solving**: Strengthening decision-making skills enhances critical thinking and equips you to analyse complex situations effectively. This ability helps reduce feelings of overwhelm and fosters a sense of control over life's challenges.
- **Stress Reduction**: Making confident decisions alleviates anxiety and eliminates the mental energy wasted on second-guessing or indecision. Lower stress levels contribute to better overall health and emotional stability.
- **Enhanced Self-Confidence**: Practicing decision-making builds trust in your judgment, fostering self-esteem and resilience when faced with difficult choices.
- **Better Coping Mechanisms**: Decision-making skills help you evaluate situations objectively, empowering you to make healthier choices that align with your goals and values.
- **Long-Term Success**: Consistently making positive decisions strengthens your ability to avoid harmful habits or triggers, supporting personal growth and sustained wellbeing.

By honing this skill, you can foster a sense of empowerment that positively impacts relationships, career development, and overall quality of life. There are plenty of engaging ways to practice decision-making skills that are both practical and fun. Here are some methods to get started:

1. **Daily Life Decisions** - Start by consciously reflecting on small everyday choices:
   - What should I eat for lunch?
   - How should I spend my free time today?
   - What's the best way to approach a task at work?

Take a moment to weigh the pros and cons before making these decisions, focusing on the reasoning behind your choice.

2. **Thought-Provoking Activities** - Try exercises that stimulate critical thinking:
   - *Would You Rather*: Pose hypothetical scenarios that require choosing between two options (e.g., "Would you rather live in the mountains or by the sea?"). Reflect on why you made your choice.

- *How the Story Goes*: Create a short story with decision points where you choose what happens next—this encourages creative thinking while practicing decision-making.

3. **Games That Build Decision Skills** - Engage in strategy-based games that simulate real-world challenges:
   - *Chess*: Develops strategic thinking by requiring players to anticipate consequences several moves ahead.
   - *Risk*: Combines elements of negotiation, probability, and long-term planning.
   - *Monopoly*: Teaches financial decision-making through investment strategies and resource management.

Decision-making is not just about solving problems, it's about building confidence in your ability to navigate life's uncertainties with clarity and purpose. Here's why it matters:
1. Empowerment: Practicing decision-making gives you a sense of control over your choices, reducing feelings of helplessness or indecision.
2. Growth Mindset: Each decision—whether successful or not—provides an opportunity for learning and improvement, fostering adaptability in various situations.
3. Better Relationships: Strong decision-making skills improve communication and collaboration with others, enhancing personal and professional connections.
4. Resilience: Making thoughtful decisions equips you to handle setbacks more effectively, building emotional strength over time.

If traditional methods feel too structured, try incorporating these enjoyable activities into your routine:
Musical Chairs - Quick thinking under pressure - Encourages adaptability
Tic-Tac-Toe - Simple strategy-building - Develops pattern recognition
Team Flag Design - Collaborative creativity - Enhances group decision-making
Hide-and-Seek - Strategic planning - Sharpens problem-solving skills

These activities provide a low-risk environment for practicing decisions while having fun! Have a look around as there are opportunities to develop decision-making skills through local workshops or online platforms focused on personal development. Consider exploring community events or organisations that offer team-building exercises or leadership training.

Practicing decision-making is more than just improving how you choose—it's about fostering confidence, reducing stress, and building resilience in all areas of life. Whether through games, daily reflections, or collaborative activities, this skill empowers you to approach challenges thoughtfully while embracing opportunities for growth. Next time cravings strike, or stress feels overwhelming, take six minutes to practice decision-making—you'll not only distract yourself but also strengthen your ability to navigate life with clarity and purpose!

Activity 161. Research a Dream Destination

Dreaming about travel gives the mind room to play, hope, and discover. By researching a place you'd love to visit, you can escape daily pressures, experience excitement, and build skills that boost well-being and recovery. This activity can be as in-depth or as imaginative as you want, with zero pressure to actually book a trip.

Mental and Emotional Benefits

- Imagining yourself somewhere new boosts happiness through anticipation and dopamine release.
- Dreaming up journeys provides a mental break from stress and routines, helping you recharge.
- Immersing yourself in culture, local food, or language lets you be present in the moment, which is great for mindfulness.
- For those in recovery, having future travel goals can serve as inspiration—keeping your focus rooted in possibilities and progress.

Cognitive and Personal Growth

- Researching a destination sparks creativity—it introduces new ideas, climates, foods, and histories.
- Planning itineraries and budgets exercises decision-making and organisational skills, building confidence for future real-world planning.

Step-by-Step Guide to Your Dream Escape

1. Pick a Destination
Dream big: a remote mountain retreat, a bustling city, or a soothing beach—where have you always wanted to go? No place is too wild or too simple.

2. Do Your Research
- Browse travel sites or apps to learn about where to stay, what to see, and how to get around.
- Watch travel videos or documentaries for visuals, vibes, and local voices.
- Read blogs or books to uncover hidden gems, local customs, or off-the-beaten-track stops.

3. Create an Itinerary
- List your must-see attractions (famous landmarks, museums, parks).
- Add less-famous gems to personalise your imaginary journey.
- Sketch a rough daily plan ("Morning: market visit; Afternoon: beach walk").

4. Budget for Fun (and Practice!)
- Look up sample prices for flights, hotels, food, and excursions.

- Calculate a rough budget—even if you're not going now, it's great real-world practice.

Making Your Destination Real—Without Booking a Flight
Engage with Local Culture—From Home
- Learn greetings and phrases in the destination's language using apps or YouTube.
- Cook a traditional meal or order takeout that reflects the region's cuisine.
- Explore the area's music—find playlists or live performances online.
- Watch films, documentaries, or series set in your dream destination.

Visualise and Get Inspired
- Make a vision board: Print off images, stick them in a notebook, create a Pinterest or digital collage, or use magazine cutouts.
- Include photos, fun facts, food pics, maps, and personal notes about why this place matters to you.

Expand and Adapt
- Consider "micro-adventures" inspired by your research—visit a local botanical garden if you dream of tropical forests, or a city walk if urban travel excites you.
- Use the experience to try new hobbies, like cooking or music, even before you set foot abroad.

Recovery-Focused Ideas
- Let researching destinations distract and uplift on difficult days—swap cravings for curiosity about local art or street food.
- Use future travel as a reward milestone: "When I reach this goal, I'll take steps toward this trip."
- Planning (even when not travelling) builds resilience, patience, and adaptability—crucial skills for lasting well-being.

Researching a dream trip isn't just escapism—it's an active way to spark hope, learn, and create new emotional anchors for the future. In six focused minutes, pick a place, start exploring, and let each detail become a stepping stone on the journey to a more joyful, empowered self. No matter where life leads you, the world remains yours to discover—one dream at a time.

Activity 162. Create a sound map

Sound mapping is all about connecting deeply to your environment by tuning in to the world of sound around you. By sitting quietly and documenting what you hear—whether in nature, the city, or inside your own home—you practice presence, soothe your mind, and celebrate creativity. This gentle activity is especially supportive for managing stress, anxiety, or recovery challenges.

How to Create Your Sound Map
1. Choose Your Spot - Pick a place full of sounds. This could be a peaceful park, a bustling street, your garden, or a favourite sunny spot indoors. Make sure it feels safe and comfortable for you to sit quietly for a while.

2. Gather What You Need
- For drawing: Paper, pencils, markers, or crayons.
- For digital mapping: Use your phone for voice memos and platforms like Google My Maps or SoundCloud if you want to get high-tech.

3. Settle In and Listen - Take 5–30 minutes to sit, close your eyes, and focus solely on what you hear. Attend to:
- Nature (birds, wind, water)
- Human sounds (conversations, footsteps, vehicles)
- Far-away noises (planes, distant traffic)
- Close-up sounds (rustling leaves, an insect buzzing)

4. Map Your Experience
- Draw an "X" in the center to show where you are.
- Draw arrows or lines pointing out in the direction of each sound.
- Use colours or shapes to show different types (maybe green for birds, blue for water, red for traffic).
- For digital maps, record sounds and mark or upload them to a map or sharing platform later.

5. Pause and Reflect - When you've filled your map, sit and notice how each sound made you feel, how the space's mood shifted, or if anything surprised you. Jot down a few words or a short paragraph about your experience right on your map if you wish.

The Well-Being Benefits
- Sound maps foster *mindfulness* by anchoring you in the 'now'.
- Listening deeply is a form of meditation that soothes the nervous system and lowers anxiety.
- The creative translation from ear to page (or app) inspires your imagination and problem-solving skills.

- Paying attention to pleasant or interesting sounds can break cycles of stressful thinking and boost emotional balance.

Physical and Emotional Effects
- Concentrated listening sharpens focus and attention to detail.
- Exposure to nature sounds—like bird song or water—can help relax body and mind, reducing heart rate and blood pressure.
- The process heightens awareness of all senses, gently shifting your state from tense to calm.

Sound Map Variations
- **Nature Map:** Head to a green space, documenting every bird call, babbling brook, or breeze.
- **City Map:** Chronicle the urban symphony—from street vendors and music to footsteps and horns.
- **Home Map:** Notice the hum of appliances, ticking clocks, or laughter in the next room.
- **Theme Map:** Focus on just one type of sound, like water or wind, and explore its character in different places.

Try These Creative Twists
- Add a journal reflection, write how each sound made you feel or what memory it triggered.
- Create mixed media with sketches, found objects, or photos to bring your map to life.
- Invite others to create sound maps beside you and share what you each noticed—everyone perceives the world a little differently!
- Revisit a favourite location in a different season or weather and create a new map—a mindful way to see (and hear) how the world changes.

Success Tips
- Be patient: The more you listen, the more you hear.
- Don't strive for perfect; focus on playfully capturing the feel of your experience.
- Use this activity when feeling anxious or unfocused, as they are grounding and easy to do anywhere, anytime.

Sound mapping is a wonderful, therapeutic practice that builds awareness, renews your appreciation for everyday life, and supports both creative and personal well-being. Whenever you need grounding, inspiration, or a mindful pause in your day, let the act of listening—and mapping what you hear, bring you back to the present and deepen your sense of connection to the world around you.

Activity 163. Try colour therapy

Colour therapy (chromotherapy) is a holistic approach that taps into how different colours can affect mood, energy, and healing. Used since ancient times, this technique uses the unique energy of each hue to support emotional balance, relaxation, creativity, and recovery. By intentionally exposing oneself to certain colours—whether through home decor, art, nature, clothing, or mindful activities—people can gently shift their mental state or support recovery from stress, anxiety, or addiction.

How Colours Can Help

- **Blue** brings calm, peace, and mental clarity. Being surrounded by blue—like wall colours, artwork, or even the sky—can help lower stress and anxiety and encourage restful sleep. Try incorporating blue into your bedroom or workspace or enjoy time by water for natural blue hues.
- **Green** soothes and restores. It represents renewal, growth, and emotional harmony. Add plants to your home, decorate with green accents, or take daily walks in parks to feel grounded.
- **Yellow** boosts optimism and energy. This cheerful shade inspires happiness and stimulates the mind. Try adding yellow through flowers, clothing, or creative supplies—but use sparingly if you're sensitive to overstimulation.
- **Red** energises and motivates. Great for boosting confidence or getting active, red can add warmth and drive—think a red mug, exercise band, or bold accessory. Use with care in spaces where calm is needed.
- **Purple** encourages creativity and reflection. Perfect for a meditation corner or creative space, purple shades can inspire introspection and inner peace.
- **Orange** brings warmth and sociability. Use orange in dining or gathering spaces, or as a playful accent in your accessories, to create an inviting and confident atmosphere.

Colours have different wavelengths and psychological effects. For instance, cool tones genuinely calm the mind and body, while vibrant hues spark engagement and positivity. Intentionally choosing colours to surround yourself with can subtly but meaningfully affect your mood and energy over time.

Practical Colour Therapy Activities

Choose one or try them all over the next week:

1. **Colour Visualisation Meditation:** Sit comfortably and close your eyes. Think of a colour that feels supportive (blue for calm, yellow for joy, green for harmony). Imagine breathing this colour in with every inhale, letting it fill your whole body as you focus on relaxation. Exhale and release tension, continuing for several minutes.

2. **Mindful Colour Walk:**
   Head outdoors, pick a focus colour, and spend 10–20 minutes noticing all the places you see that colour—leaves, flowers, doors, clothing. Pause at each discovery and notice how it affects your mood.

3. **Expressive Colour Art:**
   Using coloured pencils, pens, or paints, freely fill a page with whichever colours feel right for you at this moment. Let yourself choose shades based on your feelings (not overthinking it). Afterwards, reflect: did certain colours make you feel calmer, happier, or more reflective?

Creative Ways to Apply Colour for Well-being
- Add soft blue or green tones to your bedroom, living room, or meditation space for relaxation and emotional grounding.
- Plant green herbs, keep a vase of yellow daffodils, wear a favourite red or orange scarf, let colours become little rituals supporting your mood and motivation.
- Use yellow or orange accents in kitchens or creative spaces to energise your mornings and lift your spirits.
- Decorate your journaling area with purple or lavender hues to boost creativity and reflective thinking.

Journalling for Colour Awareness
At the end of each day, jot down which colours you noticed most, welcomed into your life, or wore. Briefly describe any changes in your mood or energy. After a week, notice which colours seem to help you most—add more of those to your environment or routines.

Making Colour Therapy Your Own
- Experiment: Try new colours in small ways, like a mug, notebook, or artwork, and pay attention to your response.
- Personalise: Everyone's reaction to colour is unique. Choose shades that work for you—even if they're different from common recommendations.
- Be consistent: The more you're exposed to supportive colours, the more benefits you may see for mood, sleep, energy, and coping.

Colour therapy is creative, accessible, and easy to adapt to your lifestyle. Whether you're seeking calm, clarity, energy, or hope on your recovery journey, using colours intentionally—in your space, art, wardrobe, or self-care—can gently support emotional and physical well-being.

Activity 164. Start coin collecting

Coin collecting, also called **numismatics,** is an engaging hobby that brings together history, curiosity, and mindful focus. Sometimes, stories of rare or misprinted UK coins send people hunting through their pocket change and create a sense of excitement across the country. Whether you're after mythical rarities or enjoying themed collections, this activity adds relaxation and a sense of discovery to everyday life.

Coin collecting (numismatics) provides a calming escape from daily worries, encourages mindfulness, and can boost self-esteem when you find or complete part of a collection. Examining details on coins sharpens memory and builds problem-solving skills. It also helps with fine motor coordination, and the peaceful pace of collecting can lower stress. Clubs and online communities turn this hobby into a way to connect, share, and learn.

How to Start
1. **Check Your Change:** Look for commemorative 50p or £2 coins (like Paddington Bear or Olympics designs) and rare errors in your everyday money.
2. **Coin Roll Hunting:** Exchange cash for bank coin rolls and search for special finds at home—great for rainy days or quiet weekends.
3. **Pick a Theme:** Collect coins by subject (animals, music legends, historic periods) or special editions.
4. **Attend Coin Shows:** See rare finds up close, chat with other collectors, and learn more about numismatics.
5. **Use Tech Tools:** Try apps or social platforms to join auctions, ask questions, or trade coins with others.

Every coin has a unique story—about historical events, famous people, or even manufacturing quirks. Coin collecting isn't about having lots of money but about noticing surprises and learning something new.

Real-Life Finds
- A rare "leopard" coin from the 1300s was found in market change and fetched over £100,000.
- A one-metal King Charles III £1 error sold for £1,250.
- Special misprints like the Peter Rabbit 50p have caused bidding frenzies online.

Tips for Beginners
- Start with fun, affordable themes (Paddington Bear, dinosaurs, music icons).
- Research what you find—every coin teaches you something.
- Make it a group activity—kids or family can join the hunt.

Success Tips
- Check rare coins for authenticity with guides or trusted websites.
- Store coins in albums or cases to keep them safe and organised.
- Enjoy the process—the main rewards are discovery, learning, and mindfulness, not profit.

Why It's Great for Recovery
- Numismatics is a positive, soothing ritual. It creates gentle routines, builds focus, and celebrates small achievements—perfect for those building resilience or needing uplifting distractions.
- Every little discovery is a reminder that patience and curiosity turn ordinary moments into something special.

Coin collecting transforms spare change into mindful adventures and newfound confidence. Whether sparked by legendary headlines or quiet interest in themed sets, let numismatics bring calm, learning, and joy—one coin at a time.

Activity 165. Sign Up for a Volunteer Opportunity

Volunteering is a rewarding way to give back to your community while improving your own mental and physical wellbeing. Whether you're helping others face-to-face or contributing remotely, volunteering fosters a sense of purpose, builds connections, and enhances personal growth. It's an activity that benefits both the giver and the receiver, making it a powerful tool for creating positive change in your life and the lives of others. Volunteering offers numerous benefits that can significantly enhance your overall wellbeing:

Mental Health Benefits
- Reduces Stress: Helping others shifts focus away from personal worries, releasing dopamine to promote relaxation and positivity.
- Combats Depression and Anxiety: Studies show that volunteering reduces symptoms of depression and anxiety by fostering accomplishment and motivation.
- Boosts Self-Esteem: Learning new skills and contributing to meaningful causes increases confidence and provides a sense of purpose.
- Prevents Isolation: Volunteering connects you with others, combating loneliness and expanding your social network.

Physical Health Benefits
- Improves Heart Health: Volunteering has been linked to lower cholesterol, reduced inflammation, and better overall cardiovascular health.
- Encourages Physical Activity: Many volunteer roles involve movement, improving flexibility, circulation, and fitness levels.
- Extends Lifespan: Research shows volunteers have lower mortality rates than non-volunteers due to improved physical and emotional health.

Follow these steps to find and sign up for a volunteer opportunity that suits your interests and schedule:

1.Identify Your Interests - Think about causes you care about, whether it's animal welfare, environmental, educational, or healthcare and choose roles aligned with your passions.

2. Search for Opportunities
   - Use online platforms like Do-it.org or Volunteer Scotland to find local opportunities.
   - Contact local charities or community centres directly for available roles.
   - Explore remote options like crisis counselling or transcription projects if you prefer working from home.

3. **Commit to a Role** - Choose a role that fits your availability and skills, whether it's tutoring students, organising food bank donations, or helping at an animal shelter.

4. **Prepare Yourself** - Attend any required training sessions or orientations for your chosen role. Familiarise yourself with the organisation's mission and goals.

5. **Start Volunteering** - Dedicate time regularly to your chosen activity, whether weekly or monthly, and reflect on the impact you're making.

Here are some examples of volunteering opportunities to inspire you:

Community Service - Tutoring students, assisting at food banks, mentoring youth
Environmental Work - Cleaning parks, conducting wildlife surveys
Animal Welfare - for shelter animals, assisting with wildlife rescue
Healthcare Support - Volunteering at clinics or mental health initiatives
Remote Roles - Crisis counselling via text lines, transcribing historical documents

Volunteering isn't just about helping others, it's also about enriching your own life through meaningful experiences. Here's why it's worth doing:

1. Build Community Connections: Volunteering fosters relationships within your local area while promoting social awareness.
2. Develop New Skills: Many roles offer opportunities to learn valuable skills like leadership, communication, or project management.
3. Enhance Personal Growth: Giving back provides a sense of purpose that boosts self-esteem and emotional resilience.

Suggestions for Roles (Even If You Have a Job)

If you're balancing work commitments but still want to volunteer, consider these flexible options:

1. Weekend Roles: Help at charity events or clean-up drives on weekends.
2. Remote Volunteering: Participate in online roles like proofreading e-books or managing social media for non-profits.
3. Short-Term Projects: Join seasonal initiatives like holiday gift drives or fundraising campaigns.
4. Micro-Volunteering: Spend just a few hours on tasks like writing letters of encouragement or knitting items for charity.

Volunteering is more than an act of kindness—it's an opportunity to grow as an individual while making a tangible difference in the world around you. By dedicating just six minutes today to researching opportunities near you, you can take the first step toward improving your wellbeing while positively impacting others.

Activity 166. Create a DIY pet toy

Creating DIY pet toys is an enjoyable and cost-effective activity that benefits both pets and their owners. These homemade toys provide mental stimulation, physical engagement, and emotional bonding for pets, while offering a therapeutic outlet for individuals, especially those managing mental health challenges or recovering from addiction. Additionally, crafting toys for other people's pets can be a thoughtful gesture—just ensure the pet has no allergies or sensitivities to the materials used.

For Pets
- **Mental Stimulation**: Interactive toys like treat dispensers or puzzle feeders challenge pets to use problem-solving skills, keeping their minds active.
- **Physical Activity**: Tug toys, chase games, and snuffle mats encourage movement, helping to maintain a healthy weight and muscle tone.
- **Reduced Stress**: Engaging with toys can alleviate boredom and reduce anxiety in pets, especially those prone to separation anxiety.

For Owners
- **Mindfulness**: Crafting pet toys is a calming activity that promotes focus and creativity.
- **Bonding**: Playing with pets using homemade toys strengthens the emotional connection between owner and pet.
- **Therapeutic Benefits**: For individuals in addiction recovery or managing mental health challenges, creating something tangible fosters a sense of accomplishment and purpose.

Here are some simple ideas for crafting pet toys using everyday items:

Interactive Treat Toys
1. Toilet Tube Treat Dispenser - Take an empty toilet paper roll, cut small holes into it, place treats inside, and fold the ends closed. Pets will roll and paw at the tube to retrieve treats.
2. Shoebox Hide-and-Seek - Cut holes in the lid of an empty shoebox, place treats inside, and let your pet figure out how to retrieve them.

Tug Toys
1. T-Shirt Rope Toy: Cut an old T-shirt into strips, braid them tightly, and knot the ends. For added fun, incorporate a tennis ball into the design.
2. Towel Tug Toy: Cut a sturdy towel into strips, braid them together, and tie knots at both ends for a durable chew toy.

Foraging Toys
1. Snuffle Mat - Use a rubber sink mat as a base and tie fleece strips through the holes to create a "fleece forest." Hide treats in the fleece for your pet to sniff out.

2. Destruction Box - Fill a cardboard box with scrap materials like paper or fabric strips and hide treats inside for your pet to forage.

Chase Toys
1. Sock Octopus - Roll one sock into a ball (the "head"), cover it with another sock, and attach additional socks as tentacles by cutting them into strips.
2. Plastic Bottle Tug Toy - Wrap an empty plastic bottle in fabric or an old sock for a crinkly toy that pets love.

Crafting pet toys is more than just an economical alternative to store-bought options, it's an opportunity to engage creatively while improving wellbeing for both pets and owners. You can tailor toys to your pet's preferences (e.g., adding catnip for cats or treats for dogs). It is eco-friendly, as you are repurposing household items like cardboard boxes or old clothing instead of discarding them and it is a very thoughtful gift. Making toys for other people's pets is a wonderful way to show you care, just ensure the materials are safe and allergy-free.

For individuals managing mental health challenges or recovering from addiction, crafting DIY pet toys offers unique benefits:

1. Therapeutic Creativity: The process of designing and assembling toys encourages mindfulness and reduces stress by focusing on the present moment.
2. Sense of Purpose: Creating something tangible fosters feelings of accomplishment—a vital aspect of recovery.
3. Social Connection: Sharing homemade toys with friends or local shelters can build community ties while spreading joy.
4. Routine Building: Incorporating toy-making into daily routines provides structure, which is crucial during recovery.

Safety Tips When Crafting Pet Toys

Whether making toys for your own pet or someone else's, keep these precautions in mind:
- Use non-toxic materials suitable for pets (e.g., avoid sharp objects or choking hazards).
- Ensure all parts are securely attached—loose pieces can be swallowed accidentally.
- Check for allergies before gifting toys to other people's pets (e.g., avoid wool if the pet has sensitivities).
- Supervise playtime when introducing new toys to ensure safety.

Crafting DIY pet toys is not only fun but also a meaningful way to enhance wellbeing for both humans and animals alike. By combining creativity with care, you can create engaging toys that promote physical activity, mental stimulation, and emotional bonding, all while supporting your own journey toward better mental health or addiction recovery.

Activity 167. Create a found object sculpture

Found object sculpture is a fun, eco-friendly way to express creativity by turning everyday objects into art. This activity, also called "assemblage," is particularly valuable for boosting mindfulness, motor skills, and self-esteem, making it a perfect mood-boosting project for those in recovery or dealing with stress.

Why Create a Found Object Sculpture?
- **Mindfulness & Stress Relief:** Collecting and arranging objects encourages presence in the moment, which reduces anxiety and fosters relaxation.
- **Creative Expression:** Sculptures can tell a personal or social story—there's no right or wrong way to make them.
- **Achievement:** Completing a piece delivers a strong sense of accomplishment and growth.
- **Dexterity:** Handling and attaching a range of materials enhances hand-eye coordination.
- **Physical Activity:** Gathering materials means moving around the home or outdoors, supporting gentle exercise.
- **Connection:** Sharing finished sculptures with others can build social ties and spark meaningful conversations.

Materials You'll Need
- **Base:** Cardboard, wood, or any sturdy foundation.
- **Adhesive:** Choose based on materials—PVA glue for lightweight, hot glue or super glue for heavier items.
- **Found Objects:**
  - *Natural Materials:* Stones, driftwood, shells, leaves
  - *Man-made/Industrial:* Scrap metal, broken ceramics, bottle caps, gears
  - *Everyday Items:* Buttons, toys, clock parts, electronics

Step-by-Step Instructions

1. **Gather Materials** - Explore your surroundings, indoors and outside, for items with fun shapes, textures, or personal meaning. Try parks, beaches, or your recycling for inspiration.
2. **Plan Your Design** - Arrange pieces on a table or tray, experimenting with different layouts. Consider a theme—like nature, technology, or a particular emotion—or just create intuitively.
3. **Prepare the Base** - Select a study base. Cardboard is excellent for small or lightweight sculptures; for heavier works, opt for a wooden block or stand.
4. **Start Assembly** - Use the right glue for your objects and attach the largest or most important parts first. Build upward and outward, checking stability as you go.

5. **Layer and Balance** - Add more objects, playing with colour and texture for variety. Layer items to create interesting focal points, but be mindful of balance so the sculpture stands securely.
6. **Add Details** - Fill small gaps with buttons, beads, or patterned scraps to give the sculpture extra detail and personality.
7. **Secure and Finish** - Check that all parts are firmly attached. Reinforce weak spots with extra glue if needed.
8. **Embellishments (Optional)** - Try painting parts of your sculpture or adding decorations like glitter, stickers, or small LED lights for dramatic effect.

Examples of Materials
- **Nature:** Driftwood, stones, shells, dried plants
- **Industrial:** Scrap metal, gears, nails, bolts
- **Home/Everyday:** Bottle caps, broken dishes, toys, kitchen tools, wires
- **Artistic:** Resin, coloured glue, paint, LED lights

Therapeutic Benefits
- *Sustainability:* Reduces waste by repurposing items.
- *Personal Meaning:* Adds depth if using sentimental or symbolic objects.
- *Routine and Focus:* Structure and routine are healing in recovery; creative projects fill free time and offer purpose.
- *Community & Giving:* Finished sculptures make unique gifts or donations, fostering a sense of contribution and belonging.

Recovery-Specific Tips
- Use the process to symbolise your personal journey; e.g., objects representing challenges or strengths.
- Gift sculptures to others (or charities) for connection and self-worth.
- If crafting for pets or others, use only safe, non-toxic, allergy-free materials, and avoid choking hazards for animals.

Safety & Best Practice
- Avoid sharp or toxic materials; supervise young helpers.
- Check adhesives for allergens and use suitable glue for object weight.
- For pet art: avoid small, detachable pieces and supervise animals.

Creating a found object sculpture transforms the mundane into the meaningful. This mindful, sustainable craft delivers calm, creative joy, and a chance to connect with yourself and others. Each piece tells a story—make yours part of a positive, restorative journey.

Activity 168. Practice interview questions

Practicing interview questions involves preparing responses to common and challenging questions you might face during a job interview. This process helps you refine your communication skills, anticipate potential questions, and develop strategies for presenting yourself effectively. Even if you're not actively seeking a job, practicing interview questions can be a valuable exercise for personal growth, self-reflection, and improving your ability to articulate your thoughts in various situations.

Mental & Physical Wellbeing Benefits
- Reduces Stress and Anxiety: Familiarising yourself with interview scenarios in a low-pressure environment helps you feel more prepared and calmer when facing real-life interviews.
- Boosts Confidence: Repeated practice reinforces your belief in your abilities, making you feel more assured when presenting yourself to others.
- Encourages Self-Reflection: Crafting thoughtful answers allows you to assess your strengths, weaknesses, and achievements, fostering greater self-awareness.
- Improves Resilience: Learning how to handle challenging questions builds mental strength and adaptability.
- Promotes Relaxation Techniques: Practicing interviews often involves learning breathing exercises or other methods to stay calm under pressure, which can benefit overall health.
- Enhances Communication Skills: Improved verbal articulation and body language contribute to better interactions in both professional and personal settings.

Step 1: Identify Common Questions
Start with frequently asked interview questions such as:
- "Tell me about yourself."
- "What are your strengths and weaknesses?"
- "Describe a challenge you've faced at work."

Step 2: Use the STAR Method
Structure your answers using the STAR method (Situation, Task, Action, Result):
- Situation: Describe the context of the example you're sharing.
- Task: Explain the problem or goal you were addressing.
- Action: Detail the steps you took to resolve the issue or achieve the goal.
- Result: Highlight the positive outcome of your actions.

Step 3: Conduct Mock Interviews
Simulate real interviews with a friend, mentor, or career coach:
- Ask them to pose questions relevant to your field or goals.
- Record the session so you can review your performance later.

Step 4: Focus on Weaknesses
Practice answering questions about weaknesses by framing them as areas of growth:
- For example, "I tend to be overly critical of my own work, but I've learned to use this as motivation for continuous improvement."

Step 5: Tailor Responses
Customise your answers based on specific roles or industries:
- Highlight skills and experiences that align with the job description.

Step 6: Refine Delivery Skills
Work on verbal and non-verbal communication:
- Speak clearly and concisely while maintaining appropriate eye contact.
- Pay attention to tone of voice, posture, and gestures.

Even if you're not actively job hunting, practicing interview questions can benefit other areas of life:

Self-Assessment Tools
Reflect on past experiences and achievements to identify patterns of success or areas for improvement. Use online personality tests or skills assessments for deeper insights into your strengths.

Behavioural Question Practice
Focus on answering behavioural questions that require specific examples (e.g., "Tell me about a time when you worked as part of a team"). This helps develop storytelling skills that are useful in both professional and personal conversations.

Feedback Mechanisms
Seek constructive feedback from mock interviewers or mentors:
- Ask for advice on improving clarity, confidence, or impact in your responses.

Examples of Strengths and Weaknesses You Can Practice Framing Positively

Strengths
1. Leadership skills demonstrated through team projects.
2. Problem-solving abilities showcased in high-pressure situations.
3. Strong communication skills used to resolve conflicts effectively.

Weaknesses (Framed Positively)
1. Perfectionism: "I sometimes focus too much on details but have learned to balance this by prioritising deadlines."
2. Difficulty Saying No: "I'm eager to help colleagues but have improved my ability to set boundaries while maintaining collaboration."
3. Impatience: "I value efficiency and have learned to channel this energy into streamlining processes while practicing patience with others."

Sample Interview Questions for Practice

General Questions
- "Why do you want this role?"
- "What do you know about our company?"

Strengths and Weaknesses
- "What is your greatest strength?"
- "How do you handle criticism?"

Behavioural Questions
- "Give an example of how you handled a difficult situation at work."
- "Describe a time when you had to meet a tight deadline."

Situational Questions
- "How would you handle conflict with a coworker?"
- "What would you do if given feedback that you disagreed with?"

Tips for Success in Practicing Interview Questions

1. Set aside regular time for practice, this ensures steady improvement over time.
2. Record yourself answering questions to identify areas for refinement.
3. Practice answering confidently without sounding rehearsed, aim for authenticity.
4. Use feedback constructively, apply suggestions from mock interviews immediately.

Practicing interview questions is more than just preparing for job applications. It's an exercise in self-improvement that builds confidence, sharpens communication skills, and enhances self-awareness. Whether you're actively seeking employment or simply looking for ways to grow personally and professionally, dedicating time to this practice can unlock new opportunities while fostering resilience and clarity in all aspects of life!

Activity 169. Create a paper quilling design

Paper quilling, also known as paper filigree, is an artistic technique that involves rolling, shaping, and gluing strips of paper to create decorative designs. This intricate craft is not only visually rewarding but also offers numerous benefits for mental and physical wellbeing. Whether you're looking for a relaxing hobby or a therapeutic outlet, paper quilling can be an excellent choice. It's accessible to beginners, inexpensive to start, and provides endless opportunities for creativity.

Mental, Physical & Social Benefits

- **Stress Relief**: The repetitive motions of rolling and shaping paper strips can have a calming effect, helping to reduce stress and anxiety.
- **Mindfulness**: Quilling encourages focus on the present moment, promoting a meditative state that quiets the mind.
- **Creative Expression**: Designing unique patterns allows you to express yourself artistically, boosting self-esteem and providing a positive outlet for emotions.
- **Fine Motor Skills**: Manipulating small paper strips improves hand-eye coordination and dexterity.
- **Cognitive Function**: The detailed planning and execution required in quilling enhance problem-solving skills and memory.
- **Sharing your quilled creations with others**: whether as gifts or through community crafting groups, can foster social bonds and alleviate feelings of loneliness.

Materials Needed

- Quilling Paper Strips: Available in various widths and colours; 1/4" wide strips are ideal for beginners.
- Quilling Tool: A slotted tool makes rolling paper strips easy; advanced crafters may prefer needle tools for intricate designs.
- Glue: Use a needle-tip bottle for precise application.
- Tweezers: Helpful for handling small pieces.
- Circle Sizing Board (Optional): Ensures consistent coil sizes.

Steps to Get Started

1. **Gather Supplies** - Assemble your materials in a quiet workspace. Starter kits are budget-friendly options that include everything you need.

2. **Learn Basic Shapes** - Master fundamental quilling shapes such as:
  - Tight Coil: Roll the paper strip tightly around the tool, then glue the end.
  - Loose Coil: Create a tight coil, then let it expand slightly before gluing.
  - Teardrop: Make a loose coil and pinch one end to form a point.
  - Marquis: Pinch both ends of a loose coil to create an almond shape].

3. **Plan Your Design** - Choose a simple pattern or draw your own design on paper. Arrange the shapes before gluing them down to ensure balance and composition.

4. **Assemble Your Artwork** - Glue each piece carefully onto your base design using minimal adhesive to avoid messiness. Add details with smaller shapes or fringed paper for texture.

5. **Optional Embellishments** - Enhance your design by painting certain areas or adding decorative elements like glitter or beads.

Paper quilling is a versatile craft that can be used to create a wide range of projects, from decorative floral patterns and geometric designs for cards and wall art, to functional items like clocks and jewellery. It also allows for the creation of charming 3D figures such as mushrooms, turtles, and ladybugs by combining basic quilled shapes.

Engaging in paper quilling goes beyond creating beautiful designs—it's an opportunity to nurture your mental health while exploring creativity. It is an accessible hobby, requiring minimal materials, making it easy for anyone to start without significant investment. It provides structure and focus during challenging times, particularly beneficial for individuals recovering from addiction or managing mental health conditions. Finished quilling pieces boost confidence and provide a sense of accomplishment.

For individuals dealing with mental health challenges or recovering from addiction, paper quilling can be transformative as the rhythmic nature of quilling promotes relaxation while keeping the mind engaged in positive activity. Incorporating quilling into daily routines provides stability during recovery processes and when using specific colours or shapes can represent personal struggles or triumphs, adding deeper meaning to your creations.

Tips for Success

1. Start with simple patterns like flowers or geometric shapes before attempting complex designs like 3D figures or typography.
2. Use high-quality materials to ensure durability in your projects.
3. Work in a calming environment, light music or candles can enhance the therapeutic experience.
4. Join crafting communities online or locally to share ideas and gain inspiration.

Paper quilling is more than just an art form, it's a journey into mindfulness, creativity, and self-expression that benefits both mental and physical wellbeing. Whether you're crafting delicate flowers or intricate 3D sculptures, this versatile hobby offers endless possibilities while nurturing your emotional health along the way!

Activity 170. Practice mime techniques

Mime therapy, rooted in physiotherapy and performance art, offers a unique blend of physical movement and emotional expression. Originally developed to treat facial nerve disorders, its principles are now being adapted to support mental health and addiction recovery in the UK. This guide combines evidence-based techniques with practical applications, emphasizing mindfulness, emotional regulation, and community building.

Why Mime Therapy Benefits Mental Health and Recovery

Emotional Expression and Regulation
- Non-Verbal Communication: Mime therapy allows individuals to articulate complex emotions (e.g., grief, anger) without words, which is particularly valuable for those struggling to verbalise trauma or cravings.
- Symbolic Release: Exercises like miming "breaking free" from chains or walls provide a safe, metaphorical outlet for processing addiction-related struggles.

Stress Reduction and Mindfulness
- Breathing Techniques: Synchronised breathing with exaggerated diaphragm movements activates the parasympathetic nervous system, reducing anxiety.
- Present-Moment Focus: The meditative nature of controlled movements helps ground individuals during emotional triggers or cravings.

Improved Self-Esteem and Body Awareness
- Mirror Feedback: Practicing facial expressions and movements in front of a mirror helps reconnect individuals with their physical presence, countering dissociation common in trauma.
- Skill Mastery: Learning precise techniques (e.g., "fixed point" exercises) rebuilds confidence eroded by addiction.

Social Connection
- Group Synchronicity: Collaborative exercises, like mirroring movements or creating joint narratives, foster trust and reduce isolation, a cornerstone of recovery.

Core Exercises for Recovery
To be completed in front of a full length mirror

1. **Emotional Mask Work** - Explore suppressed emotions non-verbally.
    - Assign an emotion (e.g., fear, hope).
    - Convey it through facial expressions and body language.
    - Discuss physical and mental manifestations post-exercise.

2. Narrative Mime - Process personal recovery milestones.
- Create a routine symbolising a challenge (e.g., pushing through an invisible barrier).
- Use imaginary props like ropes to represent addiction.

3. Breathing and Relaxation Sequences
- Sit comfortably, mimic slow diaphragmatic breathing.
- Pair with gentle neck stretches to release tension.

4. Mirror Exercises
- Practice neutral expressions, then transition to exaggerated smiles/frowns.
- Observe how subtle changes alter perceived emotions.

Why Integrate Mime Therapy into UK Recovery Programs?

1. Trauma-Informed Care - Non-verbal methods are less confrontational for trauma survivors, making mime ideal for individuals resistant to talk therapy.
2. Cost-Effective Accessibility - Requires only mirrors and open spaces, aligning with NHS initiatives for low-cost mental health support.
3. Holistic Healing - Addresses both physical (posture, muscle tension) and psychological (self-esteem, stress) aspects of recovery.
4. Complement to Existing Therapies - Enhances EMDR by providing a physical outlet for emotional release.

Mime therapy, originally developed to help people with facial palsy (weakness or paralysis of facial muscles), has been shown to improve both facial movement and social confidence. In a 2003 clinical trial, patients who practiced mime therapy experienced not just better control of their facial muscles, but also became more comfortable socially, smiling, communicating, and expressing emotions became easier and more natural.

- **Boosts Social Confidence:** Patients felt more at ease interacting with others, which greatly improved their quality of life.
- **Improves Emotional Expression:** By practicing facial movements and expressions, people found it easier to communicate feelings.
- **Rehabilitation:** The exercises support both physical recovery and social reintegration, offering hope for those coping with changes in their appearance or abilities.

Mime therapy, by focusing on expressive movement, doesn't just train muscles—it unlocks confidence and helps people reconnect with others through the power of nonverbal communication.

Activity 171. Learn to tie different knots

Tying knots is an ancient, practical skill still relevant and rewarding in modern life. Whether securing a parcel, camping, or transforming cord into art, knot-tying builds both practical confidence and personal wellbeing. This mindful activity blends cognitive challenge with hands-on creativity and is especially helpful for fostering focus and routine during recovery.

Why Try Knot-Tying?
- **Cognitive Development:** Following knot sequences sharpens spatial awareness, memory, and attention to detail.
- **Stress Relief:** Repetitive hand motions help calm the mind and promote relaxation.
- **Creativity & Expression:** From functional tasks to artistic projects, knots expand imaginative problem-solving.
- **Fine Motor Skills:** Handling and manoeuvring cord improves dexterity and hand-eye coordination.
- **Strength Building:** Pulling and tightening knots works hand muscles, supporting everyday tasks like writing and tool use.
- **Social Connection:** Teaching others or collaborating on projects builds teamwork and communication.
- **Structure & Confidence:** Mastery of knots delivers a sense of accomplishment—essential for those rebuilding structure during recovery.

Materials Needed
- **Rope or Cord:** Start with a medium-thickness, soft rope for ease of use.
- **Anchor Object:** Use a chair leg, pole, or even your hand for practice.
- **Visual Aids:** Diagrams or step-by-step videos can help beginners follow each move.

Basic Knots to Master
1. **Overhand Knot:**
   A stopper knot to prevent ropes slipping through holes.
   - Form a loop, pass the end through, and tighten.
2. **Square (Reef) Knot:**
   For joining two ropes or securing bandages.
   - Right over left, then left over right and pull tight.
3. **Figure-Eight Knot:**
   A strong stopper for climbing or boating.
   - Make a loop, wrap the end around the rope, and thread it through the loop.
4. **Bowline Knot:**
   Creates a stable loop that won't slip.
   - Make a loop ("hole"), bring the end ("rabbit") up through, around the rope ("tree"), and back down the loop.

5. **Clove Hitch:**
   A quick way to attach rope to a post.
   - Wrap around, cross over to form an X, wrap below, tuck under, and tighten.
6. **Taut-Line Hitch:**
   Adjusts for tension—great for tents or tarps.
   - Wrap around the anchor, form two sliding loops on the standing rope.

Practical Uses
- **Everyday:** Tie shoelaces, secure parcels, fix clotheslines
- **Outdoors:** Set up tents/tarps, climbing, fishing, boating
- **Craft & Art:** Macramé, bracelets, nets, decorative wall hangings
- **Emergency:** Secure bandages, improvise stretchers, build shelters

Wellbeing Benefits
- **Mindfulness:** Focusing on each step keeps intrusive thoughts at bay and fosters calm.
- **Routine:** Regular practice adds structure—key for recovery and ongoing self-care.
- **Confidence:** Achieving new knots, even simple ones, boosts self-esteem.
- **Symbolism:** Knots metaphorically represent resilience—progress in "untangling" challenges.

What To Use
- Shoelaces or string for basic knots
- Paracord or tent lines for outdoor practice
- Macramé cord or yarn for creative projects
- Table legs, poles, or tree branches as anchors

Tips for Success
- Start simple, like overhand or square knots, before trying more complex knots.
- Use visual guides or online tutorials for clarity.
- Practice regularly to develop muscle memory and coordination.
- Join workshops or online forums to share progress and learn from others.

Mastering knots is more than a practical feat, it cultivates patience, creativity, mindfulness, and readiness for daily challenges. Each knot, from a basic stopper to a decorative braid, is a step toward improved focus and accomplishment on the journey to well-being.

Activity 172. Do a Sensory Awareness Exercise

Sensory awareness is a powerful mindfulness practice that invites attention to the present moment by exploring what is seen, heard, felt, smelled, or tasted—one sense at a time or several together. By slowing down and tuning into senses without judgment, this activity helps reduce stress, calm cravings, and foster a deeper connection with body and environment.

Why Practice Sensory Awareness?
- **Calms the Mind:** Focusing on senses grounds awareness, making anxious or racing thoughts less intrusive.
- **Promotes Mindfulness:** Engages attention fully with immediate surroundings, pulling you out of autopilot mode.
- **Improves Mood:** Sensory experiences evoke pleasure, comfort, or curiosity, supporting emotional balance.
- **Aids Craving Management:** Redirecting focus to the senses helps ride out urges or difficult moments in recovery.

Step-by-Step Exercise
1. **Find a Quiet Space** - Sit comfortably in a distraction-free spot.

2. **Choose One Sense**
   - *Sight:* Notice colours, shapes, and patterns nearby.
     - *Touch:* Feel the surface beneath, the air on skin, or the texture of an object.
     - *Sound:* Listen for layers in your environment: close, distant, steady, or intermittent.
     - *Smell:* Identify subtle or bold scents in the air.
     - *Taste:* Savor any lingering flavours or take a slow bite of food.

3. **Observe with Curiosity** - Act as if this is your first time experiencing these sensations.

4. **Refocus When Distracted** - If your thoughts wander, return attention to the chosen sense—kindly and without frustration.

5. **Practice Frequently** - Start with a few minutes daily and increase as you feel comfortable.

Sensory Awareness Activities
1. The Raisin Exercise
- Hold a raisin (or similar food) and discover it with all senses: sight (wrinkles, color), touch (surface), smell (aroma), and taste (slow, attentive chewing).
- Use this for mindful eating or whenever a craving hits.

2. The Five Senses Grounding
- Name 5 things you see.
- Name 4 things you feel.
- Name 3 things you hear.
- Name 2 things you smell.
- Name 1 thing you taste.
- This quick scan can anchor you during anxiety or overwhelm.

3. Nature Sense Meditation
- Sit outdoors with eyes closed for 5–20 minutes.
- Listen deeply, notice smells, feel air or sun on skin.
- Open your eyes and take in the scene without moving your head.

4. Blindfolded Exploration
- With a blindfold in a safe space, walk slowly and use touch, hearing, and smell to discover your surroundings freshly.

5. Barefoot Walking
- Walk barefoot on grass, sand, or another safe surface.
- Focus on each step—the changing temperatures, textures, and how your muscles respond.

6. Stillness Practice
- Sit totally still for 30 seconds to 5 minutes.
- Notice all the subtle and obvious sensations and sounds around and within you.

Tips for Success

- Don't worry about "doing it right." Curiosity, not perfection, is the goal.
- If you're feeling overwhelmed or craving, pause and use any of the above exercises for at least 6 minutes.
- Use everyday moments, waiting for the kettle, pausing on a walk, as mini-practices.

Practicing sensory awareness makes each day richer, and helps interrupt stress or cravings by rooting attention firmly in the here and now. Over time, these mindfulness skills become reliable tools for self-care, building resilience and enjoyment in daily life.

Activity 173. Update Your Budget

Reviewing and updating a budget is much more than balancing numbers—it's a proactive way to reduce stress, boost financial confidence, and support your overall wellbeing. This practice helps ensure your spending, saving, and goals reflect your real life, so you feel empowered and prepared for everyday needs and future plans.

Why Regular Budget Updates Matter?
- **Reduces Financial Stress:** Knowing where your money goes helps ease anxiety and uncertainty about bills or unexpected costs.
- **Builds Confidence:** Taking charge of your finances fosters self-esteem and enables informed decision-making.
- **Encourages Mindfulness:** Tracking income and spending encourages awareness, helping align purchases with values.
- **Supports Healthy Choices:** Greater stability means more freedom to choose healthier foods, wellness programs, or healthcare.
- **Improves Sleep & Focus:** Minimising money worries supports better rest and concentration.

Step-by-Step: How to Update Your Budget

1. Review Your Current Budget
- Check existing categories: housing, food, transport, savings.
- Spot any areas where you've overspent or come in under budget and note why.

2. Gather Up-to-Date Information
- Collect pay slips, recent bank/credit card statements, and receipts (covering 3–6 months if possible) and use this data to ensure accuracy.

3. Update Your Income
- Adjust for any job changes, freelance work, or one-off payments (bonuses, side gigs).

4. Reassess Expenses
- Fixed: Rent, bills, insurance, subscriptions.
- Variable: Groceries, utilities, transport, entertainment.
- Add new recurring costs (childcare, pet insurance) or remove outdated ones.

5. Adjust Savings Goals
- Review and prioritise both short-term (holidays, gift funds) and long-term savings (home deposit, pension).
- Allocate a practical percentage, even if small, toward these goals.

6. Use Helpful Tools - Try UK-friendly apps like Moneyhub, YNAB, or Snoop, as they can link with your bank for automatic updates.

7. Optimise Spending
- Identify expenses you can reduce (dining out, unused gym memberships).
- Redirect savings toward debts and your emergency fund.

Practical Ways to Save While Budgeting
- **Energy:**
  - Switch to LED bulbs and programmable thermostats (Hive or Nest).
  - Turn off appliances when not in use.
- **Groceries:**
  - Meal-plan before visiting the supermarket.
  - Opt for store brands, collect loyalty points (Nectar, Clubcard).
- **Transport:**
  - Use price comparison apps for fuel.
  - Save with public transport passes (e.g., Oyster in London).
- **Entertainment:**
  - Cancel or share unused subscriptions (like streaming services).
  - Find free local events or use libraries for books and DVDs.

Benefits of a Regular Budget Routine
- **Stay Prepared:** Updates ensure readiness for unexpected expenses while keeping other goals on track.

- **Achieve Your Goals:** Strategic allocation moves dream purchases or travel plans forward faster.

- **Feel Empowered:** Being on top of finances gives peace-of-mind and control during life's surprises.

Helpful UK Resources
- **MoneySavingExpert.com:** Expert guides and savings tips on UK living costs.
- **Which? Magazine:** Independent product/service reviews and consumer advice.
- **Citizens Advice Bureau:** Free support for budgeting and handling debt.
- **Local Council Sites:** Check for grants, discounts, or special support schemes (e.g., council tax relief).

Budgeting isn't restrictive, it's liberating. Take an hour this week to review and update your budget and repeat every few months. Whether you use a notebook or an app, you'll immediately feel more organised and empowered, setting yourself up for both small wins and long-term success.

Activity 174. Try ink blowing art

Ink Blowing Art is a playful, spontaneous technique that uses air—usually from a straw—to move and shape liquid ink or watercolours on paper. Each creation is beautifully unpredictable, with flowing lines and bursts of colour forming abstract designs, floral patterns, or whimsical creatures. This activity is perfect for expressing creativity and embracing the joy of artistic accidents.

Why Try Ink Blowing Art?
- **Mental Wellbeing:** The process is mesmerizing and meditative, helping to quiet worries and anchor your focus in the present moment.
- **Physical Wellbeing:** Blowing through a straw encourages steady breathing and gentle breath control, which promotes calm. Manipulating materials strengthens hand-eye coordination and fine motor skills.
- **Emotional Benefits:** The unpredictable nature nurtures adaptability, acceptance, and a sense of fun—a great way to let go of perfectionism.
- **Creativity Boost:** Embrace experimentation; no two ink pieces are ever the same!

Materials Needed
- **Paper:** Heavy or watercolour paper stands up best
- **Liquid Ink/Watercolours:** Any vibrant, free-flowing ink
- **Straws:** Cut in half for better control
- **Dropper/Pipette:** For placing ink
- **Workspace Covering:** Newspaper, tray, or an old tablecloth
- **Optional:** Hairdryer (on cool/low), compressed air, markers/pens for extra details

Step-by-Step - To Create Ink Blowing Art
1. **Set Up** - Place paper on a covered surface. Keep good ventilation, especially with alcohol inks.
2. **Apply Ink** - Drip small ink puddles with a dropper or pipette. Add a splash of water for softer blending.
3. **Blow the Ink** - Hold the straw close and gently blow in different directions. Experiment with strength, distance, and angles. For bolder effects, try a hairdryer or compressed air gently.
4. **Add More Layers** - Once dry, add and blow new colours to layer effects. Watch how they collide, mix, and branch out.
5. **Refine Your Art** - Use markers, pens, or brushes to turn blots into flowers, monsters, trees, or textured backgrounds for cards. Let your imagination free!

Tips & Tricks for Success

- **Straw Control:** Halved straws give finer direction—add a tiny vent hole to keep kids safe.
- **Paper Variety:** Try glossy, recycled, or textured paper for unique effects.
- **Ink Consistency:** Thin with water for subtle, flowy patterns; thicker ink produces bolder looks.
- **Use Gravity:** Tilt and rotate for directional flow—let gravity help design your art.
- **Keep Trying:** Every artwork is unique—embrace surprises, happy mistakes, and creative detours.

Creative Variations

- **Abstract Designs:** Blow layered colours in various directions for dynamic, abstract pieces.
- **Floral Patterns:** Place a circular ink drop, blow outward for petals, and add stems with a brush.
- **Tree Silhouettes:** Start at the paper's bottom edge, blow ink upward to mimic trees; draw branches when dry.
- **Ink Monsters:** After drying, add eyes and mouths to blots for imaginative, playful characters—fun for all ages.
- **Backgrounds:** Use flowing ink as a striking backdrop for calligraphy, collage, or cards.

Ink blowing art is a joyful, accessible way to relax, play, and let creativity flow. Suitable for all skill levels—from mindful solo sessions to group fun—this technique provides a visually stunning, therapeutic outlet for expression. So gather your inks and straws, protect your workspace, and breathe colour onto the page—discovering vibrant new worlds in every burst!

Activity 175. Do A Strengths and Weaknesses Analysis

A strengths and weaknesses analysis is a straightforward yet deeply impactful tool for self-reflection. By regularly observing where you excel and where you struggle, you gain greater self-awareness, reduce stress, and become better equipped to reach your personal and professional goals.

Why Do a Self-Analysis?
- **Enhances Self-Awareness:** Identifying abilities and limitations increases emotional intelligence.
- **Reduces Stress:** Pinpointing challenges enables proactive problem-solving and relieves uncertainty.
- **Boosts Confidence:** Focusing on strengths builds resilience and self-assurance.
- **Improves Focus:** Helps target effort toward tasks that suit your abilities, while managing weaker areas constructively.
- **Clarifies Goals:** Accurate self-understanding leads to more realistic, motivating plans for growth.

Step-by-Step - How To Conduct Your Strengths & Weaknesses Analysis
1. Set the Scene
   - Find a calm spot and take a few quiet minutes. Use a notebook, worksheet, or digital document to jot down thoughts.
2. Identify Strengths
   - Ask: What do I naturally excel at? What have others complimented me on? Which activities make me feel capable and positive?
   - Examples: Communication, creative thinking, organisation, reliability, empathy.
3. Identify Weaknesses
   - Ask: What do I find most challenging? Where have I received constructive feedback? Which habits hold me back?
   - Examples: Procrastination, stress management, avoidance of conflict, time management.
4. Organise & Reflect
   - Make two clear lists or columns—one for strengths, one for weaknesses.
   - Reflect on how each affects work, relationships, hobbies, or wellbeing.
5. Set Growth Goals
   - Use strengths intentionally in upcoming opportunities—e.g., volunteering for public speaking if that's a strong suit.
   - Choose one or two weaker areas to address—through learning, mentorship, or setting specific habits (e.g., a focus timer if procrastination is a challenge).

Why It's Worth the Effort
- **Personal Growth:** Embracing weaknesses is key to lifelong learning, while developing strengths unlocks new opportunities.
- **Career Development:** Focused growth helps direct your career path and improve job satisfaction.
- **Stronger Relationships:** Honest self-knowledge enables open communication and empathy with others.
- **Resilience:** Facing weaknesses directly—rather than ignoring them—builds confidence for new challenges.

Tips for Success
- **Be Honest & Kind:** True progress comes from candid, judgment-free self-reflection.
- **Ask for Feedback:** Trusted friends, mentors, or colleagues may see strengths (and blind spots) you've missed.
- **Repeat Regularly:** Revisit this process every few months—growth is continual, and your skills will evolve.
- **Use Available Resources:**
    - UK National Careers Service: Guidance for identifying career strengths.
    - Mind UK: Self-awareness advice for mental health.
    - Local workshops: Look for community centres offering personal development events.

A strengths and weaknesses analysis is more than a list—it's a launch point for positive change. Set aside six minutes today to jot down your strengths and weaknesses, reflect honestly, and commit to one small step for growth. Over time, these insights can empower you to set realistic goals, build resilience, and unlock your unique potential.

Activity 176. Learn basic sign language

Sign language is a visual language that uses hand gestures, facial expressions, and body movements to communicate. While primarily used by the Deaf and hard-of-hearing communities, learning basic sign language offers significant cognitive, social, and emotional benefits for everyone. For individuals navigating mental health challenges or recovering from addiction, incorporating sign language into their lives can foster communication, mindfulness, and inclusivity.

Why Learning Sign Language Is Beneficial for Mental Health and Recovery?

1. **Improved Communication Skills**
   - Sign language bridges communication gaps in noisy environments or situations where silence is required.
   - For individuals struggling with verbal expression due to trauma or addiction, sign language provides an alternative way to articulate thoughts and emotions.
   - It promotes inclusivity by enabling communication with the Deaf community, fostering empathy and understanding.

2. **Cognitive Benefits**
   - Learning sign language stimulates brain function, enhancing memory retention, spatial awareness, and mental agility.
   - The visual nature of sign language improves peripheral vision and reaction times, which can be beneficial in daily tasks like driving or sports.

3. **Emotional Regulation**
   - Expressing emotions through gestures can help individuals process feelings that may be difficult to verbalize.
   - Sign language encourages mindfulness by requiring focused attention on movements and expressions, reducing stress and anxiety.

4. **Social Connection**
   - Learning sign language fosters inclusivity and builds relationships with diverse groups of people.
   - For individuals recovering from addiction, it can provide a sense of purpose through community engagement and shared learning experiences.

5. **Self-Esteem and Confidence**
   - Mastering a new skill like sign language boosts confidence and provides a sense of accomplishment—vital for individuals rebuilding their lives during recovery.

Step-by-Step Guide - How to Learn Basic Sign Language

Materials Needed
- Access to online resources or apps (e.g., British Sign Language [BSL] courses).
- Flashcards or printed diagrams of signs.
- A quiet space for practice.

1. Learn Basic Signs
Start with everyday phrases:
- *Hello:* Wave your dominant hand near your head in an arc.
- *Thank You:* Touch your chin with your fingertips and move your hand forward.
- *Sorry:* Make a fist and rub it in a circular motion on your chest.

2. Practice Fingerspelling
- Learn the BSL alphabet to spell out names or words you don't know the signs for. This is especially helpful when expanding vocabulary.

3. Numbers and Colours
- Practice signing numbers (e.g., 1–10) and basic colours like red, blue, and green using online tutorials or flashcards.

4. Use Facial Expressions
- Work on matching facial expressions with signs to convey emotions effectively (e.g., smiling while signing "happy").

5. Engage in Interactive Activities
- Play fingerspelling games or quizzes online to reinforce learning.
- Join beginner-friendly BSL courses or workshops for structured practice.

6. Connect with the Community
- Attend Deaf events or practice with native signers to improve fluency and cultural understanding.

Examples of Signs You Can Use
- Greetings - *Goodbye:* Same as "Hello," using an arc motion near the head.
- Common Phrases - *What is your name?* Sign "name" by placing the tips of your index and middle fingers to your forehead and twisting forward; then point at the person you're asking.
- Emotions - *Happy:* Use open hands to pat your chest lightly while smiling.
- Practical Words - *Help:* Place one hand flat (palm up) while lifting it slightly with the other hand's thumb extended upward.

Why Learn Sign Language?

1. **Mental Health Support**: For individuals struggling with verbal expression due to trauma or addiction, sign language offers a non-verbal way to communicate emotions effectively.

2. **Inclusivity**: Learning BSL promotes understanding of Deaf culture, breaking down barriers between communities while fostering empathy.

3. **Therapeutic Benefits**: The physical movements involved in signing encourage mindfulness, which can reduce stress levels during recovery journeys.

4. **Practical Application**: Whether communicating in noisy environments or engaging in group therapy sessions, sign language enhances accessibility for all participants.

For individuals recovering from addiction or managing mental health challenges:

1. **Mindfulness Practice**: Signing requires focused attention on movements, creating a meditative effect that helps ground individuals during emotional triggers or cravings.

2. **Community Engagement**: Joining Deaf events or practicing sign language with others fosters social connection—a vital component of recovery programs.

3. **Accessible Therapy Options**: Therapists fluent in BSL can provide tailored support for individuals who struggle with verbal communication due to trauma or substance use disorders.

4. **Symbolic Expression**: Sign language can be used metaphorically during therapy sessions (e.g., signing "strength" while discussing personal growth), offering catharsis without verbal confrontation.

Tips for Success

1. Start small: Focus on learning basic greetings and phrases before progressing to complex sentences or conversations.
2. Practice daily: Regular repetition helps reinforce memory retention.
3. Use visual aids: Flashcards, videos, and apps are excellent tools for beginners.
4. Join workshops: Structured courses taught by qualified instructors provide guidance tailored to your skill level.
5. Stay patient: Learning any new language takes time—celebrate progress along the way!

Learning basic sign language is more than just acquiring a new skill—it's an opportunity to enhance communication, foster inclusivity, and support mental health recovery through mindfulness and connection!

Activity 177. Try Beatboxing

Beatboxing, the art of creating percussive sounds using one's mouth, is more than just a musical skill, it's a form of self-expression that offers significant physical, mental, and emotional benefits. Whether you're exploring it as a hobby or using it as a therapeutic tool, beatboxing can be an accessible and enjoyable way to enhance wellbeing. For individuals managing mental health challenges or recovering from addiction, beatboxing provides a unique opportunity to build confidence, regulate emotions, and foster creativity, plus no materials needed, just your voice.

How is it good for mental and physical wellbeing?

- **Improved Breath Control**: Beatboxing requires precise breath management to produce sounds and rhythms. This practice strengthens lung capacity and improves overall breath control, which is beneficial for physical fitness and relaxation.
- **Vocal Health**: Unlike singing, which relies heavily on vocal cords, beatboxing engages pharyngeal muscles, reducing strain on vocal folds and potentially protecting them from overuse injuries.
- **Core Strength**: The diaphragmatic breathing involved in beatboxing engages core muscles, offering light cardiovascular exercise that contributes to physical fitness.
- **Stress Relief**: The rhythmic and repetitive nature of beatboxing can be cathartic, helping to release tension and promote a sense of calm.
- **Enhanced Focus**: Practicing complex rhythms improves concentration and attention to detail—skills that can be applied in daily life.
- **Creativity Boost**: Experimenting with sounds and patterns fosters innovative thinking and encourages self-expression.
- **Confidence Building**: Mastering beatboxing techniques boosts self-esteem by providing a tangible skill that can be shared with others.
- **Emotional Regulation**: Creating beats allows individuals to channel emotions constructively, offering an outlet for feelings like frustration or sadness.

Beatboxing can be practiced collaboratively in groups, fostering teamwork and communication. It provides opportunities for bonding through shared musical experiences.

Basic Sounds to Learn
1. Kick Drum (B): Say "Boom" with emphasis on the "B." Gradually transition to producing the sound without vocalizing by using just your lips.
2. Hi-Hat (T): Make a sharp "ts" sound by placing your tongue behind your front teeth and releasing it. This mimics the crisp sound of a hi-hat cymbal.

3. Snare Drum (K): Produce a hard "K" sound on an outward breath. For variation, try the inward K snare by sucking air in while making the "K" sound.

Simple Patterns for Beginners
1. Boots and Cats Pattern: - Say "boots-and-cats" repeatedly, emphasizing "b" (kick drum), "ts" (hi-hat), and "c" (snare). This foundational pattern helps build rhythm skills.
2. BTK Pattern:
   a. Combine kick drum (B), hi-hat (T), and snare (K) in sequences like:
   b. B t K t
   c. B t t K t B K t
3. Song Covers: - Practice simple beats from popular songs like *Billie Jean* by Michael Jackson or *Drop It Like It's Hot* by Snoop Dog.

Beatboxing is an accessible art form that requires no instruments or costly equipment, making it an inclusive skill that anyone can learn using just their voice. It offers therapeutic benefits, providing structure, focus, and a creative outlet for individuals recovering from addiction or navigating mental health challenges. The breath control involved in beatboxing promotes physical relaxation and engages the core muscles, offering light exercise. Additionally, sharing beats with friends or performing in public settings helps build confidence and fosters meaningful social connections.

For individuals navigating recovery, beatboxing can serve as a grounded mindfulness practice by requiring focused attention on breath control and rhythmic patterns, helping to anchor awareness in the present moment and manage cravings or intrusive thoughts. It also offers symbolic expression, allowing beats to represent personal struggles or victories—such as mimicking the sound of breaking chains—providing a powerful and cathartic outlet without the need for words. Additionally, joining local beatbox groups or workshops like the BAC Beatbox Academy encourages community engagement and builds social connection through shared, creative music-making experiences.

Tips for Success

1. Start slow: Focus on mastering individual sounds before combining them into patterns.
2. Record yourself: Listen back to help identify areas for improvement & progress.
3. Practice daily: Consistency is key, try incorporating short sessions into your routine even if only for 5–10 minutes.
4. Experiment creatively: Don't be afraid to invent your own rhythms or mimic sounds from your environment.

Beatboxing is more than just vocal percussion—it's a dynamic art form that nurtures creativity, builds confidence, and supports emotional wellbeing through rhythm and self-expression!

Activity 178. Design a mandala

A mandala—meaning "circle" in Sanskrit—is a geometric design that symbolises balance, harmony, and the universe. Creating mandalas is more than an art project; it is a meditative process that fosters mindfulness, self-expression, and relaxation, making it especially valuable for individuals managing mental health challenges or recovering from addiction.

Mental Wellbeing

- **Stress Relief:** The focus on repetitive patterns and symmetry encourages calm, eases anxiety, and provides a gentle distraction from racing thoughts.
- **Mindfulness:** Drawing a mandala requires attention to detail, helping anchor awareness in the present moment and promoting mental stillness.
- **Emotional Expression:** Pattern and colour choices provide a non-verbal outlet for emotions, allowing feelings to surface and be processed safely.

Physical Wellbeing

- **Improved Motor Skills:** Designing intricate patterns develops fine motor control, dexterity, and hand-eye coordination.
- **Physical Relaxation:** The slow, repetitive actions often slow breathing and heart rate, supporting a state of rest and relaxation.

Emotional and Social Benefits

- **Confidence & Achievement:** Completing a mandala fosters accomplishment and self-esteem, even for beginners.
- **Symbolic Healing:** Mandalas are often used in therapy to represent growth, resilience, or a journey towards balance and wholeness.
- **Social Connection:** Group mandala sessions or sharing designs can foster community, support, and non-verbal communication.

How to Design a Mandala

Materials
- Paper or sketchbook
- Pencil and eraser
- Compass and ruler for circles (optional)
- Markers, coloured pencils, or paints

1. Prepare Your Workspace
- Choose a quiet space. Decide on a centre for your mandala on the paper.
- Gather materials—compass for circles, ruler for dividing sections.

2. Create the Structure
- Draw several concentric circles (with a compass, or trace round objects for guidance).
- Use a ruler to draw two lines through the centre at right angles, dividing the circle into four. For more sections, use a protractor for even spacing.

3. Start Drawing Patterns

- Begin at the centre with dots, small circles, or shapes.
- Add outward rings of petals, triangles, or geometric forms, repeating each shape around the circle for symmetry.
- Layer different shapes, letting the design grow from the centre.

4. Add Intricate Details
   - Use fine pens or pencils for delicate lines, dots, or textures within each section.
   - Colour some spaces fully, leave others plain for contrast and depth.

5. Colour Your Mandala
   - Choose colours based on mood - bright for energy, soft for calm.
   - Blend colours or keep sections bold and graphic.
   - Reflect on your choices and what they represent emotionally or symbolically.

Inspiration and Examples

- **Simple Shapes Mandala:** Central circle with rings of petals, triangles, and curved lines.
- **Nature-Inspired Mandala:** Incorporate leaves, tree rings, flower petals, or water ripples.
- **Geometric Mandala:** Fill divided spaces with repeating diamonds, squares, or hexagons.
- **Dot Mandala:** Build patterns using only dots radiating outward.
- **Doodle Mandala:** Add stars, hearts, swirls, or creative doodles in a balanced way.

Mandala Making in Recovery and Wellbeing

- **Accessible Creativity:** No advanced art skills necessary—just willingness to experiment.
- **Therapeutic Outlet:** Structured but flexible, mandalas can safely anchor emotional processing.
- **Symbolic Growth:** Use the mandala's expanding form to reflect personal progress or aspirations.
- **Mindfulness Tool:** Promotes deep focus and can help manage cravings or intrusive thoughts.
- **Group Connection:** Mandala making in groups nurtures a sense of belonging while sharing creativity.

Tips for Beginners

- Start simple; let confidence and complexity grow over time.
- Rotate your paper often to keep patterns balanced.
- Look to nature or online for visual inspiration.
- Embrace imperfections—they add character and authenticity.
- After finishing, pause to reflect on the design's meaning for your journey.

Designing mandalas is a gentle, accessible way to nurture mindfulness, creativity, and personal growth—helping to restore balance and joy, one pattern at a time.

Activity 179. Make homemade pet treats

Creating homemade pet treats is a fun and rewarding way to bond with your furry friends while ensuring they enjoy healthy, nutritious snacks. Beyond the practical benefits, this activity can also serve as a therapeutic outlet for individuals managing mental health challenges or recovering from addiction. The process of crafting treats fosters mindfulness, creativity, and a sense of accomplishment, making it an ideal addition to self-care routines in the UK.

Why Making Pet Treats Is Good for Mental and Physical Wellbeing?

1. Mental Benefits
    - Mindfulness: The step-by-step nature of preparing treats encourages focus on the present moment, helping to reduce stress and anxiety.
    - Creativity: Experimenting with recipes and shapes allows for self-expression and innovation.
    - Sense of Purpose: Providing for your pet through homemade treats fosters a sense of achievement and strengthens the human-animal bond.

2. Physical Benefits
    - Fine Motor Skills: Measuring, mixing, rolling, and shaping ingredients improve hand-eye coordination and dexterity.
    - Relaxation Response:* Engaging in repetitive tasks like kneading dough or cutting shapes can have a calming effect on the body.

3. Emotional Benefits
    - Connection: Strengthening the bond with your pet through homemade care can boost mood and emotional resilience.
    - Confidence Building: Successfully completing recipes enhances self-esteem, especially during recovery journeys.

4. Social Connection - Sharing recipes or participating in pet treat-making workshops provides opportunities for community engagement.

Step-by-Step Guide - How to Make Homemade Pet Treats

Materials Needed
- Mixing bowls, measuring cups, rolling pin, cookie cutters (optional).
- Fresh ingredients tailored to your pet's dietary needs.

Recipes for Dogs

1. Peanut Butter & Carrot Dog Treats
Ingredients: 2 large carrots, 2 cups oats, ½ cup natural peanut butter.

Boil carrots until tender; blend with oats and peanut butter in a food processor. Roll out dough, cut into shapes, and bake at 150°C (300°F) for 20–25 minutes.

2. Banana Peanut Butter Dog Treats
Ingredients: 2 ripe bananas, ½ cup natural peanut butter, 2 cups oats.
Mash bananas; mix with peanut butter and oats. Form small balls or discs and bake at 175°C (350°F) for 15 minutes.

3. Cheesy Dog Biscuits
Ingredients: 1 cup grated cheese, 1½ cups whole wheat flour, ½ cup water.
Combine ingredients into a dough; roll out and cut into shapes. Bake at 175°C (350°F) for 20 minutes.

Recipes for Cats

1. Tuna Cat Treats
Ingredients: 1 can tuna (drained), 1 egg, 1 cup whole wheat flour.
Blend tuna and egg; add flour to form dough. Roll out and cut into small shapes; bake at 175°C (350°F) for 20 minutes.

2. Salmon Cat Treats
Ingredients: ½ cup cooked salmon (flaked), 1 egg yolk, ½ cup oat flour.
Mix ingredients; form small balls or discs and bake at 175°C (350°F) for 15 minutes.

3. Pumpkin Cat Treats
Ingredients: ½ cup cooked pumpkin puree, 1 egg yolk, ½ cup coconut flour.
Combine ingredients; roll out dough and cut into small pieces. Bake at 175°C (350°F) for 20 minutes.

Why Make Homemade Pet Treats?

1. Health Benefits: Homemade treats allow you to control the ingredients, ensuring your pet enjoys safe and nutritious snacks without harmful additives or preservatives.
2. Personalised Care: Tailor recipes to suit your pet's dietary needs or preferences (e.g., grain-free options for sensitive stomachs).
3. Therapeutic Process: The structured steps involved in making treats provide focus and relaxation—ideal for individuals recovering from addiction or managing mental health challenges.
4. Eco-Friendly Option: Using fresh ingredients reduces reliance on commercial packaging, aligning with sustainable practices.

For individuals navigating recovery journeys:

1. Mindful Creativity: The act of measuring ingredients, mixing dough, and shaping treats engages the senses while promoting mindfulness—a valuable tool for managing cravings or intrusive thoughts during recovery.
2. Symbolic Connection: Making treats mirrors the process of nurturing oneself—just as you care for your pet's wellbeing, you're also fostering your own healing journey through creative acts of kindness.
3. Community Engagement: Sharing recipes or gifting homemade treats to friends' pets builds social connections while reinforcing feelings of purpose and contribution.
4. Routine Building: Incorporating treat-making into daily or weekly routines provides structure—a key element in maintaining stability during recovery.

Tips for Success

1. Use pet-safe ingredients: Avoid toxic foods like chocolate, xylitol, onions, garlic, grapes, or raisins.
2. Start simple: Begin with easy recipes before experimenting with more complex ones.
3. Store properly: Refrigerate treats for up to one week or freeze them for longer storage.
4. Introduce gradually: Monitor your pet's reaction when trying new recipes.
5. Consult your vet: Discuss any dietary changes or ingredient concerns specific to your pet's health needs.

Making homemade pet treats is more than just an activity—it's an opportunity to nurture creativity while strengthening bonds with your furry companions through mindful care!

Activity 180. Read poetry

Not all poetry is the same or is 'stereotypical' poetry, there is a wide variety of exciting and inspiring poetry across different forms, styles, and themes.

Many poems are known for their ability to inspire and excite readers:

1. **"Still I Rise" by Maya Angelou**: A powerful poem about resilience and strength in the face of adversity.
2. **"If" by Rudyard Kipling**: An inspirational poem presenting rules for adulthood and overcoming challenges.
3. **"Hope is the Thing with Feathers" by Emily Dickinson**: A beautiful metaphorical poem celebrating the power of hope.
4. **"The Road Not Taken" by Robert Frost**: A famous poem about making choices and forging one's own path.
5. **"Invictus" by William Ernest Henley**: A stirring poem about the indomitable human spirit.

These poems, among many others, use vivid imagery, powerful language, and relatable themes to connect with readers emotionally and intellectually. They often address universal human experiences, challenges, and aspirations, making them resonate with people across different cultures and time periods.

Poetry's diversity in form, style, and content ensures that there is something to excite and inspire nearly every reader, from those who enjoy structured classical forms to those who prefer more experimental, contemporary approaches.

As well as being powerful, reading poetry can significantly benefit mental health by providing a medium for expressing complex emotions, helping individuals cope with feelings of anxiety, depression, and loneliness. It allows individuals to reflect on their lives and find new perspectives on their experiences.

Reading rhythmic poetry aloud can slow breathing and activate the relaxation response, it can also lower physiological stress indicators such as muscle tension, perspiration, blood pressure, and heart rate

Poetry therapy has shown positive effects for patients dealing with chronic illness, pain management, and end-of-life care. It can boost mood, improve emotional resilience, and enhance overall quality of life

By engaging with poetry through reading, writing, or sharing, individuals can access a powerful tool for improving mental health and well-being. Here are a few poems to think about:

"One Day at a Time" by Anonymous

This simple yet powerful mantra is often recited in recovery circles:

"One day at a time— This is enough.
Do not look back
And grieve over the past,
For it is gone;
And do not be troubled about the future,
For it has not yet come.
Live in the present, draw breath
Know in this moment, and every moment:
You matter.
And make it so beautiful
That it will be worth remembering."

"The Uses of Sorrow" by Mary Oliver

While not explicitly about addiction, this poem resonates deeply with many in recovery:

"Someone I loved once gave me a box full of darkness.
It took me years to understand that this, too, was a gift."

These poems offer comfort, hope, and reflection for those on the journey of recovery. They speak to the transformative power of adversity, the importance of living in the present moment, and the unexpected gifts that can arise from our darkest experiences.

But this is my favourite, and it is the most powerful poems I have ever read. It is a poem that sends me back to darkest of dark times but brings so much light with knowing what I have been through and where I am now. If you have no experience of addiction, here is a glimpse of the cunning and baffling disease, with the hold it has on you waiting to strike. I hope you enjoy reading it!

I AM YOUR DISEASE - Author Unknown

You know who I am, you've called me your friend
Wishes of misery and heartache I send
I want only to see that you're brought to your knees
I'm the devil inside you, I am your disease.

I'll invade all your thoughts, I'll take hostage your soul
I'll become your new master, in total control
I'll maim your emotions, I'll run the whole game
Till your entire existence is crippled with shame

Life Re-Imagined

When you call me I come, sometimes in disguise
Quite often I'll take you by total surprise
But take you I will, and just as you've feared
I'll want only to hurt you, with no mercy spared

If you have your own family, I'll see it's destroyed
I'll steal every pleasure in life you've enjoyed
I'll not only hurt you, I'll kill if I please
I'm your worst living nightmare, I am your disease

I bring self destruction, but still you can't tell
I'll sweep you through heaven, then drop you in hell
I'll chase you forever, wherever you go
And then when I catch you, you won't even know

I'll sometimes lay silent, just waiting to strike
What's yours becomes mine, cuz I take what I like
I'll take all you own and I won't care who sees
I'm your constant companion... I am your disease

If you have any honor, I'll strip it away
You'll lose all your hope and forget how to pray
I'll leave you in darkness, while blindly you stare
I'll reduce you to nothing, and won't even care

So, don't take for granted my powers sublime
I'll bend and I'll break you, time after time
I'll crumble your world with the greatest of ease
I'm that madman inside you...I am your disease

But today I'm real angry...you want to know why?
I let this treatment center full of Addicts entirely slip by
How did I lose you? Where did I go wrong?
One minute I had you...then next you were gone

You just can't dismiss all the good times we've shared
When you were alone...wasn't it I who appeared?
When you sold those possessions you knew you would need
Wasn't I the first one who stepped in and agreed

Now look at you bastards, you're all thinking clear
You escaped with your lives when you found your way here
Only fools think they're winners when admitting defeat
It's what you must say when you're claiming that seat

Emma Gardner

Go ahead and surrender, if that's what you choose
But, I'm not giving up. cuz I can't stand to lose
So stand in your groups and support hand in hand
Better choices will save you...leaving me to be damned

Well, be damned all you people seeking treatment each week
Be damned inner strength, however unique
Be damned all your sayings, be damned your cliches
Be damned every addict, who back to me strays

For I know it will happen, I've seen it before
Those who love misery will crawl back for more
So take comfort in knowing, I'm waiting right here
But next time around, you'd just better beware

You think that you're stronger or smarter this time'
There isn't a mountain or hill you can't climb
Well if that's what you're thinkin, you ain't learned a thing
I'll still knock you silly if you step back in my ring

But you say you've surrendered, so what can I do?
It's so sad in a way, I had big plans for you
Creating your nightmare for me was a dream
I'm sure gonna miss you...we made quite a team

So please don't forget me, I won't forget you
I'll stand by your side watching all that you do
I'm ready and waiting, so call if you please
I won't let you forget me...I am your disease.

About the Author

Emma is a passionate entrepreneur and founder of Evolve Recovery, whose life and work shine a beacon of hope for anyone navigating the complexities of addiction and healing. As an adult child of an addict and someone in recovery,

Emma knows firsthand what it takes to transform pain into purpose and strength. Years spent coaching others, hosting the Healing Odyssey podcast, and creating safe spaces for self-discovery have shaped an authentic voice that resonates deeply with readers and clients alike.

From growing up amidst the silence and secrecy of addiction, Emma emerged as a fierce advocate for recovery, mental wellness, and family support.

Today, her story blends lived experience and empowering coaching, inviting people to reimagine their lives, embrace resilience, and break cycles for future generations.

When not writing or supporting people on their recovery journeys. Emma enjoys life in the beautiful valleys of South Wales with her husband and their spoilt cats, exploring new places together, watching the rugby and finding joy in everyday moments. You'll often find her hosting podcasts, meeting fellow advocates, and building welcoming communities where hope and healing truly thrive.

Website: http://www.evolve-recovery.co.uk

Facebook: https://www.facebook.com/EvolveRecoveryTogether/

Instagram: https://www.instagram.com/regainatevolverecovery/

LinkedIn: https://www.linkedin.com/in/emma-gardner-75554624/

My Contingency Plan

1. Identification of Triggers
- Internal Triggers:

- External Triggers:

2. Coping Strategies
- Relaxation Techniques:

- Physical Activity:

- Creative Outlets:

- Social Support:

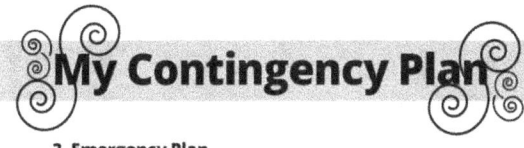

My Contingency Plan

3. Emergency Plan

- Contact Information:
  _____
  _____
  _____

- Safe Places:
  _____
  _____

- Immediate Actions:
  _____
  _____
  _____

4. Relapse Warning Signs

- Emotional Changes:
  _____
  _____
  _____

- Behavioural Changes:
  _____
  _____
  _____

My Contingency Plan

5. Regular Self-Assessment
- Weekly Reflections:
_____
_____
_____

6. Healthy Lifestyle Practices
- Nutrition and Sleep:
_____
_____
_____

- Leisure Activities:
_____
_____
_____

7. Professional Support
- Therapy Sessions:
_____
_____
_____

- Support Groups:
_____
_____
_____

Journalling Page for Recovery Activities

Below is a journaling page designed for individuals to use alongside each activity from your book. The prompts are informed by the "How to Use This Book" section and the book's holistic, flexible approach, encourages you to reflect before, during, and after each activity, track progress, and support habit formation.

My Recovery Activity Reflection

Date:

Activity Name/Page No:

1. How do I feel right now, before starting this activity?
(Check in with yourself: Are you feeling anxious, hopeful, low, restless, curious, etc.?)

2. What made me choose to do an activity today?
(Was it curiosity, a craving, a need for distraction, or something else?)

3. Did I adapt or change the activity in any way to suit my mood, ability, or environment?

4. How did I feel while doing the activity?
(Did any emotions, memories, or thoughts come up? Did you feel engaged, frustrated, surprised, joyful?)

Journalling Page for Recovery Activities

5. What did I like about this activity?
_____
_____
_____

6. What didn't I like (if anything)? Would I do anything differently next time?
_____
_____
_____

7. How do I feel now, after completing the activity?
(Do you feel more relaxed, energised, distracted, or is your mood unchanged?)
_____
_____
_____

8. Did this activity help with my cravings or low mood? How?
_____
_____
_____

9. Could this activity become a regular part of my routine? Why or why not?
_____
_____
_____

10. Any additional thoughts, insights, or ideas for next time?
_____
_____
_____

Journalling Page for Recovery Activities

Progress & Self-Care Check

Did I use any coping strategies or urge surfing techniques today? ☐ Yes ☐ No
If yes, which ones?

_____
_____
_____
_____
_____

Did I skip any activity today? ☐ Yes ☐ No
If yes, why?

_____
_____
_____
_____
_____

What is one thing I am grateful for today?

_____
_____
_____
_____
_____

What is one positive thing I noticed about myself today?

_____
_____
_____
_____
_____

Tip: Use this page daily or as often as you need. Over time, your journal will become a powerful record of your journey, helping you spot patterns, celebrate growth, and discover what works best for you.